Sport Marketing
A Canadian Perspective

NORM O'REILLY
School of Sports Administration,
Laurentian University

BENOIT SÉGUIN
University of Ottawa

NELSON / EDUCATION

NELSON / EDUCATION

Sport Marketing: A Canadian Perspective, First Edition
by Norm O'Reilly and Benoit Séguin

Associate Vice President, Editorial Director:
Evelyn Veitch

Editor-in-Chief, Higher Education
Anne Williams

Acquisitions Editor:
Amie Plourde

Marketing Manager:
Kathaleen McCormick

Developmental Editor:
My Editor Inc.

Permissions Coordinator:
Shelley Wickabrod

Content Production Manager:
Christine Gilbert

Production Service:
GEX Publishing Services

Copy Editor:
Elaine Freedman

Proofreader:
GEX Publishing Services

Indexer:
GEX Publishing Services

Manufacturing Manager:
Joanne McNeil

Design Director:
Ken Phipps

Managing Designer:
Katherine Strain

Interior Design:
Tammy Gay

Cover Design:
Martyn Schmoll

Cover Image:
ASSOCIATED PRESS

Compositor:
GEX Publishing Services

Printer:
Thomson West

Library and Archives Canada Cataloguing in Publication Data

Main entry under title:

O'Reilly, Norm, 1973-
Sport marketing : a Canadian perspective / Norm O'Reilly, Benoit Séguin.

Includes bibliographical references and index.
ISBN 978-0-17-610458-0

1. Sports--Canada--Marketing--Textbooks. I. Séguin, Benoit, 1963- II. Title.

GV716.O74 2007   796.06'98
C2007-906447-7

ISBN-13: 978-0-17-610458-0
ISBN-10: 0-17-610458-5

Table of Contents

PART TWO: STP and the Canadian Sport Marketing Mix

Chapter 5: Segmentation, Targeting, and Positioning in Canadian Sport   97

Executive Perspective: Dale Hooper, Vice-President, Marketing, PepsiQuakerTropicanaGatorade Canada   98

Chapter 18: Marketing Plan Example   383

Preface

Thank you for selecting sport marketing as a potential career or just out of interest. This book lets us share our passion for sport marketing and the knowledge, contacts, and concepts we have built over a combined 50 years in sport.

For us, this book comes out of our many years of work, study, and volunteer time in sport, particularly in sport marketing. As former athletes and coaches and current administrators, we feel privileged to share our views on marketing in Canadian sport. And we are especially proud that many colleagues and experts in marketing and in sport have also shared their views in this book in the form of case studies and executive perspectives. We both strongly support the concepts of applied learning and believe that this book will provide you with the tools necessary to begin or enhance a career in sport marketing. Why a Canadian book? Marketing is driven by its environment; therefore, material specific to the Canadian environment is important to any Canadian student of sport marketing.

Thank you and enjoy the read.

Norm O'Reilly and Benoit Séguin
December 2007

Acknowledgments

The authors acknowledge the significant contributions of two colleagues to this book:

- Dr. Robert Wanzel, founding director of the Institute of Sport Marketing at Laurentian University, for contributing to Chapters 9 and 10 and for providing the resources to conduct the case study research.
- Dr. Ann Pegoraro, associate director of the Institute of Sport Marketing at Laurentian University, for her authorship of Chapter 4.

We also note the contribution of these experts who generously provided their time and knowledge in the many executive perspectives throughout the book:

Dave Bedford, executive director of marketing and communications, Canadian Olympic Committee

Krista Benoit, director, iSPARK Consulting

Ian Bird, senior leader, Sport Matters Group

Claire Carver-Dias, marketing director, Bobsleigh Canada

Linda Cuthbert, principal, Breakthrough Performance Group and president, Aquatic Federation of Canada

Jean Dupré, director general, Speed Skating Canada

Mark Harrison, president and CEO, TrojanOne

Peter Hellstrom, athletic director, Laurentian University

Dale Hooper, vice-president, marketing, PepsiQuakerTropicanaGatorade Canada

Terry Kell, president, Kanatek Technologies

Phil Legault, vice-president, communications, Ottawa Senators

Ann Pegoraro, associate director of the Institute of Sport Marketing at Laurentian University

Richard Pound, chair of World Anti-Doping Agency and member of International Olympic Committee

Gavin Roth, senior director of partnerships, Canadian Football League

Blaine Smith, vice-president of hockey operations, Sudbury Wolves

Scott Smith, senior vice-president of operations, Hockey Canada

Chris Walling, director of marketing, Callaway Golf

We sincerely thank these research associates for their contributions that helped make this book a reality.

- Jeff Barsevich, BComm (sports administration) candidate, School of Sports Administration, Laurentian University (Chapter 18)

- Alex Campbell, BComm (sports administration) candidate, School of Sports Administration, Laurentian University (Chapter 18)
- Courtney Cohoon, MA (human kinetics) candidate, School of Human Kinetics, University of Ottawa (editing support)
- Donald Desloges, MBA candidate, Faculty of Management, Laurentian University (Chapters 3 and 8)
- Dana Ellis, MA (human kinetics), School of Human Kinetics, University of Ottawa (Chapters 2 and 7)
- Tim Horton, BComm (sports administration) candidate, School of Sports Administration, Laurentian University (Chapter 18)
- Allison King, BComm (sports administration) candidate, School of Sports Administration, Laurentian University (Chapter 18)
- Brandon Mazerall, BComm (sports administration) candidate, School of Sports Administration, Laurentian University (Chapter 18)
- Ryan Rahinel, BComm candidate, School of Information Technology Management, Ryerson University (Chapters 14 and 15)
- Rob Reimer, BComm (sports administration) candidate, School of Sports Administration, Laurentian University (Chapter 16)

We are also grateful to these groups for their support:

- University of Ottawa's masters level sport marketing class of winter 2007 (review)
- The Institute of Sport Marketing at Laurentian University's 2007 research associates (edit)

Finally, we thank the reviewers for their comments and feedback, which played an important role in guiding the development of this first edition:

- Cheri Bradish, Brock University
- Karen Danylchuk, University of Western Ontario
- Liz MacDonald, York University
- Richard Powers, University of Toronto
- Ernie Rainbow, Durham College
- Ian Reid, University of New Brunswick
- Harold Riemer, University of Regina
- Joanne Schroeder, Malaspina University-College
- Marijke Taks, University of Windsor

We view this book as a work in progress and welcome any comments or feedback you may have as you work your way through its pages.

Dedication

This book is dedicated to Chantal, Nadège, Geneviève, Marc-André, Alexandre, Emma, and Kian.

Foreword

The time is right for a book like this, and the two authors are the right professors to undertake such a comprehensive project.

The concept of marketing has been around for centuries, probably millennia. A study of past experience encourages making deductions as to why some enterprises have been successful, and others not, and drawing contemporary inferences within an increasingly mercantile society where consumers regularly choose between competing products or services. Fundamental principles of marketing have been identified over the years and much has been written about them.

Comprehensive application of these fundamental principles and concepts to the field of organized sport, however, has been a more recent phenomenon. Sport is increasingly concerned with effective marketing. It is clear that private-sector support is essential to generating both public interest and the revenue streams required to organize events and remunerate players (and owners), where the activity is sufficiently important to become a livelihood. As with other products and services in the marketplace, sport must compete for attention and support. Consumers of entertainment have a vast array of choice. How can sport capture its share of disposable incomes? How can it maintain its "market share" and avoid becoming a one-time experience? What attributes of sport encourage regular consumption and loyalty? How is sport's message to be developed, crafted, and communicated?

Marketing may be the expression of a global strategy, but local tactics are required in the successful application of that strategy. There can be little quarrel with such a thought, given the vast differences of a cultural and economic nature that exist throughout the world, within countries, and even within cities. Each segment is comfortable with its own traditions and vocabularies and responds accordingly to marketing messages. While elements of any marketing program can be original, in the sense of attracting attention and "connecting" with the intended targets, they must not be so foreign that they risk missing the mark.

O'Reilly and Séguin have developed a systematic and comprehensive approach to the elements of marketing. They have adopted the useful device of illustrating the basic principles with case studies drawn, for the most part, from Canadian experience and first-hand descriptions from Canadian sport figures. For the Canadian student or reader, this has the double advantage of reinforcing the discipline and demonstrating that, with the application of the discipline, success is possible, whether on a local, regional, national, or even international scale.

However, make no mistake about it—sport marketing is hard work. Money does not fall from trees. Good, even brilliant, marketing ideas do not come to magical fruition on their own, but only with careful tending and meticulous attention to basic marketing principles.

Richard W. Pound
December 2007

Introduction

Baseball game today 2:00 p.m. Wanzel Field.

A can of peas—on special.

The two notices above are related. And therein lies the development of the field of sport marketing. Historically, a sporting contest such as a baseball game was just "announced," and a packaged goods item was noted at a special price at the local store. The proliferation of packaged goods products (and other grocery/non-grocery items) available to the public through the development of super-store distribution brought sophisticated product marketing to the industry. Sport marketing development lagged behind several other industry marketing thrusts for many years.

Eventually, as media platforms developed, and sport and event growth surged, the necessity for sophisticated sport marketing became essential. The convergence of product, entertainment, and sport marketing became the norm. Because sport can now deliver an audience/target market, the "Wanzel Field" (or venue) noted above has itself become sponsored/named as a business marketing tool (e.g., Rogers Centre).

As the founding director (1974) of Canada's first university (and business) degree program in sports administration (Laurentian University senate approved 1972), I discovered a dearth of information on sport marketing. At that time, only three universities in the United States had sport management programs (none offering a business degree). To build a curriculum meant importing articles from the sport and business sections of newspapers and extrapolating from textbooks on business marketing. Slowly the development of sport and event marketing led to specific information being written about the field. This information was, for the most part, chronicling the development of the field in the US.

This text by professors O'Reilly and Séguin is important: It has information and case examples drawn from Canadian experiences, which are essential for not only Canadian students but also students/practitioners worldwide in this field. The authors' background experiences in sport/event marketing bring a very interesting perspective to the information conveyed in this text. The text, covering as it does, a sport marketing landscape introduction, the sport marketing mix, and strategic elements in several areas, offers a broad insight into the field. The executive perspectives adds to the in-depth knowledge presented for all components of the text.

Since 2001, the Institute for Sport Marketing (ISM) at the School of Sports Administration at Laurentian University has worked to improve private-sector sponsorship and investment in the Canadian sport system. This text is an important extension of ISM research and contribution to the sport marketing field.

Dr. Bob Wanzel
Professor Emeritus Laurentian University and Founding Director Institute
of Sport Marketing
December 2007

Chapter

An Introduction to Sport Marketing

Source: Matthew Jacques / Shutterstock

Learning Objectives

- To be able to define a market, marketing, and sport marketing
- To understand the role of marketing in sports
- To be able to distinguish marketing of sport from marketing through sport
- To understand the importance of target markets, market research, STP, fan loyalty, the marketing mix, and sponsorship

Introduction

Marketing and sport: A marriage meant to last

Every day, we are hit by thousands of messages about products, ideas, activities, services, and entertainment. Many of these make sense; many do not. Some catch our attention; others do not. Some make us think "I should get one of those." And sometimes we even stop what we are doing and impulsively make an immediate purchase. At the same time, in the marketing offices of organizations across Canada, marketers plan how they can get their product offerings to attract our attention and ideally lead to a purchase.

This is **marketing**. Marketing involves an exchange between two parties that provides a win–win benefit to both. This is typically an **exchange** of some product—tangible good, service, idea, or behaviour—in return for money. This process is supported by a marketing mix, composed of the strategic elements of **product**, **price**, **promotion**, and **place**, commonly referred to as the 4 Ps of marketing, which are developed to support and ultimately achieve an exchange.

marketing: an exchange between two parties that provides a win–win benefit to both.

exchange: a transaction in which both parties receive value that they perceive to be greater than what the exchange costs them.

product: tangible good, service, idea, or behaviour.

price: a cost that leads to perceived value.

promotion: communication that will reach the target market.

place: the ability to purchase and/or receive the product at a convenient and accessible location; ensuring distribution is set up to get the product to consumers.

Although sport had been "sold" since the days of the ancient Olympics in Greece and gladiators in Rome, it is only recently that the marriage between sport and marketing became a formal arrangement worth billions of dollars annually. Regardless of the industry in which the marketer works, sport has the ability to provide marketing benefit beyond that of other properties. It is the mission of this text to describe this advantage and provide tools that allow marketers to take it.

EXECUTIVE PERSPECTIVE

Trojan One
integrated brand activation.

Mark Harrison, President and CEO, TrojanOne

I refer to sport, or sports, marketing as a subset of marketing that presents a unique opportunity to marketers to activate their brands. With the power of sports, a marketer can conduct strategic initiatives using any of the key marketing tactics—public relations, celebrity spokespeople, sampling, advertising, corporate hosting, contesting, and so on.

So what makes sport marketing unique? Powerful? Dynamic? Why is it that sport marketing is more studied and practised than say entertainment marketing or cause-related marketing? The answer lies in the fact that it is different from those other areas of marketing.

I propose, and I am not the first person to do so, that sport has a unique attribute, unseen in all other properties in marketing, that drives its appeal. That attribute is the power of uncertainty in sport. Sport has no predetermined outcome. It has no set conclusion. There is no confirmed ending. Think about it. A concert has a start and an end with very few surprises. A play or a movie may be new, but it is driven by a script, and you can find the outcome ahead of attending (by the way, she dumps the good looking guy for the nice guy in the end!). A fundraiser marches to a particular drummer: We listen to the speeches, we eat the food, we bid on the auction items, we dance, we go home feeling worthwhile. These examples are from the more dynamic forms of marketing, not even the more traditional forms such as TV advertising, in-store displays, or billboards.

Sport has no script. It has no screenwriter. It has no predetermined plot. Yet it does have a stage. It does have directors. It does have performers. But best of all, it has circumstance. It is affected by the weather. It hinges on the physical and mental well-being of the competitors. It has uncontrollable variables, such as officiating and coaching. It is unpredictable due to momentum and how it changes within the game or competition, when spontaneous reactions erupting from the athletes add to the pressure of the moment.

Coupled with the unpredictability of sport are the overpowering emotions associated with it. But what drives these emotions? Surely uncertainty on its own cannot be enough to drive men to behave like lunatics, to encourage fans to act like children, to result in women holding their hands in prayer, to lead the media to debate mundane stats till sunset, and to drive commentators to act like Elvis had been spotted in the building. Beyond the "Go Team Go." Beyond the cheering for an individual elite athlete in an international competition. Beyond the "She's my favourite player" is something more fundamental, more personal, more involved. That is the connection between the athlete and the team and the individual fan.

That team or athlete represents not just my country or my region or my city or my school. They represent me. And because they represent me, the team in black represents the other guys. Not the other city or the other country or the other school. They represent everybody I want to be better than. If my team or my hero conquers all, not only are they more powerful, smarter, stronger, and better looking, but magically I am as well. Magically I can deal with my boss, my neighbour, my family, my annoying cable man, with a bit more authority, a little more confidence, and a touch more swagger. Why? Because I'm a winner.

I worked just as hard as my team or favourite athlete did in training. I sacrificed the same late nights and early mornings, strict diets and intense workouts, demanding coaches and intimidating trainers. I sacrificed and I won. I bled for this. Now I am more than a fan. I am the coach, the quarterback, the boxer, the racecar driver. I made that 11-foot putt on the 18th. Or at least I believe deep down inside that if I had been taught to golf when I was three and had 72 000 hours of range time, I could have made that putt!

In the end, the sports arena provides an unparalleled opportunity for fans to transpose themselves to another place, to ride every emotion possible upwards and downwards until the outcome is determined, and then to be encased by the resulting emotion. As a marketer, you have a unique opportunity to become part of this experience, to demonstrate that your brand is just as involved in this modern day tragedy as the fan is, and to communicate that your brand is helping the consumer's team to win, to play better, and to overcome all odds. And if their brand is doing that for my heroes, they must be doing it for me.

Mark Harrison has an MBA in entrepreneurship and strategic marketing and 17 years of experience in sponsorship, event marketing, and consumer promotions. He has worked with such brands as Coca-Cola, CFL, BMW, Esso, HBC, and Johnson & Johnson.

Some Underlying Marketing Theory

Marketing

The American Marketing Association (AMA) updated its definition of marketing in the fall of 2004 to:

> Marketing is an organizational function and a set of processes for creating, communicating and delivering value to customers and for managing customer relationships in ways that benefit the organization and its stakeholders[1].

This definition clearly describes marketing as not only an organizational function but also a set of processes that enable the creation of relationships between an organization and its stakeholders, both internal (e.g., employees, consultants) and external (e.g., suppliers, customers). Value is a key construct in the definition, which explicitly appreciates that the benefits provided to both parties in the exchange result from the delivery of value to customers. A recent

---

[1] American Marketing Association (2004) A new definition of marketing. *Marketing News,* Sept. 15.

development in marketing is also emphasized in the AMA definition—the move from an exchange to a relationship, emphasizing the objective of seeking long-term relationships with loyal customers rather than one-time purchases.

Development of Marketing

Marketing has been around as long as some people have been selling and others buying. In older times, barter was often at the heart of the exchange. For example, a corn farmer would exchange five bushels of corn for a quarter of beef from a nearby beef farmer. Some marketers have even traced the roots of marketing as far back as 3000 years to the Lydians, who were known to be the first to use coins as a form of value[2].

Bartels suggests that the term "marketing" was coined around 1910[3]. And about 60 years ago, we began to observe in the literature and in practice the early developments of the field. Now known as marketing management, it has evolved considerably, and today we know that business is most profitable when both the organization and the customer are satisfied and happy.

Marketing Theory

This book assumes that the reader has limited understanding of marketing. Therefore, we will now highlight some key concepts and tools of marketing theory.

Exchange

The marketing exchange, a key concept of marketing theory, articulates that both sides must receive value from the transaction that they perceive to be greater than what the exchange is costing them. For example, if Susan is considering spending $119 on a ticket to a Calgary Flames hockey game, she will only make the exchange if she believes that the value she'll receive back (e.g., entertainment, seat location, team, associated activities, telling her friends she went to the game) is worth more than $119 to her. This concept of value varies from one individual to the other or from one group to the next.

Value and Utility

Marketing theory has always worked with the four well-established utilities (or value provided from satisfying a need or want) of marketing. When met, these four utilities—form, time, place, and possession—are what provide value to the customer. Form refers to the tangible properties of the product. For example, the form properties of a running shoe include comfort, durability, look, colour, ease of use, and packaging. Time describes the consumer's ability to access the product at the right time. From the organization's end,

utility: value provided from satisfying a need or want.

---

[2] Dewan, T., K. Jensen, C. Farrell, & N. O'Reilly (2005) *Marketing: What is it Good For?* Copley.

[3] Bartels, R. (1976) *The History of Marketing Thought*, 2nd ed. Grid.

this includes such considerations as inventory, delivery, and warehousing. An example is the concession stands at the 2006 Canadian Women's Hockey Championships, where fans want to be able to purchase cold beer, warm hot dogs, and salted popcorn without missing any of the action on the ice. Place is the utility of being able to purchase and/or receive the product at a convenient and accessible location. Buying tickets for a sporting event is a good example, as those that are easily accessible (available through TicketMaster, Internet, in-person, stores) are more likely to sell than those with only a single outlet. Possession is the value created by giving the consumer the ability to actually take ownership of the product immediately. Possession becomes more important in high-involvement decisions like purchasing a Montreal Canadiens season ticket package.

Needs and Wants

A key idea in marketing is the satisfaction of consumer needs and wants. At a most basic level, people have needs (e.g., shelter, food, drink) and wants (e.g., ego, self-actualization) that organizations in capitalist societies seek to meet. In the western world, where technology, disposable income, and free time have led to a consumer-based society, one could argue that many wants have become needs. For example, an individual who golfs five times a year does not require a set of high-end Tiger Woods–endorsed clubs to play a round; however, given the advances of our materialistic culture, for some this may be a necessity. Right or wrong, it is a reality.

Applied Sociology

Some view marketing as the application of sociology. As marketers, we seek to understand society and how it functions and then work within it. Our understanding of how it is structured, how people live, and what people need and want allows us to help our organizations be successful. On this point, it is important to note that marketers do not critique society; they work within it.

Relationship Marketing (1:1 Marketing)

In the recently developed notion of relationship marketing, organizations use technology to market to individual consumers through databases, online ordering, and Internet/phone communication (e.g., Dell Computers). Quite simply, technology has enabled mass market offerings to be customized. Although impossible with certain products and in certain industries, it is widely viewed as the ideal form of marketing—providing an offering that is designed to meet the needs of specific customers.

The Two Tasks of Marketing

Marketers work is a two-stage process—discovering customer needs/wants and then satisfying them. The first task is driven by discovery through market research; the second by strategy development and implementation through the application of marketing principles.

The 3 Cs

When looking internally, marketers focus on the 3 Cs—company, competition, and consumers. To be successful, they must understand each. Company refers to the firm or organization of the marketer and is described based on its assets (e.g., skilled employees, physical structures, patents) and its competencies, things it is good at (e.g., software development, supply chain management). The things it does better than its competition are called competitive advantages. Competition involves understanding who the company is competing against for customers. It takes three forms: direct competitors, substitutes, and future competition. For example, in seeking to increase ticket sales, the marketing director of the Toronto Argos CFL team would consider nearby professional football clubs (e.g., Buffalo Bills and Hamilton Tiger-Cats) as direct competition; any entertainment activity that could replace going to the game (e.g., other sport events, going to a movie, going on a date, watching television) as substitutes; and a possible NFL or Arena Football League team (again) setting up shop in Toronto as future competition. For consumers, the third C, the marketer uses various concepts of consumer behaviour to understand the individuals in their market and why, for example, these people might attend an Argos game.

competition: another organization or product competing with you for customers.

consumer: a person who purchases a product (good and/or service).

substitute: as a form of competition, this refers to any entertainment activity that could replace going to the game.

PEST

Marketers must understand their organization's external environment to develop and implement effective strategy. PEST—political, economic, social (demographic), and technological—is a useful tool to describe and organize the forces whose opportunities and threats the marketer must consider.

STP (Segmentation, Targeting, Positioning)

This is the process of building from the background research (PEST and 3 Cs) to define the target market(s) and demonstrate how the offering will be positioned vis-à-vis the competition, which in turn, provides the basis for developing the marketing strategy.

segmentation: dividing up the market into distinct homogeneous groups.

targeting: selecting the segment(s) to target.

positioning: developing a marketing strategy that positions the product in the minds of consumers in relation to competition.

marketing mix: comprises the strategic elements: product, price, promotion, and place.

The Marketing Mix

Also known as marketing strategy, the mix involves the well-known 4 Ps—product, price, promotion, and place. Any marketing plan needs to consider these four elements to develop a strategy based on the product attributes desired by the target market(s), a price point that leads to perceived value, promotional techniques that will reach the target market(s), and making sure that distribution plans are set up so that the product can get into the hands of consumers. Figure 1-1 illustrates the relationship between the 4Ps, STP, PEST, and the 3Cs.

Marketing as a Revenue Generator

Marketing scholars and practitioners stress that marketing is the only revenue-generating activity in an organization.

FIGURE 1-1

external analysis		marketing strategy
PEST		product
competition	STP	price
substitutes		promotion
market analysis		place
consumer behaviour		marketing tactics
opportunities		
threats		

The Uniqueness of Sport Marketing

Marketing theory is applied in most, if not all, industries. Sport marketing, however, is one of a few industry-based subfields of marketing that has developed its own body of literature and methods of common practice. Why is sport marketing different? Why does it merit its own text and its own courses?

Simply, sport marketing provides organizations—both those marketing sport directly (e.g., learn-to-swim programs selling lessons to children) and those marketing indirectly through sport (e.g., Buick selling more cars through its sponsorship of Tiger Woods)—with access to properties where people have unbridled passion for their team, their sport, their favourite players, their favourite coaches, their favourite equipment, and/or their favourite ball cap. For example, the strong attachment fans have to the Toronto Maple Leafs is rarely found with other products. Sport marketing is thus about more than just the needs and wants; it is about connecting to emotions, building passion, and leveraging images.

A number of factors further elevate the importance of sport marketing. First, the ability of sport organizations to provide means by which a nonsport organization can associate itself with attractive sports and sports heroes is on the rise. Second, sport is increasingly accessible through such media technologies as television, radio, the Internet, and satellite phone[4]. Third, sport has been shown to generate considerable excitement and emotional attachment by its consumers, which may render them more susceptible to product-based messages and other marketing initiatives[5]. Fourth, sport and its events have the ability to provide significant leveraging opportunities (e.g., merchandise, cross-promotions, brand extensions, licensing, dealer incentives) to nonsport

sport marketing: activities that provide organizations—both those marketing sport and those marketing through sport—with access to properties where people have unbridled passion for their team, their sport, their favourite players, their favourite coaches, their favourite equipment, their favourite ball cap, etc.

---

[4] Quester, P. & B. Thompson (2001) Advertising and promotion leverage on arts sponsorship effectiveness. *Journal of Advertising Research*, 41(Jan–Feb):33–47.

[5] O'Neal, M., P. Finch, J.O. Hamilton, & K. Hamilton (1987) Nothing sells like sports. *Business Week*, Aug. 31:48–53.

organizations[6]. Fifth, interest in leisure-type events and properties has been increasing since the mid-1990s[7], and today it is very difficult to find a sporting event that is not sponsored[8]. Sixth, sport spectators are exposed to messages in favourable conditions, where there is enthusiasm, excitement, and enjoyment, and where they are relaxed and receptive to sponsors' messages[9]. Finally, a sport can be adopted to reach specific target market segments of narrow demographics in a more diverse and cost-efficient manner[10].

A Definition of Sport Marketing

"Sport marketing is the specific application of marketing principles and processes to sport products and to the marketing of non-sports products associated with a sport[11]."

Case: Athletes CAN and Sport Marketing

Background

Athletes CAN is Canada's only fully independent and inclusive organization representing athletes on Canadian national teams, including Commonwealth, Aboriginal, Olympic, Pan American, and Paralympic athletes. The organization was developed to provide a voice for Canada's top athletes, who previously had not been represented at many levels of decision making (e.g., government, NSO, MSO). With a membership of nearly 3000 athletes, the organization set its mission to ensure a fair, responsive, and supportive system for Canadian high-performance athletes by working with their partners in the areas of leadership, advocacy, and education.

Athletes CAN is governed by an 11-member board of directors, with day-to-day operations run by two staff members and a chief executive officer. At present, one staff member is responsible for marketing, while all are involved in sponsor servicing and relations. The dedication of staff to marketing demonstrates the importance of that function.

Athletes CAN as a Marketing Property

From a marketing point of view, Athletes CAN is an attractive property to some organizations. It has direct access to 3000 Canadian high-performance athletes through its database of all national team athletes in Canada, including well-known stars—Alexandre Despaties, Cindy Klassen, Simon Whitfield, Hailey Wickenheiser, and Clara Hughes. In sport, Athletes CAN is respected and is recognized as the collective voice for all Canadian amateur athletes.

[6] Stotlar, D.K. (1993) Sponsorship and the Olympic Winter Games. *Sport Marketing Quarterly*, 2(1):35–43.

[7] Gwinner, K.P. (1997) A model of image creation and image transfer in event sponsorship. *International Marketing Review*, 14(3):145–58.

[8] Kover, A.J. (2001) Editorial: The sponsorship issue. *Journal of Advertising Research*, 41(Jan–Feb):5.

[9] Nicholls, J.A.F., S. Roslow, & S. Dublish (1999) Brand recall and brand preference at sponsored golf and tennis tournaments. *European Journal of Marketing*, 33(3/4):365–86.

[10] Crompton, J.L. (2004) Sponsorship ambushing in sport. *Managing Leisure*, 9:1–12.

[11] Shank, M. (2005). *Sports Marketing: A Strategic Perspective*, 3rd ed. Pearson-Prentice-Hall.

Athletes CAN recognizes the importance of marketing to achieve its mission, in both generating the resources necessary to support its programs and promoting its existence and its members to the Canadian sport community. For example, Athletes CAN is committed to supporting the sponsorship efforts of athletes, in an attempt to rely less on government funding.

Athletes CAN – Bell Canada Athletes Connect Program

One of Athletes CAN's marketing activities is its partnership with Bell Canada on the Athletes Connect Program. Canada's largest telecommunications company, Bell is a sponsor of both the 2010 Vancouver Olympic Games and the Canadian Olympic Committee. Bell provides Athletes CAN with an annual contribution of over $5 million in cash and in-kind value. The program offers comprehensive telecommunications services to Canada's senior national team athletes competing in the Olympics, Paralympics, Aboriginal, Commonwealth, or Pan American Games, where eligible athletes may receive at no charge:

- A limited edition Samsung a660 handset for 12 months
- Digital North America 800 Rate Plan for 12 months; airtime value about $80–100 a month
- Bell Sympatico high-speed Internet (to athletes in Ontario and Quebec) at a value of about $40–50 a month

In exchange, Bell can access all Canadian athletes at one time through its association with Athletes CAN. It also leverages this investment toward being the number 1 telecommunications company in Canada under the tag line "Connecting athletes to something that they care more about than medals: their families." Given the diversity of Athletes CAN's membership and the fame of these members in their home communities, Bell also sees the sponsorship as a way to reach potential customers in all regions of Canada.

Bell dedicates six full-time employees to servicing the program. They work on these leveraging activities:

- During the Olympic Games, Bell offers a special limited-edition cell phone in partnership with Olympic sponsor Samsung. It is a fundraising opportunity, with a portion of profit from the sales of these cell phones directed to Athletes CAN.
- During the Olympic Games, Bell implements a fully integrated communication program consisting of newspaper, television, radio, and Internet advertising.
- Bell sponsors nine athletes (beyond the Athletes CAN sponsorship), who act as athlete ambassadors for the program.
- Bell creates a program during the Olympic Games to connect athletes to the public by purchasing in-program capsules (advertising) where athletes connect with family and/or friends through the Internet.
- Bell manages a website for the program.

Source: Institute for Sport Marketing Case Studies. Laurentian University 2003-2005

Case Questions

1. Why is this case an example of sport marketing?
2. What product does Athletes CAN offer? Why is it of value to Bell?
3. What properties (assets and competencies) of Athletes CAN might be of value to potential marketing partners?
4. In addition to sponsorship, what kind of marketing activities could Athletes CAN consider doing in the future?
5. Could Bell have partnered with another nonsport property to achieve the same marketing benefits as it does with Athletes CAN? If so, name it and decide which you would recommend to Bell.
6. Could Athletes CAN have partnered with another sponsor to achieve the same marketing benefits as it does with Bell? If so, name it and decide which you would recommend to Athletes CAN.

Chapter Summary

This chapter introduces marketing and sport marketing. It assumes that the reader has little experience or background in marketing and therefore provides a brief overview of marketing and its key concepts. The goal of marketing is to satisfy the needs and wants of consumers by engaging them in an exchange process to build long-term relationships. While sport marketers also aim to satisfy needs and wants, they seek to connect emotions and build passion with consumers. Sport marketing happens in two distinct ways: the marketing of sport products and services directly to consumers of sport (e.g., Wilson tennis racquets) and marketing through sports, or using sport to market other consumer and industrial products through promotions (e.g., General Mills using its sponsorship of Olympic athletes to put their pictures on its Cheerios boxes).

Test Your Knowledge

1. What does the STP stand for? Describe each term and explain how it fits into marketing theory.
2. Analyze the 2004 AMA definition of marketing. From your review, list at least four key points of that definition.
3. A smart marketer considers which element first: product, positioning, segmentation, price, place, targeting, or distribution?
4. In fewer than 50 of your own words, describe what marketing is.
5. What is the competition for:

   a. Toronto Blue Jays
   b. Callaway Golf
   c. Sport Canada
   d. Jim's Bike Store in Kelowna, BC
   e. The Ottawa 67s Junior A Hockey Club

    f.   Alpine Canada

    g.   A player's agent

    h.   Any coach

6. What makes sport marketing unique? Are there any reasons you can think of that are not in this text?

7. Define and give examples of these concepts:

    a.   marketing

    b.   exchange

    c.   consumer

    d.   competition

    e.   substitute

    f.   segmentation, targeting, and positioning

    g.   product, price, promotion, and place

    h.   utility

For more review questions, go to http://www.sportmarketing.nelson.com.

Key Terms

competition	product
consumer	promotion
exchange	segmentation
marketing	sport marketing
marketing mix	substitute
place	targeting
positioning	utility
price	

A full glossary of key term definitions is located at http://www.sportmarketing.nelson.com.

Internet Resources

Get acquainted with marketing and sport sites:

International Olympic Committee, http://www.olympic.org

National Hockey League, http://www.nhl.com

Major League Baseball, http://www.mlb.com

National Basketball Association, http://www.nba.com

Athletes CAN, http://www.athletescan.com

American Marketing Association, http://www.ama.org

Canadian Marketing Association, http://www.the-cma.org/

Sport Marketing Quarterly, http://www.fitinfotech.com/smq/smq.tpl

International Journal of Sport Management and Marketing,
https://www.inderscience.com/browse/index.php?journalID=102

International Journal of Sports Marketing & Sponsorship,
http://www.imr-info.com/SM/IJSM/

The Sport Journal, http://www.thesportjournal.org/

NASSM, http://www.nassm.com/

Journal of Sport Management,
http://www.humankinetics.com/JSM/journalAbout.cfm

European Sport Management Quarterly,
http://www.tandf.co.uk/journals/titles/16184742.asp

International Journal of Sport Finance,
http://www.fitinfotech.com/IJSF/IJSF.tpl

Sports Marketing on Wikipedia,
http://en.wikipedia.org/wiki/Sports_marketing

Brand Noise (Sport Marketing),
http://brandnoise.typepad.com/brand_noise/sports_marketing/index.html

Sports Marketing: The motor that drives the sports business,
http://www.wharton.universia.net/index.cfm?fa=viewfeature&id=
966&language=english

Octagon Sports Marketing, http://www.octagon.com/

Q Sports, http://www.qsports.net/

Sports marketing in India,
http://www.indianchild.com/marketing/sports-marketing.htm

Chapter 2

The Canadian Sport Industry

Source: Kathy Willens / AP Photo / CP Images FILE

Learning Objectives

- To understand the complexity, scope, and variation of Canadian sport
- To be able to speak knowledgeably about and understand the differences between professional, Olympic, university, college, and grassroots sport
- To be well versed in the important organizations, facilities, events, and policies driving sport in Canada
- To understand the role of governments in Canadian sport
- To understand the role of corporate Canada in sport
- To understand the roles of coaches, athletes, and administrators in sport in Canada

Introduction

In Canada, sport is important

From a child playing hockey on a frozen pond to a sprinter at the starting line of the Olympics or a professional athlete hoisting the championship trophy, sport engages and fascinates people on an individual, national, and global scale. In Canada, sport is deeply rooted in our past, present, and future and, as such, it plays an important role in the lives of millions of Canadians. Bloom,

Grant, and Watt remarked[1]: "Sport touches many aspects of Canadians' lives, yet many people are unaware of how powerfully sport affects them ... it changes individuals ... it affects communities ... it has an impact on the economy ... [and] it helps to shape our national and cultural identities." The significance of sport in Canada makes it an important topic for study, with no shortage of subject matter to examine. The purpose of this chapter is to provide a comprehensive overview of sport in Canada.

Four distinct yet interconnected facets make up Canadian sport:

- **Professional sport** refers to leagues and athletes that represent private enterprise and/or who compete in exchange for economic gain.
- University and **collegiate sport** pertains to competitions that involve student-athletes competing on behalf of the postsecondary institution in which they are enrolled.
- **Olympic sport** covers high-performance athletic competition in which athletes typically compete more for personal than economic, gain, although many Olympic athletes do experience significant financial benefit from their athletic careers..
- **Grassroots sport** refers to sport that is based around local communities and participation by the general public.

In addition to the four facets of our sport system, this chapter discusses sport events and facilities in a Canadian context to provide a comprehensive view of sport in Canada.

A Brief Introduction to Canada

To explain sport in Canada, it is important to describe the country in which sport exists. Canada is widely known as a nation of vast distances, natural resources, and peace keeping. Diversity prevails in everything from population to climate and topography. As a member of the British Commonwealth, Canada is both a constitutional monarchy and a parliamentary democracy. However, despite our tie to Britain, Canada's closest ally is the United States, with whom it shares its southern border. Canada is also bordered by three oceans: the Atlantic to the east, the Pacific to the west, and the Arctic to the north. Measuring 9 984 670 square kilometres, Canada is the second largest country in the world[2]. Its vast expanse comprises a wide diversity of topography, with mountains in the west, prairies in central Canada, tundra to the north, and lowlands in the southeast. The climate is similarly diverse and varies between arctic and sub-arctic in the north and temperate in the south[3].

professional sport: leagues and athletes that represent private enterprise and/or who compete in exchange for economic gain.

collegiate sport: competitions that involve student-athletes competing on behalf of the postsecondary institution in which they are enrolled.

Olympic sport: a high-performance athletic competition in which athletes compete for personal, rather than economic, gain.

grassroots sport: sport that is based around local communities and participation by the general public.

---

[1] Bloom, M., M. Grant, & D. Watt (2005) *Strengthening Canada: The Socio-economic Benefits of Sport Participation in Canada*. Conference Board of Canada.

[2] Central Intelligence Agency (2006) The World Factbook: Canada. Retrieved November 15, 2006 from https://www.cia.gov/cia/publications/factbook/geos/ca.html.

[3] ibid.

The population of Canada is estimated at almost 33 million people[4]. The majority (70%) are between the ages of 15 and 64[5], with a median age of 38.9[6]. Canada has a low population density of about 3.1 people per square kilometre. (For comparison, the US has 29.4 people per square kilometre, and the Netherlands 390.3)[7]. However, 80 percent of the Canadian population lives in urban areas[8], with 90 percent within 160 km of the US border[9].

Canada is a highly developed nation with a literacy rate of 99 percent[10] and an average life expectancy of 78 years[11]. Language plays a major role in Canadian society, as the country recognizes two official languages, English and French. About 67 percent of the population speaks English and no French, 13 percent speak French and no English, 18 percent speak both languages, and 1.5 percent speak neither[12]. Canada also has a diverse ethnic population, with 18.4 percent being foreign-born[13]. About 230 000 immigrants arrived in Canada in 2002[14]. The multicultural nature of Canadian society is a major facet of Canadian identity and plays a large role in the generally diversified character of the country.

An economically affluent country, Canada operates in a market-oriented economic system that represents about 2 percent of the world's economy. The gross domestic product (GDP) in 2005 was $1.111 trillion, or $33 900 per capita, with an annual growth rate of 2.9 percent[15]. Canada's closest neighbour, the US, is also its largest trading partner, accounting for 85 percent of exports and 56.7 percent of imports[16]. Canada possesses vast natural resources, including iron ore, zinc, copper, nickel, gold, lead, diamonds, silver, fish, timber, wildlife, coal, petroleum, natural gas, and hydro electric power[17], which makes it a valuable global trading partner and ensures relative affluence in the future.

The demographics, diversified nature, and economic situation of the country all have a large impact on sport, and so the above examination of these aspects will contribute to a better understanding of sport in a Canadian context.

---

[4] Statistics Canada (2006) Population by year, by province and territory. Retrieved November 15, 2006 from http://www40.statcan.ca/l01/cst01/demo02a.htm?sdi=population.

[5] ibid.

[6] Central Intelligence Agency (2006) The World Factbook: Canada.

[7] ibid.

[8] Statistics Canada (2001) Population urban and rural, by province and territory. Retrieved November 15, 2006 from http://www40.statcan.ca/l01/cst01/demo62a.htm.

[9] Central Intelligence Agency (2006) The World Factbook: Canada.

[10] ibid.

[11] Statistics Canada (1996) Disability-free life expectancy, by province and territory. Retrieved November 15, 2006 from http://www40.statcan.ca/l01/cst01/health38.htm.

[12] Statistics Canada (2001) Population by knowledge of official language by province and territory. Retrieved November 15, 2006 from http://www40.statcan.ca/l01/cst01/demo15a.htm.

[13] Statistics Canada (2001) Proportion of foreign-born population by province and territory 1991–2001. Retrieved November 15, 2006 from http://www40.statcan.ca/l01/cst01/demo46a.htm.

[14] Citizenship and Immigration Canada (2002) Facts and Figures 2002, Immigration Overview. Retrieved November 15, 2006 from http://www.parl.gc.ca/information/library/PRBpubs/bp190–e.htm.

[15] Central Intelligence Agency. (2006). The World Factbook: Canada.

[16] ibid.

[17] ibid.

Canadian Sport

Canada's former secretary of state (amateur sport) Denis Coderre once declared that[18]:

> Sport is at the heart of Canadian life. It's an activity that has benefits for each and every Canadian, for our communities, and for our country. Sport puts front and centre the qualities we value as Canadians—fairness, team spirit, hard work, dedication, and commitment.

This quote indicates the position of sport as a vital thread in the fabric of Canadian society. The following overview of Canadian sport will provide a valuable outline of the sport community, as it examines professional sport, university and college sport, Olympic sport, grassroots sport, sport facilities, and **sport events** in Canada.

sport events: opportunities for numerous social, economic, and cultural benefits including facility legacies, job creation, and volunteer development.

Professional Sport

Professional sport in Canada can be divided into five categories:

- tier one professional sport
- tier two professional sport
- tier three professional sport
- professional sport competition
- sports entertainment

This section looks at each of these categories and discusses the challenges facing professional sport in Canada.

Tier One Professional Sport

Tier one professional leagues are considered the highest level of professional sport competition in North America and usually the highest level of professional competition globally. Canadians have been an increasing presence in all professional leagues; in 2006, Canadian athletes were voted as the National Basketball Association MVP, National Hockey League MVP, and Major League Baseball American League MVP.

National Hockey League (NHL): Currently six Canadian teams compete in the National Hockey League. From 1992 to 1995, there were eight Canadian teams; however, the Quebec Nordiques moved to Denver in 1995, and the Winnipeg Jets to Phoenix, leaving the Calgary Flames, Edmonton Oilers, Montreal Canadiens, Ottawa Senators, Toronto Maple Leafs, and Vancouver Canucks. Despite being home to only one-fifth of the leagues teams, Canada's influence on the league is unmatched. For instance, during 2005–2006 season, over half of the players on NHL rosters were Canadian born. In addition, five

---

[18] Culture Statistics Program (2000) *Sport Participation in Canada: 1998 Report.* Public Works and Government Services Canada.

of the six Canadian teams were in the top ten for average attendance during the same season[19], and Canadian teams represent three of the top ten Forbes franchise valuations[20]. Despite these positive figures, many of the Canadian teams have experienced financial difficulties, as Edmonton, Calgary, and Ottawa are considered to be small-market teams. However, a new collective bargaining agreement signed by the NHL after the lockout of the 2004–2005 season is expected to assist these teams in competing with the larger markets.

Major League Baseball (MLB): The Toronto Blue Jays is the only Major League Baseball team in Canada. From 1977 to 2005, there were two teams; however, after the 2004 season, the Montreal Expos moved to Washington. The Blue Jays won back-to-back World Series in 1992 and 1993. Since then, the team has not been back in the post season and, as a result, has seen its attendance drop. The average game attendance for the 2006 season was 28 422, which put it 18th out of the 30 league teams[21]. The Blue Jays home games are at the Rogers Centre in downtown Toronto, which it shares with the Toronto Argonauts of the Canadian Football League.

National Basketball Association (NBA): The Toronto Raptors is the only National Basketball Association team in Canada. It joined the league in 1995, along with the Vancouver Grizzlies, which moved to Memphis in 2001. The team has yet to win a league championship and has made the playoffs in only three of its first 11 seasons, never advancing beyond the second round. Despite this, the team has a large fan base, particularly among younger generations with whom basketball has become an increasingly popular sport. The arrival of NBA stars in Toronto over the years has also raised the profile of the club. The Raptors' home games are in Toronto's Air Canada Centre. During the 2005–2006 season, their average attendance was 17 054[22], 17th out of 30 teams in the league.

Tier Two Professional Sport

Tier two professional leagues include leagues that represent a high level of professional sport in Canada or North America but not the world.

Canadian Football League (CFL): The CFL is a professional football league made up entirely of Canadian teams. There are eight teams in two divisions: The East Division consists of the Hamilton Tiger-Cats, Montreal Alouettes, Toronto Argonauts, and Winnipeg Blue Bombers; the West Division consists of the BC Lions, Calgary Stampeders, Edmonton Eskimos, and Saskatchewan Roughriders. Founded in 1958, the league has seen numerous franchises come

---

[19] ESPN (2006) NHL Attendance Leaders. Retrieved November 13, 2006 from http://sports.espn.go.com/nhl/attendance?sort=home_avg&year=2006.

[20] Ozanian, M.K. & K. Badenhausen (2006) The business of hockey. Retrieved November 13, 2006 from http://www.forbes.com/lists/2006/31/biz_06nhl_NHL-Team-Valuations_land.html.

[21] ESPN (2006) MLB attendance leaders. Retrieved November 13, 2006 from http://sports.espn.go.com/mlb/attendance.

[22] ESPN (2006) NBA attendance leaders. Retrieved November 13, 2006 from http://sports.espn.go.com/nba/attendance?year=2006.

and go, including six now defunct teams in American cities. The league championship, called the Grey Cup, takes place each November, and the all-Canadian nature of the league has led the event to become a powerful symbol of Canadian sport. The numerous differences between the football of the CFL and that of the National Football League (NFL) include the size of the field (the Canadian field is 110 by 65 yards, the American 100 by 53.5 yards) and the number of downs (to advance the ball ten yards, Canadian football allows three downs, American four downs). Recent years have seen an increase in attendance levels for most of the CFL teams. The average attendance in 2006 was over 28 000, with western franchises enjoying the highest level of support[23].

American Hockey League (AHL): The American Hockey League is composed of the minor league affiliate teams of the NHL. Three Canadian teams in the AHL are affiliates of Canadian NHL teams: The Manitoba Moose are affiliated with the Vancouver Canucks, the Hamilton Bulldogs with the Montreal Canadiens, and the Toronto Marlies with the Toronto Maple Leafs. Attendance for the three Canadian teams for the 2005–2006 season averaged 5853, which is slightly higher than the league average of 5487[24].

Major League Soccer (MLS): The newest addition to Canadian professional sports is the first Canadian Major League Soccer franchise, Toronto FC. Currently, Canada and the US are among the few countries whose most popular spectator sport is not soccer. MLS is North America's highest level of professional soccer, but it does not compare to leagues such as the English Premiership or Spanish La Liga in terms of status, support, or financial capability. For example, MLS average attendance in 2006 was 15 502[25], while the average attendance in the English Premier League was 34 099[26]. The 2007 MLS season will be Toronto FC's first since the city was granted a franchise in 2006. They will be playing their home games in Toronto's new soccer-specific stadium, BMO Field.

National Lacrosse League (NLL): The National Lacrosse League consists of 13 teams, three located in Canadian cites. The Calgary Roughnecks and the Edmonton Rush are in the West Division, while the Toronto Rock is in the East Division. The Rock is the most successful team in the history of the league, having won the championship five times in the nine seasons since the league's inauguration in 1998. The average attendance for the Canadian teams is 12 894, significantly higher than the league average of 10 703[27].

[23] Canadian Football League (2006) Schedule. Retrieved November 13, 2006 from http://www.cfl.ca/index.php?module=sked&func=view&year=2006.

[24] Hornstein, H. (2006) 2005–06 AHL attendance. Retrieved November 13, 2006 from http://www.mib.org/~lennier/hockey/leagueatt.cgi.

[25] Kenn.com. (2006). Basic numbers. Retrieved November 13, 2006 from http://www.kenn.com/soccer/mls/basic.html.

[26] ESPNsoccernet (2006) Premiership attendance 2006/07. Retrieved November 13, 2006 from http://soccernet.espn.go.com/stats/attendance?league=eng.1&year=2006&cc=5901.

[27] Pointstreak.com. (2006). League attendance. Retrieved November 13, 2006 from http://www.pointstreak.com/prostats/attendance.html?leagueid=230&seasonid=977.

Tier Three Professional Leagues

Tier three professional leagues represent a lower level of professional competition in a specific sport in North America. They are also often leagues in a stage of growth that have yet to establish themselves as major sport entities.

United Soccer League: First Division (USL): Until the arrival of the MLS in 2006, the USL was the highest level of soccer competition in Canada. Currently, there are two Canadian teams in the USL, the Montreal Impact and Vancouver Whitecaps. With the arrival of Toronto FC in MLS, the USL's Toronto franchise, the Lynx, dropped to the premier development league as of 2007. In 2006, USL average attendance was 4667, while Montreal's was 11 554 and Vancouver's 5085[28].

Women's Professional Leagues: Even at the highest levels of professional competition available for women in sports, the women's professional leagues in Canada are third tier. They simply do not have the status or visibility of the comparable men's leagues, and in most cases, the women are not full-time athletes. Two women's professional leagues in Canada are the National Women's Hockey League (NWHL) and the W-League (semiprofessional soccer). There are ten Canadian teams in the NWHL: the Brampton Thunder, Etobicoke Dolphins, Toronto Aeros, Oakville Ice, Montreal Axion, Ottawa Raiders, Quebec Avalanche, British Columbia Breakers, Calgary Oval X-treme, Edmonton Chimos, and Saskatchewan Prairie Ice. The W-League has seven Canadian teams: the Vancouver Whitecaps, London Gryphons, Toronto Lady Lynx, Hamilton Avalanche, Laval Comets, Ottawa Fury, and Sudbury Canadians.

Canadian Tire NASCAR Series: Previously called the CASCAR Super Series, this Canadian professional stock car racing series was relaunched as the Canadian Tire NASCAR Series for 2007. The series consists of 10 to 12 races a year and targets a Canadian NASCAR fan base of about 5.8 million people.

Professional Sport Competition

Professional competition represents those sports that have no major professional league or tour operating exclusively in Canada but rather have specific professional events on their world tours that take place in Canada.

- *Tennis:* The Rogers Cup is the Canadian stop on the Men's Association of Tennis Professionals Tour and the Women's Tennis Association Tour.
- *Golf:* The Canadian Open is the annual Canadian stop in the Professional Golf Association Tour (PGA), while the CN Canadian Women's Open is the annual Canadian stop for the Ladies Professional Golf Association (LPGA).
- *Car racing:* Several Canadian cities host annual races including Formula One in Montreal and CHAMP car in Edmonton, Toronto, Vancouver and Mount Tremblant.
- *Other:* Many other professional competitions take place annually in Canada, including boxing, figure skating, equestrian, and extreme sports.

---

[28] Kenn.com (2006) USL First Division attendance. Retrieved November 13, 2006 from http://kenn.com/sports/soccer/usl/usl1.html.

Sport Entertainment

Sport entertainment represents sports which do not fit the mould of traditional professional sports but whose popularity has made them an important aspect of Canadian professional sport culture. Most notably, professional wrestling has become a huge business dominated by World Wrestling Entertainment, Inc. (WWE). (To emphasize that they are in the business of sport entertainment, the World Wrestling Federation changed its name in 2002 to World Wrestling Entertainment[29].) While the matches are staged and the outcomes predetermined, the athletic ability of the performers is unquestionable. The WWE makes frequent visits to Canadian cities for live performances, and many of its weekly and pay-per-view programs are regulars on Canadian television. The numerous other examples of sport entertainment in Canada include ultimate fighting, professional rodeo, extreme sports, poker, and strongest man competitions.

Challenges for Canadian Professional Sport

Many factors work together to challenge the Canadian professional sport community. The first is the *value of the Canadian dollar* in comparison with the American dollar. While there has been a resurgence of the Canadian dollar in recent times, it has often been worth significantly less than the American dollar, which poses problems for Canadian teams in professional leagues based primarily in the US. For example, while Canadian team revenues are collected in Canadian dollars, players are paid in American dollars, and to attract and hold onto players in the competitive marketplace, Canadian teams must pay similar salaries to those offered in the US. *Taxation policies* are a second challenge facing Canadian professional teams. Taxes are generally higher in Canada than the US, and professional sport is typically given fewer favours (e.g., new stadiums paid by taxpayers). While many American teams are exempt from municipal taxes, Canadian teams must pay municipal as well as federal and provincial taxes. In addition, the large salaries of major professional athletes are taxed at a higher level in Canada than the US. This poses a problem for the Canadian teams competing to attract the best players, since many players do not want to come to Canada and have a larger portion of their salaries taxed. The *level of public subsidy* is a third challenge to Canadian professional teams. According to Brown and Paul[30], American taxpayer dollars compose the majority of finances used to build new professional sports complexes and facilities. Public subsidies in Canada are much lower, and so make Canadian cities much less attractive for new franchises. This is unlikely to change in the future, as the Canadian public has voiced major concerns over the public subsidy of professional sport.

---

[29] World Wrestling Entertainment, Inc. (2002) World Wrestling Federation Entertainment drops the "F" to emphasize the "E" for entertainment. Retrieved November 15, 2006 from http://corporate.wwe.com/news/2002/2002_05_06.jsp.

[30] Brown, C. & D. Paul (2002) The political scorecard of professional sports facility referendums in the United States, 1984–2000. *Journal of Sport & Social Issues*, 26(3): 248–67.

Phil Legault, Vice-President Communications, Ottawa Senators

The Face of Professional Sports—Not Just a One-Game Business

Eugene Melnyk has been the owner of the National Hockey League's Ottawa Senators Hockey Club and its home arena (now known as Scotiabank Place) since August 2003. But that is only a small part of the business picture. One must consider the many elements of a professional sport franchise, including facilities, marketing programs, ownership objectives, and surviving in the highly competitive entertainment marketplace.

Prior to Melnyk taking over as owner of the National Capital Region's (NCR) NHL franchise, the club passed through the hands of founder Bruce Firestone and then Rod Bryden. Each owner played an important role in developing the business of the operation. As is proven by the suburban location of Scotiabank Place, Firestone's dream of reviving Ottawa's turn-of-century NHL success[31] was closely tied to developing the land his company owned in the west end of the city. As CEO and chairman of Terrace Investments in 1989, Firestone not only filed a letter of intent with the NHL for an expansion team, but also submitted to the Ottawa-Carleton regional government the official plan for the approval of the Palladium site. At the time, plans for Palladium included rezoning 600 acres for more than just a world-class arena and entertainment venue. He also sought approval for a luxury hotel, retail stores, office complex, business park, housing, and more.

By the time Firestone and the Senators had received full NHL membership in December 1991, it was evident that the success of professional hockey in the NCR would be driven by the team's ability to draw fans to the city's west end from Ottawa, Gatineau, and surrounding areas. The difficulty of the business challenge became evident in August 1993, when Firestone, who had brought the NHL back to the region, resigned as chairman and governor of the Ottawa Senators and sold his remaining interest to Rod Bryden, who then became the majority owner of the club and arena.

In the 10 years (1993–2003) that he was the majority owner of the hockey club and facility, Bryden continued Firestone's "diversity of business" plan as a means of survival and, hopefully, profit. Under his direction, the organization took over sole operation and management of Scotiabank Place, added office towers to the 600-acre property and continued to look at strengthening its core business, the hockey team, through outside ventures, such as adding more concerts and events to the building schedule.

Regrettably, the same fate that befell Firestone also ended Bryden's tenure as owner. In August 2003, just three months after the Senators were just one goal and one game away from the Stanley Cup finals, ownership of the team was transferred to Canadian pharmaceutical entrepreneur, Eugene Melnyk.

The business side of the operation has taken a major shift under Melnyk and, today, after four years under his direction, the structure of the various business elements has evolved. Capital Sports Group comprises four operating entities under Capital Sports Holdings Inc.: Capital Sports & Entertainment Inc. (CSEI), which owns the Senators and its related assets; Capital Sports Properties Inc. (CSPI), which owns Scotiabank Place; Capital Sports Management Inc., the management division of the Bell Sensplex and other sports facilities; Capital Tickets Inc. (CTI), which operates www.CapitalTickets.ca.

While the Senators on the ice continue to be a competitive team, the business side of the operation is as strong as it has ever been. In seeking success and profitability in diverse business ventures, the financial stability and security created by Melnyk's ownership model has provided the executive management team with the ability to strengthen itself from within its own talents and properties. One strong example is CapitalTickets, which has been a resounding success and revenue generator for the

---

[31] Ottawa was first home to a professional hockey franchise in 1893. It joined the NHL in 1917 but moved to St. Louis in 1934 and eventually folded. From 1893 to 1934, the Ottawa franchise, known as both the Senators and the Silver Seven, were very successful on the ice, winning the Stanley Cup nine times between 1909 and 1927.

® Registered trade-mark of Capital Sports & Entertainment Inc., used under license.

organization. In January 2004, less than four months into Melnyk's ownership, the Ottawa Senators and Scotiabank Place announced that CapitalTickets was the ticketing agent for all events held in the building. Capital Tickets developed quickly, becoming the ticketing agent for other entertainment events in the NCR outside of Scotiabank Place, including the Canadian Football League's Ottawa Renegades, Ottawa Bluesfest, and the Ontario Hockey League's Ottawa 67's. These events, coupled with the 50 home games for the Senators in a season and another 60 events (e.g., concerts, family shows) at Scotiabank Place, means that about 1.8 million tickets are being sold in-house (1.3 million for Scotiabank Place events alone) rather than through an external agency.

It is not surprising that, as Capital Sports Group went through an extensive planning and self-evaluation process with all levels of every entity, it developed corporate and department scorecards[32] through in-depth SWOT analyses (strengths, weaknesses, opportunities, and threats) with an eye on continuous improvement of our core business and developing more ventures. Using the strengths and opportunities of the core business—the Senators and Scotiabank Place—assisted the business to grow, despite Ottawa being considered a small-market NHL city (28th out of 30).

And we're not the only professional sport organization operating in this context. In Toronto, Maple Leafs Sports and Entertainment (MLSE) describes itself as "Canada's most successful sports and entertainment empire[33]." It has done so by effectively using its core business, the Toronto Maple Leafs, to own and operate the Air Canada Centre, NBA's Toronto Raptors, Leafs TV, Raptors NBA TV, and Ricoh Coliseum. And they continue to expand with the acquisition of Toronto FC, an MLS franchise.

To summarize, long gone is the day that the professional sport franchise can rely solely on the sale of tickets and hope to survive in this age of the Internet, multimedia entertainment, and 24-hour sport access. Developing and growing your business has become as important on the corporate scorecard as your team's scouting and prospects drafting.

Legault graduated from Laurentian University's sports administration program in 1986. Starting his career with the CFL's Ottawa Rough Riders, he moved to the Canadian Soccer Association, Canadian Hockey Association (Hockey Canada), and now the Ottawa Senators, where he has been since 1996.

University Sport

Canadian Interuniversity Sport (CIS) Overview

Canadian Interuniversity Sport (CIS) is the governing body for university athletics in Canada. The first Canadian university sport organization, the CIAU Central, was founded in 1906 and represented only universities from Ontario and Quebec[34]. Over the years, the organization grew, developed, and changed names many times. The last name change came in June of 2001, when the Canadian Interuniversity Athletic Union became Canadian Interuniversity

---

[32] Scorecards are outlined the month before the next financial year as the organizations develop department scorecards to support the corporate one. All scorecards are updated and presented monthly.

[33] Maple Leafs Sports and Entertainment (MLSE) describes itself as "Canada's most successful sports and entertainment empire."

[34] Canadian Interuniversity Sport (2006) History. Retrieved November 9, 2006 from http://www.universitysport.ca/e/about/history.cfm.

Sport. The organization felt that this name better represented its mission and function, as athletics is typically used when discussing only track and field events, and union typically applies to labour organizations[35].

The CIS currently represents over 10 000 student-athletes at 51 universities across the country. It offers championships in 11 sport disciplines: field hockey, rugby, cross-country skiing, soccer, football, wrestling, ice hockey, swimming, volleyball, basketball, and indoor track and field. In total, university sport recognizes a schedule of about 3000 events during each school year[36]. University sport in Canada is divided into four regional associations: Ontario University Athletics (OUA) represents Ontario's 18 universities; Atlantic University Sport (AUS) represents 11 universities in New Brunswick, Nova Scotia, Newfoundland & Labrador, and Prince Edward Island; the Quebec Student Sport Federation (QSSF) represents Quebec's 8 universities; and Canada West represents 14 universities in British Columbia, Alberta, Saskatchewan, and Manitoba. Champions from each of these regions meet every year in national championships sanctioned by the CIS. The largest of these are the Utek Bowl (QSSF and AUS football semifinal), Mitchell Bowl (CW and OUA football semifinal), Vanier Cup (national football final), and University Cup (national men's ice hockey final).

The CIS mission is "to enrich the educational experience of the athlete through a national sport program that fosters excellence[37]." Its five core values are:

- quality educational and athletic experience
- unity of purpose, respect for autonomy
- integrity and fair play
- trust and mutual respect
- equity and equality of experience

Finally, it is the vision that "CIS is the destination of choice for Canadian student-athletes to pursue excellence in academics and athletics. The CIS is recognized as one of the influential leaders in sport in Canada[38]."

The CIS seeks to ensure that student-athletes who have attained a high level of success both in academics and athletics are recognized for their achievements, though the Academic All-Canadians Program. To be named an Academic All-Canadian, student-athletes must maintain a grade point average of 80 percent or better during the school year while competing for a varsity team. During the 2005–2006 varsity season, about 2000, or over 20 percent, of

[35] ibid.

[36] Canadian Interuniversity Sport (2006) Canadian Interuniversity Sport mission statement. Retrieved November 9, 2006 from http://www.universitysport.ca/e/pol_proc/documents/001_MISSIONSTATEMENT_OBJECTIVES.pdf

[37] Canadian Interuniversity Sport (2006) Programs and services. Retrieved November 9, 2006 from http://www.universitysport.ca/e/about/index.cfm.

[38] ibid.

amateur sport: sport in which athletes are not remunerated.

all CIS student-athletes were named Academic All-Canadians[39]. In addition, every year the CIS names the top eight Academic All-Canadians by selecting the top male and female from each regional association. The CIS also honours All-Canadians who are the top athletes in each sport, a CIS Male and Female Athletes of the Year, student-athletes deserving of community service awards, and gives out numerous sport- and championship-specific awards.

EXECUTIVE PERSPECTIVE

Peter Hellstrom, Athletic Director, Laurentian University Athletics

Media Coverage and Website to Substitute for Zero Marketing Dollars

A challenge that many of us in sport marketing, particularly those in **amateur sport**, face is to achieve marketing objectives with very limited resources. In some cases, this has to be done with zero dollars. Recently, I have developed different methods for marketing Voyageur Athletics with a very small budget. It was a daunting challenge at first, but, after some research and planning, I was able to creatively work with the resources I had to be successful. Our first method was partnering with the local media and using their coverage as a free marketing tool, although there was and still is a lack of media personnel to cover all the sports in the city of Sudbury. Sudbury is a middle-sized city of just under 200 000 people, where the media are one TV station, one major newspaper, a couple of radio stations, and a few minor publications. The sport market is dominated by the local Junior A hockey club, the Sudbury Wolves. So, we set a goal of one article/story per day in the local media and identified a solution to do so—to develop our own sports information department.

To make this happen, we hired a marketing/sports info coordinator to head this area and gave him a staff and policies to follow. We had to be creative, so we hired a few sports administration and human kinetics students as our event reporters. Their main duty was to report results to local media, the OUA and CIS. We instituted fines (docked pay) if our home results were not reported to the OUA and CIS as per policy. We then developed relationships with the local print, television, and radio media. We drafted partnership agreements whereby we would write the articles and send them in by their deadlines in exchange for guaranteed coverage. They need content, and we want promotion, so the partnership works. All local media signed on, and now we average six to seven articles in the local paper weekly (paper is printed six times a week) and four to five stories a week on television, and our scores are reported on the radio the day after each event. In our estimate, this partnership provides us with roughly $400 000 worth of media coverage per year. The benefits, however, do not stop there. We also were able to feature sponsors in our articles and provide extra exposure (value) for them. For example, The Keg Athlete of the Week appears in all print, television, and radio coverage. In addition, we advertise our website in all promotions and average 120 000 unique views a month.

Our efforts have continued as our success has grown. We've recently hired a staff photographer on an event contract to shoot action pictures to add to our articles and website. Through these partnerships, we also developed contra advertising agreements. For example, we advertise

---

[39] Canadian Interuniversity Sport (2006) Academic All-Canadians. Retrieved November 9, 2006 from http://www.universitysport.ca/e/awards/academic/index.cfm.

upcoming games and special events on average four to five days a week and six to eight times a day leading into one of our events with our print, TV, and radio part– ners. These agreements are estimated to be worth about $70 000. Combined with our actual marketing budget of $20,000, we have leveraged the value of our promotions to $550 000, or 27 times our actual marketing budget.

Peter holds a bachelor of arts in physical education and a masters of science in physical education with a concentration in athletic administration. He was manager of marketing, events and sports information at Laurentian University Athletics until his promotion to athletic director in 2001.

Scholarships

Canada has historically been far behind the US in the number and size of athletic scholarships that are distributed annually to student-athletes. This has contributed to the brawn drain[40], the large number of talented Canadian athletes choosing to attend college or university in the US where they receive large athletic scholarships. More recently, the regulations concerning Canadian athletic scholarships have begun to reflect the desire of Canadian institutions to keep the best athletes in Canada by increasing maximum award amounts. CIS regulations state that the maximum amount a student-athlete can receive annually covers their tuition and compulsory fees for the academic year[41]. However, as athletic scholarships are the responsibility of each university and also subject to regulations from each of the four regional associations, the number and value of scholarships varies widely from one university to another across Canada. CIS reported that for the 2005–2006 academic year, 27 percent of student-athletes received an athletic financial award, averaging $1 957.68[42]. The sport with the largest percentage of athletes receiving an award was women's basketball at 48 percent; however, the average value of awards was highest for men's hockey at $2726.05[43]. To receive any funding, student-athletes must meet the minimum academic requirements. CIS regula– tions state that first-year student-athletes must have a minimum 80 percent entering average[44]. After their first year of eligibility, student-athletes must have maintained a minimum 65 percent average in the preceding year's aca– demics to be eligible for an athletic financial award in the next season[45]. While

[40] Scholfield, J. (2000) Raising the stakes: A move to boost the value of university athletic awards could help slow Canada's "brawn drain." *Maclean's*, 113(July 1):70.

[41] Canadian Interuniversity Sport (2006) Athletic financial awards. Retrieved November 9, 2006 from http://www.universitysport.ca/e/student/index.cfm#financial.

[42] Canadian Interuniversity Sport (2006) Award statistics. Retrieved November 9, 2006 from http://www.cisport.ca/e/research/documents/TeamByTeamSummary.pdf

[43] ibid.

[44] Canadian Interuniversity Sport (2006) Athletic financial awards.

[45] ibid.

these are the regulations set in place by the CIS, individual universities and regional associations may place further restrictions on academic eligibility. While these changes have allowed Canadian universities to compete on a more level playing field with smaller American universities, there remains a sizable difference in both award quantity and value between Canadian universities and larger universities in the US.

College Sport

Canadian Colleges Athletic Association (CCAA) Overview

The Canadian Colleges Athletic Association (CCAA) was founded in 1974, and the first national championship competitions were held for hockey and basketball in 1975[46]. As the solitary governing body for college sport in Canada, the CCAA states its primary objectives are[47]:

- To provide a framework through which interprovincial, national, and international college athletic competitions may be conducted, developed, and promoted.
- To seek full and effective representation on committees, boards, study groups, and other like bodies, which make decisions concerning the development of college athletics in Canada.
- To provide for the recognition and achievement of intercollegiate athletic excellence on a national level.

The CCAA represents the interests of 104 member institutions, which provide services to 9000 intercollegiate athletes, about 700 coaches, and over 150 sport administrators[48]. Its membership comprises community colleges, universities, university-colleges, CEGEPs, and technical institutions, making it the largest postsecondary sport organization in the country[49]. The member institutions are organized into five regional conferences: the Atlantic Colleges Athletic Association (ACAA) comprising nine colleges and universities in New Brunswick and Nova Scotia[50]; the Ontario Colleges Athletic Association (OCAA) representing 27 colleges across the province; the Alberta Colleges Athletic Conference (ACAC) made up of 17 colleges throughout Alberta and Saskatchewan51; the British Columbia Colleges Athletic Association (BCCAA) which includes 14 colleges in British Columbia; and the Quebec Student Sports Federation (QSSF) made up of 37 universities, colleges, and CEGEPs in Quebec[52].

---

[46] Canadian College Athletics Association (2006) National championships. Retrieved November 9, 2006 from http://www.ccaa.ca/national.htm.

[47] Canadian Colleges Athletic Association (2006) About the CCAA. Retrieved November 9, 2006 from http://www.ccaa.ca/profile.htm.

[48] ibid.

[49] ibid.

[50] ibid.

[51] ibid.

[52] ibid.

Every year, the CCAA sponsors nine national championship tournaments for men's soccer, women's soccer, men's basketball, women's basketball, men's volleyball, women's volleyball, badminton, cross-country running, and golf[53].

The CCAA sponsors several academic- and athletic-based excellence awards. Like CIS, the CCAA recognizes individuals as Academic All-Canadians. To receive this honour, student-athletes must demonstrate excellence in both academic and athletics at their institution. Specifically, they must be named to their provincial college athletic association all-star team in a CCAA-recognized sport and maintain a GPA standing of 3.5 or equivalent[54]. The institution with the most CCAA Academic All-Canadians in each year is presented with a CCAA Academic All-Canadian Recognition Award.

Olympic Sport

Sport Canada

Sport in Canada is governed at a federal level under the Department of Canadian Heritage. Within this department, Sport Canada is a branch of International and Intergovernmental Affairs. Sport Canada's mission is "to enhance opportunities for Canadians to participate and excel in sport[55]." Its stated strategic directions are to[56]:

- Strengthen sport leadership
- Provide strategic support for high-performance programming
- Promote technically sound sport development
- Enhance opportunities for sport participation
- Maximize the benefits of hosting
- Promote linguistic duality in the Canadian sport system
- Strengthen the ethical foundation of sport
- Expand the body of knowledge about sport
- Harmonize the Canadian sport system

The Canadian government invests about $140 million annually in Canadian sport through Sport Canada[57]. Sport Canada is organized into three parts: Sport Programs, Sport Policy, and Major Games and Hosting.

---

[53] ibid.

[54] Canadian College Athletics Association (2006). Awards. Retrieved November 9, 2006 from http://www.ccaa.ca/awards.htm.

[55] Sport Canada (2006) Canadian Heritage (Sport Canada) quick facts. Retrieved October 30, 2006 from http://www.pch.gc.ca/progs/sc/info-fact/2004-2005_e.cfm.

[56] Sport Canada (2005) Mission. Retrieved October 30, 2006 from http://www.pch.gc.ca/progs/sc/mission/index_e.cfm.

[57] Government of Canada. (2006) Canada's new government announces the creation of Podium Canada. Retrieved November 26, 2006 from http://www.news.gc.ca/cfmx/view/en/index.jsp?articleid=258109.

Sport Programs

Sport Programs is responsible for distributing funding for national sport organizations, multisport organizations, athletes, and events through three funding programs: the Sport Support Program, Hosting Program, and Athlete Assistance Program. In 2004–2005, Sport Canada contributed $123.3 million in grants and contributions to these programs[58].

Sport Support Program: In 2004–2005, the Sport Support Program received $81.9 million in funding from Sport Canada, which was divided among 55 national sport organizations (NSOs), 20 multisport/service organizations (MSOs), and 9 Canadian sport centres[59]. To identify which Canadian sport organizations are eligible for funding, Sport Canada uses the Sport Funding and Accountability Framework (SFAF), introduced in 1995 and currently in its third edition, for the April 1, 2005 to March 31, 2010 funding cycle[60]. Funding is divided into the national sport organization component, the multisport organization component, and the project stream component (referring to such projects as ethics strategies, events, and research). To determine the funding entitlement of each NSO and MSO applicant, the SFAF looks at eligibility, assessment, funding, and accountability. The first step in the process is ensuring eligibility, or whether the organization or project meets specific criteria set out by the government. The next step is assessment, for which the organizations must complete several questionnaires to determine the level of funding to be provided: For NSOs, the "scope and performance of the NSO across key areas of high performance, sport participation/development and organizational management"[61] are examined to make this determination; for MSOs, "the nature, scope, volume and leadership associated with the MSO's delivery of core services within the Canadian sport system"[62] is assessed. The third step is funding where eligible NSOs and MSOs are required to provide a complete funding application. The final step in the process is accountability. Here, Sport Canada provides specific guidelines on policy, which the sport organizations must incorporate to ensure that their funding will be granted and sustained[63]. Created in accordance with the goals of the Canadian Sport Policy, these guidelines consider such issues as official languages, women in sport, harassment and abuse, Aboriginal sport, and participation access and opportunity[64].

Athlete Assistance Program: The purpose of this program is to provide direct financial assistance to Canada's high-performance athletes. The Athlete Assistance Program states that its main goal is "[contributing] to improved Canadian performances at major international sporting events such as the Olympic Games, Commonwealth Games, Pam Am Games, Paralympic

---

[58] Sport Canada. (2006). Canadian Heritage (Sport Canada) quick facts.

[59] ibid.

[60] Sport Canada (2005) Sport Funding and Accountability Framework. Retrieved October 30, 2006 from http://www.pch.gc.ca/progs/sc/prog/cfrs-sfaf/index_e.cfm.

[61] ibid.

[62] ibid.

[63] ibid.

[64] ibid.

Games and World Championships[65]." In 2004–2005, the program received $19.9 million from Sport Canada[66]. The total number of carded athletes from April 1, 2004 to March 1, 2005 was 1566, competing in 75 sports or disciplines. To qualify for this assistance, athletes must be identified as among the top 16 in the world in their sport, or they must show the potential to be among the top 16. Further athlete eligibility requirements include their availability to compete for Canada in international competition[67]. The athlete's sport must also meet such requirements as being funded under the SFAF and having a sanctioned world championship or equivalent[68]. Assistance is provided to athletes to cover living and training expenses, tuition, and identified special needs. The amount given for living and training expenses depends on the carding status of the athlete. Those who have had a senior card for more than one year receive $1500 a month, while first-year senior carded athletes and development athletes receive $900 per month[69]. Athletes who are attending a public postsecondary institution at the same time as meeting the requirements for their carded status are also eligible to receive tuition support. Athletes may also defer this support and use it when they have retired from competition[70]. Subsidized special needs include relocation expenses and child-care assistance[71].

Sport Policy

The second area of Sport Canada's focus is sport policy. To understand the current policies, it is important to examine the evolution of the federal government's involvement in sport in Canada. The first significant government sport policy is considered to be the *Fitness and Amateur Sport Act* of 1961, created to "encourage, promote, and develop fitness and amateur sport in Canada"[72] as a response to concern over the health of Canada's population as well as the declining status of Canadian athletes in international competition. By most standards, the act had almost no major impact on sport, and very little change occurred. The issue of the government's involvement in sport was raised again in 1968, when Prime Minister Pierre Trudeau commissioned the Task Force on Sport for Canadians. This report had a significant impact on national sport organizations as it led to an era of direct promotion of high-performance sport by the federal government[73]. However, this impact was

---

[65] Sport Canada (2005) *The Athlete Assistance Program: Policies and Procedures*. Government of Canada Depository Services Program.

[66] Sport Canada (2006) Canadian Heritage (Sport Canada) quick facts.

[67] Sport Canada (2005) The Athlete Assistance Program: Backgrounder. Retrieved November 2, 2006 from http://www.pch.gc.ca/progs/sc/prog/paa-aap/info_e.cfm.

[68] ibid.

[69] Sport Canada (2005)The Athlete Assistance Program: Support. Retrieved November 2, 2006 from http://www.pch.gc.ca/progs/sc/prog/paa-aap/all-sup_e.cfm.

[70] ibid.

[71] ibid.

[72] Sport Canada (2003) *Fitness and Amateur Sport Act* 1961. Retrieved November 2, 2006 from http://www.pch.gc.ca/progs/sc/pubs/act_e.cfm.

[73] Macintosh, D., & D. Whitson (1994). *The Game Planners*. McGill-Queen's University Press.

both positive and negative.[74] While the increased funding to the organizations improved professionalism, it also led to greater complexity and a decrease in their established autonomy.

The next 20 years saw numerous other government papers and sport funding plans, some of which were considered a success and others that were not. These include *Game Plan 1976* and *Partners in Pursuit of Excellence: A National Policy on Amateur Sport* (1979). Later, the Ben Johnson doping scandal at the 1988 Seoul Olympics was the catalyst for the creation of another important government sport report: The *Report of the Commission of Inquiry into the Use of Drugs and Banned Practices Intended to Increase Athletic Performance* (Dubin Inquiry) was released in June 1990 and provided a critical evaluation of the government's emphasis on high performance and excellence over participation in sport[75]. The recommendations of the report forced the sport community to re-evaluate its priorities and responsibilities and eventually led to three phases of implementation: The first two phases dealt directly with the issue of doping, while the third focused on the structure of sport in Canada and led to the creation of *Sport: The Way Ahead: The Minister's Task Force on Federal Sport Policy* in 1992. This report recommended a decreased role for the federal government and an increased role for national sport organizations to create future Canadian sport policy[76]. The next major report on Canadian sport was *Sport: Everybody's Business*, also known as the Mills Report, released in 1998 and widely accepted by the sport community[77]. Its purpose was to "[examine] the industry of sport in Canada. It [provided] an analysis of the various sectors of sport, [described] the challenges these sectors faced, and [offered] recommendations for the future"[78].

The next major government policy project was a Canada-wide consultation in 2000–2001 of sport organizations and athletes at six regional conferences regarding their vision and views on sport in Canada. The outcome of these consultations led to the National Summit on Sport in 2001 and eventually to the development and adoption of *The Canadian Sport Policy* in 2002, the framework that guides Sport Canada and the Canadian sport community. For the first time, the federal government and all 13 provincial and territorial governments agreed on a far-reaching sport policy and adapted their organizations accordingly. The mission of the policy is "to have by 2012 a dynamic and leading-edge sport environment that enables all Canadians to experience and enjoy involvement in sport to the extent of their abilities and interests and, for increasing numbers, to perform consistently and successfully

---

[74] ibid.

[75] Semotiuk, D. (1994) Restructuring Canada's national sport system: The legacy of the Dubin Inquiry. In Wilcox, R.C. (ed.) *Sport in the Global Village*. Fitness Information Technology Inc.: 365–75.

[76] Thibault, L. & K. Babiak (2005) Organizational changes in Canada's sport system: Toward an athlete-centred approach. European *Sport Management Quarterly*, 5(2):105–32.

[77] Athletes CAN (2006) History of Canadian sport and accomplishments of Athletes CAN. Retrieved November 2, 2006 from http://www.athletescan.com/Images/Publications/History_Cdn_Sport_ACAN_Achievements.doc.

[78] Mills, D. (1998) *Sport in Canada: Everybody's Business*. Standing Committee on Canadian Heritage.

at the highest competitive levels[79]." The policy is built on four goals, or pillars of achievement. The first is enhanced participation, ensuring that Canadians from all segments of society are getting involved with sports at all levels and in all forms[80]. The second is enhanced excellence, expanding the pool of talented Canadian athletes and teams and ensuring they are "achieving world-class results at the highest levels of international competition through fair and ethical means[81]." The third is enhanced capacity, making certain "the essential components of an ethically based, athlete/participant-centred development system are in place and are continually modernized and strengthened as required[82]." The final pillar is enhanced interaction, ensuring that "the components of the sport system are more connected and coordinated as a result of the committed collaboration and communication amongst the stakeholders[83]." The realization of these goals is at the heart of any new sport policy and program. As well, eligibility requirements for previously created programs such as the SFAF have been adjusted to reflect the overall vision of *The Canadian Sport Policy*.

The *Physical Activity and Sport Act* (introduced as Bill C-54 in 2002 and approved as Bill C-12 in 2003) replaced and modernized the *Fitness and Amateur Sport Act* of 1961. Its goal was to "encourage, promote and develop sport and physical activity in Canada[84]." The bill also declared the establishment of the Sport Dispute Resolution Centre of Canada and provided details of the full configuration of the organization.

The previous paragraphs highlight the most important sport policies and reports commissioned by the Canadian government. Numerous other policies and reports also exist, including those that focus on specific issues in the sport system, such as the Federal Government Policy on Tobacco Sponsorship of National Sport Organizations (1985), Women in Sport Policy (1986), Canadian Strategy for Ethical Conduct in Sport (2002), the Canadian Policy Against Doping in Sport (2004), Sport Canada's Policy on Aboriginal People's Participation in Sport (2005), and the Policy on Sport for Persons with a Disability (2006). Each of these policies deals with issues in Canadian sport, and to receive funding from Sport Canada, sport organizations must adhere to each to be considered under the SFAF.

Major Games and Hosting

In the mid-1990s, the Canadian government realized that hosting international sporting events presented an opportunity for numerous social, economic, and cultural benefits, including facility legacies, job creation, and

---

[79] Sport Canada (2002) *The Canadian Sport Policy*. Retrieved November 2, 2006 from http://www.pch.gc.ca/progs/sc/pol/pcs–csp/2003/polsport_e.pdf.

[80] ibid.

[81] ibid.

[82] ibid.

[83] ibid.

[84] Department of Justice Canada (2003) *Physical Activity and Sport Act*. Retrieved November 6, 2006 from http://laws.justice.gc.ca/en/p-13.4/254499.html.

volunteer development[85]. At the same time, it recognized the need to ensure that those events receiving government funding provided a return of the positive benefits they were seeking. This led to the creation of the Federal Policy for Hosting International Sport Events (2000), to provide "a decision-making framework for determining federal involvement in the hosting of international sport events. The policy clarifies the federal government's role in hosting and provides a transparent, decision-making tool for the government to assess proposals against strict criteria[86]." The federal government has identified eight tenets which must be examined for an event to receive government funding[87]:

- potential to accrue net benefits
- fiscal reality
- proactive partnerships
- provision of legacies
- no deficit guarantees
- compliance with federal standards (e.g., languages, environmental law)
- demonstrable community support
- sound management

By ensuring these requirements are in place before providing funding, the government reduces its risk in making a safe investment from which it can expect a positive contribution toward Sport Canada's objectives.

In 2004–2005, the federal government contributed $21.5 million to the international hosting program, funding 43 international single sport events (e.g., world championships) and one international strategic focus event, the North American Indigenous Games[88]. Of these 44 events, only two received funding in excess of $250 000, while over 85 percent received less than $50 000[89]. In addition to international sporting events, the hosting program also plays a role in supporting the Canada Games by providing funding and other assistance to the organizing committee.

National Sport Organizations

National sport organizations (NSOs) are the individual nonprofit sport governing bodies for all Olympic and non-Olympic sports in Canada. In total, 55 national sport organizations of all sizes are funded by the federal government through Sport Canada, including large NSOs like the Canadian Soccer Association and smaller ones such as Ringette Canada. There are also numerous NSOs not funded by the government, including Ski Jumping Canada and the Canadian Handball Association. To be funded by the government, the organizations must meet the requirements of the SFAF, discussed earlier in

[85] Sport Canada (2003) International activities. Retrieved November 6, 2006 from http://www.pch.gc.ca/progs/sc/inter/02_e.cfm.

[86] Sport Canada (2000) Federal Policy for Hosting International Sport Events. Retrieved October 30, 2006 from http://www.pch.gc.ca/progs/sc/pol/accueil-host/Hosting%20Policy%20Dec%202000%20Eng.pdf.

[87] ibid.

[88] Sport Canada (2006) Canadian Heritage (Sport Canada) quick facts.

[89] ibid.

this chapter. For the current 2005–2010 funding cycle, the top three NSOs in the high-performance assessment are speed skating, hockey, and swimming. In the sport development area, the top three are hockey, soccer, and figure skating[90]. The operating budgets of Canadian NSOs widely vary from a few thousand dollars to millions of dollars. Besides government funding, NSOs rely on sponsorship, fundraising, merchandising, event hosting, and membership fees to make up the remainder of their budgets. However, increased government funding of NSOs may have caused an overdependence on government funds for many of these organizations, threatening their autonomy as they are increasingly required to meet government regulations under the threat of having their funding pulled[91].

The responsibilities of NSOs include policy development, program development, national team selection, and national and international event hosting. NSOs also maintain membership in their sport's international federation. To compete at an internationally sanctioned event, athletes are required by the international federation to be a member of their sport's NSO. The majority of Canada's NSOs are headquartered in Ottawa; however, some are strategically located elsewhere, such as Bobsleigh Canada Skeleton situated in Calgary, where the Olympic bobsleigh facilities are located.

Provincial and Territorial Sport

Each of Canada's 13 provincial and territorial governments plays a large and important role in sport in the country. While the organizations responsible for sport, in each province vary in size and capability, they all seek to accomplish similar goals. It is the provincial/territorial government's responsibility to promote and develop sport in its jurisdiction and ensure that sport services are delivered on a provincial and territorial scale. While Canada's national sport organizations tend to focus more on high-performance sport, the provincial and territorial governments focus on developing of young athletes, grassroots sport and on sports participation and recreation. The structure of sport at a provincial/territorial level is similar to that of the national level. In each province or territory, sport is a division of a larger government department. Each province and territory then has a provincial sport body whose membership includes the sport-specific organizations. For example, sport in Alberta falls under the Department of Community Development, the Division of Alberta Sport, Recreation, Parks and Wildlife Foundation, and is administered by Sport Alberta, which is tied to over 75 provincial sport organizations. Table 2-1 lists the sport organizations in each provincial and territorial government.

The major contributions and responsibilities of the provincial and territorial governments to sport are funding, hosting policies, high-performance and amateur sport development, provincial team selection, and award recogni-

---

[90] Sport Canada (2005) 2005–2020 funding cycle: Assessment points and ranking lists—mainstream. Retrieved October 30, 2006 from http://www.pch.gc.ca/progs/sc/prog/cfrs-sfaf/financement-funding_2005-2010/regulier-mainstream_e.pdf.

[91] Macintosh, D. & D. Whitson (1994) *The Game Planners*.

tion. Each provincial/territorial sport organization has a direct connection to the national sport governing body (e.g., Basketball Ontario is connected to Basketball Canada), and they work together to support the development of their sport.

TABLE 2-1

Provincial and Territorial Government Sport Departments

PROVINCE	GOVERNMENT DEPARTMENT	GOVERNMENT DIVISION	PROVINCIAL SPORT BODY
Alberta	Department of Community Development	Alberta Sport, Recreation, Parks & Wildlife Foundation	Sport Alberta
British Columbia	Ministry of Tourism, Sport & Arts	Sport & Physical Activity Branch	Sport BC
Manitoba	Department of Culture, Heritage & Tourism	Recreation	Sport Manitoba
Newfoundland & Labrador	Department of Tourism, Culture & Recreation	Recreation & Sport	Sport Newfoundland & Labrador
New Brunswick	Wellness Culture & Sport	Sport, Recreation & Active Living	Sport New Brunswick
Northwest Territories	Department of Municipal & Community Affairs	Sport, Recreation, Youth & Volunteerism	Sport North
Nova Scotia	Health Promotion & Protection	Physical Activity Sport & Recreation	Sport Nova Scotia
Nunavut	Department of Culture, Language, Elders & Youth	Recreation & Leisure	Sport Nunavut
Ontario	Ministry of Health Promotion	Sports & Recreation	Sport Alliance
Prince Edward Island	Department of Community & Cultural Affairs	Sport & Recreation	Sport PEI
Quebec	Éducation Loisir et Sport	Loisir et Sport	Sports Québec
Saskatchewan	Department of Arts Culture, & Recreation	Sports/Recreation	Sask Sport

Multisport organizations (MSO) in Canada represent a diversity of interests and provide a variety of services to the Canadian sport community. There are MSOs responsible for such things as athlete interests (Athletes CAN), doping control (WADA), ethics (CCES), Aboriginal sport (ASC), wheelchair sport (CWSA), coaching (CAC), and women in sport (CAAWS) among others. Table 2-2 lists Canada's MSOs. Like NSOs, many of these MSOs receive funding from the federal government as long as they meet the requirements set out in the SFAF. In 2004–2005, for example, 20 MSOs received funding from the federal government. Other sources of funding for these organizations include sponsorship, fundraising, and corporate philanthropy.

TABLE 2-2

Canadian Multisport Organizations

Aboriginal Sport Circle (ASC)

Athletes CAN

Arctic Winter Games

Calgary Olympic Development Association (CODA)

Canadian Association for the Advancement of Women in Sport (CAAWS)

Canadian Blind Sport Association

Canadian Centre for Ethics in Sport (CCES)

Canadian Deaf Sports Association

Canada Games Council (CGC)

Canadian Olympic Committee (COC)

Canadian Paralympic Committee (CPC)

Canadian Sport Centres

Canadian Sport Resource Centre

Canadian Special Olympics

Canadian Sport Tourism Alliance

Canadian Wheelchair Sport Association (CWSA)

Coaching Association of Canada (CAC)

Commonwealth Games Canada (CGA)

Sport Dispute Resolution Centre (ADRSportRED)

Sport Matters

Vancouver Organizing Committee (VANOC)

World Anti-Doping Agency (WADA)

Canadian Olympic Committee

The Canadian Olympic Committee (COC) is arguably the most influential of all Canadian MSOs. The COC focuses on high-performance sport and is responsible for all facets of Canada's participation in the Olympic Movement.

This includes Canada's involvement in the Olympic and Pan American Games, managing numerous cultural and educational programs that seek to advance the Olympic Movement in Canada, selecting and supporting Canadian cities in bidding for Olympic and Pan American Games, and providing athletes with services that assist them in sport and in life[92]. The COC also provides athletes, coaches, NSOs, and MSOs with about $11 million annually in funding and program support[93]. The mission of the COC is "to achieve podium success at Olympic Games and to advance the Olympic Movement in Canada[94]." All of its programs are created to push the organization toward the achievements set out in this mission statement. The COC also seeks to promote seven values to the Canadian sport community: excellence, fun, fairness, respect, human development, leadership, and peace[95].

The COC is a national, private, nonprofit organization, which seeks revenue from various sources to fund its programs. Matching the timing of the Olympic Games, the financial activities of the organization follow a quadrennial planning cycle. The current cycle began January 1, 2005 and continues until December 31, 2008. The cycle always ends on the last day of the year in which the Summer Olympic are held. During this cycle, it is projected that partner (sponsor) revenues will provide 59 percent of the COC's revenue, while segregated funds (i.e., investments) will provide 35 percent and grants and other contributions will provide 6 percent[96].

Own the Podium Program: This initiative brings together all major funding providers in the Canadian sport system to support Canada's goals for the 2010 Vancouver Olympic Winter Games. These funding providers include all 13 winter-sport-specific NSOs, the Vancouver Organizing Committee for the 2010 Olympic and Paralympic Games, the Canadian Olympic and Paralympic Committees, Sport Canada, and the Calgary Olympic Development Association[97]. The purpose of the program is to "set the vision and strategy for Canada to be the number one nation in total medals at the 2010 Olympic Winter Games in Vancouver[98]." To achieve this goal, it is estimated that an additional $21 million will have to be invested in the Canada sport system annually[99].

Grassroots Sport

Every Olympic medalist's and professional star's first experience with sport was at the community level. Across Canada, hockey rinks, soccer fields, baseball diamonds, pools, and more are filled with the young Canadians, the next

---

[92] Canadian Olympic Committee (2006) About us: Role of the COC. Retrieved November 6, 2006 from http://www.olympic.ca/EN/organization/aboutus.shtml.

[93] Canadian Olympic Committee (2005) *Canadian Olympic Committee Annual Report 2005*. Retrieved November 6, 2006 from http://www.olympic.ca/EN/organization/publications/reports/2005report.pdf.

[94] ibid.

[95] Canadian Olympic Committee (2006) About us: Role of the COC.

[96] Canadian Olympic Committee (2005) Canadian Olympic Committee Annual Report 2005.

[97] Canadian Olympic Committee (2006) Own the podium 2010. Retrieved November 6, 2006 from http://www.olympic.ca/EN/organization/news/2005/0121_background.shtml.

[98] ibid.

[99] ibid.

generation of superstars alongside those just out to stay healthy and have fun. The grassroots sport movement, however, is not just about playing the game; it is about being a part of the whole experience. Coaches, referees, administrators, parents, and athletes are all part of grassroots sport, and without the contribution of any one of these groups, it would not be possible. The grassroots movement can also be connected to spectatorship. Cities and towns all over the country support teams in various sports at various levels, and in many cases, those teams have come to be a defining presence in the community.

In Canada, grassroots sport is fast becoming one of the most important pursuits for governments, researchers, and practitioners. It is a common topic at conferences and is on the agenda of governments. Recognizing the importance of grassroots sport to both high-performance sport and the health of all Canadians drives this increased interest. Specific to high-performance sport, an effective grassroots sport system: increases talent identification opportunities; provides for the development of athletes, officials, and coaches; and enhances sport–community linkages. With respect to the general health of Canadians, grassroots sport systems provide opportunities and incentives for people of all ages to participate in an active lifestyle.

We define grassroots sport as sport that is based around local communities and participation by the general public. This section outlines three aspects of Canadian grassroots sport: participation, spectatorship, and organizations.

Participation

At the grassroots level, participation in sport is not limited by age or ability and can arguably provide numerous social, economic, cultural, and physical benefits for the participants and the community. Donnelly and Kidd[100] describe the individual highlights of grassroots participation as "the joys of effort, the emotional drama of competition, the satisfactions of self-mastery and accomplishment, the lifelong friendships, and the adventures and learning of travel." In 1998, a Statistics Canada general social survey declared that 34 percent of adults over the age of 15 participated in sport on a regular basis; as did 54 percent of children aged 5 to 14[101]. These statistics compare favourably with those of the US and Australia, where sport participation levels are notably lower. In Australia, the participation rate is 30 percent; in the US, it is only 22 percent[102]. In Canada, golf, hockey, and baseball are the most popular sports among adults at the grassroots level, while soccer, hockey, and swimming are the most popular among children[103]. Hockey Canada boasts more than 1.5 million games played and 2 million practices every year in over 3000 rinks throughout the country. One of the fastest growing sports in Canada is soccer,

participation: getting involved with sports at all levels and in all forms; sport consumers' primary method of engagement.

---

[100] Donnelly, P. & B. Kidd (2003). Realizing the expectations: Youth, character, and community in Canadian sport. In *The Sport We Want: Essays on Current Issues in Community Sport in Canada.* Canadian Centre for Ethics in Sport: 25–44.

[101] Culture Statistics Program (2000) *Sport Participation in Canada: 1998 Report.* Public Works and Government Services Canada.

[102] ibid.

[103] ibid.

in which the annual number of registered players has been climbing for many years and to the current 841 466, significantly more than hockey's 551 655[104]. The largest growth in soccer registration is coming from typically under-represented groups: women with a 2.76 percent increase and players over 18 with a 3.35 percent increase[105]. Grassroots participation is not just about the athletes, however; it is also about those who keep the programs running. The 1998 Statistics Canada general social survey reported that 7 percent, or 1.7 million, of Canadians were coaching amateur sport, and the same number were involved as administrators or helpers (volunteer and paid positions), while 4 percent, or 940 000, were involved with refereeing. Volunteering is an important aspect of grassroots sport, as community leagues are run almost entirely by volunteers, without whom the programs would cease to exist. In fact, 18 percent of all volunteers in Canada volunteer with organized sport, and they contribute a total of 167 million hours to sport alone[106].

While large numbers of Canadians are able to enjoy sport at a community level, many do not have the opportunity. Numerous barriers to participation exist in community sport, and this should be of concern to Canadians. Researchers suggest that the most important barrier to access is the "increasing inequity in the distribution of wealth among Canadians[107]," confirmed by statistics reporting that 51 percent of people in households earning more that $80 000 annually participate in sport, while only 25 percent of those in households with an annual income less than $20 000 participate[108]. Other barriers include disability, location, gender, and ethnocultural heritage[109].

spectatorship: commonly associated with professional sport, opportunities in communities all over the country for people to get out and support local teams.

Spectatorship

The second aspect of grassroots sport is spectatorship. While most people associate this solely with professional sport, opportunities exist in communities all over the country for people to get out and support local teams. For example, it is not unusual in Canadian towns for the population to come out and enjoy a midget or juvenile hockey game, or to get spectators out to a local curling bonspiel. Even the smallest towns have sports pages in their newspapers, which report the achievements of local athletes and the scores of all minor sport games from the previous week. As the wealth and power of professional athletes continue to increase, people can still identify with local teams and athletes. The star of the local baseball team might live next door and walk your dog, while the star quarterback serves coffee at the local Tim Hortons.

---

[104] Canadian Soccer Association (2005) *2005 Demographics*. Retrieved November 13, 2006 from http://www.canadasoccer.com/eng/docs/2005_demographics.pdf.

[105] ibid.

[106] Doherty, A. (2005) A Profile of Community Sport Volunteers: Executive Summary. Retrieved November 13, 2006 from http://prontario.org/PDF/reports/FinalReport_ExecutiveSummary_PhaseOne.pdf.

[107] Donnelly, P. & B. Kidd (2003) Realizing the expectations.

[108] Culture Statistics Program (2000) *Sport Participation in Canada: 1998 Report*. Public Works and Government Services Canada.

[109] Donnelly, P. & B. Kidd (2003). Realizing the expectations.

The professional sports world, however, does have ties to the grassroots movement, particularly the Canadian Football League and the Grey Cup. Essentially, it is the "Canadianness" of the league that distinguishes it and pulls its support mainly from a grassroots level. Canadians are looking for ways to differentiate themselves from Americans, and the "league of our own" claim to the CFL is one way to do that. The league seems to thrive in smaller cities and creates a sense of pride and identity in those communities[110]. Many CFL franchises are community owned, and salaries in the CFL are comparable to average Canadian salaries, so the players are not far from the realities of the fans. The Grey Cup is the largest Canadian sporting event. The 2006 version was the 94th Grey Cup game, which means it has a longer history than the Stanley Cup finals[111]. While the game is televised nationally, it usually takes on the character of the host city, which gives the local citizens an opportunity to show the country how great their city is. It is these aspects of the CFL that make it a professional league that communities can really get behind.

IN THE KNOW

BIRGing and CORFing: Fan Identity Conceptualized!
Why is it that when Team Canada won hockey's Olympic gold at the 2002 Olympic Winter Games in Salt Lake City the sales of Hockey Canada merchandise skyrocketed to unprecedented highs? And why is it that after a big win against the Maple Leafs, formerly 'lost' Montreal Canadiens' fans are quick to jump back on the bandwagon, take their old jerseys out of the closet, and refer to "our big win" when talking about the game? On the other hand, why is it that these same people are nowhere to be found following a big loss to the Leafs?

These phenomena have been labeled BIRGing and CORFing. BIRGing, or basking in reflected glory, is "the phenomenon of enhancing or maintaining self-esteem through associating with winning teams[112]." CORFing, or cutting off reflected failure, is the phenomenon of "spectators who dissociate themselves from losing teams because they negatively affect self-esteem[113]." In other words, we all enjoy being associated with winners but are quick to dissociate from losing teams.

---

[110] Deacon, J. (2004) Three-down nation: The Grey Cup stays true to its true north roots. *Maclean's*, 117 (November 24):43.

[111] ibid.

[112] Shank, M.D. (2005) *Sports Marketing: A Strategic Perspective*, 3rd ed. Prentice Hall: 162.

[113] ibid.

The concept of BIRGing is closely related to social identity theory, which explains how one's self-esteem and self-evaluation can be enhanced by identifying with another person's success[114]. An additional interesting aspect of BIRGing is the tendency of people to publicize their connection with successful others (e.g., the team), when they have not contributed to the (team's) success[115], where they are truly basking in reflected glory, not earned success. CORFing is described as cutting off reflected failure, which is accomplished by distancing oneself as far as possible from the losing team[116]. CORFing fans distance themselves physically, mentally, or emotionally, with the intent of avoiding negative relationships with the unsuccessful entity (e.g., the team)[117].

Grassroots Organizations

Numerous grassroots organizations look to develop, protect, and advance the cause of community sport. The majority of these organizations are nonprofit, volunteer-directed, and funded by all levels of government and through sponsorship and donations. Grassroots organizations exist on national, provincial, and local levels; some even have international connections.

Local: The Edmonton Sport Council is one grassroots support organization working at a local level. Its purpose is to serve and represent the local Edmonton sport community, specifically to: advocate for sport and promote sport development in Edmonton; advocate and support the development of stable and ongoing funding for sport in Edmonton; facilitate effective communication among Edmonton sport organizations and other key organizations including all levels of government; and assist sport organizations and individuals by linking them to, or providing them with, sport-related education and sport services[118].

Provincial: KidSport Ontario represents the Ontario chapter of the National KidSport initiative. Run in each province as an independent organization, the program follows the outline provided by KidSport Canada. Its mission is to "help disadvantaged kids overcome social and economic barriers preventing or limit their participation in organized sport, through the issuance of registration fees and/or equipment grants[119]." KidSport Ontario has four objectives: raising funds, gathering resources, and building program partnerships;

---

[114] Jacobson, B. (2003) The social psychology of the creation of a sports fan identity: A theoretical review of the literature. *Athletic Insight,* 51(2).

[115] Hirt, E., D. Zillman, G. Erickson, & C. Kennedy (1992) The costs and benefits of allegiance: Changes in fans' self-ascribed competencies after team victory versus team defeat. *Journal of Personality and Social Psychology,* 63: 724–38.

[116] ibid.

[117] ibid.

[118] Edmonton Sport Council (2006) About the ESC. Retrieved November 13, 2006 from http://www.edmontonsport.com/about.

[119] KidSport Ontario (2006) About us. Retrieved November 13, 2006 from http://www.kidsport.on.ca/about-us.html.

establishing local chapters throughout the province; partnering with other charitable and community-based programs; and identifying and alleviating social and economic barriers to help a child participate in sport[120].

National: True Sport is a national initiative that involves parents, teachers, athletes, officials, coaches, organizers, and community leaders working together to make sure that sport participation lives up to its potential for benefits[121]. It is described as: "a national movement of communities and groups across Canada working to ensure a positive meaningful and enriching experience for all who participate in sport[123]."

International connections: Play Soccer is an Ontario-based community soccer program, that seeks to "enhance what is truly great about the sport in [Ontario]—it's about family, recreation, fun and learning about ourselves as individuals and team members[124]." The program has developed international connections with the Everton Football Club of the English Premiership Soccer League in a deal that benefits both parties. Everton provides coaches and coaching systems and commercial expertise to Play Soccer; in exchange, it looks for exposure in the Canadian marketplace to help in its pursuit of a more global brand[125].

EXECUTIVE PERSPECTIVE

Linda Cuthbert, Principal, Breakthrough Performance Group; President, Aquatic Federation of Canada

A View from Many Angles: Sport Excellence in Canada

When I first reflected on the Canadian sport landscape and what I should write about, I thought back to when I was an athlete. As an athlete, you're very narrowly focused on your own performance and you have little time to learn about the larger sport system and the many people who make it work.

When I retired in 1980, I was the national champion in Olympic diving, and Canada had just boycotted the 1980 Olympic Games in Moscow. After a few months of retirement, I stopped by the pool to visit some of my former teammates and coaches and, not being one to sit idle, embarked on what would become a rather long career as a sport volunteer. I felt part of something, part of a community—and community is created when people connect and contribute. When I was an athlete, people were working behind the scenes to make things happen, and I wanted to give back and make things happen for the next generations of athletes. I've been a sport volunteer for 25 years and, as I've gone from one role to another (official, coach, administrator, etc.), what amazes me is, no matter what I've done or how much experience I have, there are always new challenges to tackle, great new people to meet, and interesting new things to learn.

---

[120] ibid.

[121] True Sport (2006) About True Sport. Retrieved November 13, 2006 from http://www.truesportpur.ca/index.php/language/en/category/39.

[122] ibid.

[123] Everton Football Club (2006) Ontario Soccer Association. Retrieved November 13, 2006 from http://evertonfc.com/club/ontario-soccer-association.html.

[124] ibid.

[125] Case compiled using secondary data sources (e.g., Sport BC website, BC Ferries website) and in-depth interviews with Peter Simpson, manager of marketing and sponsorship at Sport BC and Maury Kask, director of marketing and sales at BC Ferries.

Going from technical official to PSO president, to NSO president, and to AFC president involved a huge learning curve with each new role. Now, as a new board member of Commonwealth Games Canada, I face another learning curve, and I welcome the opportunity to expand my horizons again. I never mapped out a course for myself—I never had the goal of becoming president of an organization, but one thing led to another. I guess it is performance punishment! I recall when I was first asked to be president of the PSO, Nancy Brawley, a dedicated sport volunteer herself, encouraged me and said I should do it "because it would be good for me."

I strongly believe that athletes should get involved in their sport community after they retire from competition—start locally, in your club and in your provincial sport association. Keep your motives pure, and then just see where it leads you. The Canadian sport community is a great place to devote your energy, and, besides, it's easier to make change and improvements when you're part of the process rather than sitting on the sidelines. I welcome opportunities to mentor athletes and encourage them to get involved and develop their own leadership. And while I respect their focused headspace while they're athletes, if they're ever curious or wondering about what lies beyond, I'm ready to help expand their horizons.

Aquatic Federation of Canada (AFC)

The AFC is FINA's (Fedération Internationale de Natation, which governs the aquatic sports internationally) representative member in Canada. The AFC's members are the NSOs (National Sport Organizations) for swimming, diving, water polo, and synchronized swimming. While each sport would be represented by a different committee of the aquatic federation in most countries, in Canada, each of the four NSOs is autonomous—responsible for its own plans, budgets, policies, funding, performance results, and so on. The AFC is the umbrella organization representing the NSOs to external stakeholders and promoting common interests. The AFC has three main business areas:

Events: This has two components—hosting and participating. In terms of participating, the AFC nominates the Canadian team that will compete at the FINA World Aquatics Championships held every two years. For hosting, the AFC is the Canadian rights holder for FINA events. In 2005, Montreal hosted the magnificent FINA

World Aquatics Championships, the first time to be held in North America.

Representation (international and domestic): Internationally Canada has representatives on various FINA committees and the continental zone (i.e., the North and South American region) of the Americas (ASUA). Collectively within the AFC, we determine how we can play a leadership role with our international partners to ensure we represent both the best interest of Canada and the long-term development of our sports internationally. Domestic representation is an area receiving greater attention now than in the past. While we continue to have representation on the COC, we are devoting more energy to working with other stakeholders in aquatic activities (e.g., Red Cross, Royal Life Saving, Canadian Parks and Recreation Association) to increase participation. We are also developing resident expertise and advocacy tools to influence the building of aquatic facilities, as infrastructure is key to growing aquatic sport in Canada.

Promotion: This involves strategies for the NSOs to collaboratively promote our sports. A number of AFC awards recognize the accomplishments of outstanding athletes, coaches, and volunteers from the aquatics community. We are also involved with the Canadian Aquatic Hall of Fame and Museum and an Aquatic Foundation.

Being an umbrella group, the AFC struggles with the dichotomy of its structure: the opportunity to work together as members to improve aquatic sport coupled with the competition between the members for marketing dollars, government dollars, and even pool time. With this reality, it's important to focus on the areas that benefit us all. We are blessed with a very competent and committed board of directors who see the big picture and realize that if we focus on expanding opportunities and resources for all of us, we will each be better positioned for growth and performance.

The AFC itself has no staff and relies on the efforts of its volunteer board of directors and the staff of the member NSOs. The board comprises ten people—the president, the FINA bureau member, and a director and senior staff person from each of the four NSOs. We hold an annual general meeting, bi-monthly meetings via conference call, and one face-to-face planning meeting annually. We develop a plan and budget and share expenses equally among the four member NSOs.

Hierarchy of Sport

The International Olympic Committee (IOC) governs the Olympic sports; the COC is the IOC member in Canada; and the NSOs are members of the COC. In most cases, the NSO members are the provincial chapters or sections and, in some cases, their stakeholder and technical committees. The athletes are trained and developed through the club system at the local level. While we'd like to think this hierarchy represents a seamless sport system, it does not, at least not yet. We are constantly trying to ensure the appropriate body has the appropriate rights and responsibilities in the appropriate jurisdiction. This is very relevant from a sport marketing perspective. For example, a local club is hosting the national championships in partnership with the NSO. Prior to the event, the NSO representatives want to erect their sponsor signage in the facility only to learn that the facility has an agreement with a competitor in one of the categories. The hierarchy (or mosaic) of rights needs to be clearly articulated and understood. Sponsors want to direct their marketing efforts where they will get return on their investment as well as help sport development. If they become an Olympic sponsor, they get rights to the rings but may not get access to the athletes. If an athlete has a personal sponsor, they have to coordinate how that relationship may complement or conflict with a sponsor of their NSO. The athletes' needs, the long-term development of the sport, and the objectives of the sponsor and other stakeholders must work in sync. Putting together the pieces of this puzzle is the great opportunity and challenge for people working in sport.

My Advice to You, as a Student of Sport Marketing

Very often people say they want to work or volunteer in sport because of their passion for it. I'll take passion any day over apathy, but we have to ensure that our passions and energy are focused in a positive direction rather than making us competitive to the point of being nearsighted. Our passions need to be tempered in community values with our long-term objectives in mind. Rather than wasting our resources competing among ourselves, it's far better to pool our passions and compete externally to be the best in the world. I believe that most Canadians don't understand or appreciate the inherent value of sport and what sport contributes to Canadian society. Besides the health benefits of sport participation, sporting excellence builds character, citizenship, community, and pride. Those of us who are part of the sport community need to work together to convince Canadians to be as passionate about sport as we are.

Linda was the president of Diving Plongeon Canada for six years and is currently president of the Canadian Federation of Aquatic Sports. In 2004, she was named by CAAWS as one of Canada's 20 most influential women in sport and physical activity.

Sport Organizations in Canada

This chapter discussed five main sectors of sport in Canada: professional, Olympic, grassroots, university and college, and events. Each of the five plays an integral role in shaping Canadian sport, and, without one aspect, holes would appear and the system would be drastically weakened. Each sector is interconnected with the others, and it is the strengths and weaknesses of these connections that will help or hinder the progress of the overall system. For example, a strong university and college sport sector can produce an excellent feeder system for future Olympic or professional athletes. For Canadian sport to reach its full potential, cooperation, communication, and interaction between all these elements are essential. Figure 2-1 below describes sport in Canada.

FIGURE 2-1

The Canadian Sport Landscape

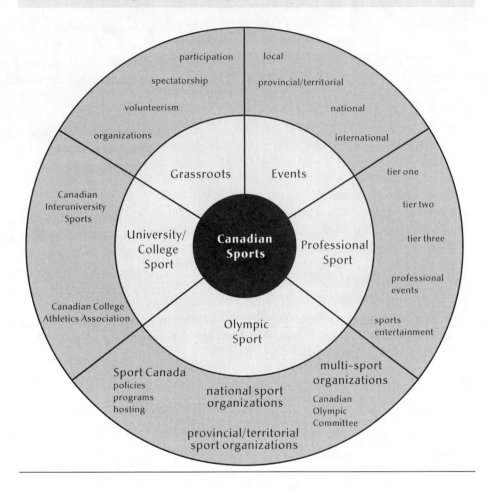

Sport Facilities in Canada

A wide variety of sport facilities can be found across Canada, ranging from local rinks and soccer fields to Olympic-calibre training and competition venues and stadiums that seat more than 65,000 spectators. Tables 2-3 to 2-5 list the major Canadian sport facilities that cater to professional sport, Olympic sport, and sometimes recreation.

TABLE 2-3

Tier One and Tier Two Professional Facilities

FACILITY	CITY	USE	CAPACITY*	BUILT
Air Canada Centre	Toronto	hockey, basketball, lacrosse	19 800	1999
BC Place Stadium	Vancouver	football	59 841	1983

Bell Centre	Montreal	hockey	21 273	1996
BMO Field	Toronto	soccer	20 000	2007
Canada Inns Stadium	Winnipeg	football	29 503	1953
Commonwealth Stadium	Edmonton	football	60 081	1978
Copps Coliseum	Hamilton	AHL hockey	19 000	1985
GM Place	Vancouver	hockey	18 630	1995
Ivor Wynne Stadium	Hamilton	football	30 000	1930
McMahon Stadium	Stampeders	football	35 650	1960
Mosaic Stadium at Taylor Field	Regina	football	28 800	1927
MTS Centre	Winnipeg	AHL hockey	15 003	2004
Pengrowth Saddledome	Calgary	hockey, lacrosse	19 289	1983
Percival Molson Memorial Stadium	Montreal	football	20 202	1916
Rexall Place	Edmonton	hockey, lacrosse	16 839	1974
Ricoh Coliseum	Toronto	AHL hockey	N/A	2003
Rogers Centre	Toronto	football, baseball	53 506	1989
Scotiabank Place	Ottawa	hockey	19 153	1996

* The number refers to largest possible capacity.

TABLE 2-4

Canadian Sport Centres

NAME	CITY
Canadian Sport Centre Atlantic	Halifax, Fredericton, St. John's, Charlottetown
Canadian Sport Centre Calgary	Calgary
Canadian Sport Centre Ontario	Toronto
Canadian Sport Centre Saskatchewan	Regina
Canadian Sport Centre Winnipeg	Winnipeg
National Multisport Centre	Montreal
Pacific Sport	Victoria
Pacific Sport	Vancouver

Canadian Sport Centres, high-performance training centres in cities across the country, represent a joint effort between Sport Canada, the COC, and the Coaching Association of Canada and offer athletes a wide range of training facilities and sport services.

TABLE 2-5

Other Facilities

NAME	CITY	PURPOSE
Olympic Park	Calgary	multisport
Calgary Oval	Calgary	speed skating
Olympic Stadium	Montreal	baseball/football
National Sports School	Calgary	multisport
Spruce Meadows	Calgary	equestrian
Rexall Centre	Toronto	tennis
Lansdowne Park	Ottawa	football/hockey
Whistler/Blackcomb	Alberta	alpine skiing

While these lists cover the majority of major sport facilities across the country, numerous smaller facilities cater to third-tier professional and semi-professional leagues and teams. In addition, the Vancouver 2010 Winter Olympics will offer a new set of world-class winter sport facilities to match those in Calgary.

Sport Events in Canada

Through the creation of its hosting policy, the Canadian government has shown that it recognizes the contribution of international events. In addition to international events, numerous national and local events, as well as annual professional championships, also take place. Table 2-6 lists some of the annual events that have been hosted by Canadian cities in the past (or will be in the near future). This list includes international multisport events, international single sport events, national multi- and single sport events, and specialty games. The list gives a general overview of the Canadian sport event landscape.

TABLE 2-6

Major Events

	WHERE	WHEN
Major Single Sport Events		
IAAF World Championships	Edmonton	2001
FINA World Championships	Montreal	2005
World Figure Skating Championships	Calgary	2006

World Women's Hockey Championships	Winnipeg	2007
World Men's Curling Championships	Edmonton	2007
World Junior Hockey Championships	Ottawa	2007
FIFA Under 20 World Cup	Various	2007
World Men's Hockey Championships	Various	2008
Annual/Continuing Events		
Brier (curling)		March
Calgary Stampede		July
Canada Summer/Winter Games		Biennial
Grey Cup (CFL champlonshlp)		November
Memorial Cup (CHL championship)		May
Provincial Summer/Winter Games		Biennial
Rogers Cup (tennis)		August
Scott Tournament of Hearts (curling)		March
Vanier Cup (CIS football)		November
Specialty Games		
Gay Games	Montreal	2006
World Transplant Games	London	2005

Case: M&M Meat Shops and Canadian Curling

Grassroots Sport Sponsorship

M&M Meat Shops, a supermarket-style butcher, first opened its doors in Kitchener, Ontario in 1980. At supermarket prices, M&M sells choice cuts of flash-frozen meat. Because the meet is frozen quickly and at extremely low temperatures, its freshness and flavour are preserved at the moment of freezing and remain when the food is cooked.

By 1992, M&M had expanded to Quebec, under the banner of Les aliments M&M. This quickly led to the establishment of 37 franchises in the province. M&M expansion continued with the purchase of the Calgary-based Jeffery's Foods in 1997 and the opening of franchises in British Columbia. By 1999, M&M had opened its fiftieth store in BC alone. By 2001, M&M Meat Shops was included in the list of Canada's 50 best-managed companies, and today it is Canada's largest retail chain of specialty frozen foods.

The communities in which M&M franchises are located have benefited from the company's success. The owners are adamant that building a strong community is not a privilege but a civic responsibility. At the local level, franchise owners are urged to support local charities, nonprofit organizations, school programs, and amateur sports teams. Grassroots soccer programs in particular seem to have benefited with M&M support. In the Kitchener-Waterloo area, for example, the company supports 30 teams. In addition, M&M Meat Shops is the major corporate sponsor of the Crohn's and Colitis Foundation of Canada (CCFC). The annual 2003 Charity BBQ Day raised over $1.2 million, and since 1989, M&M has raised $8 million for CCFC research projects.

Marketing through Curling at M&M Meats

M&M Meat Shops has a marketing advisory council (MAC) comprising representatives from the individual franchises. The MAC dictates what sports sponsorships will be supported at the national level, and to which sponsorship each individual franchise owner will financially contribute. With such a responsibility, it is important that the MAC provide solid reason why a particular sponsorship is undertaken.

Curling has been designated the national sport of choice by MAC but not without consideration of other major Canadian activities. Skating was given serious attention but, in the end, was eliminated because its sponsorship properties were too expensive. The Blue Jays of Major League Baseball and the Canadian Football League Grey Cup Game have received sponsorship in the past. But since 1996, the national corporate sponsorship has been with the sport of curling.

Curling was chosen because it was a game that appealed to both men and women. Both sexes were active participants at all skill levels of the game. Curling was one of those sports that made good television, with excellent audience ratings among both men and women. It was also a game that was readily identifiable as part of Canadiana, an identity M&M wished to cultivate for itself. Curling was also a relatively low-cost grassroots sport with a wide participatory base; again qualities that M&M reiterated for itself through its corporate advertising.

The first major national commitment that M&M made to curling was sponsoring the Kitchener-based Wayne Middaugh curling team in 1996. Team Middaugh had been World Champion in 1993 and 1998, and, with the sponsorship support of M&M, it had become one of Canada's premier rinks. Prior to this relationship with Team Middaugh, M&M had extensive involvement in curling at the local and provincial levels through individual franchise support. Team Middaugh billed the national commitment as a great match—"champion Canadian curlers in partnership with a champion Canadian company."

Such sponsorships are renewable but are reviewed on an annual basis. This was obviously a good partnership. Not only was M&M the official sponsor in 2001–2002 of Team Middaugh in its quest to represent Canada at the 2002 Salt Lake City Olympics, but M&M Meat Shops also partnered with the Sherry Middaugh rink in its quest as the Canadian Olympic women's team. The sponsorship supplied the curlers with athletic clothing and performance-based financial incentives. The rinks in return were expected to appear at M&M promotional events (e.g., charity golf tournaments, franchise promotions, merchandise advertising) and to represent the company on the curling rink.

The M&M–curling relationship extends beyond the financial support of curling teams. M&M has a strong commitment with curling's "skins games": It became the title sponsor for the $75 000 Canadian Skins competitions, the first of which was held in February 2001. Prior to that, the company had been an associate sponsor of the World Curling Tour in 1999 and 2000. M&M had taken out a silver sponsorship for the Canadian Curling Olympic trials held in Regina in December 2001, a generous involvement given its support of two serious contenders in the Middaugh rinks. Finally, M&M made a major contribution to the 2002 production of the acclaimed full-length film *Men with Brooms*, produced by Alliance Atlantis Broadcasting.

Source: Institute for Sport Marketing Case Studies. Laurentian University 2003-2005

Case Questions

1. Why is M&M Meats marketing through curling a good example of a grassroots sponsorship initiative?
2. Is grassroots marketing effective for M&M Meats? Why or why not?
3. Name four other grassroots marketing initiatives in Canada.
4. Do you agree that M&M Meats and curling are "a good fit" for marketing action?
5. Comment on M&M Meats grassroots efforts in terms of participation, spectatorship, and other grassroots organizations?

Chapter Summary

This chapter provides an extensive review of the landscape that is Canadian sport. The four major facets of Canadian sport are professional sport, university and college sport, Olympic sport, and grassroots sport. Each has its own set of organizations, events, and participants. Professional sport includes leagues (e.g., NHL) and athletes (e.g., Sidney Crosby), which provide entertainment for an economic gain. In Canada, professional sport can be divided in five categories: tier one professional sport (e.g., NHL, MLB, NBA), tier two professional sport (e.g., CFL, AHL, MLS), tier three professional sport (e.g., USL, Women's professional leagues), professional sport competition (e.g., Rogers Cup in tennis, Canadian Open in golf), and sports entertainment (e.g., WWE). While a number of challenges face professional sport in Canada (e.g., value of Canadian dollar, taxation policies), its ultimate goal is to make a profit.

University and college sport are those competitions (e.g., Vanier Cup) involving nearly 20 000 athletes in Canada. To be eligible to compete, athletes must be enrolled in postsecondary institutions. The Canadian Interuniversity Sport is the national organization that manages university sport, while the Canadian Colleges Athletic Associations manages college sports. Both organizations have regional associations, or conferences, across the country.

Olympic sport covers high-performance athletic competition in which athletes compete, for the most part, for personal rather than economic gain. The Canadian government (Sport Canada) provides funding ($140 million) to national sport organizations and athletes through various programs (e.g., sport support, athlete assistance) and direction to sport through various policies (e.g., Canadian Sport Policy, Women in Sport Policy). National sport organizations are the individual nonprofit bodies (e.g., Swimming Canada) that manage Olympic sport (e.g., swimming) and non-Olympic sport (e.g., squash). Multisport organizations represent a diversity of interests and provide a variety of services to the Canadian sport community (e.g., Coaches Association of Canada, Canadian Centre for Ethics in Sport). While the federal government is involved at the national level, the 13 provincial and territorial governments play a large role in sport in the country by promoting and developing sport in their own jurisdictions and ensuring that sport services are being delivered on a provincial and territorial scale.

Grassroots sport is based around local communities and participation by the general public. The three aspects of Canadian grassroots sport are participation, spectatorship, and organizations.

Finally, sport facilities are paramount to all four facets of sport in Canada. These facilities may be financed by the various levels of government (municipal ice rinks) or privately by the owners of professional sport teams (e.g., Bell Centre in Montreal).

Test Your Knowledge

1. What is the role of the Canadian government in sport in this country?
2. What is the role of the provinces of Quebec, British Columbia, and Nova Scotia in sport in this country?
3. Provide an example of each type of organization shown in Figure 2-1.
4. How do each of the following groups fit into Figure 2-1?
    a. coaches
    b. elite athletes
    c. developing athletes
5. Describe the size of the sport industry in Canada.
6. Distinguish between professional, Olympic, and grassroots sport.
7. What role do universities and colleges play in Canada's sport system?
8. In your opinion, what are the 10 most important sport organizations in Canada? Describe each and support your selection.
9. In the coming years, a number of important sporting events are coming to Canada. Identify two of these events and describe what kind of impact they could make on sport in Canada?
10. Is corporate Canada involved in sport? If so, how?

W W W For more review questions, go to http://www.sportmarketing.nelson.com.

Key Terms

amateur sport

collegiate sport

grassroots sport

Olympic sport

participation

professional sport

spectatorship

sport events

A full glossary of key term definitions is located at
http://www.sportmarketing.nelson.com.

Internet Resources

Professional leagues:

National Hockey League, http://www.nhl.com

Canadian Football League, http://www.cfl.ca

Major League Baseball, http://www.mlb.com

National Basketball Association, http://www.nba.com

Major Soccer League, http://www.mlsnet.com

American Hockey League, http://www.theahl.com

National Lacrosse League, http://www.nll.com

United Soccer League, http://www.uslsoccer.com

Provincial/territorial sport:

Ontario, http://www.sportsalliance.com

Alberta, http://www.athleticsalberta.com

Saskatchewan, http://www.sasksport.sk.ca

Manitoba, http://www.sportmanitoba.ca

British Columbia, http://www.sport.bc.ca

Quebec, http://www.sportsquebec.com

Nova Scotia, http://www.sportnovascotia.ca

New Brunswick, http://www.sport.nb.ca

Prince Edward Island, http://www.sportpei.pe.ca

Newfoundland & Labrador, http://www.sportnl.ca/

Territories, http://www.sportnorth.com

University / college sport:

Canadian Interuniversity Sport, http://www.universitysport.ca

Canadian College Athletic Association, http://www.ccaa.ca

Canadian sport organizations:

Sport Canada, http://www.pch.gc.ca/progs/sc/index_e.cfm

Canadian Olympic Committee, http://www.olympic.ca

Canadian Paralympic Committee, http://www.paralympic.ca

Aboriginal Sport Circle, http://www.aboriginalsportcircle.ca

Canadian Association for the Advancement of Women in Sport, http://www.caaws.ca

Sport Matters, http://www.sportmatters.ca

World Anti-Doping Agency, http://www.wada-ama.org

Vancouver Winter Games 2010, http://www.vancouver2010.com

Canadian Centre for Ethics in Sport, http://www.cces.ca

Coaching Association of Canada, http://www.coach.ca

Sport Dispute Resolution Centre, http://www.adrsportred.ca

Canadian Sport Tourism Alliance, http://www.canadiansporttourism.com

Canadian Sport Resource Centre, http://www.canadiansport.com/resources/index_e.cfm

Canadian sport centres:

Alberta/Calgary, http://www.canadiansportcentre.com

Manitoba, http://www.nscm.ca

Quebec/Montreal, http://www.multisport.qc.ca

British Columbia/Greater Vancouver, Greater Victoria, http://www.pacificsport.com

Ontario/Toronto, http://www.cscontario.ca

Atlantic Provinces, http://www.cscatlantic.ca

Saskatchewan/Regina, http://www.sasksport.sk.ca/csc-sk

Other:

National Sport School, http://www.nationalsportschool.ca

Olympic Oval, http://www.oval.ucalgary.ca

Calgary Olympic Park, http://www.canadaolympicpark.ca

Chapter **3**

Sport Market Research

Learning Objectives

- To appreciate the importance of market research in making business decisions
- To identify the role of market research in the marketing process
- To recognize the different types of research and techniques available
- To learn the steps in the market research process
- To understand the online methodology known as netnography, why it is used, and how it is carried out in practice

Introduction

Marketing research: What is it good for?

The objective of this chapter is to discuss the importance of market research and its uses. Marketing research is heavily used in academic inquiry and in business practice. Therefore, all marketers must be familiar with the basic types of market research and the research process. They must also understand that marketing research is a highly tailored process designed specifically for individual research questions. In practice, each research study will be different and will require a customized approach to be successful.

Marketers use research to gather information about their industry, products, competition, and clients to make educated and timely business decisions. Table 3-1 lists questions that market research can help answer.

TABLE 3-1

The Six Questions of Sport Marketing Research

Who?	Who is my consumer/audience/fan?
	Who will make the final decision in this purchase?
	Who is my competitor?
	Who is my competitor's consumer/audience/fan?
What?	What features does my consumer look for in my product?
	What is my consumer willing to pay?
	What benefits does my consumer seek?
Where?	Where does my consumer learn about my product?
	Where does my consumer shop for my product?
	Where will my consumer use my product?
When?	When does my consumer purchase my product?
	When does my consumer use it?
How?	How many of my products will my consumer purchase?
	How is my product consumed?
Why?	Why does the consumer buy my product?

Source: Adapted, with permission, from B. J. Mullin, S. H. Hardy, and W. A. Sutton, 2000, Sport Marketing, 2nd ed. (Champaign, IL: Human Kinetics), page 81

By acquiring specific information from market research, people involved in sports, such as sport equipment manufacturers, official NHL novelty suppliers, sport promoters, and sport drink suppliers, can make business decisions to improve their competitive edge. With research, they can find new opportunities for existing products, identify new market segments for new products, or identify the needs of customers to serve them better. For example, the Toronto Blue Jays used telephone interviews to small-business clients and potential clients to determine what kind of business package (e.g., suite, tickets, game times) would be of interest to this target market. With this information, the Jays are able to alter their marketing mix to cater to these needs and wants.

EXECUTIVE PERSPECTIVE

Krista Benoit, President, iSPARK

Sport Marketing Research—My View

As a consultant working with the sport community, I am constantly dealing with clients who have restricted marketing budgets and high goals. The challenge is to develop an effective, yet economical, marketing plan that will achieve their ultimate objective while maximizing the available human and financial resources. Tradeoffs often have to be made. For example, do we do a costly direct mail campaign with a reach of 3000, or do we go for the inexpensive e-mail blast that reaches an audience of only 1000? I am constantly trying to come up with creative approaches for my clients. In sport, saving money is always a critical part of the marketing plan.

I am not a fan of ad hoc approaches to marketing. I prefer to have an intelligent strategy that is based on knowledge of the market and the audience—market research. In an ideal world, my clients would be armed with mountains of market research to help guide them with their marketing strategies, but this is not the reality in the sport community, where marketing budgets are small and every dollar must be spent wisely. One of my favourite ways to gather the data I need is the telephone interview. You would be amazed at how much information you can obtain from a few casual, chatty phone calls to some key stakeholders!

Recently, I was hired by Synchro Canada, the national governing body for the sport of synchronized swimming, to develop a national promotional campaign for their new learn-to-swim program offered in conjunction with Canadian Red Cross. My first objective was to find out how people felt about this new program. AquaSquirts had been launched 12 months earlier but had not really taken off. My gut feeling was that it was a great product that needed a strong sales push; but directed to whom—pool programmers, instructors, parents? Who were the decision makers when it came to deciding if this program would be offered at the local pool?

I hired a student for one month to call pools all across Canada. He talked to over 100 pool programmers, life guards, and instructors. He had no experience in market research, but he was a certified water safety instructor, so he spoke their language. He was also an outgoing and talkative guy who was able to engage people over the phone. Within one month, I had a binder full of notes, contact info for 200 people, and the information that we needed. First, awareness in the market was low, but interest in the program was high. Second, a number of pool facilities had tremendous success with AquaSquirts as a summer camp program—an exciting piece of information. The best part about the telephone interview project was that it was inexpensive to conduct—the long-distance charges were part of the client's general administration expenses and not part of the marketing budget, and the student's hourly wages were reasonable—yet the outcome

was significant. As a result of the calls, I had the information I needed to develop a comprehensive and targeted marketing plan to increase awareness about this new swim program.

The Internet and e-mail can also be a quick and efficient way to do market research. When I was hired by Laurentian University's Institute for Sport Marketing to conduct a survey of national sport organizations about their experience with corporate sponsorship, I used technology to collect the data. A similar survey had been conducted two years prior, but it was done in hard-copy format: Completed surveys had been faxed in and results tabulated by hand. I hired a web developer to design an electronic survey to be sent via e-mail. The software would automatically track who replied and who didn't and send friendly reminders to members of the target group prompting them to complete the survey. This software also tabulated the results, which simplified reporting. The response rate for the electronic survey was 65 percent versus 43 percent for the faxed version. Although there was an initial investment for software development, it was later adapted for a second survey to a different target group, and it can easily be used again for a follow-up survey in the future.

I sometimes wonder if I should consider expanding my client base beyond sport. I'm told that in the corporate world, budgets are seemingly limitless, the pay is higher, and the latest tools and resources are readily available. It is tempting, but I'm taking a pass for now. I have carved out a niche in the sport community and I secretly thrive on the challenge of balancing the restrictive parameters.

Krista holds a bachelor of commerce degree in sports administration from Laurentian University and a bachelor of arts degree in French from Carleton University. In 2000, she launched iSPARK Consulting, whose clients include community-based sporting events and national and multisport organizations.

Market Research: An Introduction

Market research can be defined as the collection and evaluation of data about a particular product, target market, competitor, or environment[1]. Its purpose is to provide supporting information to management so that they can make better decisions. For example, the president of the University of Manitoba commissions surveys of the student body and residents of Winnipeg to get their opinions on starting a women's varsity hockey team at the university.

Market research focuses on answering questions about product, price, promotion, and place, but it can also address economic trends, technological advances, and potential risks. Determining the proper question to collect accurate data can be complex. Therefore, many companies offer their experience in various forms of market research: Some companies may focus on specific industries such as automotive, medical, or financial services; some may concentrate on ethnic research, online research, international research, or other specialized areas. Table 3-2 lists some market research consultants that specialize, or have a component of their business, in the sport industry.

These companies provide public and private industries with strategic information by successfully acquiring the data, analyzing it, and communicating the results to the recipient who use it to support their business decisions. Two marketing research firms A.C. Nielsen and Ipsos Reid are profiled here.

TABLE 3-2

Market Research Companies with an Interest in Sport

COMPANY	SPECIALIZATION	WEBSITE/CONTACT
Ipsos Canada (international, with an office in Toronto)	Advertising, marketing, and public affairs research	http://www.ipsos.ca/reid
iSPARK (Canada)	Sport management research	ispark@sympatico.ca
IEG (US, with offices in Toronto and Vancouver)	Sport sponsorship marketing research	http://www.sponsorship.com
Charlton Engel (US, with an office in Toronto)	Retail advertising, branding, strategy, political, etc.	http://www.charltonmarketing.com
Decima Research (Canada)	Many marketing research segments	http://www.decima.com

---

[1] Market Research Portal (2006) Definition of market research. Retrieved November 1, 2006 from http://www.marketresearchworld.net/index.php?option=com_content&task=view&id=14&Itemid.

A.C. Nielsen and Ipsos Reid Profiles

A well-known marketing firm, A.C. Nielsen collects data for television and publishes ratings which are widely used to determine the success of individual television programs. However, some marketing firms like Ipsos Reid are recognized for offering survey-based market research in Canada. Ipsos Reid "offers timely and cost effective data collection through close to 600 staff members in eight cities, the biggest network of telephone call-centres in Canada, and the largest pre-recruited household and on-line panels[2]." Ipsos Reid also specializes in market research for certain industries, including automotive, energy, financial services, health care, and retail.

A marketer must always consider the value of market research information, weighing its cost against the economic benefits it may provide. Although research can be delegated to a market research firm, it can also be executed by an individual, group, or team to accomplish their goals. Numerous texts and papers present techniques and options for performing market research.

Time is important in market research and in the decision-making process. Marketers attempt to gather research to make better business decisions to gain a competitive advantage. Many times, firms require the information quickly to be a first-mover in the industry or to react to a competitor's new marketing strategy. These situations demonstrate that time can mean the difference between success and loss. A successful market research firm will understand, acquire, and present research findings in a timely manner.

Simply put, a well planned and properly implemented market research program will reduce the business risk of an organization by eliminating potential errors and saving both financial resources and, often more important, time.

Accumulating data is an important part of the market research process. This chapter discusses the types of data required and how to accumulate them. First, it presents the three main types of research—exploratory, descriptive, and causal—and the two general research methodologies—primary and secondary. Second, it examines the marketing research process, including several popular techniques.

---

[2] Ipsos Reid (2006) About Ipsos Reid. Retrieved November 1, 2006 from http://www.ipsos.ca/reid/.

Types of Market Research

The three principal types of market research are exploratory, descriptive, and causal[3]. Exploratory research is typically used initially to determine the "real" problem or issue, such as assessing if there is a market for the expansion of the Canadian Football League into Halifax. Descriptive research is used to find the answer to a specific problem, for example using customer satisfaction surveys to poll guests at the host hotel of a local five-pin bowling event to determine if the hotel should consider sponsoring the event the following year. Causal research is used to determine the relationships between known variables, such as assessing the cause and effect between a proposed change in ticket prices and forecast ticket sales to Toronto Raptors' games.

Exploratory, Descriptive, and Causal Research

Exploratory research

exploratory research: research used initially to determine the real problem or issue.

Exploratory research is often used when the type of problem or issue faced by the marketer is vague. Therefore, marketers often use it to define the initial issue for a larger marketing research project. For example, a manufacturer like Nike is unsure whether it should size the potential market for a new product or find a new product for its existing markets. Exploratory research helps to clarify problems by gathering ideas, details, explanations, and insights to form hypothetical solutions that can be further researched. During the process, it can unexpectedly discover new ideas, opportunities, and problems faced by the company. Exploratory research is usually relatively inexpensive and is rarely used to draw conclusions. Techniques include include observation (such as ethnography), pilot studies[4], literature searches, interviews, expert interviews, focus groups, and case studies[5]. For example, exploratory research can be used to determine the change in consumer purchase behaviour as more consumers rely on the Internet to gather information: Interviewing 50 potential clients will enable researcher to determine where, when, and how they acquired their information.

Descriptive research

descriptive research: research used to determine the answer to a specific problem.

Descriptive research is typically used after the exploratory research is complete and the problem faced by the marketer has been better defined. It generally asks specific questions about the who, what, where, when, why, and how; and it accurately answers them. A common complaint about descriptive research is that it merely acquires analytical and statistical data but does not address the behaviours and motivations that have caused the problem or issue[6]. The most common techniques of descriptive research are surveys, experiments, secondary data searches, and observation. For example, a marketer observes patrons at a local tennis club to determine where to best locate vending machines for beverages and snacks.

---

[3] Zikmund, W.G. (2003) *Esssentials of Marketing Research*, 2nd ed. Thomson South-Western: 92.

[4] ibid.

[5] ibid.

[6] ibid.

Causal research

Causal research is used when the problem faced by the marketer is well understood and clearly defined. It is used primarily to discover the cause and effect relationships between two known variables—why one event occurs after the marketer does something in particular. The researchers attempt to discover the relationships that predict future events. The most common technique in causal research is the experiment, where one variable's relationship to another is tested. For example, the relationship between gender and spending habits on Hockey Canada merchandise at Christmas could be determined using follow-up mail surveys.

causal research: research used to determine the cause and effect of relationships between known variables.

Secondary Research

Secondary research is typically used in marketing research to quickly and inexpensively find data about the research topic. Secondary data are those that have been collected for other uses but that contain information pertinent to the current marketing research project. A common source of secondary data is **census** information collected by Statistics Canada (http://www.statscan.ca/menu-en.htm). Table 3-3 lists topics on the Statistics Canada website.

Libraries, the Internet, industry associations, and competing organizations are also principal sources of secondary data since they have access to abundant statistics, studies, and facts. Sometimes these sources of secondary data can fully answer the marketing problem at a fraction of the cost of primary research; however, they often do not have enough detailed information to be of

secondary research: research of data already collected for other uses.

census: secondary research information collected by Statistics Canada.

TABLE 3-3

The Statistics Canada Website Topics

1. Agriculture	15. National accounts
2. Arts, culture, and recreation	16. Personal finance and household finance
3. Business enterprises	17. Population and demography
4. Communications	18. Prices and price indexes
5. Construction	19. Primary industries
6. Education	20. Reference
7. Energy	21. Science and technology
8. Environment	22. Service industries
9. Geography	23. Social conditions
10. Government	24. Statistical methods
11. Health	25. Trade
12. Justice	26. Transport and warehousing
13. Labour	27. Travel and tourism
14. Manufacturing	

Chapter 3: Sport Market Research

use and are merely a convenient stepping stone in the market research process. This is often the case because competing organizations do not share detailed information, and industry data (associations or libraries) are often dated and developed for other purposes.

Primary Research

primary research: accumulating data created specifically for the purpose of the research.

sampling: examining a smaller, randomly chosen selection (the sample) of group members to obtain information about a large group.

Primary research is accumulating data specifically for the purpose of the research[7] through such means as surveys, observations, questionnaires, and focus groups. Researchers use it to find solutions and answers when secondary data are inadequate or inappropriate. The primary research process includes planning a research design, **sampling**, and collecting specific data and information on the topic of interest. Primary research is typically more costly and takes longer to complete since it is more labour intensive.

The Market Research Process

The marketing research process usually consists of six steps (Table 3-4). However, the actual number of steps and each one's importance depends on the project's needs. For example, secondary data may sufficiently answer the issue, so steps 3 and 4 would not be required. Or time constraints and budgets may affect the shape and direction of the final process.

Step 1: Define the Marketing Issue

The initial stage of designing a market research project is defining the marketing issue—a problem or an opportunity facing the marketer. This step is crucial: Failure to properly define the issue will result in useless data. And the marketer and researchers must ascertain the proper direction for further analysis. For example, the marketer may notice that game attendance is diminishing and ask: "Why? Are fans finding new, more exciting sports or entertainment options? Are attendance prices too high? Is access to the new sports dome problematic?"

TABLE 3-4

Basic Steps of the Marketing Research Process

Step 1	Define the marketing issue
Step 2	Set objectives and budge
Step 3	Select research type, technique, and design
Step 4	Collect data
Step 5	Organize and analyze data
Step 6	Prepare and present market research findings

Source: Zikmund, W.G.,(2003). Essentials of Marketing Research.(2nd ed.) United States: Thomson South-Western, p.47

[7] Mullin, B., S. Hardy, & W. Sutton (2000) *Sport Marketing*, 2nd ed. Human Kinetics: 88.

Properly defining the issue, or cause, without confusing it with the symptoms can be difficult. At this stage, exploratory research is often used (e.g., literature research, interviews, focus groups, case studies), not to draw final conclusions but merely to confirm the defining issue. By gathering ideas, details, explanations, and insights to form hypothetical solutions, the researcher is able to clarify problems and make further decisions in the market research process. At the end of this stage, the researcher should have a precise definition of the issue to set objectives and a budget.

Step 2: Set Objectives and Budget

At this stage, a market researcher must formulate specific objectives for the research project based on the issue definition. These objectives must state the type of information required and several potential hypotheses to help answer the issue—the researcher must make educated guesses as to methods and direction that could acquire the necessary information. The objectives must limit the scope of the research project to control its size and costs. For example, if a midget boys soccer team in Red Deer, Alberta needs to find sponsors for its annual tournament in Vancouver, an extensive and costly market research program to identify and describe all potential sources is beyond the team's resources. Once the limits of the project have been defined, the market researcher can calculate the probable costs to proceed with the research. The cost for the marketing research process should not exceed any expected benefits that the information could deliver. For example, it is not cost effective to spend $10 000 on a research project which could not result in increased revenues of at least the same amount. Therefore, the market researcher must find a new balance between the type of research (and its costs) and the relative importance of the data, or else cancel the research project.

Step 3: Select Research Type, Technique, and Design

The next step is to finalize a design plan to proceed with the research. This plan should delineate the details, including the type of research, technique to be used to gather the data, and the sample size. It also involves determining the analytical methods to be used to analyze the data.

Type of Research

Depending on the type of issue to be investigated, the researcher has two options for collecting primary data—descriptive research or causal research. *Descriptive research* is used when the problem is partially defined, typically when the researcher is aware of the who, what, where, when, why, and how. In descriptive research, one can ask fairly precise questions. *Causal research* is used when the problem is well understood and clearly defined, primarily to discover the cause and effect relationships between known variables. The selection of descriptive or causal research depends on the type of question that must be answered and the amount of uncertainty associated with it.

Chapter 3: Sport Market Research

Research Techniques

The researcher then chooses a technique for gathering the required data. The choice will be influenced by the technique's limitations and effectiveness, as well as budget and time constraints. The researcher's experience is an asset in determining the proper technique: A seasoned one will have been exposed to a variety of research questions, methodologies, and protocols. Table 3-5 lists some research techniques.

Sampling

After deciding on the technique, the researcher determines the sample. Since it is not cost effective to obtain the data from every individual in a target population, we choose to obtain the data from a subset. Sampling enables the researcher to obtain information about a large group by examining a smaller selection (sample) of group members. If the sampling is conducted correctly, the results will be representative of the whole group[8]. There are two methods to choose the sample: probability sampling and non-probability sampling.

TABLE 3-5

Sampling of Research Techniques

TECHNIQUE	DESCRIPTION
Questionnaire	Also known as a survey, this is administered to a sample of respondents who are asked to answer a number of questions on a given topic. It often includes scale questions, open-ended questions, and questions about demographic characteristics.
Interview	A qualitative method in which the researcher asks an individual respondent a variety of questions (typically open ended) and records answers.
Expert interview	Like an interview, except the respondent is an expert in their field.
Secondary data	Search of studies completed by others.
Experiment	Controlled research in which the researcher views consumer behaviour under controlled conditions to examine the relationships between two or more variables.
Observation	Non-intrusive technique (e.g., ethnography) in which the researcher observes consumer behaviour in real-life environments.
Focus groups	A qualitative technique in which several respondents sit at a table with a facilitator to discuss a topic. The discussion is recorded and analyzed as qualitative data.

[8] Hawaii Department of Education (2006) Assessment terminology: A glossary of useful terms. Retrieved December 3, 2006 from http://www.k12.hi.us/~atr/evaluation/glossary.htm.

In *probability sampling*, which includes simple random sampling, stratified random sampling, and cluster sampling, every member of the population has the same chance of being chosen for the sample. This method typically gives the most accurate representation of the actual population but may not be possible in all circumstances[9].

In *non-probability sampling*, which includes convenience sampling, judgment sampling, quota sampling, and snowball sampling, the sample is chosen for a particular criterion determined by the researcher. Although this method carries a higher risk of error, it is acceptable for certain research projects[10]. A researcher can usually judge the most appropriate method for sampling based on recommendations, experience, required degree of accuracy, budget, and time constraints. The final sample size will be determined by common statistical concepts or the researcher's experience and budget constraints.

Step 4: Collect Data

Following the design plan, researchers initiate the chosen technique to gather the data while trying to minimize errors by maintaining consistency and accuracy. They ensure that the data gatherers are properly trained in the methodology. They may also do a test run to identify potential problems in the technique. Fatigue and even boredom of both researchers and participants must be addressed when designing the plan to minimize their effects on the data collection process.

Step 5: Organize and Analyze Data

Once the data are collected, the researcher must organize them into a usable format. Responses or observations can be tabulated by computer programs that can rapidly calculate percentage, frequency distributions, mean, median, mode, range, variance, and standard deviation. The needs of the research study determines the selection of metrics and methods. Table 3-6 names several methods of displaying data.

TABLE 3-6

Tabular and Graphic Methods to Display Data

tables	bar graphs
contingency tables	pie charts
scatter diagrams	histograms
line charts	stem and leaf displays
box plot	ogives

Source: Keller,G. (2005), Statistics for Management and Economics (7th ed.) United States: Thomson South-Western, pp.23-61.

---

[9] Zikmund, W.G. (2003) *Esssentials of Marketing Research*: 297.
[10] ibid.

Further analysis of the data depends on the type of information that was collected and the potential requirements of the methodology. Statistical techniques include calculating the standard deviation and multiple regressions on two or more variables. The complexity is that it is often left to the professional market researcher to explain the meanings from the results to their clients or management.

Basic Statistical Analysis

Numerous tools for statistical analysis are available to marketers, including frequency distributions, probabilities, proportions, measures of central tendency (mean, median, mode), measures of dispersion (range, variance, standard deviation), normal distribution, sampling distribution, central limit theorem, hypothesis testing, structural equation modelling, regression analysis, and chi-square test for goodness of fit. Any market research textbook will contain information on these techniques and others. Students of marketing are encouraged to study market research.

Step 6: Prepare and Present Market Research Findings

At this stage, the researcher prepares a report on the market research project and summarizes the conclusions. If the research was properly designed and executed, the data should answer the marketer's questions. The research findings may prove or disprove hypotheses, locate new segments, identify customer needs, or answer any number of questions.

Market Research Techniques

The Questionnaire

The questionnaire is considered one of the most economical methods of collecting data[11]. Researchers prepare a list of questions, which can be delivered to any size of sample by hand, mail, fax, or Internet. It permits a certain flexibility as its confidential and anonymous nature allows for specific questions on opinions, satisfaction, and demographics. The final design of the questionnaire must take into consideration these limitations: Does the respondent fully understand the questions? Should it be kept simple? Should it ask the respondent to elaborate? Is the respondent motivated to return the questionnaire? The greatest challenge with questionnaires is achieving a good response rate.

The Interview and the Expert Interview

Interviews can be an expensive method for collecting data since they are labour intensive: The larger the sample size, the larger the number of interviewers required. Training and experience are critical factors in selecting

---

[11]Wong, K.B., S.J. Shapiro, W.D. Perreault, & E.J. McCarthy (2005) *Basic Marketing: A Global Managerial Approach*, 11th ed. McGraw-Hill Ryerson: 230.

interviewers. The interviews are done primarily in person or by telephone to allow the interviewer to elaborate when a respondent encounters some difficulty. By allowing the interviewer to probe for further clarification, this interactive technique enables new ideas to arise from the replies. Technique limitations include interviewer prejudice and time and budget constraints.

The Focus Group

The focus group is a facilitator-led group "interview" of about four to nine people who are encouraged to interact through discussion[12]. This method can lead to the generation of new ideas, as individuals reflect and build on the others' comments. This technique typically leads to a more stimulating dialogue, which can result in a wide array of information. Focus groups can be planned to run for more than one session, where participants go away, think further on the topic, and return to make additional contributions. Limitations of focus group usefulness include the size and composition of the group and the experience of the facilitator. Simply, the effectiveness of the focus group can be undermined if the discussion wanders off topic or if any of the participants does not contribute—both possible if the group is not cohesive or the facilitator is unable to manage it.

The Experiment

One of the best methods for carrying out causal research, the experiment allows the researcher to vary one factor while controlling all others to prove cause and effect during[13]. As this method can be costly and complex, it must be subject to stringent guidelines. It is important that any experiment be designed and executed by experienced researchers.

Observation

Observation typically requires no interaction between the researcher and the subject. Yet, the qualitative or quantitative data can easily be acquired by the observer[14]. This method is widely used when the subject, such as children and animals, are not capable of expressing their opinion. It allows the observer to note their behaviour. The following case provides an example of an observation research methodology.

Case: "Citizens and Netizens?"

Background

People wear many different hats. In addition to a sport marketer, you might also blossom to become a civic volunteer, an astute fan, or an expert cook. Becoming any of these things often requires that you be schooled by veterans

---

[12] Aaker, D.A., V. Kumar, & G.S. Day (1998) *Marketing Research*, 6th ed. John Wiley & Sons: 191.

[13] ibid.

[14] Zikmund, W.G. (2003) *Esssentials of Marketing Research*: 56–7.

in the trade. An effective way to do this is to become a member of a community organized around your chosen activity, like a fan club or recipe swap group. These clubs and groups used to meet personally, perhaps in a community centre or even casually on the street. While this still holds for some, the Internet has allowed many of these communities to become virtual entities, congregating in online forums, sometimes in lieu of physical meetings. These virtual communities have implications not only for community members, but also for organizations that market products to them. In this chapter, you'll learn how netnography helps marketers learn about these communities and their cultures in a boundless and timeless online environment. In practice, understanding how to research online communities will help you make better decisions about your products, brand, and organization.

The Importance of Culture

Culture is not a difficult concept to understand, although it may be a relatively difficult term to define. Basically, culture describes the particulars of a distinct population: These particulars might include shared beliefs, meanings, customs, norms, patterns, or other nuances that both shape and are shaped by people's behaviours and attitudes. For example, Canadians understand that when people say "Canada's game," they are referring to hockey; and as do other countries with other sports, we exuberantly celebrate on the streets after significant major league feats (e.g., Canadian team wins the Stanley Cup). It is also common for people to wear hockey jerseys (known in general cultural jargon as cultural artifacts) while consuming games. Underlying these practices and meanings is a shared belief that the game of ice hockey is important in Canada, certainly over and above other sports, and possibly many other entertainment options as well. Collectively, these points could serve as a preliminary description of Canada's "ice hockey culture."

Members of Canada's ice hockey culture do another thing: They congregate online in chats, discussion boards, and other forms of computer-mediated communication. In this virtual arena are many strata of fandom, from Toronto Maple Leafs fans to collectors of legendary hockey cards. These groups, or subcultures, enforce certain standards of attitudes, online conduct, or consumption decisions for their members. In a netnography of European football (soccer) fans, for example, Brendan Richardson found that one of the truest signs of a "real" fan, from the perspective of the subculture, was the choice to attend away games. Since only the real fans attended these games, this was a way one could "climb the ladder" in the subculture. Subcultural standards were also developed on which teams should be ostracized and how to do it. For example, in European football, the City Cork FC fans often referred to the Shamrock Rovers as the scum. Through this example, we see that peering into this window of subculture can help marketers gain insights into the tastes and desires of specific segments, especially where intense consumption is concerned. But before we can arrive at findings of our own, we have to learn how to carry out a netnography.

The Methodology

Netnography is a relatively new research methodology that originated in the 1997 paper by Robert Kozinets[15] on the culture of fans devoted to the television show *The X-Files*. Since then, netnography has been applied to many other subcultures from Napster users to soccer fans. Similar to their physical counterparts, ethnographers, netnographers become "flies on the wall," watching their subjects as they go about their routine interactions in online forums. In doing this, the researcher also becomes part of the virtual subculture, sometimes participating in the peripheral activities associated with being a bona fide member. From a research design perspective, this makes netnography contextualized, fast, simple, and unobtrusive, a combination that is absent in many other options.

Kozinets outlines four key aspects of a netnography:

1. cultural entrée
2. data collection and analysis
3. research ethics
4. member checks

Cultural Entrée

All good researchers need questions to investigate. As a sport market researcher, you will find your questions undoubtedly shaped by the sport organization carrying out the research initiative. They might be to find out what functionalities or benefits are sought after in the next product line, what fans thought about your last acquisition, or what the current perception of your brand is compared to those of your regional competitors. In any case, solidifying your objectives through a list of questions of interest is a basic step in carrying out a netnography.

Once you have decided on the questions, the next step is to find online forums that can help you to answer them. In 1999, Kozinets suggested five main types of forums: bulletin/discussion boards, chat rooms, e-mail lists, rings (organizations of websites clustered by interests), and dungeons (characterized by role and game playing). Blogs, or online journals, also provide an environment that is suited to this type of investigation. No matter what form or structure, as long as consumers can interact online, there is opportunity for netnography to take place.

In selecting appropriate sources of data, Kozinets recommends that researchers consider four variables:

1. *Relevance to the research question(s):* "Is the data in this forum going to help me answer my question(s)?"
2. *Traffic and homogeneity of posters:* "How many different people actually visit/post on the forum?"

---

[15] Kozinets, R.V. (1997) "I want to believe": A netnography of the X-Philes' subculture of consumption. *Advances in Consumer Research*, 24: 470–5.

3. *Detail and richness of data:* "How descriptive are the data on the forum? Do people just post questions and have them answered, or do posters often talk about feelings, try to influence others, or share in symbolic exchanges with other members?
4. *Amount of social interaction:* "How many posts are there?"

Data Collection and Analysis

There are three potential sources of data in netnography. First is the downloaded messages copied verbatim from the online forum. Because of the overwhelming amount of text from this source, you may have to filter out irrelevant items, chunk together similar posts, or add notes and comments to sentences just to keep it organized, both in the text document and in your head. The second source of data is your written "field notes," which may include shared meanings (recall "Canada's game" equals hockey), names/pseudonyms of key members, and things that would otherwise go undocumented like details from your physical participation in events. The depth and amount of note taking would depend on your involvement in the community. In fact, a healthy netnography can be conducted without any field notes at all. As the third source of data, online forum members can be interviewed via e-mail, instant messaging, or private messaging (a feature similar to e-mail offered by many discussion boards).

Data analysis techniques used in netnography include symbolic, interpretive, and metaphoric methods. In much of the literature, netnographies are grouped thematically, profiling the subculture through select quotations and descriptions of cultural characteristics. Content analysis, in which posts are classified into groups based on factors the researcher wishes to study (e.g., counting posts including product feedback), is certainly welcome in a netnography study but should be used to supplement other types of culturally penetrating methods and not be generalized beyond the online culture of which the subjects are a part. Ultimately, Kozinets suggests, the choice of method(s) depends on both the researcher's strengths and the questions they want to answer.

Research Ethics

Kozinets[16] raises two concerns in the use of netnography—the public or private nature of the online forums and the nature of consent from online forum members. Researchers should pay close attention to the individuals whose lives they prod and err on the side of conservatism. It is our view that consent from members is *essential* when using direct quotations whether the online forum is private or public. Pseudonyms and actual names of the members should be disguised in the final report. If there is a clear "owner" of the online forum, specific permission should also be solicited to conduct the study.

---

[16]Kozinets, R.V. (2002) The field behind the screen: Using netnography for marketing research in online communities. *Journal of Marketing Research,* Feb: 61–72.

Member Checks

In this final stage, a researcher presents select online forum members with a copy of some or all of the report's findings. While this is useful for gaining additional insights into their culture, it can also work as an ethical control to give members a say in how they are presented to the outside world. As with interviewing procedures, member checks can be conducted via electronic means.

Summary: Relevance of Netnography to Sport Marketers

It is helpful to understand what research questions a new methodology *can* answer and hence why it should be used at all. Netnography offers sport market researchers a way to gauge reactions to elements of the marketing mix. Consider, for example, some hypothetical utterances by forum members:

- *Product:* "Trust me, our team is going to trade for a marquee player, it is in their best interests!" "How come my soccer ball doesn't stay inflated as long as the other ones on the market?"
- *Place:* "Where do I get tickets to the game and how come they're not even posted on the team website?" "Does anybody know where I can get these golf clubs? I live in a really small town and can't find them anywhere."
- *Price:* "If you were a true hardcore fan, you wouldn't care about the price! Show some loyalty!" "I don't know, but I don't think you should really invest a ton of cash in those pads just because that brand makes skates. Why don't you shop around a bit more?"
- *Promotion:* "lol Did you see that commercial they just aired? I could have taken better shots with my cell phone." "The stick looks like a pretty good buy, but I doubt that player who sponsors it even uses it on the ice."

More generally, examining macro-issues relating to culture can show sport market researchers how patterns of consumption work. You may, for example, be able to discover:

- unknown purchases and attitudes shaped by the subculture that precede purchases of your product
- what types of purchases characterize the avid or astute subculture member versus the newbie
- how subculture members can change each other's attitudes about your brand, organization, or products

Although your first few will likely be constrained by a deadline, netnographies can (and should) extend as long as new insights are being found. It is not often that market researchers can find primary data literally at their fingertips.

Source: Case Developed by Norm O'Reilly and Ryan Rahinel building from their work published as: O'Reilly, N., Rahinel, R., Foster, M. and Patterson, M. (2007). "Connecting in Mega-Classes: The Netnographic Advantage", Journal of Marketing Education, 29 (1), 69-84.

Case Questions

1. Based on the Internet's rise in popularity as a medium for communication year after year, do you think methodologies like netnography will continue to grow, or will security and anonymity issues limit them?
2. In your opinion, can data from online sources be trusted more, less, or the same as data from other sources (e.g., phone, in-person, mail)?
3. Name five online forums a sport marketer could use as data sources.
4. Visit the website of a professional sport team of your choice and find their fan forum. Select a recent quote from the forum and suggest how it could be used by the marketing director of that team?

Chapter Summary

To meet the needs and wants of consumers, sport marketers must thoroughly understand them. Market research provides information that helps sport marketers make appropriate decisions about the type of product, price, place, and appropriate ways to communicate (promote) to consumers. The marketer may design research programs (exploratory research, descriptive research, causal research) to collect primary data or look for information from available sources (secondary research) such as Statistics Canada. The decision to use primary or secondary research or both depends on the kinds of information needed and available budget and time. Marketers go through six steps in conducting research—defining the marketing issue; setting objectives and budget; selecting research type, technique, and design; collecting data; organizing and analyzing data; and preparing and presenting market research findings. Data collection methods include questionnaires (quantitative) and focus groups and interviews (qualitative). With the increased importance of the Internet in consumers' lives, a new research technique called netnography is being used by marketers to observe consumers in a unobtrusive way.

Test Your Knowledge

1. What market research firms have you encountered recently?
2. Name and describe the three different types of research.
3. Describe the differences between primary and secondary research.
4. List the steps involved in the marketing research process.
5. Name and describe five different marketing research techniques.
6. Name three statistical techniques used in market research.

 For more review questions, go to http://www.sportmarketing.nelson.com.

Key Terms

causal research	primary research
census	sampling
descriptive research	secondary research
exploratory research	

A full glossary of key term definitions is located at
http://www.sportmarketing.nelson.com.

Internet Resources

Statistics Canada, http://www.statcan.ca/start.html

2006 Sports Business Market Research Handbook,
http://www.ucalgary.ca/lib-old/business_pdfs/2006sports.pdf

Epiar Market Research Blog (Sports),
http://www.epiar.com/market-research-blog/category/arts-culture/sports/

Sports Business Market Research Reports,
http://www.marketresearch.com/browse.asp?categoryid=789&g=1

Sports Marketing Surveys – Market Research,
http://www.sportsmarketingsurveys.com

Sports Business Research Network,
http://www.sbrnet.com/sbr/guest_page.cfm

About the ESPN sports poll,
http://www.sportspoll.com/about_sportspoll.htm

Interactive sports marketing leverages STATS fantasy sports for targeted
market research,
http://www.allbusiness.com/marketing-advertising/3924051-1.html

Chapter 4

The Canadian Sport Consumer

by Dr. Ann Pegoraro, Laurentian University

Source: AP Photo / Ryan Remiorz, CP

Learning Objectives

- To build on the information presented in Chapter 2 to describe the Canadian sport consumer
- To understand why the consumer is the focus of marketing
- To provide details on why Canadians are engaged in sport
- To realize the need to understand the "minds" of consumers to develop marketing strategy

Introduction

Hockey is Canada's "religion"

The Canadian sport industry offers a wide variety of options for consumers. The level, reasons, and types of engagement vary for each person. The "actions performed when searching for, participating in, and evaluating the sports activities that consumers feel will satisfy their needs and desires" is known as participant consumption behaviour[1]. Understanding this process is essential for sport marketers. Whether consuming sport as a participant, spectator, or volunteer, the consumer goes through this process. Consider these two examples.

Participant: Mary is a five-year-old girl who is excited about beginning the downhill ski lessons her parents signed her up for. While Mary looks forward to her first lesson, her parents had chosen this activity for her after considering a number of others, including skating, gymnastics, and music.

---

[1] Shank, M.D. (2005) *Sports Marketing: A Strategic Perspective*, 3rd ed. Prentice Hall.

When making the decision, Mary's parents considered such factors as time involved (driving, skiing), risks for Mary, costs involved (lessons, equipment, concessions, gas, etc.), and which ski hills would be available. Mary's father, who has not skied for 10 years, saw this as a great opportunity to get back into skiing and engage in an activity that could be enjoyed as a family. In this situation, it is important for sport marketers to find out why Mary is taking ski lessons and the decision process that took place prior to her starting them.

Spectator: Jimmy is a 45-year-old businessman who lives in Calgary. Despite finding the prices high, Jimmy continues to purchase tickets to the Calgary Flames two or three times a year. He loves going to the games; in fact, he usually gets excited hours before. When going to a "big" game (usually against the Edmonton Oilers), the level of stress, the excitement, and the anticipation go up a notch. Jimmy loves to wear his Flames jersey at the games. He cheers, yells, celebrates, and usually has a great time. In addition, when the team is on the road, Jimmy watches some of the games on television. He listens to the radio sport talk shows and often goes to the Internet for more information. All in all, Jimmy follows his team and is an engaged consumer.

These two examples demonstrate the different types of engagement and the importance of knowing why consumers make the decision they do. In Mary's case, why is she choosing skiing? Will she be influenced by the choices made by her parents later in life? And with Jimmy, how can the Flames make him even more engaged? Is Jimmy a potential season ticket holder? Can the Flames develop programs for consumers like Jimmy to get them to buy more products? A committed participant or fan will "think more, feel more, and do more"[2]; hence nurturing the committed consumer is a key goal. The 80/20 rule, where 80 percent of the products are purchased by 20 percent of the customers, supports this point.

EXECUTIVE PERSPECTIVE

Ann Pegoraro, Associate Director, Institute for Sport Marketing (ISM) at Laurentian University

Canadian Sports Consumers

Everyone has a friend or family member who is a die-hard Toronto Maple Leafs fan or a Montreal Canadiens fan. These team loyalists are easy to identify. But what about the less visible sport fans who consume all types and variety of sports events, merchandise, and related services in Canada each and every year.

Sports organizations are no different from those that offer consumer products: They must understand who their consumers are, what value these individuals seek in exchange for their dollar, and what influences their purchase decisions. Therefore, sport organizations must delve into the consumer market to identify segments other than the obvious fan and understand the consumption patterns of these various groups.

---

[2] Mullin, B., S. Hardy, & W. Sutton (2000) *Sport Marketing*, 2nd ed. Human Kinetics.

So who are Canadian sport consumers? In an attempt to differentiate the market and develop a more detailed understanding of the sport consumer, we present the following descriptions to provide a psychographic and attitudinal segmentation of the Canadian sport consumer market.[3]

FANatics: These are the most visible of all sports consumers. They are largely young males who are fervent in their pursuit of sporting events, news, and scores. They are not necessarily loyal to one team or one sport but rather have a vast interest and knowledge of various sports teams and statistics. They represent the most valued consumers for any sports organization, as they spend most of their entertainment dollar on team-related merchandise and products.

Loyalists: These are die-hard, true-blue team fans. These consumers are very loyal to their sports team, which they ardently follow. They use various media to gather every news item and statistic pertaining to that team. Loyalists frequently attend live sports events and are willing to pay top dollar for event tickets and related merchandise.

Star-struck: These consumers are passionate about a sports star rather than a team or a specific sport. For example, legions of Tiger Woods fans congregate to watch him play, either in person or on television. To achieve long-term benefit from this segment, sport organizations need to transfer the interest of these consumers from the star to the sport, as stars have a finite tenure in their sport.

Socialites: To these consumers, sports are a means to a social end. Major sporting events provide the opportunity to socialize with friends, business contacts, or clients: They provide a venue to be seen at. This social motivation usually translates into heavy spending on status items like corporate box seats or related services.

Opportunists: Consumers who have never met an offer they could refuse, opportunists do not seek out sports events but will not turn down the opportunity to attend when offered. Their focus is on viewing sports events as a source of entertainment, one that competes with all other sources for both their attention and their dollar.

Disinterested: These consumers are usually vaguely aware of major sporting events, but show little or no interest in following sports with any continuity. Therefore, they provide the biggest challenge and the largest opportunity for sports organizations—the undecided consumer. If an organization can engage this segment, changing them from disinterested to interested, the resulting increased revenue could be significant.

The challenge for Canadian sport organizations is to move consumers up the loyalty ladder, engaging new consumers while maintaining their loyal fan base. The segments can be grouped into three categories on that ladder: At the top are the traditionalists (fanatics, loyalists); in the middle are the new kids on the block (socialites, star-struck, opportunists); and at the bottom are the undecided (disinterested). The key is to find the right offerings to move the undecided and the new kids up the ladder to the top position of traditionalists through a process of continually creating and maintaining a consumer-centred marketing strategy and organization. Perhaps this concept is best illustrated by the words of Mark Cuban, the owner of the NBA's Dallas Mavericks and one of the biggest fans of the game[4]: "We basically amped up every interaction that the organization had with fans to a level where we hoped and tried [to] over deliver value to our customers and fans. We made it clear to everyone that we no longer sold basketball. We sold fun."

Dr. Ann Pegoraro received her doctorate from the University of Nebraska-Lincoln and is currently the associate director of the Institute for Sport Marketing (ISM) at Laurentian University.

---

[3] Based on and adapted from A.T. Kearney (2003) *The New Sports Consumer.*

[4] Cuban, M. (2006) Some thoughts on the NBA. Retrieved March 4, 2006 from http://www.blogmaverick.com/ 2006/03/04/some-thoughts-on-the-nba/.

The Psychological Relationship between Consumers and Sport

To understand how consumers make sport-related consumption decisions, sport organizations need to first understand how they build relationships with sport. Funk and James proposed a model (Table 4-1) that identifies four levels for classifying the relationship a consumer has with a sport or sport organization[5]. At the initial level, a consumer first learns about a sport and/or specific team: This *awareness* is just the beginning, and no relationship to a favourite team or sport has been made. The next level, *attraction*, is where a consumer first begins to acknowledge a preference for a sport or a team, created through various psychosocial and demographic motives and the beginning of a visible relationship. At the third level, a psychological connection begins to form, and an *attachment* is made between the consumer and the favourite team or sport. At the top level, a consumer becomes a loyal devotee of the team or sport, forming a strong relationship: This *allegiance* results in consistent and valuable behaviour related to sport consumption and is the ultimate goal for sport organizations.

TABLE 4-1

The Psychological Continuum Model – A Conceptual Framework for Understanding an Individual's Psychological Connection to Sport

LEVEL OF CONNECTION	DESCRIPTION OF CONSUMER RELATIONSHIP
4 Allegiance	Consumer is a loyal fan of a sport and/or organization
3 Attachment	Consumer has a visible relationship with a sport and/or organization
2 Attraction	Consumer begins to acknowledge a preference for a sport and/or organization
1 Awareness	Consumer first learns of a sport and/or organization

Source: Adapted from Funk, D.C. and James, J. (2001)The Psychological Continuum Model- A conceptual framework for understanding an individual's psychological connection to sport. Sport Management Review 4 119-150.

Consumer Gateways to Sport[6]

Understanding how consumers form relationships with sport is the first step to understanding sport consumption. The next step is understanding how consumers engage with sport. For example, how does a consumer become

---

[5] Funk, D.C & J.James (2001) The psychological continuum model–A conceptual framework for understanding an individual's psychological connection to sport. *Sport Management Review*, 4:119–50.

[6] The consumer gateways to sport are based on those proposed in Rein, I., P. Kotler, & B. Shields (2006) *The Elusive Fan.* McGraw-Hill.

aware of a sport or sport organization and then engage with it? This section outlines five gateways to sport engagement and shows how Canadian sport consumers use them.

Participation

The primary method of engagement with sport for the majority of sport consumers is through participation at some stage of their lives. This traditional gateway often provides Canadian sport consumers with their first interaction with sport, whether through Timbits hockey or house league soccer. Participation in sport gives consumers intimate knowledge of sport, an opportunity to bond with other participants, and an enhanced appreciation for the skills, abilities, and performance of athletes at higher levels. The participation gateway is usually first accessed in childhood and then often through adulthood, as the consumer continues to engage in the sport they are so fond of. As consumers age and move through the life cycle, they are often introduced to new sports that provide new gateways to engagement. For example, over 6.5 percent of the Canadian adult population participates in golf primarily, seeking to improve their personal performance and occasionally participating in formal competitions[7].

Overall Canadian men are much more likely than Canadian women to be active participants in sport: In 2005, almost two-fifths of men actively participated versus less than one quarter of women[8].

Attendance

Consumers can attend sport in a range of environments, from small local venues used in a local children's soccer league, where spectators watch the game from the sidelines, to large high-end venues provided for National Hockey League games, complete with a variety of food outlets, memorabilia shops, expensive video and sound systems, and dedicated parking facilities. Whatever the venue, the sport consumer has a set of expectations for the experience. And for the sport organization to successfully manage this consumer gateway, the experience must be in line with these expectations. For the children's soccer game attendee, it may be as simple as an enjoyable interaction with other spectators and a hassle-free access to the facility. For the NHL spectator, expectations would be at a higher level and might include items related to entertainment and the overall "NHL experience."

Attending a sport event as a spectator requires less time and much less energy than actively participating in sport; as such, it attracts many individuals who are not athletically inclined but who are still interested in sport. Seventeen percent of the Canadians who participate in sport limit themselves to the role of attendee[9]. In addition, since no physical requirements or skills

---

[7] Bloom, M., M. Grant, & D. Watt (2005) *Strengthening Canada: The Socio-economic Benefits of Sport Participation in Canada.* Conference Board of Canada.

[8] ibid.

[9] ibid.

are involved in this role, the rate of attendance remains high during the later stages of the consumer life cycle. Therefore, the participation rate can remain as high as 50 percent among people 60 and over[10].

Media

The pervasiveness of media, including such new forms as the Internet, has provided the most accessible gateway to sport for the consumer and for sport organizations to access the consumer. To be successful, a sport must be available on television, no longer a barrier with the rise in such specialty cable sports channels as the SPEED channel, NHL network, and Golf channel. Sport consumers now demand more than just television coverage from sport organizations; they require an Internet presence and increasingly the integration of the "third" screen or cell phones and/or other mobile devices. While this is perhaps the greatest opportunity for sport organizations to engage the consumer, it is also an enormous burden to manage the constant need for timely information.

Television retains the number one medium for sport, with Internet-using Canadians averaging 14.3 hours of viewing a week. The gap between Internet and TV usage is closing (a difference of 1.6 hours per week in 2006 compared to 4.5 hours in 2002), with the Internet threatening to overtake television should this trend continue[11]. Research pertaining to media use in viewing the Olympic Games shows that 39 percent of Canadians would be interested in watching coverage via webcasts and 10 percent would want to receive information on their cell phones. The trends related to new media depend on gender and age, with males and youth more open to their use in the future[12].

Word of Mouth

Word of mouth is one of the most powerful gateways to sport that consumers have. This gateway involves personal recommendations from influential individuals in a sport consumer's life. Traditional forms of word of mouth include a recommendation from a family member, close friend, work colleague, or other acquaintance. New forms include the Internet, chat groups, instant messaging, and blogs: While these technology-mediated forms are not personal, they are relatively unfiltered, enabling real discussion among sport consumers. Table 4-2 lists some sport blogs related to the Toronto Raptors.

Canadians have embraced blogs: About 42 percent have read a blog and among these:

- A majority (58%) believe blogs influence public opinion, and many believe they influence mainstream media (45%) and politics and public policy (41%).

---

[10] ibid.

[11] Ipsos Reid (2005) The Internet continues to impact consumers' usage of other media. Retrieved May 23, 2007 from http://www.ipsos-na.com/news/pressrelease.cfm?id=2749.

[12] Honey, C. (2006) *Canada 2006 Olympic Global Brand Research*. Sponsorship Intelligence.

- Almost four in ten (37%) describe blog content as "accurate."
- Over half (52%) trust the content of these websites either somewhat (49%) or very much (3%)[13].

Thus, the new forms of word of mouth create a powerful gateway to sport for Canadian sport consumers.

TABLE 4-2

Some Toronto Raptors Blogs

http://www.raptorscity.com/blog/

http://www.raptorblog.com/

http://raptorsforum.com/

http://www.hooplife.ca/raptorshq/

http://raptors.aolsportsblog.com/

http://www.raptorslocker.com/

Influencers

Each consumer considers some individuals as key influencers in their lives—a family member, close friend, coach, mentor, or teacher. A key influencer with a keen interest in sport provides another gateway to sports for consumers. This could be as simple as a father who takes his daughter to the local golf course to learn the game, thereby fuelling her interest in taking lessons, or more complex like a physical education teacher who inspires students to participate in lacrosse and begin to follow the NLL. In the case of Mary, her father's experience with skiing influenced Mary into becoming exposed and engaged in the sport. While this is a rich gateway to sport, it is perhaps the hardest for sport organizations to access or affect.

Model of Participant Consumption Behaviour

5 steps

Shank suggests that consumers are influenced by a number of internal (psychological), external (sociological), and situational factors when making decisions to participate in sports (Figure 4-1)[14]. The decision-making process at the centre of this model consists of five steps: **problem recognition**, information search, evaluation of alternatives, participation, and post-participation. Depending on the experience of the consumers, some decisions take more time than others.

problem recognition: the first step in the consumer decision-making process related to sport consumption occurs when an individual perceives a difference between their ideal and actual states that is large enough to trigger the process.

---

[13] Ipsos Reid (2005) Blogs and the influence on news and the media. Retrieved May 23, 2007 from http://www.ipsos-na.com/news/pressrelease.cfm?id=2729.

[14] Shank, M.D. (2005) *Sports Marketing*.

Step 1: Problem Recognition

decision-making process: at the centre of Shank's participant consumption behaviour model; consists of five steps: problem recognition, information search, evaluation of alternatives, participation, and post-participation.

The first step in the consumer **decision-making process** related to sport consumption occurs when an individual perceives a difference between their ideal and actual states that is large enough to trigger the process. Sport participants often search for their desired, or ideal, state of fitness or skill level. If the discrepancy between the actual and ideal is large enough and the problem important enough, the consumer will initiate the decision-making process.

Step 2: Information Search

After recognizing their problem or need, the consumer begins to search for information to help solve it. This search usually starts with an *internal* memory scan for previous related experiences and solutions. For routine purchases like sport related consumables (e.g., hockey tape), this internal search suffices, as the consumer will remember previous experiences with a brand and use this information to complete the purchase. For more complex decisions that involve more risk or ones where they have no experience, consumers undertake a more extensive *external* search. This leads the consumer to various sources: *personal sources* (e.g., family and friends whom the consumer trusts); *public sources* (e.g., *Consumer Reports*, Internet sites that rate products or events); and *marketing-related sources* (e.g., advertising, salespeople, promotional information, such as websites, provided by sport organizations).

FIGURE 4-1

Model of Participant Consumption Behaviour

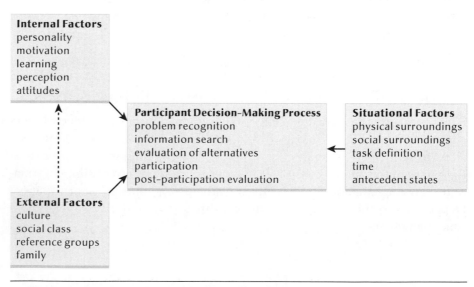

Source: Shank, Mathew, Sports Marketing: A Strategic Perspective, 3rd ed. © 2005. Electronically reproduced by permission of Pearson Education Inc., Upper Saddle River, New Jersey.

Step 3: Evaluation of Alternatives

Once the search is complete, the consumer has information to help set criteria for evaluating purchase options. For a consumer choosing to participate in a new sport, these criteria might include the cost of required equipment, costs to join the league/take lessons, availability of the activity and fit with personal time schedule, and friends participating. Once these criteria are established, the consumer evaluates the available options and usually selects the one that maximizes the value received.

Step 4: Participation

After the consumer has evaluated the alternatives and settled on a choice, the next step is participation in the sport or event. For marketers, this is the most important outcome of the consumer decision-making process. In the example of Mary, the participation decision involved choosing skiing over other sport options. Once the decision was made, Mary's parents signed her up for ski lessons, which probably triggered other buying decisions pertaining to equipment (skis, poles, boots) and apparel (ski suit, toque, gloves). Often the decision to participate or attend a sporting event triggers other consumption decisions, and marketers need to be aware of how the original decision is followed by other purchasing actions.

Step 5: Post-Participation

After participating in the sport or event, a consumer evaluates it, comparing the actual experience with their expectations of the event and determining whether they were satisfied. Marketers' main objective is to have satisfied consumers. Studies have shown that, on average, satisfied consumers tell three other people about their experience and dissatisfied consumers will complain to nine[15].

Sport Consumer Decision Factors

Internal Influences

In the decision-making process, consumers determine the most important internal factors when they are making a choice. These internal factors include **perception**, **learning**, **personality**, **motivation**, and **attitudes**.

Perception

Perception is how consumers see themselves in the world they live in. It is the process by which they select, organize, and interpret information to create a picture of their world. The main issue for marketers is that consumers are

perception: how consumers see themselves in the world they live in.

learning: repeated experiences and thinking leading to consumer's behaviour.

personality: an individual's personal characteristics (behaviours or responses) that are consistently exhibited in recurring situations.

motivation: the force that spurs consumers to a certain action to satisfy the identified need.

attitudes: what a consumer feels or believes about something and how they act on those feelings.

---

[15] Shiffman, L.G., L.L. Kanuk, & M. Das (2006) *Consumer Behaviour*, Cdn ed. Pearson Prentice Hall.

bombarded with information daily. To manage this, consumers use filters to select which information to store, resulting in their recollection of an event differing from the actual event. Thus, perception is the way consumers filter stimuli (e.g., marketing messages such as advertisements on television, radio, and the Internet, stories in the newspaper, or conversations heard at work) and then make sense of it.

Perception has four stages[16]:

1. Exposure: sensing a stimulus (e.g., hearing an ad on the radio on the drive to work)
2. Attention: recognizing the stimulus (e.g., recognizing you are hearing an ad on the radio)
3. Awareness: assigning meaning to the stimulus (e.g., laughing at the humour in the ad)
4. Retention: adding the meaning to internal memory (e.g., that product has humorous ads)

Learning

behavioural learning: developing automatic responses to a situation built up through repeated experiences; its four key variables are drive, cue, response, and reward.

Learning refers to consumer's behaviour that results from repeated experiences and thinking. Repeated experiences involve **behavioural learning** where the consumer develops automatic responses to a situation built up through the repeated experiences. The four key variables for behavioural learning are drive, cue, response, and reward. For example, a consumer attending a hockey game is hungry (drive), sees a cue (ad on the jumbotron for popcorn at the concession stands), takes action (goes to concession stand and buys popcorn), and receives a reward (popcorn tastes great). Consumers also learn by thinking, reasoning, and problem solving without direct experience; this is called **cognitive learning**. With this type of learning, a consumer makes connections between two or more ideas by observing the outcome of the behaviour of other individuals and then adjusting their own accordingly. From the previous example, the consumer at the hockey game is hungry and has observed many people nearby leaving their seats and returning with popcorn. Observing this behaviour allows the consumer to learn that there is popcorn in the building and that others are using this as a means to solve their hunger problems. The consumer then adjusts their own behaviour by purchasing popcorn.

cognitive learning: learning by thinking, reasoning, and problem solving without direct experience.

Personality

Personality is an individual's personal characteristics (behaviours or responses) that are consistently exhibited in recurring situations. There are numerous theories of personality, but most identify key traits or enduring characteristics within an individual or their relationships with others. For

---

[16] Solomon, M.R., J.L. Zaichkowsky, & R. Polegato (2008) *Consumer Behaviour,* 4th Cdn ed. Pearson Prentice Hall.

example, an individual might be extroverted, assertive, and dominant, or conversely compliant. Personality can involve both what others observe—how individuals talk, act, or react in situations—and what individuals think of themselves—how they observe their own actions in the situation—and this self-concept may or may not be the same as how others view them.

Motivation

Motivation is the force that spurs consumers to a certain action to satisfy an identified need. Consumers have many needs; however, without motivation, they would never act to satisfy them. Many internal factors can influence motivation in purchasing decisions. For example, while a consumer may be motivated to attend an MLS soccer match, when it comes to purchasing the ticket, this motivation may be affected by financial issues (Can I afford the ticket?), time constraints (The game is tomorrow, can I go?), value (Will I get my money's worth?), and perceived risk (What if I buy a ticket and cannot attend?).

Attitude

Attitude is what a consumer feels or believes about something and how they act on that feeling. Once formed, attitudes can be very difficult to change. If a consumer has a positive attitude toward an issue (soccer is the greatest game), it would be hard to change this attitude (substitute hockey as the greatest game in their mind). This is also true if the consumer has a negative attitude toward an issue; it would take consider effort to change this attitude.

External Influences

Consumer purchasing decisions are often influenced by external factors, which are outside of their control. External factors that can either directly or indirectly influence a consumer's decision include culture, social class, **reference groups**, and family.

Culture

Culture is the set of values, ideas, beliefs, and attitudes that are accepted by a homogeneous group of individuals, who pass them on to the next generation. Culture is a very broad concept, and marketers tend to focus on understanding what occurs within smaller groups, or subcultures, to which most consumers belong. Subcultures have shared values and exist where groups share similar values in terms of age (generation Y), ethnicity (French Canadian), religious beliefs (Catholic), geographic location (Atlantic Canada), and special interests (snowboarders). The Canadian national culture is difficult to define due to its pluralistic tradition where ethnic groups do not necessary join the cultural mainstream. Therefore, many ethnic-based subgroups exist across the country and should be of prime interest to marketers.

reference groups: groups of people others emulate or would like to become like (e.g., star athletes).

culture: set of values, ideas, beliefs, and attitudes that are accepted by a homogeneous group of individuals and which they pass on to the next generation.

Other Group Membership

In addition to cultural groups and subgroups, consumers belong to many other groups with which they share certain characteristics and which may influence their purchase decisions. These groups may contain an opinion leader or other leaders who have a major influence on what an individual consumes.

Social class: Represents the social standing an individual has within society and is based on such factors as income, education, and occupation. Consumers in the same social class exhibit similar attitudes, lifestyles, and consumption patterns.

Reference groups: Refers to people whom consumers look to as a basis for self-appraisal or as a source of personal standards. Examples of these groups are family, teams, and fan clubs. Reference groups have an important influence on the purchase of luxury items but little on necessities[17].

Family

Family is a reference group to which most consumers belong and which has a strong influence on how purchase decisions are made. The notion of family has changed over time. Statistics Canada defines a census family as[18]:

> a married couple and the children, if any, of either or both spouses; a couple living common law and the children, if any, of either or both partners; or, a lone parent of any marital status with at least one child living in the same dwelling and that child or those children. All members of a particular census family live in the same dwelling. A couple may be of opposite or same sex. Children may be children by birth, marriage or adoption regardless of their age or marital status as long as they live in the dwelling and do not have their own spouse or child living in the dwelling.

Today, 61 percent of the 11.6 million households in Canada are family households (couples with or without children). According to many sources, the *family* remains the central or dominant institution that provides for the welfare of individuals[19].

Although *families* are sometimes referred to as *households*, not all households are families. A household might consist of a single person or of persons who are not related by blood, marriage, or adoption, such as unmarried couples, family friends, or roommates. However, within the context of consumer behaviour, households and families are usually treated as synonymous, and this text will follow this convention.

---

[17] Berkowitz, E.N., F.G. Crane, R.A. Kerin, S.W. Hartley, & W. Rudelius(2003) *Marketing*, 5th Cdn ed. McGraw–Hill Ryerson.

[18] Statistics Canada (2007) Key definitions—Census Family. Retrieved May 24, 2007 from http://www.statcan.ca/english/concepts/definitions/cen-family.htm.

[19] Statistics Canada (2001) *Census of Canada*.

How Does Household Composition Affect Canadian Sport Participation?

In Canadian households, the presence of children has a significant impact on the pattern of adult participation in sport, especially adult volunteerism: 32 percent of adults in households with children volunteer versus 16 percent of adults in childless households (Table 4-3). Men are especially likely to volunteer: Over 38 percent of men in households with children volunteered.

The presence of children also has a significant impact on rates of attendance at sporting events. Sixty-six percent of households with adults and children attend sporting events, compared with only 47 percent of households without children (Table 4-3).

TABLE 4-3

Impact of Children in the Household on Adult Participation Rates

HOUSEHOLD MAKEUP	ACTIVE PARTICIPANTS%	VOLUNTEERS%	ATTENDEES%o
No children	37.0	15.9	47.4
With children	37.6	31.9	66.3
Women with no children	27.0	12.8	42.6
Women with children	27.1	26.8	62.7
Men with no children	47.8	19.2	52.5
Men with children	50.7	38.2	70.8

Source: The Conference Board of Canada, National Household Survey on Participation in Sport, December 2004.

The presence of children in the household also affects the sport participation rate of Canadians, as about 80 percent of "other people" in the household participate in sport when an adult sport participant has children. Participation might be children attending a parent's sporting event, parents attending or volunteering at a child's sporting event, or the entire family participating in a sport or attending a sporting event together.

Situational Influences

An individual's consumption decision can be strongly affected by the situation in which they find themselves. Since situations are not always controllable, the consumer may not follow the normal process for making a consumption decision. Shank[20] noted five situational influences on the sport consumer decision making: physical surroundings, social surroundings, task definition, time, and antecedent states.

Physical surroundings: The physical and spatial aspects of the participation environment. Sport marketers can control some of these factors, such as the atmosphere in a facility, but many others are outside their control, such as weather. Other aspects of the physical surroundings that may affect a participation decision include noise, density/crowding, and location.

Social surroundings: Other people at the decision point who can have an impact on the sport consumer. In addition to individuals the consumer may know, the presence of others can also have an impact. Large crowds at a participation venue may have either a negative impact (e.g., long waits for golf tee off) or a positive impact (e.g., large crowds for a footrace provide the competition many runners enjoy)[21].

Task definition: Reflects the reason for participation or the purpose for engaging the consumption behaviour. The reason the consumer is participating also affects their decision. For example, a consumer may make a participation decision based on special occasion (e.g., while on vacation) or situational reasons (e.g., special roadrace for charity).

Antecedent states: Refers to the temporal state a consumer may be in. These temporal states include moods, such as temporary states of depression or high excitement, or physiological issues, such as tiredness, illness, or general malaise. Temporal states can provide a positive impact on participation decisions, such as feeling 'stressed out' and using sport to alleviate this state. The important factor for marketers is that antecedent states are 'prior' to the decision to participate and that consumers may use sport participation to change these states[22].

Time: Involves the effect of time on a sport consumer's behaviour. Time has become an increasingly important factor as shifts in family structure and work life have brought time pressures to the majority of sport consumers. Table 4-4 gives an overview of how Canadians spend their average day. With limited time for active sports (1.1 hours a day) or sport entertainment events (0.2 hours a day), time is a critical factor in Canadian sport consumers' decision making.

TABLE 4-4

How Canadians Spend Their Day

ACTIVITY	HOURS PER DAY		
	TOTAL	MALE	FEMALE
Paid work	3.9	4.7	3.1
Household work	3.1	2.3	3.8

[20] Shank, M.D. (2005) *Sports Marketing.*
[21] ibid.
[22] ibid.

Civic and volunteer work	0.3	0.3	0.4
Education-related work	0.6	0.5	0.6
Total work	7.9	7.8	7.9
Sleep, meals, and other personal activities	10.6	10.4	10.8
Socializing, including restaurant meals	1.7	1.7	1.8
Television, reading, and other passive leisure	2.5	2.6	2.4
Sports, movies, and other entertainment events	0.2	0.2	0.1
Active leisure (sports and other)	1.1	1.3	0.9
Total free time	5.5	5.7	5.3

Source: "How Do Canadians Spend their Day", adapted from the Statistics Canada publication "Overview of the Time Use of Canadians", 2005, Catalogue 12F0080XWE, released July 12, 2006, 1990http://www.statcan.ca/english/freepub/12F0080XIE/ 2006001/tables/tables.htm.

Summary

Returning to the example of Mary in the chapter opening, her parents' decision may have been influenced by a number of factors such as family, social class (costs related to skiing), perception (risk), attitudes (father likes to ski, family activity), motivation, and the physical surroundings (hills, snow). They may further have been influenced by internal or psychological factors (personality, motivation, attitudes), external or sociological factors (culture, social class, family), participant decision-making process (problem recognition, participation), and situational variables (task definition, time, social and physical surroundings).

Sport Consumer Buying Roles

During the participant decision-making process (Figure 4-1), sport consumers can take on different buyer roles. These are interchangeable, and consumers can play one or multiple roles[23]:

1. Initiator: recognizes a problem, need, or opportunity and introduces the idea of a sports activity.
2. **Gatekeeper**: conducts the information search and controls the flow of information to the group.
3. **Influencer**: tries to sway the outcome of the decision by searching for more information and validating the initiator's idea of a sports activity.
4. Decision maker: evaluates alternatives and has the formal authority to make decisions.
5. Approver: can approve or reverse a decision.
6. Real buyer: makes the final decision and must make the purchase.
7. User: ultimately uses the purchase (include family, friends, clients, or colleagues).
8. **Evaluator**: reflects on the quality of the experience and takes further action depending on levels of satisfaction or dissatisfaction.

gatekeeper: one who conducts the information search and controls the flow of information to the group.

influencer: one who tries to sway the outcome of the decision by searching for more information and validating the initiator's idea of a sports activity.

evaluator: one who reflects on the quality of the experience and takes further action depending on levels of satisfaction or dissatisfaction.

---

[23] This list of roles is adapted from Schiffman, L.G., L.L. Kanuk, & M. Das, (2006) *Consumer Behaviour* and from Rein, I., P. Kotler, P., & B. Shields (2006) *The Elusive Fan*.

It is essential that sport organizations understand who are involved in a sport-related purchase and what roles these individuals might play in the decision-making process. In the example of Mary, her parents have played to roles of initiator, gatekeeper, influencer, decision maker, approver, and buyer, but Mary is the actual user of the ski lessons and will probably be an evaluator as well. To illustrate how sport consumers assume different roles in a sport consumption decision and the nuances of these roles, we present a hypothetical example of a decision to attend a hockey.

IN THE KNOW

What to Do on a Wednesday Night in Kingston

THE SITUATION

Four friends—Nick, Anne, Steve, and Pierre—are deciding what to do on a Wednesday night in Kingston, Ontario, a small city of about 100 000 people halfway between Toronto and Montreal. A relatively affluent community, Kingston is home to one of Canada's most prestigious universities, Queen's University, as well as a Junior A hockey team in the Canadian Hockey League—the Kingston Frontenacs.

THE SCENARIO

It is the fall of 2006, and the Sudbury Wolves are in town for a rare preseason Wednesday night match up. Of note for fans is the chance to see two of the four famous Staal brothers—Mark and Jared—who play for the Wolves. Mark is a top draft pick of the New York Rangers, and young Jared, at 15, is touted to be the best of the brothers. It is also the last season for the Frontenacs to play at the Kingston Memorial Centre. Some details for the game:

- Tickets cost $16.00
- Programs cost $5.00
- The arena is in walking distance to the university and close to local restaurants, pubs, and bars
- Popcorn, hot dog, and pop cost $5.00

THE ROLES

Initiator: "Wouldn't it be fun to go to a hockey game?"
Gatekeeper: "Wednesday night games are half-price"
Influencer : "I've been to a game at that arena. It is a lot of fun"
Decision maker: "Wednesday night? Half price? Let's go. I'm in!"
Approver: "I think we can afford it. Sounds like a good idea to me. Count me in."

Real Buyer: "I'll use my credit card to pay."

User: "Thanks for the tickets to the game"

Evaluator: "I had a good time at the hockey game. We should do it again"

THE EVALUATOR ISSUES

Evaluator issues: seats were not great; good thing they are building a new arena; sat beside an obnoxious fan; became a part of the experience after a while; food was okay; game was great; Staal brothers were as advertised; and the home team won in overtime

THE EXERCISE

Develop a story using the characters and the roles provided to create a plausible explanation of how this scenario may have unfolded. Based on the evaluator issues, what do you think happened?

Canadian Sport Consumers

In 2005, the Conference Board of Canada published a report called *Strengthening Canada*, which provides excellent information on the Canadian consumer. The key drivers of sport participation in Canada include age, gender, household composition, educational attainment, and income[24]. In 1998, 34 percent of Canadians 15 years of age and over (8.3 million) participated regularly in sports[25], though research suggests that active participation falls steadily through to the senior years. Men are much more likely than women to be active participants in sport, with 43 percent of men versus 26 percent of women participating regularly[26]. The presence of children in the household has a significant impact on the pattern of adult participation in sport, especially adult volunteerism, which doubles. People with high incomes are much more likely to participate in sport than people who earn less. On the other hand, lack of time is the reason most often given for not participating in sports, followed by lack of interest and health[27]. For people aged 55 and over, age and health/injury concerns were the reason most frequently given for not participating in sports. As suggested earlier, consumers can engage in sports as a participant, spectator, or/and volunteer. Table 4-5 indicates that Canadians prefer to attend events rather than participate or volunteer for sport organizations.

---

[24] Bloom, M., M. Grant, & D. Watt (2005) *Strengthening Canada.*

[25] Statistics Canada (1998) *General Social Survey (GSS) on Time Use.*

[26] Bloom, M., M. Grant, & D. Watt (2005) *Strengthening Canada.*

[27] Statistics Canada (1998) *General Social Survey (GSS) on Time Use.*

TABLE 4-5

Activity of Canadian Adults in Sport, by Type of Participation, Adult Population

TYPE OF PARTICIPATION			
ATTENDEES	ACTIVE PARTICIPANTS	VOLUNTEERS	CANADIAN ADULTS No. (%)
X			4 240 000 (17.0)
	X		1 821 000 (7.3)
		X	249 000 (1.0)
X	X		3 068 000 (12.3)
X		X	1 472 000 (5.9)
	X	X	299 000 (1.2)
X	X	X	2 569 000 (10.3)
Total number (%) 11 324 000 (45.4)	7 732 000 (31.0)	4 565 000 (18.3)	13 718 000 (54.9)

Source: The Conference Board of Canada, National Household Survey on Participation in Sport, December 2004.

Canadians participate in nearly 100 different sports, but tend to focus on ice hockey, golf, soccer, baseball, basketball, volleyball, skiing, swimming, and cycling. Nearly half of active participants (47.1%) take part in only one sport. The overwhelming majority of the multisport active participants take part in only two or three sports (44.3%); a mere 8.7 percent compete in four or more.

The most popular sports for adult participants in Canada are golf, hockey, baseball, and swimming. Statistics Canada reported the following in 1998:

- 4.6 million (19%) belonged to an amateur sport club or organization.
- 3.0 million (12%) participated in competitions or tournaments.
- 1.7 million (7%) were amateur sport coaches.
- 1.7 million (7%) were amateur sport administrators or volunteers.
- 0.9 million (4%) were amateur sport officials.

IN THE KNOW

Sports Popularity and Trends in Canada

A 2004 report by Ipsos Reid identified these trends in sports and their popularity in Canada:

- Most Canadians (85%) follow NHL hockey either very or somewhat closely, making it by far the most popular sport in the country. Other popular sports are major league baseball (40%), figure skating (40%), NFL football (29%) , and CFL football (29%).

- CFL and NFL, though enjoying the same level of popularity across Canada, each have a distinct fan base.
- "Hot" sports, those gaining momentum, are such "extreme" sports as skateboarding, street luge, and BMX biking as well as men's golf, junior hockey, lacrosse, and professional wrestling.
- The Toronto Maple Leafs is the hockey team most closely followed by Canadians (35%), succeeded by the Montreal Canadiens (21%), and Vancouver Canucks (9%).
- Trending results from 1998 to 1999 demonstrate that team performance plays a pivotal role, alongside regional loyalties and winning tradition, in determining which team a sport's fan is most likely to follow.

Canadian Sports Fans versus Non-Fans

The *Canadian Sports Monitor* report produced by Angus Reid[28] classified Canadians into two main groups: sports fans and non-fans.

Sports fans: Canadians who consider themselves to be avid sports fans and confirm this through reporting regular consumption of sport. Sports fans follow a wide range of sports, tend to be younger than non-fans, and are more likely to be male and live in English Canada.

Non-fans – The rest of the Canadian population surveyed. Non-fans either do not consider themselves to be "avid" sports fans or do not typically access sports media coverage in a typical week[29].

Sports fans can also be distinguished from the rest of the population by their lifestyles, **values**, and attitudes. For example, sports fans are more likely to participate in sport, are more competitive, and see themselves as team players. These are the group of individuals that sport marketers consider the mainstays in terms of consumption habits. The biggest challenge for sport marketers is engaging the non-fans on the sport consumer loyalty ladder. There exist a number of ways by which to break down the market of sport fans. This will be presented in Chapter 5.

values: ideals that dictate how people conduct themselves, interact with others, and set the benchmark as to how they gauge right from wrong.

In the late 1990's, Sport Canada commissioned a study about the Canadian sport fan's lifestyles, values and attitudes. Although this study has never been repeated, its results are still relevant today. The study found that Canadians group into 4 distinct groups of people when considering sport. These are *Active Thrill Seekers* (young males, identify as fans, enjoy action/contact, often also participate, consume by Internet), *EZ Chair Quarterbacks* (avid fans, very young, often consume by television, do not participate, follow a wide range of sports), *Patriotic Traditionalists* (mostly female, older, self-identify as traditional, patriotic when watching Team Canada, prefer amateur sport), and

---

[28] Angus Reid (1999) *The Canadian Sports Monitor Report.*
[29] ibid.

Cultured Individualists (most male and from Quebec, prefer individual sports, also participate in individual sports, not interested in other sports than those they play, typically prefer tennis, Formula 1 car racing or golf).

Case: Casino Nova Scotia—Nokia Brier

Background

To illustrate the nature of the Canadian sport consumer, we describe a short case outlining a sponsorship in Eastern Canada. The sponsor is Casino Nova Scotia; the sponsored is the Nokia Brier.

The 2003 Nokia Brier

In January 2003, Halifax, Nova Scotia hosted Canada's largest and most prestigious annual curling event, the Nokia Brier. Held yearly, the Brier is Canada's national men's championship that brings all provincial champions (12 teams from the 10 provinces plus Northern Ontario and Team Canada as defending champion) to compete for the national title and the right to represent Canada at the World Championship. The 2003 Brier was the 74th Canadian men's curling championship, the fifth held in Halifax, and third under the title sponsorship of Nokia, the world's largest supplier of mobile communications.

The Brier is a nine-day event that includes two weekends, various associated events, and an overall festival feel. It has tremendous impact on the host community and is broadcast annually on TSN and CBC.

Casino Nova Scotia

Casino Nova Scotia is a hotel/entertainment facility of the kind that is rapidly coming to characterize the global economy prototype, which seeks to provide a comprehensive "experience" package rather than merely quality accommodation for its guests. The 140 000-square-foot structure includes many features that promote the experiential theme: an architectural design that incorporates features of the many historical buildings of Halifax; an expansive casino gaming floor; several excellent restaurants and pubs catering to the varied cuisine and dining preferences of guests; live entertainment in the Schooner Room, a 6000-square-foot entertainment area with a fully-equipped stage to accommodate a variety of performers; 25 000 feet of flexible space that can be used for business meetings, conventions, banquets, and weddings, accommodating groups as small as 20 or as large as 800.

The hotel itself contains 352 guestrooms, including 21 suites with all the amenities of a first-class facility, including boutiques, shops, businesses, and a swimming pool. And the facility is monitored 24 hours a day by a highly qualified security department. The $100 million Canadian Casino Nova Scotia complex opened April 24, 2000 and replaced the interim casino and Sheraton Hotel facilities that had occupied the waterfront site. The casino itself is under the authority of Park Place Entertainment, one of the world's premier gaming companies, whose US$4.7 billion annual revenue surpasses the GNP of many Third World countries and whose international reach embraces four continents with 54 000 employees. All told, Park Place is the world's largest gaming company as measured by casino square footage and revenues.

The sponsorship objectives are clearly linked to the overall business plan of Park Place Entertainment, the owner of Casino Nova Scotia. The latter's corporate governance mandate is concise: "The business of Park Place Entertainment will be conducted in the most ethical manner. Our associates will seek to achieve for the company the highest degree of respect and esteem of the public in general and those with whom Park Place does business." Similarly, the Casino Nova Scotia complex seeks to provide an all-inclusive experience for guests who can legally game in the province, those 19 years or older. Sponsorships should augment this experience through trickle-down benefits to the guests and normally strictly adhere to a policy of adult-only relationships. That is, Casino Nova Scotia may donate to local minor sport as a good corporate citizen, but normally it would not enter into a sponsorship with such organizations.

Case Questions

1. Perform a consumer segmentation of the fans for the Nokia Brier, using the two examples provided in the guest author perspective and the end of chapter.
2. Which consumer segment(s) do you think are the targets for Casino Nova Scotia through their sponsorship of the Nokia Brier? Why?
3. Provide an example of the consumer decision-making process for this segment.
4. Using the answer to question 3 and the five gateways to sport presented in this chapter, develop a marketing plan to target the segment you have selected for Casino Nova Scotia.

Chapter Summary

This chapter examined some of the theory behind why individuals consume sport either as a spectator or as a participant. It presented the psychological relationship individuals have with sport; the sport consumer consumption model; the internal, external, and situational factors affecting consumption; the roles that consumer can assume in the decision-making process; the specific gateways through which consumers engage with sport; and a portrait of the Canadian sport consumer. This was only a brief introduction to the vast complex area of sport consumer behaviour, an area of significant importance to any sport marketer.

Test Your Knowledge

1. Outline the steps in the decision-making process for sport participation. Reconstruct your most recent decision to attend a major sport event. How did your experience compare to the decision-making model?
2. What roles can consumers assume in the decision-making process?
3. Outline the internal influences on consumer consumption. Using one of these influences, discuss how it could have an affect on sport participation.
4. Define the Canadian family. How does this reference group affect sport participation? Cite specific examples where possible.
5. Explain the five situational factors that influence the sport consumer's decision-making process.
6. Use the gateways to sport participation to provide an example of how an individual might engage with hockey through each of the different methods.
7. Using the example of a consumer thinking about joining a health club, briefly comment on each step in the decision-making model.
8. Considering the psychological relationship between consumers and sport, what factors might influence a consumer to move from awareness to attraction to attention?

 For more review questions, go to http://www.sportmarketing.nelson.com.

Key Terms

attitudes
behavioural learning
cognitive learning
culture
decision-making process
evaluator
gatekeeper
influencer

learning
motivation
perception
personality
problem recognition
reference groups
values

 A full glossary of key term definitions is located at http://www.sportmarketing.nelson.com.

Internet Resources

Sport Canada, http://www.pch.gc.ca/sportcanada

Sport Information Research Council, http://www.sirc.ca

Sports in Canada, http://en.wikipedia.org/wiki/Sport_in_Canada

FanNation (online community for sports consumers), http://fannation.com/

Fan.ca (online community for sports consumers), http://www.fan.ca/

Responding to the Canadian Female Sports Consumer,
http://www.thesportjournal.org/sport-supplement/vol14no4/
09_OConnor.asp

The Daily, StatsCan Study: Consumer demand for entertainment services
outside the home,
http://www.statcan.ca/Daily/English/060627/d060627a.htm

Toronto Star article: Fans complaints sometimes valid,
http://www.thestar.com/article/189930

Fox Sports Article: Bettman risking losing Canadian fans,
http://msn.foxsports.com/nhl/story/6530664

Segmentation, Targeting, and Positioning in Canadian Sport

Source:Sebastien Kaulitzki / Shutterstock

Learning Objectives

- To learn the importance and advantages of effectively identifying target markets
- To understand the role of segmentation, targeting, and positioning (STP) in the marketing process
- To understand segmentation, targeting, and positioning and be able to apply each to any market of interest
- To be aware of the many potential bases of segmentation to divide markets into homogeneous groupings

Introduction

Different strokes for different folks

The effective sport marketer understands that their 'field of play' is in the minds, or perceptions, of consumers, whose worldview is coloured by their own background, experiences, and cultural make-up. Each sport marketer is an 'N of 1' trying to understand how hundred, thousands, millions, or even billions of people think.

Therefore, we must realize that the total market can be subdivided into homogeneous subgroups who are similar in their wants, needs, desires, behaviours, and so on. And it is usually advantageous for an organization to selectively serve one or more specific subgroups, or market segments.

As consumers, we all view the world through our own 'lens' of personal experiences, needs, wants, and desires: Our worldviews are often similar to others', but nevertheless they are unique. As marketers, we must understand this phenomenon and adopt a scientific approach to targeting our marketing effects to those consumer groups who may be interested in making the exchange we seek: Using segmentation, targeting, and positioning (STP) tactics enables us to use marketing resources effectively and efficiently.

STP as Economic Advantage

The field of economics supports STP, as it enables the marketer to relate supply to demand. The use of STP tools allows the marketer to uncover specific unsatisfied needs and wants (demand) in specific markets and, in turn, develop an offering (supply) that will meet such demand. For example, offerings of athletic apparel have grown over the years to a point where numerous manufacturers, labels, and retailers offer numerous lines of clothing and brands specific to target markets—items such as sneaker/rollerblade combos, running skirts, and triathlon shorts that target specific market groups of people of similar age, fashion consciousness, occupation, level of competition, gender, style, usage, sport interest, and so on.

EXECUTIVE PERSPECTIVE

Dale Hooper, Vice-President, Marketing, PepsiQuakerTropicanaGatorade Canada

Segmentation, Targeting, and Positioning

Every marketer who has led a major consumer brand has completed this exercise at least once for their brand. In a world of proliferation of new products, fragmentation of media, and time-starved consumers, having a clear concise understanding of your brand positioning and the consumer group that will drive growth are more important than ever.

The key to successful "partnerships" between property owners looking for sponsors and consumer brands is a clear understanding of both brands' key segments and core targets. Once there is consistency between the targets, then they can determine if the partnership will be successful. The property brand must allow the consumer brand to communicate/demonstrate its positioning to its consumers. If it only allows for a placement of a logo or some form of ad, it is not fully exploiting the opportunity, and success will be limited.

Three Types of Property/Consumer Brand Partnerships

In my mind, three types of partnerships are possible between properties and brands: philanthropy, building awareness, and positioning enhancing. In my professional life, I seek to develop partnerships of all three types.

1. *Philanthropy:* This typically involves supporting non-profit organizations with cash, product in kind, or resources in return for logo as a gold or silver brand supporter. Although some promotional value is achieved, there is no real ability to connect with the brand's audience to demonstrate the brand's core positioning.

2. *Building Awareness (Brand Awareness/Product Distribution/Hospitality):* These partnerships involve relationships where a consumer brand sponsors an event/team/entertainment property to build

awareness. The support comes with cash and/or in-kind product support. Product may be available for sale, but the brand is rarely able to influence consumer behaviour.

3. *Positioning Enhancing:* In these partnerships, the property and the consumer brand share common targets and have positioning objectives that are consistent with each other. The property also enables the brand to not only drive awareness or distribution but to have the brand reinforce its position with its target. This is often accomplished by demonstrating a desired behaviour, encouraging trial, or reinforcing a brand truth. In these situations, participants can use the product but without any accompanying communication, which may work to reinforce a positioning of "authentic" or "for the experts."

Some Great Examples of Positioning Partnerships

One of the really great things about marketing is that everyday we can see examples of how to do things all around us. In considering STP, I've seen successful positioning partnerships in:

AMJ Campbell: To enhance their positioning as a dependable mover, it sponsors the AMJ Campbell Move of the Game, an in-stadium promotion that enables two fans in the nosebleed seats to move to platinum-level seats. AMJ Campbell executes this at many different events in different locations.

Nicorette: This company sponsors no smoking areas at the Bell Centre. To enhance positioning as the number 1 smoking cessation product, Nicorette brands all the "no smoking signs" in the building.

Gatorade: Gatorade has a presence at 'point of sweat' at all key sporting events. It enhances its positioning as the hydration expert by sponsoring "sweat tests" with teams. Networks use this as content in their broadcasts as it demonstrates the athletes' game preparation

My Advice to You

In considering STP, I recommend that, as a brand marketer, you spend time with your key internal and external partners, speak to consumers, and take the time to clearly determine your brand's key growth segments, its core consumer, and what positioning will promote brand growth. If you are a property manager, you must clearly understand what type of opportunities you can offer to potential sponsors. Once you know that, you can work closely to develop positioning-enhancing programs.

Dale holds a bachelor of commerce in sports administration from Laurentian University. He has developed products and advertising campaigns that have been adapted in countries around the world, and is currently vice-president, marketing at Pepsi QTG Canada.

STP as the Bridge to Marketing Strategy

We refer to STP as the bridge to marketing strategy. STP enables the marketer to make sense of all of the background research and data so that the resulting marketing strategy and tactics (the 4 Ps) are more likely to succeed since the strategy is customized both to the target market(s) of interest and to how the marketer's offering is positioned in the minds of the target market(s) compared to competitive offerings.

The bridge analogy emphasizes the role that STP can play in taking the large 'mainland' of information and data [e.g., external analysis, PEST (political, economic, social, and technological factors), competitive analyses] to a focused, customized 'island' of market strategy, which enables the marketer to effectively and efficiently pursue their objectives. By linking the information mainland to the strategy island, STP acts as a bridge. The efficiency of the STP approach is also reflected in the bridge analogy as it provides for the cost-effective use of resources in marketing.

external analysis		marketing strategy
PEST		product
competition	STP	price
substitutes		promotion
market analysis		place
consumer behaviour		marketing tactics
opportunities		
threats		

Reflected in the graphical representation of the STP bridge analogy is timing in developing marketing strategy: STP *must* always occur *after* fully understanding the external and internal environments and *before* developing marketing strategy. The importance of this timing is intuitive. How can a marketer determine their targets and positioning without knowing the market, the competition, and their own competencies and capabilities? The necessity of completing marketing strategy after STP is equally evident: Without knowing the specifics of our target markets and how we plan to position ourselves against competing offerings in those markets, how can we develop a marketing strategy that will be successful?

Market Segmentation

Market Selection

With the possible exception of the world's largest global firms and their mass-market products (e.g., Coca-Cola, Sony), few organizations are able to fund marketing programs that involve some presence in all major international channels and markets. However, even these global organizations no longer diffuse the same message to all: Sophisticated marketing that selects market segments and tailors specific marketing programs to them has become commonplace. Further, many other organizations that could afford to reach the vast majority of global markets choose not to, since only certain parts of certain markets are interested in their offerings.

This trend to customized marketing messages is forcing organizations to determine which markets to pursue. They do not want to invest resources in marketing to segments where they have little or no competitive advantage or where there is limited opportunity for success. Success in for-profit organizations involves grouping consumers by similar needs and/or wants to increase profitability (e.g. Nike's line of running shoes); success for nonprofit organizations involves achieving their own particular goals (e.g., World Anti-Doping Agency seeking to eliminate doping from sport). In both cases, important decisions about which markets to enter are vital to success. These market selection decisions are one of the most important parts of the marketing process since they are what determines the elements of the development of the marketing mix—or marketing strategy—that will follow. STP decisions are based on the answers to these questions:

- S—How can we break our market down into homogeneous, reachable groups?
- T—Which of these groups should we commit our resources to reach?
- P—How do we want the selected target(s) to perceive our offering versus the offerings of our competition?

To answer these questions, we must remember that the three steps of STP occur in progression—segmentation then targeting then positioning—and build upon each other to reduce a full market to manageable, reachable, and profitable chunks. This process is straightforward. First, segmentation involves identifying relevant bases and using them to segment the market and develop profiles for each identified market. Second, targeting involves evaluating the attractiveness of all the identified segments to select the target market or markets to pursue. Finally, the offering is positioned against the competition in the minds of those target markets. If more than one target market is selected in the targeting stage, then the positioning step must be carried out for *each* one.

What Is Market Segmentation?

Different customers want different things (products), are able to pay different prices, have different information sources (promotion), and buy at different places (geographic, demographic). Marketers, in turn, seek to understand their target consumers to develop a targeted, tailored marketing strategy (the 4 Ps), which is more likely to be successful than an unsophisticated blanket approach. The ideal scenario is a specific marketing strategy implemented for each consumer: Although advancements in technology have virtually made this possible in certain scenarios (e.g., Dell Computers), it is generally very expensive and thus inefficient. This is where market segmentation provides support to a sport marketer and allows for the organization of people that behave similarly into groups, whether they be customers, fans, participants, sponsors, or suppliers. An easily observable example is a professional sport teams that has developed specific marketing programs for various segments of spectators, including season ticket holders (diehard local fans), box-seat holders (corporate hospitality seekers), family game-zone single game tickets (families), multi-game ticket holders (non-local diehard fans, interested fans), and so on.

Formally, we define sport marketing segmentation as the delineation of a customer, fan, spectator, participant, or business-to-business (e.g., sponsor, media partner) group or groups with homogeneous needs and/or wants which the marketing function of the sport organization has the ability to successfully satisfy. This definition demonstrates five important aspects of segmentation in sport marketing:

- *Wide product application:* Segmentation is beneficial to the sport marketer for a wide range of products, from tangible goods (Adidas segmenting the market of Canadian women for new product development) to services (Sport Canada understanding Canadian high performance and developing Olympic athletes when designing their athlete assistance funding programs) to ideas (the Vancouver Bid Committee for the 2010 Winter Olympic Games understanding local citizens prior to launching their marketing efforts leading up to a referendum on whether they should bid for the games) to behaviours (the World Anti-Doping Agency understanding athletes prior to developing a social marketing campaign to encourage anti-doping behaviour).

- *Broad reach:* Segmentation in sport can be applied to any number of potential markets—spectators, participants, business partners, and others—where tailored marketing strategies will enable more successful marketing. For example, the organizing committee for a high-profile 10-km run will use segmentation to best reach spectators (both in-stadium and via media), participants (both professional and participation), sponsors, and media partners.

- *Efficient reach:* If an organization understands its market properly, it can reach various segments with the same offering. For example, airline firms reach more than one segment with their flights (e.g., business travellers and well-to-do personal travellers in business-class seats; frequent flyers with point program benefits; and students, tourists, and lower-income travellers in economy; upper class consumers as readers of a yachting magazine).

- *Timing:* A wide variety of stimuli, both internal and external, can quickly change the benefits that individuals are looking for at any time, thus moving them into another segment. For example, a casual fan who attends a few Major Soccer League games each year may have become a season ticket holder following the move of David Beckham to the league.

- *Segment boundaries:* Only segmentations that yield segments that are both homogeneous and mutually exclusive are acceptable. Within each segment, homogeneous consumers possess similar needs and wants. Segments are mutually exclusive, each having different needs and desires, with no cross-over between them. For example, a segmentation for a golf clubs identifies a key target market as upper-class, retired women 60 years of age and older, where the analysis has found that women within that segment have very similar needs vis-à-vis golf clubs and are not members of any other segment (e.g., men, under 60, lower/middle class).

A sport marketer undertakes segmentation only when it makes financial sense, when a greater return is worth the cost in time, human resources, and financial resources committed to do the segmentation. Thus, deciding to sell T-shirts to parents of a youth soccer team to raise funds for a tournament would not justify segmentation as the revenues would not offset the research costs of the segmentation, whereas selling tickets for the World Under-17 Soccer Championships in Toronto would as the market and potential revenues are significantly higher.

Practically, market segmentation involves the aggregation of potential customers into groups, or market segments, that have similar needs and/or wants, will respond similarly to marketing action, and help the organization achieve its organizational objectives.

The segmentation process typically yields one of three scenarios.

- In the 'one product/multiple market segments' scenario, the same product is marketed in different ways to different market segments. For example, the Harry Potter books are marketed in a completely different fashion to two segments—youth and adults – through different promotional strategies. With Toronto Blue Jays ticket sales, the same seat is marketed in very different ways to a number of very different markets— single game (e.g., online, mass market promotions), corporate (e.g., phone sales to build relationships), season tickets (e.g., preseason promotions targeted a previous season ticket holders), group (e.g., reduced pricing for volume purchases).
- The 'multiple product/multiple segments' scenario involves different products for different segments. Marketers typically cite the example of Gap Jeans, which offers different brands of jeans to different markets through its three brand stores of Gap, Banana Republic, and Old Navy. Maple Leaf Sports and Entertainment of Toronto targets different sport market segments through its three professional sport franchises: the Toronto Maple Leafs National Hockey League team, Toronto Raptors National Basketball Association team, and Toronto FC Major League Soccer team.
- In the 'segment of one' scenario, the organization uses technology (e.g., online ordering, databases) or custom products (e.g., custom jewelry, custom home) to develop marketing programs specific to each customer. For example, Dell Computers allows a customer to build a custom computer with the specific options they want rather than select from a limited number of offerings, which most of their competitors do. A triathlon coach customizes training programs for individual athletes.

An Effective Tool for Sport Segmentation

In sport, like other industries, segmentation is a process: It is dynamic, as people's needs, wants, drivers, make-up, and interests change over time. This chapter presents and describes how to use a process for effective segmentation.

Market segmentation is straightforward. It involves considering every potential consumer who might purchase your product—the 'total' market—and determining how best to divide the total market into segments of individuals with similar needs and wants. This allows the marketer to invest resources in marketing to those groups that are most likely to be 'profitable' over the long term and that are 'reachable' through existing marketing channels.

As a process that aggregates prospective buyers into groups, or market segments, with common needs/wants and that will respond similarly to marketing action, segmentation enables organizations to market more efficiently.

Marketers segment markets when it makes sense, when return on investment (ROI) is greater than its cost. Reaching a mass market is very costly, so an organization that can segment its market can reach it much more efficiently: A marketing program developed to target a specific market will cost less to implement than one targeted at the mass market. However, the marketer must be careful to not over-segment, since the segments must be large enough to make them worthwhile for the organization. The four criteria for effective segmentation are:

responsiveness: how a market segment responds to marketing action.

measurability: the ability of a marketer to measure the attitudes, behaviours, and demographics of a market segment to its marketing actions.

- *Responsiveness:* Does each identified segment respond to marketing action differently from the others?
- *Measurability:* Can each segment's boundaries be identified and its size measured?
- *Accessibility:* Is each member of each segment reachable by the marketer?
- *Substantiality:* Is the segment large enough to warrant developing, implementing, and evaluating a unique marketing mix?

We know the key criteria for effective segmentation. But how do we do the segmentation? The six-question segmentation process and its steps follow.

The Six-Question Segmentation Process

Although other segmentation processes are discussed in the sport marketing literature (e.g., the market-product grid), we like the six-question segmentation process as it allows for a more comprehensive market analysis on three levels. First, it enables in-depth analysis of each segment through the six-question process. Second, it is applicable to new product development as well as existing products. Third, it enables considerable feedback throughout the process yielding better results.

The process comprises three steps: the identification of the total market of interest, the iterative identification of the most relevant bases of segmentation, and the six-question analysis of each identified segment.

Step 1: Identification of Total Market

The first step of the segmentation involves the articulation of the total market of interest. Very little, if any, research is required, as the marketer considers every person who could, even in what might be considered unlikely situations, be interested in the product offering, existing or planned. For example, the marketing director of a Canadian running series that offers 5-km runs across Canada would consider all Canadian residents capable of doing a 5-km run as the total market. To be more limited in defining the total market would risk missing a key market or potential niche market in later steps in the segmentation process.

Step 2: Bases of Segmentation

The second and most important step of the segmentation process is its bases, where the total market identified in Step 1 is divided into smaller, homogeneous, mutually exclusive groups using the most relevant characteristics that tell us why groups, or segments, differ. These differences could be in their needs, preferences, decision processes, or wants.

In terms of implementation, the marketer considers each of the potential bases of segmentation to the total market and selects those that are most relevant and will most appropriately divide the total market into segments. A minimum of two bases of segmentation are selected (e.g., age and gender); theoretically, there is no maximum. In our consulting experiences, we have seen segmentations on over 50 bases.

In addition to selecting bases, the marketer also determines the **sensitivity** of each base, or its number of categories. For example, income can be used as a base with low sensitivity, where the market is divided by low and high income; or it could be used as a high sensitivity base, where the market is divided into those earning under \$20,000k, \$20,000k to \$40,000k, \$40,001k to \$60,000k, \$60,001k to \$80,000k, \$80,0001k to \$100,000k, and over \$100,000. The determination of sensitivity is based on the market and the marketer's determination of which level of sophistication is required for effective segmentation.

How do we select the appropriate bases of segmentation? We do market research and pick the bases that make the most sense (e.g., gender and age for beer, social class and disposable income for race horses). And we typically include as many as we can that make sense (e.g., gender, age, culture, religion, sexual orientation, marital status, lifestyle). Table 5-1 lists many consumer market (**B2C**) and business market (**B2B**) bases of segmentation from which a marketer can select those that are most appropriate and relevant to their market.

sensitivity: how easily a group of consumers will alter their purchase patterns due to a price change, which is reflected in the number of categories used to assess a give base of segmentation.

B2C: business-to-consumer marketing where a product is marketed directly to the consumer, in contrast to business-to-business (B2B) marketing where organizations market directly to other organizations.

B2B: business-to-business, or industrial, marketing where organizations market to other organizations, which may market to consumers.

TABLE 5-1

Bases of Segmentation

CONSUMER MARKET (B2C) BASES OF SEGMENTATION	BUSINESS MARKET (B2B) BASES OF SEGMENTATION
Customer definition or category it belongs to (e.g., government, industry)	Industry
Geography (region, city, CMA, population, density, neighbourhood, climate)	Size
Culture	Location
Race	Organizational structure
Age	Head office location

Income	Region
Education	Store location
Lifestyle (activities, interests, opinions)	Industry classification
Media habits	Number of employees
Profession	Sales
Personality traits	Revenue
Volume of product use	Price
Customer loyalty, relationship	Benefits sought (organization)
Benefits sought	Usage rate (organization)
Consumer motivation	User status (organization)
Consumer behaviours	Loyalty status (organization)
Frequency of contact (i.e., number of visits)	Purchase method
Sensory factors (e.g., comfort, smell, etc.)	Centralization of buying process (central, de-centralized)
Sociable factors (e.g. fashionable look)	Buying decision process (individual, group)
Price sensitivity	Type of buy (new, modified re-buy, straight re-buy)
Usage rate	
User status	
Family size	
Stage of family life cycle	
Home ownership	
Values	
Attitudes	
Social class	

There are a few important points to note in Table 5-1. The B2C segmentation bases can be grouped into three general categories:

1. The market's state of being, or market bases, which includes all the demographic, geographic, and customer definition bases.
2. The market's state of mind, or psychology bases, including personality, activities, interests, opinions, and other similar bases.
3. Product-related bases, like volume of use and loyalty to brands.

There are no psychological bases on the B2B side because organizations don't think; they work on policy. For example, a buyer for Adidas purchasing toilet paper for the employee bathrooms considers price and firm policy, not on personal associations with certain brands.

Once the bases of segmentation have been determined, the marketer decides a level of sensitivity for each, given the results of market research and the understanding of the particular segment's size and composition. Although it would seem to be desirable to have high sensitivity and many bases to define precise segments, this could lead to an untenable situation. For example, two bases of segmentation with two levels of sensitivity each yields a 2×2 matrix, or four groups to analyze. However, five bases with four, five, two, five, and three levels of sensitivity each yield a 4×5×2×5×3 matrix, or 600 segments. Thus, unless one is running a complex database or is prepared for many hours of work, this decision needs to be taken carefully. Further, the marketer must also consider the size of each segment in the analysis. Segments that are too large may pose problems later on with strategy implementation, and segments that are too small may not be worth pursuing.

Step 3: Segment-by-Segment Analysis

Once the appropriate bases of segmentation and their sensitivities have been selected, the marketer analyzes each segment by determining the following the process outlined below for each permutation of the bases/sensitivities identified.

This process involves two steps: First, the bases/levels of sensitivity are organized in table format; and second, six basic but thought-provoking questions are asked about each group/segment. A table reminds us of two important points described earlier—mutual exclusivity between segments and homogeneity within segments. Although, it is quite likely that bases of segmentations have more than two levels of sensitivity with more sophisticated breakdowns, for simplicity in our example, we have kept the levels of sensitivity for each base to two simple groupings. The bases of segmentation in this example are:

- Base #1: Income (high/low)
- Base #2: Age (young/old)
- Base #3: Personality (type A/type B)
- Base #4: Geography (urban/rural)

INCOME	HIGH				LOW			
Age	Y		O		Y		O	
Personality	A	B	A	B	A	B	A	B
Geography	U R	U R	U R	U R	U R	U R	U R	U R

The breakdown clearly shows the 2×2×2×2 segmentation results in 16 segments, which are mutually exclusive: No individual in the total market appears more than once in the segmentation.

From this point, we consider six specific questions for consumers within each of the identified potential market segments:

- Who are they?
- What do they want/need?
- When to they want/need it?

- Where do they get it?
- Why do the want/need it?
- How do they go about getting it?

These questions are important as they force the marketer to consider what is happening in the minds of the consumers in each potential target market. Through this, the marketer hopes to achieve a complete understanding of each segment prior to selecting among them, or targeting.

Using this same example, we end up with a segmentation grid that looks like this:

INCOME	HIGH				LOW			
Age	Y		O		Y		O	
Personality	A	B	A	B	A	B	A	B
Geography	U R	U R	U R	U R	U R	U R	U R	U R
Who?								
What?								
Where?								
Why?								
How?								
When?								

As this chart clearly shows, for a 16-group segmentation, this process becomes very complex very quickly, and database-assisted organization is recommended for all but the simplest segmentation. In larger ones, a database program (e.g., Access) with queries would be ideal.

To help clarify the process, we present an example of a segmentation from a consulting project on the market for ice hockey nets. This involves a relatively simple 2×2 format with levels of sensitivity for Type of Hockey (ice/road) and Product Use (personal/institutional) that leads to Table 5-2.

TABLE 5-2

Segmentation Table: Market for Ice Hockey Nets

Market	Ice Hockey/ Personal Use	Ice Hockey/ Institutional Use	Road Hockey/ Personal Use	Road Hockey/ Institutional Use
Who are they?	rural families and back-yard rinks	arenas, munici-palities, parks and rec, clubs	children and young adults at home	bars, arenas, teams, leagues, clubs

What do they want?	an enabler for game-like fun, competition, and practice	regulation-size net that conforms to rules; durability, quality, and safety	an enabler for game-like fun, competition, and practice	regulation-size net that conforms to rules; durability, quality, and safety
Why do they buy it?	to keep puck in play, practice, skill development, dream, fun	to provide a regulation game to players	To keep ball in play, practice, fun, pick-up games	to provide a regulation game to players
How do they buy it?	Pressure from children, parents go to purchase	based on client need and owner-ship decision	pressure from children, parents go to purchase	based on client need and owner-ship decision
Where do they buy it?	large sporting-goods stores	wholesaler or larger retailer	large sporting-goods stores	wholesaler or larger retailer
When do they buy it?	fall or early winter	year-round	spring or early summer	year-round

Table 5-2 and this section in general underline that good segments are both homogeneous and mutually exclusive. The hockey nets example shows that each of the groups is different from one another, while individuals within each group are similar. Further, no consumer would fall in the grid more than once, and each member of the total market would fall there only once. In the case of a consumer who plays ice hockey in the winter and road hockey in the summer, they would be considered two different consumers as they would be using two different hockey net products.

Feedback Advantage

An important advantage of segmentation using the six-questions grid is that it provides for double-checks of the work. Following completion of the grid, the marketer can double-check their work by comparing responses in each column. If the chart is identical under certain rows, then we have chosen bases of segmentation that are not relevant to our market. For example, in the hockey net example above, if the responses in the two columns under ice hockey were *identical* to those under road hockey, we would know that Type of Hockey is not a useful basis of segmentation for this market. We would then revisit the analysis and seek other, relevant bases of segmentation.

Targeting

Historically, the marketing literature[1] has offered three ways to target markets.

1. *Undifferentiated Targeting:* The marketer ignores market segmentation and the differences it reveals between groups and targets the entire market with a single message. This is rarely used, and even those organizations that once did so (e.g., Coca-Cola) are now opting for more complex approaches. It is our opinion that this approach never be taken.
2. *Multisegment Targeting or Differentiated Targeting:* The marketer selects more than one of the segments identified in the segmentation process and develops distinct marketing strategies, one per selected target market, designing separate offers for each. For examples, the automakers (e.g., General Motors, Ford, Honda) develop, promote, and offer numerous vehicles, each specifically targeted to specific markets. Similarly, the footwear manufacturers (e.g., Nike, Reebok, Adidas) develop, promote, and offer numerous styles of sporting footwear, each designed for specific markets.
3. *Concentrated Targeting:* Similar to multisegment targeting, this involves focusing on only one target market. This decision may be made for resource reasons or as part of a niche strategy, and it is particularly attractive when financial resources are limited. For example, Softride bicycles are specially designed for, and marketing to, only long-distance triathletes and cyclists.

Targeting, although vitally important to the success of any marketing plan, is the simplest step in STP. It involves assessing the work done in the segmentation to determine which market or markets will be pursued in the marketing strategy. In this regard, a marketer generally seeks to consider segments that have sustainable profitability, are measurable, and are accessible through existing marketing channels. Specifically, targeting seeks to identify those segments with the greatest potential for profit or return on investment, as well as to consider the feasibility, simplicity, and cost of reaching a segment.

The 80/20 Rule

The marketing literature on targeting often discusses the 80/20 rule. In this context, the 80/20 rule reminds us that typically 80 percent of revenue comes from 20 percent of customers; our high-volume customers drive our business and must be considered in our targeting decisions[2]. In carrying out a detailed

---

[1] For example: Kotler, P. & G. Armstrong (1987) *Marketing: An Introduction.* Prentice-Hall.
[2] For example: Crane, F.G., R.A. Kerin, S.W. Hartley, E.N. Berkowitz, & W. Rudelius (2006) *Marketing*, 6th Cdn ed. McGraw-Hill Ryerson: 234.

and sophisticated segmentation, we often reveal potential target markets that are interesting but that may require significant investment to reach and whose profit potential is limited. For example, the Ottawa Senators' strategy may be to spend more time, money, and human resources on customers who have engaged in an exchange with the team by buying one or several tickets than on the ones that have never done so. Thus, by targeting those fans, the Senators can develop a number of marketing strategies to deepen the team's relationship with them. The result may be more ticket sales (ultimate goal season ticket), more merchandises sales (e.g., jerseys, mugs), and more revenues from concessions.

Using Segmentation Grid for Targeting

The six-question grid provides the marketer with a tool to analyze the various markets to consider and the data necessary to make an informed targeting decision. Specifically, targeting involves the analysis of each segment and the selection of the one or ones that will enable the marketer to achieve their goals.

The process involves two steps: assessing size, reach, profitability (or ROI), and measurability of each potential target market identified in the segmentation, and selecting target market(s).

Step One: Assessing Size, Reach, Profitability, and Measurability

This step involves going across the completed segmentation grid, segment by segment, and asking these questions of each:

Size

- Is the segment too large (i.e., difficult to differentiate from) for a marketing effort?
- Is the segment large enough to justify a marketing effort? If not, will it grow to that size in the near future?
- Is our target market too narrowly defined?

Reach

- Are we able to communicate with this segment? If not, will future technology enable this communication to happen?
- Is the segment compatible with the goals and image of our organization?

Profitability

- If we're seeking profit, can we achieve our profitability requirements from this target market?
- If we're not seeking profit, can we achieve our objectives in a cost-effective manner through this target market?
- Do we possess the resources (financial and human) necessary to pursue this segment?
- Is it possible to achieve a competitive advantage in this segment?

Measurability

- Can we measure the size of the segment?
- Can we estimate the purchasing power of the segment?
- Can we determine if we can access this segment?

A few notes to these questions. First, the largest segment may be too large to pursue if the marketer cannot find a point of difference, a specific feature to demonstrate how their product is superior to competing products. A smaller segment where a niche strategy is likely to work may be a better choice. For example, the new Major League Soccer franchise in Toronto targeted specific cultural groups in the city known to support soccer (e.g., Italian-Canadians, Brazilian-Canadians) in its ticket sales programs. Second, in considering reach, the marketer must be aware that new forms of communications and consumer engagement are developing all the time (e.g., online forums, blogs), which may change our answer to this question.

The responses to the questions above will provide the data and direction marketers require for selecting the target or targets they wish to pursue.

Step Two: Selecting Target Markets

Armed with the responses to the 12 questions above for each identified segment from the segmentation step, the marketer is able to determine which segment(s) to select for marketing action.

This involves analyzing the segments and determining which ones to pursue, based on available resources. The number of targets is specific to each target decision, which considers how attractive they are and the resources and market conditions that the marketer faces.

Positioning

Marketers assume that consumers arrange competitive offerings in their minds according to factors (e.g., price, quality, luxury) that are important and relevant to them for the product. Position is the place that each product offering occupies, relative to others, in the minds of the consumers of that target market segment.

hole in market: a niche or a particular segment whose needs and/or wants have not been adequately met.

Practically, positioning involves looking for that place in the minds of your target market(s) where you can fit your product, or where there is currently a **hole in the market**—no direct competitive offering. The trick to effective positioning is to have carried out segmentation and targeting properly to provide for clearly articulated target markets and, then, to view your product versus competitive offerings (competition and substitutes) specifically *in* the minds of the consumers in each target market.

For each target market identified in the targeting stage, a separate positioning strategy is developed. For example, if three target markets are selected, then three positioning strategies are developed, one for each target market.

Positioning Story: Clean and Clear B-Ball Skills Days

The Clean and Clear B-Ball Skills Days is an excellent example of STP in action developed by Toronto-based marketing agency TrojanOne. Clean and Clear, an acne treatment product, ran a program known as B-Ball Skills Days in high schools throughout Ontario in 2005. They went into the schools and ran basketball skills camps and scrimmage games with girls while the boys watched. No product was given out, but the name Clean and Clear was attached. Why was it brilliant STP? Research had revealed that a large segment of teenage girls did not participate in sport because they believed that sweating would cause skin problems (e.g., acne) and they were afraid this would limit their attractiveness to boys. Thus, the combination of playing a cool sport in front of the boys positioned Clean and Clear in their minds as the product to counter these fears.

Positioning Strategies

Marketing theory provides a number of strategies by which a marketer can position their product in the marketplace. Table 5-3 lists these strategies.

TABLE 5-3

Strategies for Positioning

STRATEGY	EXAMPLE
By attributes	Seek specific characteristic (e.g., Nike and high performance) by which to position
By price–quality association	Position by the value proposition offered to the target market (e.g., student discounts on ski passes at Whistler)
By use	Determine why product is purchased (e.g., Big Bertha golf club for long drives)
Advantage over competition	Seek difference from competitors or seek to mimic a successful competitor's offering (e.g., Gatorade scientifically proven to enable a runner to absorb more energy than competing products)
By benefit	Seek difference by benefits offered to consumer
Find market gap	Assess marketplace and find niche where competition is limited or absent (e.g., PowerBar and endurance sport athletes)

By usage environment	Use situations or times of use as point of difference (e.g., road hockey net)
By association with endorsers	Use endorser to position or reposition (e.g., Tiger Woods and Buick)
By association with something unique	Use unique or exotic aspect or fact to position or reposition (e.g., Mike Weir wine)
By product of choice to certain users	Select a specific product for a specific group where the product becomes their option of choice (e.g., Gatorade for athletes)
Differentiate brand	Stress your differences and avoid head-to-head competition (e.g., Softride bicycles and a comfortable ride)
Reposition	Adapt product to a new market (e.g., golf to senior women)
Be the leader	Set the tone, be the one that others follows (e.g., Speedo as the manufacturer of performance swimming products)
Appeal to lifestyle	Seek fit between lifestyle and product appeal for your target segments and use to differentiate offering (e.g., Chariot baby strollers for active parents offer a multiuse stroller for running, bicycling, hiking, cross-country skiing)

Marketers must be careful in their positioning strategies. First, positioning against a clear market leader (e.g., Brooks versus Nike, Aspirin versus Tylenol) is not recommended due to the influence of the market leader on all target markets. Second, positioning in a crowded market is unlikely to work well as confusion will reduce or limit the ability of the message to effectively reach its target. Third, over-positioning may lead to a narrow image communicated to an overly small and likely unprofitable market segment. Fourth, it is generally not recommended to position a product on an attribute that is not important to the target market (e.g., waterproof tennis racquet). Finally, product modification that is not needed or wanted by the target is likely to be ineffective.

IN THE KNOW

Canada's Teams
An example of positioning is professional sport franchises in Canada and those who take on the role of Canada's Team at certain times and with certain segments of fans. In NHL hockey, clearly the most

popular sport league in Canada, the Toronto Maple Leafs and Montreal Canadiens both take on the role of Canada's Team with market segments across the country. In many cases, residents of cities with newer franchises (e.g., Edmonton Oilers, Ottawa Senators) are fans of either Toronto's or Montreal's home team, which become their top-of-mind Canada's Team. In baseball and basketball, Toronto has the only Canadian franchises, which play the role of Canada's Team.

The Positioning Map as a Marketing Tool

In continuing the process we've developed from the six-question segmentation grid and the twelve-question targeting approach, we now move to positioning the offering in the minds of the consumers in the target market(s) selected. We consider and carry out a positioning for only the target market(s) we have selected.

Effective positioning is built on three required stages:

1. The marketer assesses a given market segment and determines where each competitive offering is currently positioned.
2. The marketer does background research to determine the important dimensions and drivers that lead to this positioning.
3. The marketer selects a position for their product to occupy in the mind of the target market segment.

As suggested by one of the authors' professors, this process can be referred to as "cherchez le creneau" (look for the hole): The marketer seeks to understand what is happening in the minds of consumers in the target market and identify holes where they can position their product for success. If all the competitors in the running-shoe market are launching high-quality shoes with big-name athlete sponsors, why not offer a low price shoe? If all the events in town are free and convenient, why not offer a prestige event?

Perceptual Mapping

The **perceptual map**, a positioning tool, displays the location of products or brands (or sometimes product classes or groups) in the minds of consumers (both current and future) in the target market of interest. Perceptual maps are usually displayed in two dimensions but can be constructed in three or more dimensions using special software.

perceptual map: a graphic representation of positioning in the minds of consumers in the target market.

One perceptual map is designed for each target market of interest. The design process involves three steps.

1. Draw the axes: The two most relevant dimensions of the target market are selected, along with ranges of each dimension, based on the views of consumers in the market of interest.

Chapter 5: Segmentation, Targeting, and Positioning in Canadian Sport

2. Plot all offerings: All competing offers (substitutes as well) are positioned on the graph in one of two ways: by feel and understanding of the market or by scoring via the perceptual mapping technique (see below). The latter is always recommended.

IN THE KNOW

Positioning Using the Perceptual Mapping Technique

In this technique, a sample of consumers from the target market of interest are asked to use Likert scale questions (e.g., putting answers on a 1–5 scale such as 1=very similar to 5=very different) to rank product pairs (e.g., Nike/Adidas, tennis/soccer) or product comparisons (e.g., the entertainment value of a Manitoba Moose hockey game), with the results used to position competing offerings in a perceptual map.

3. Determine position of product of interest in target market of interest. Based on market and research, determine position of product. With existing products, this may involve repositioning, where the product's current position is altered based on a changing market or environment.

Figure 5-1 is a typical perceptual map, based on the results of a recent exploratory study at University of Ottawa that queried consumers on the corporate brand prestige of many Ontario and Quebec universities.

FIGURE 5-1

Perceptual map of the perceptions of Canadians (random sample of general population) of the corporate brands of a sample of Ontario and Quebec universities.

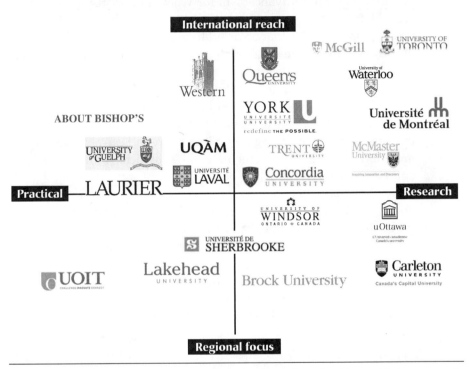

Ontario and Quebec universities corporate brand preceptual map

Note that this perceptual map is based on the opinions of a small panel and is meant to be an example of a perceptual map and not a validated representation of Canadian universities.

In Figure 5-1, two dimensions were selected to determine the perceived marketing reach (international/regional) and focus (research/applied).

Common Target Markets in Canadian Sport

Some specific target markets in Canadian sport should be well known to the Canadian sport marketer.

> *Aboriginal Canadians:* Aboriginal Canadians represent a group of considerable interest in amateur sport, particularly in participation where sport is seen by government as a way to improve the lives and health of this group. Sport Canada, the Aboriginal Sport Circle, and other organizations work in this segment. Examples of targeted activities in Canadian sports include the North American Indigenous Games, the Canadian Sport Policy which includes specific action

targeted at Aboriginal sport, and Hockey Canada youth programs to encourage Aboriginal youth to participate in hockey.

Canadian women: Female Canadians represent an important interest group to the government as well as to professional sport with initiatives to engage women at all levels of sport, ranging from the creation of new female professional sport leagues to youth programs to get girls involved in sport. For example, the Canadian Association for the Advancement for Women in Sports and Physical Activity (CAAWS), created in the early 1980s, has been successful in developing strategies that have led to more opportunities for girls and women to engage at different levels in the sport system (participants, athletes, administrators, etc.).

Young Canadians: Young Canadians, particularly due to increasing health issues (e.g., obesity) in youth, are a focus of government, particularly Health Canada and Sport Canada. Thus, developing specific strategies for engaging youth into sport and physical activity are priorities for governments (national, provincial, municipal), sport clubs, corporations, and health-care professionals.

Official language groups: Canada is a country of two official languages, and sport organizations, activities, events, and programs that cater to both are sought and supported. For example, national sport organizations must develop marketing programs that appeal to both segments.

Paralympic athletes: The emergence of the Paralympic Games has provided huge opportunities for physically challenged individuals to pursue their athletic dreams (see case on Paralympics Ontario).

IN THE KNOW

STP in Action: The ITU Toronto World Cup Triathlon

In 2000, one of the authors (O'Reilly) worked for the Toronto 2008 Olympic bid as event manager for the ITU Toronto World Cup Triathlon. He used STP extensively in developing the marketing program for the event, which ended up with six specific target markets:

1. *International decision makers:* As part of the Olympic bid, the main goal of the event was to influence those voting to determine the location of the 2008 Olympic Games. Specific marketing strategy was developed to pass Toronto's message to these individuals.
2. *Spectators:* The event was held following the Molson Indy car race in Toronto on the same course. Extensive seating was still up following the event, which organizers had to fill since empty seats look bad on television. STP identified potential Toronto fans and a marketing program developed to encourage 5000 spectators to show up.

3. *Participants—Elite:* To impress the international decision makers, a top field representing many countries was needed to participate in the event. Thus, a strategy was developed that saw the vast majority of the top 50 male and female athletes in the world, representing over 30 countries, participate.

4. *Participants—Amateur:* A further source of spectators for the elite race and of goodwill for the event is the amateur triathletes doing the event. This marketing strategy was adopted to try to attract 1000 participants that day: That objective was not achieved, and the strategy was altered for 2001.

5. *Participants—Celebrity Relay:* A few celebrities (e.g., actors, politicians, business executives) were sought to garner media attention and fanfare.

6. *Sponsors:* To access a major source of funding for the event, we developed a detailed sponsorship program and implemented it with partners. We reached the target amount, with Pizza Hut as the title sponsor.

To review an example of a marketing plan, go to www.sportmarketing.nelson.com.

Case: Paralympics Ontario

Sensitive STP…What Does the Sport Marketer Do?

In spring 2005, Andrew Greenlaw sat in his office going over marketing reports from the previous year. As director of sponsorship and events for Paralympics Ontario, he was charged with a number of tasks for the small nonprofit organization responsible for furthering the Paralympic movement in the province in Ontario. At the top of his mind was sponsorship, one of his key tasks, and the challenges in attracting, signing, and renewing both association and event sponsors. He harkened back to his studies on segmentation, targeting, and positioning—known to him as STP—and wondered how these tools could help him.

Background

Paralympics Ontario was established in 1981 under the name Sport for Disabled Ontario to act as the provincial sport organization for athletes with a physical disability in Ontario. In 2003, it formed a partnership with the Canadian Paralympic Committee and changed its name to Paralympics Ontario. With the mission of providing leadership, resources, and opportunities to ensure a strong community for people with a disability in the Ontario sport and recreation community, Paralympics Ontario offers a broad range of services along the sport continuum encompassing initiatives targeted at both grassroots and elite levels of involvement.

Ontario is Canada's most populous province, home to 12 541 400 people or 38.8 percent of Canada's population in 2005[3]. Ontario is also home to 11 of Canada's 27 census metropolitan areas— Greater Sudbury, Hamilton, Kingston, Kitchener-Watreloo, London, Oshawa, Ottawa-Gatineau (shared with Quebec), St. Catharines-Niagara, Thunder Bay, Toronto, and Windsor.

Paralympics Ontario is organized on a membership structure with four member organizations representing each of the disability-specific sport organizations in the province:

- Ontario Amputee and Les Autres Sports Association
- Ontario Blind Sports Association
- Ontario Cerebral Palsy Sports Association
- Ontario Wheelchair Sports Association

Paralympics Ontario currently has four full-time staff: an executive director, a director of sponsorship & events, a sport development manager, and an administrative assistant. The director of sponsorship & events coordinates sponsorship and marketing activities, with decisions regarding agreements finalized by the executive director.

Programs and Properties

Paralympics Ontario administers a number of programs to achieve its goals. Of these programs, two are vital to the organization's success: its Games Program and its Ready, Willing and Able initiative.

The largest, and perhaps most widely known property in Paralympics Ontario is its Games Program, which provides competitive opportunities for athletes. Each year, the organization, in conjunction with host communities, offers two sets of regional games and one set of provincial championships for summer sports. In light of the upcoming Vancouver 2010 Paralympic Games, Paralympics Ontario is working to add a Winter Paralympic Championships to the existing games program.

Ready, Willing and Able (RWA) is an initiative designed to develop awareness and participation in disability sport at the grassroots community level. This program provides introductory sessions to disability sports and gives participants the opportunity to try a variety of them with specialized sport-specific equipment provided at sessions by Paralympics Ontario. The RWA program targets both individuals with a disability and their able-bodied peers by hosting sessions at rehabilitation centres, children's treatment centres, schools, camps, and other community settings.

---

[3] Statistics Canada (2006) Canadian statistics by province. Retrieved May 7, 2006 from http://www .statscan.ca.

Sponsorship

As he glanced out his window, Andrew's thoughts drifted to sponsorship and his work in the area. Andrew defines a successful sponsorship as one in which the sponsor renews the partnership at the end of the original term. He believes it important to keep sponsors engaged at all levels, through phone calls, face-to-face meetings, and attending events.

Paralympics Ontario is very committed to sponsorship efforts and realizes that, due to the current trend of decreased government support for sport, it is necessary to secure corporate sector involvement to ensure continued quality programming and service delivery. The organization has been successful in securing many short-term sponsorship agreements, mainly in-kind and contra contribution. The organization recognizes that contra and in-kind contributions can greatly reduce budgets and believes these forms of sponsorship are as important as financial contributions. However, it has been less successful in obtaining long-term financial partnerships with corporations. It hopes that single-year contracts with corporations can be extended once they are exposed to Paralympic sport and value to the sponsor can be demonstrated.

In summary, the Paralympic brand is currently not well established, and it is difficult to sell long-term agreements to first-time sponsors. Paralympics Ontario is involved in a joint marketing agreement with the Canadian Paralympic Committee, which provides access to their sponsors and protects those in Ontario from ambushers. Further and with the recent Vancouver 2010 agreement, Paralympics Ontario must protect all of the International Olympic Committee's TOP sponsors, meaning that those categories (e.g., soft drink, credit card, etc.) are no longer available in seeking potential sponsors, although the opportunity to sell additional marketing properties related to the Olympic Games themselves to the existing TOP sponsors does exist.

Andrew feels that there is significant future potential for Paralympics Ontario due to the upcoming 2010 Paralympic Games in Vancouver. He also knows that, on the sport–cause continuum, Paralympics Ontario has the opportunity to position itself as both—sport and cause. Thus, the same property can be positioned in two ways.

Andrew's Challenge

As he thinks of what STP can do for him, Andrew considers his two most important properties—Games Program and RWA—and considers how STP can help him with both.

For Games Program, STP would be implemented to the market he wishes to target—potential sponsors or, more broadly, potential funders through donations, sponsorship, or grants. Knowing that he must start with the entire potential market, he thinks of any organization or entity who would be able to support the Games Program. He quickly jots down names of corporations, foundations, government, government agencies, charities, the Canadian Olympic

Chapter 5: Segmentation, Targeting, and Positioning in Canadian Sport

Committee, Sport Canada, and others. He is impressed with what he comes up with in terms of its scope. His mind quickly turns to the appropriate bases of segmentation by which to slice this market in to homogeneous segments which can be targeted efficiently. Bases such as fit with the Paralympic movement, size, geography, and purpose (i.e., philanthropy or sponsorship investment) go through his mind. He also considers both cash and in-kind investments.

His mind is racing, and he moves on to RWA. This is a completely different market, as its target is individuals who might participate in Paralympic activities and sport in Ontario. This is challenging as recruiting Paralympic athletes is a sensitive endeavour that requires proper planning and attention to detail. From an STP point of view, the potential targets would include such individuals as those who have recently suffered a serious injury, those who were born with serious illness, as well as those able-bodied individuals who are supportive of the movement and could be engaged as volunteers, coaches and administrators. The market is not large, and many of these individuals will be very hard to engage, let alone just communicate with. As a base of segmentation, reachability is key to Andrew's thinking, as are severity of disability, income, and family support.

For further information, visit http://www.paralympicsontario.com and related links.

Sources: Paralympics Ontario website, http://www.paralympicsontario.com; personal interview with Andrew Greenlaw, Director of Sponsorship & Events, Paralympics Ontario, February 2005, Toronto, Canada.

Case Questions

1. Complete a six-question segmentation grid for the Games Program target.
2. Complete a six-question segmentation grid for the RWA target.
3. Complete a full STP for the segmentation from Question 1.
4. Complete a full STP for the segmentation from Question 2.
5. Do you think STP is useful for Andrew?
6. What would you recommend for future marketing action at Paralympics Ontario?

Chapter Summary

Chapter 5 introduces STP, the bridge to marketing strategy, and outlines the important process of turning research data about consumers' internal and external environments of interest into effective and efficient marketing strategy to achieve organizational objectives. The three-step STP process includes, in order, segmentation, targeting, and positioning. Segmentation involves reducing the entire market of interest down to manageable groups with similar characteristics. Targeting is the selection of segments (one or more) that will have the greatest potential for marketing success. Positioning is the act of determining how to best present your product in the minds of consumers in your target market(s) of interest versus your competition. The chapter provides a number of tools for STP (e.g., perceptual mapping, six-questions segmentation grid), which enable marketing action that is efficient and reduces risk.

Test Your Knowledge

1. Selecting at least three bases of segmentation, create a segmentation grid and respond to the six questions for launching a new driver into the golf market in Canada.
2. Explain the role and give an example of each of the following in developing marketing strategy:

   - segmentation
   - targeting
   - positioning

3. If the targeting process reveals two target markets of interest, how many perceptual maps and marketing strategies must be developed?
4. Create a perceptual map that for sport entertainment options for a couple on a Saturday night in the Great Toronto Area.
5. List as many bases of segmentation as you can that might help segment the market of CFL fans.
6. What risk does a marketer take if develops his or her strategy without considering or doing an STP?

For more review questions, go to http://www.sportmarketing.nelson.com.

Key Terms

B2B
B2C
hole in market
market segmentation
market state of mind

measurability
perceptual map
positioning
responsiveness
sensitivity

A full glossary of key term definitions is located at http://www.sportmarketing.nelson.com.

Internet Resources

Frito-Lay Canada, http://www.fritolay.ca/

Canadian Association for the Advancement of Women in Sport, http://www.caaws.ca/

Canadian Paralympic Committee, http://www.paralympic.ca/

Aboriginal Sport Circle= Canada, http://www.aboriginalsportcircle.ca/main/main.html

Market segmentation, http://en.wikipedia.org/wiki/Market_segment

Market targeting, http://en.wikipedia.org/wiki/Target_marketing

Market positioning, http://en.wikipedia.org/wiki/Positioning_(marketing)

Chapter 6

The Sport Product

Source: George Doyle/Getty Images

Learning Objectives

- To understand what is meant by a product
- To expand the concept of a product to a sport product
- To become acquainted with the various product forms and the elements of product strategy

Introduction

The sport product

Nothing inspires passion and emotion quite like sport. One kick of the ball or swing of the bat can energize and excite a crowd or dash the hopes of a nation. In many cases, an ingrained emotional connection exists between the consumer and the product, something most marketing professionals can only dream of achieving. However, there is much more to the sport product than emotion: Many characteristics challenge the sport marketing professional. Sport is not a product form that can be easily defined as a good or a service, but rather it is made up of a variety of forms representing both categories. Some argue that the core of the **sport product** is an athletic event and that all other product forms support and expand on that core. It is on this basis that we discuss the sport product. This chapter begins by looking at the unique features of the core sport product: Why is this product different from all others? It then examines numerous forms of the sport product, including events, athletes, facilities, teams, leagues, clubs,

sport product: any good, service, person, place, or idea with tangible or intangible attributes that satisfy consumer sport, fitness, or recreation needs or desires.]

merchandise, media, and skilled services, providing a general description of each form along with examples taken from Canadian sport. The chapter ends with a brief overview of the concept of the sport brand and sport packaging.

As the product is the most important element of the marketing mix, it is vitally important for sport marketing professionals to clearly understand the product in all its forms. They must appreciate the aspects of sport that make it a challenge to market but that also form the basis of its appeal. This chapter outlines and highlights these aspects to provide that understanding.

EXECUTIVE PERSPECTIVE

Callaway GOLF

Chris Walling, Director of Marketing, Callaway Golf Canada Ltd.

It seems simple. A man walks into a store, goes to the section that carries what he needs, looks over the options in front of him, picks one, takes it to the counter, and pays for it.

But in looking deeper into consumer purchasing habits, it's essential to understand what affects their judgment and influences their loyalties leading up to their actually handing over their hard-earned money at the till.

In sport marketing, understanding consumers and what goes into their buying habits is even more crucial than for a typical consumer product good (CPG) type of model (like soft drink or deodorant): The size of overall market is generally smaller than that of a CPG, and many other pre-purchase factors are involved. What we have on our side, however, is the emotional connection the consumer makes with sport and our ability to tug on those heartstrings.

We look further into the consumer process of buying sporting goods equipment. Many factors come into play, all becoming a vital part of the product development and consumer marketing behind the success of a product. For the sake of this example, let's use the process of buying a driver (one of golf's key product categories since it typically defines the success of a brand) and the various steps involved in convincing customers to purchase one.

Consumer research tells us that from beginning to end, the entire purchase process takes from 35 to 50 days, and in over 85 percent of consumers we've surveyed, the process remains the same:

1. Brands matter: While many feel drivers are too expensive, brand legitimacy is key in the consideration set.

2. Process: Understanding the consumer and the reasons for buying a driver is essential. Knowing that the average golfer will spend over $300 and will replace a driver every 2.5 years allows product teams to build technological life cycles and features into the product that cater to what golfers are looking for (i.e., their needs and/or wants).

3. Professional use: The use of your product by those who play your sport for a living is key to legitimizing your brand and product. If pros (e.g., PGA Tour players) are using your product, why would a consumer chance their own performance with anything else?

4. Competitive set: The need for initial and constant brand reinforcement through print and television advertising, public relations and buzz creation, the Internet, tour presence, retail presence, and recently the realization and importance of 1:1 direct consumer marketing is key to ensuring that consumers put your product into their purchase consideration sets early.

5. Choice: At the end of the day, the consumers need to try before they buy. Surveyed consumers tell us that product demonstration and trying a friend's club are the two most influential means to gathering information and perception of a product. Considerable time is invested in consumer interface events, including demo days, fitting events, and retail events to ensure that at every consumer touch point, the ability to try an array of product is available.

6. Performance: Product performance, in terms of feel and results, generally outweighs many other factors. If your product genuinely performs better than others within the consideration set, price will often become a secondary factor.

7. Product availability: During the trial stage and at the point of sale, this is critical. A sound distribution strategy is essential to ensure that when all the previous consideration sets come together for potential buyers, they can get what they want, when they want it. It crucial to ensuring the sale.

All in all, the purchase process can be articulated into something that looks like this.

In the end, buying a driver is a poignant experience for golfers. How long and straight players drive the ball give them a mental edge and a feeling of confidence and euphoria unparalleled by any other single action in individual sport. Understanding this emotional experience allows us as marketers to develop strategies that allow consumers to not only see first hand through the use of professional endorsement and validation what they can aspire to be, but to live an exhilarating experience where price no longer stands in the way. They simply must have it!

Chris began his career with Spalding Canada, where he held the positions of product manager, category manager, and marketing manager for their Top-Flite and Ben Hogan brands. He is currently the director of marketing with Callaway Golf Canada, overseeing the Callaway Golf, Odyssey, Top-Flite, and Ben Hogan Brands.

INITIAL INFO GATHERING (21–28 DAYS)	NARROWING DOWN (10–15 DAYS)	MAKING FINAL DECISION (5–10 DAYS)
Including brand experience, tour validation, research, and retail exploration	Including trial, word-of-mouth recommendation, retail shopping, and media/buzz	More trial, including the ability to demo exactly what they want to buy, availability, and price

Source: Some data and process references supplied by the Golf Digest Companies Research Resource Centre (2004) "The process of buying drivers—From couch to cash register" prepared for Callaway Golf.

The Sport Product

What Is a Product?

Sport is a product like no other; however, to understand it, we must examine the more general definitions and elements of a product. The numerous definitions of product all contain similar elements. Central to the definition is the assertion of Pitts and Stotlar[1] that a product should be understood as a concept, rather than a singular item. Solomon and colleagues[2] define a product as "a tangible good, a service, an idea, or some combination of these that, through the exchange process, satisfies consumer or business customer needs; a bundle of attributes including features, functions, benefits and uses."

---

[1] Pitts, B.G. & D.K. Stotlar (1996) *Fundamentals of Sports Marketing*. Fitness Information Technology.

[2] Solomon, M.R., E.W. Stuart, A. Carson, & J.B. Smith (2003) *Marketing: Real People, Real Decisions*, 2nd Cdn ed. Prentice Hall.

Similarly, Graham[3] defines a product as "anything that can be offered to a market for attention, acquisition, use or consumption that might satisfy a want or need. The term product may refer to a service, idea, organization, person, place, or activity."

Central to these definitions are the ideas that a product is something that satisfies a need and that it exists in more than one form—a good, service, idea, person, organization, place, or activity. A product may be made up of any one or a variety of these forms. This is a particularly relevant observation in the context of the sport product, which encompasses a wide variety of these forms. To gain an even deeper understanding of a product, we can also define critical elements of these definitions—goods and services. A good is a tangible, physical entity that offers specific benefits to the consumer. For example, a pair of shoes is a physical, tangible object that offers the consumer something to cover the feet with. A service, on the other hand, represents the opposite, a non-physical entity that is intangible but that still offers specific benefits to the consumer. For example, a piano lesson does not offer the student a physical object but rather a new skill that benefits them.

Since the tangibility of the product is the most important determinant in classifying it as a good or service, it is important to understand the meaning of tangibility. Pitts and Stotlar[4] define a tangible product as "something that is concrete, definite, discernible, and material ... it physically exists." The same authors describe an intangible product as "something that is indefinite, indiscernible, indistinguishable, and imperceptible. It is not a physical object." All of these definitions and concepts are key to understanding the product and will be discussed again in the context of the sport product.

Product Life Cycle

The product is the core of the marketing mix. It is important for marketers to not only define the product they are dealing with but also understand how it evolves over time so they can adapt it accordingly. The most widely accepted way of explaining the evolution of a product is with the product life cycle model (Figure 6-1). This consists of four stages—introduction, growth, maturity, and decline—each representing distinct challenges for the marketing professional. Therefore, marketers must recognize where their product fits in the cycle so they can respond to those challenges. In the *introduction stage*, the product first enters the market, few consumers have heard of the product, and sales are low. A product in this stage requires extensive promotion to create awareness; and if this is successful, then a slow but steady increase in sales should be expected. In the *growth stage*, the product has been recognized and accepted by most consumers. This stage is characterized by a

---

[3] Graham, P.J. (1994) *Sport Business: Operational and Theoretical Aspects.* Brown and Benchmark: 4.
[4] Pitts, B.G. & D.K. Stotlar (1996) *Fundamentals of Sports Marketing*: 141.

steady, rapid increase in profits; however, it also entails the introduction of competitors and a resulting peak in profits followed by a decline. During the growth stage, marketers must appreciate the impact of the arrival of competitors on the profitability of the product[5] and take measures to counteract such an impact. When sales have leveled off and the competition is firmly established, a product has reached the *maturity stage*. During this stage for tangible products, the majority of purchases are made to replace worn-out products, and so the number of new consumers is relatively low[6]. While the leveling of profits symbolizes the beginning of the maturity stage, competition is the most pressing issue, and the costs of promotion and competitive pricing strategies eventually lead to further profit decline. Finally, the *decline stage* is reached when a product becomes obsolete. New technologies may mean that a significantly improved product is taking over and sales will steadily decline. During this stage, it is up to the marketer to realize when a product should no longer be produced. Table 6-1 describes sport products in various stages of the product life cycle.

FIGURE 6-1

The Product Life-Cycle

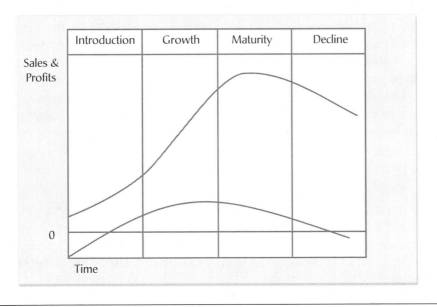

Source: Solomon, M.R.,Stuart,E.W.,Carson,A & Smith,J.B. (2003) Marketing: Real Pople, Real Decisions (1st Canadian Ed.) Toronto, Ontario: Pearson Prentice Hall. Reprinted with permission by Pearson Education Canada Inc.

5 Shapiro, S.J., W.D. Perreault, & E.J. MacCarthy (1999) *Basic Marketing: A Global-Managerial Approach* (9th Cdn ed). McGraw-Hill Ryerson.

6 Solomon, M.R., E.W. Stuart, A. Carson, & J.B. Smith (2003) *Marketing: Real People, Real Decisions.*

TABLE 6–1

Examples for Stages of Product Life Cycle

STAGE	PRODUCT ATHLETE	EQUIPMENT	LEAGUE
Introduction	Angelo Esposito	hybrid golf clubs	Major League Soccer
Growth	Sidney Crosby	yoga	National Lacrosse League
Maturity	Wayne Gretzky	snowboards	National Hockey League
Decline	Gordie Howe	scooters	Women's National Basketball Association

Source: Adapted from Pitts,B.G. & Stotlar, D.K. (1996). Fundamentals of Sports Marketing. Morgantown, WV: Fitness Information Technology Inc. p.152

What else can we learn from the product life cycle model? First, a product can leave or enter the marketplace in any stage. Products that are a duplicate of an original idea can skip the introduction stage and come in later in the cycle. For example, a new brand of snowboard may be introduced to the market, but it does not have to gain consumer recognition for the product, and the majority of its sales may come from replacing boards that have worn out. This means the product has joined the cycle at the maturity stage and so should be marketed in a way that reflects this. As well, different products will move through the life cycle at different speeds, product life cycles are getting shorter, and the early bird generally makes the greatest profit[7]. Since all of these must be considered when creating a marketing plan, marketing professionals must be aware of them.

The Sport Product

In the introduction to this chapter, we noted that sport is a product like no other, and this is part of what makes its study complex. The purpose of this section is to examine the numerous forms that make up the sport product. It begins, however, by defining the sport product and discussing what makes it unique.

What Is the Sport Product?

The definition of a sport product is similar to that given earlier for general products but placed in a sport context. Pitts and Stotlar[8] define the sport product as "any good, service, person, place, or idea with tangible or intangible attributes that satisfy consumer sport, fitness, or recreation needs or

---

[7] Shapiro, S.J., W.D. Perreault, & E.J. MacCarthy (1999) Basic Marketing.

[8] Pitts, B.G. & D.K. Stotlar (1996) Fundamentals of Sports Marketing: 142.

desires." Key to this definition, like the generic product definition, are the concepts of the product taking many forms and fulfilling the needs or desires of the consumer. For example, one form of the sport product is sport equipment, which fills the needs of athletes as it provides the material necessary to facilitate their participation in a sport.

Why Is Sport Special?

Despite the existence of numerous sport product forms, the core sport product is the production of an athletic **event**, and it is elements of this core product that give the sport product its unique nature. Mullin[9] lists eight specific characteristics that make the sport product unique.

event: the core sport product form which stimulates and drives production of all other sport products.

1. The sport product is intangible and subjective: A sport event is intangible in that consumers are unable to physically touch the experience of attending or viewing a sport event. Instead, the benefit they receive from the product is the entertainment they have been provided. A sport event is subjective: What one person considers a positive experience, another may perceive as negative. For example, if the Toronto Blue Jays beat the New York Yankees, then, despite the fact that they attended the same game, the Blue Jays fans may be pleased with the product, while the Yankees fans may be disappointed.

2. The sport product is inconsistent and unpredictable: The human element of sport makes it impossible to predict from one game to the next. This is true in both the spectator and the participant aspect of the sport product. While the Blue Jays may have beaten the Yankees one week, that is no guarantee that the next game will bring the same outcome. Similarly, a person participating in figure skating may skate the same routine at every competition but may win at some and not at others. So many factors go into the outcome and production of a sport event that it becomes unpredictable. The weather, injuries, the crowd atmosphere, or unexpected events can have a huge impact on a game. For instance, a professional team in a hotel may be woken at 3 a.m. by a fire alarm and be forced to stand outside for an hour before going to bed. That is something that cannot be predicted and could possibly affect the outcome of the next day's game. It is this unpredictability that makes sport so exiting, as Whannel[10] describes, "sport entertains, but can also frustrate, annoy and depress. But it is this very uncertainty that gives its unpredictable joys their characteristic intensity."

3. The sport product is simultaneously produced and consumed. It is also perishable and must be presold: Both a spectator sport event and a participant event are being produced as they are being consumed. The crowd at a football game is watching the sport product as the players

---

[9] Mullin, B. (2000) Characteristics of sport marketing. In Appenzeller, H. & G. Lewis (eds) *Successful Sport Management*, 2nd ed. Carolina Academic Press: 127–49.

[10] Whannel, G. (1992) *Fields Vision: Television Sport and Cultural Transformation*. Routledge.

on the field are creating it. This leads to the sport product being classified as perishable, which means that it has a limited shelf life. Once the football game is over, the sport product is no longer able to be sold. Even the most talented marketer cannot sell a ticket for a game that has already taken place. Similarly, for a participant event, the experience of playing a game of golf is being consumed by the golfers as they make their way around the course. When they are finished, the product no longer exists.

4. For marketing professionals, there is a greater emphasis on product extensions than the core product: The inconsistent and unpredictable nature of the sport product cannot be controlled by the marketer. Therefore, there tends to be a focus on product extensions, which can be controlled to a great degree. The marketing professional has no say on which players will be signed or how the team may perform, and, as these things can significantly alter the core product, it does not make sense for a marketing plan to centre on them. Instead the **packaging** of the event becomes even more important. The experience of attending the game can be affected by product extensions like cheerleaders, mascots, and promotions.

packaging: how the product is presented to the potential customer; ranges from the design of the cardboard box or plastic container for a tangible good (e.g., golf balls) to the pageantry and ambiance around a live event.

5. Sport is generally consumed in public and so the experience is affected by group dynamics: For the most part, sport is a social product, which is consumed by a large group of people in a public location. The behaviours and activities of the other consumers can have a significant impact on an individual's experience. It is the job of the marketer to ensure that programs and plans are in place to facilitate the needs of different groups so that they have a positive experience. For example, the Ottawa Senators have created Coca-Cola Family Fan Zone seating section to meet the needs of families coming to the games. Special features of the section include low ticket prices, no alcohol in the section, and fun games for children on the concourse[11].

6. The emotional attachment and personal identification associated with sport in incomparable: Whannel[12] states that: "while there are clearly aesthetic pleasures in merely watching a sport performance, the real intensity comes from identifying with an individual or team as they strive to win." In many cases, committed sports fans feel as though they are part of the team and often use phrases like "*We* won the other day in Edmonton" in an effort to affiliate themselves with a win that they technically had no part in[13]. The strong degree of emotional attachment makes sport an excellent opportunity for selling product extensions like merchandise and collectibles because, in purchasing these items, fans often feel like they are supporting their team. However there is also a negative side to such an attachment. The backlash that can result from

[11] Ottawa Senators (2006) Tickets–Gameday. Retrieved November 27, 2006 from http://www2.ottawasenators .com/eng/Tickets/gameday.cfm.

[12] Whannel, G. (1992) *Fields Vision*.

[13] Mason, D. (1999) What is the sport product and who buys it? The marketing of professional sport leagues. *European Journal of Marketing*, 33(3/4): 402–18.

selling a team's best player or losing an important game can have a negative impact on the sport product. For example, when Wayne Gretzky was traded from the Edmonton Oilers to the Los Angeles Kings, the grief of Canadian sports fans was so great that it prompted *Sports Illustrated*[14] to write an article titled "A nation in mourning."

7. Sport pervades all elements of life and enjoys an almost universal appeal: Across all provinces and territories, among the many cultures, and through all classes in Canada, sports fans exist. This is the same in every country all over the world and is one of the few things which all countries have in common. Soccer is often referred to as the world's game because of its universal appeal and popularity. The World Cup is one of the few events that stops life in hundreds of countries all over the world to focus on the host city and 32 nations competing for the title of world champions. Mullin[15] also notes that sport is associated with numerous elements of life, such as relaxation, entertainment, eating, drinking, sex, gambling, drugs, violence, social identification, religion, and business and industry.

8. Sport is both a consumer and industrial product: A consumer good is typically classified as the end product, which is consumed after production, while an industrial good is a product that is manufactured for use in creating another product[16]. In most cases, a product is either an industrial good or a consumer good; however, different forms of the collective sport product represent both. For example, a hockey game is a consumer product as it is consumed by the fans as it is produced; however, it is also an industrial product as it fuels the production of other products such as sport media. This interaction will be discussed further in the next section.

These eight elements make the sport product unique and provide special advantages and challenge for a sport marketer. The key to marketing success is to recognize these elements and capitalize on those that offer an advantage and preempt the possible negative impact of those that offer a challenge.

Sport Product Forms

The sport product takes a variety of forms—goods and services, consumer and industrial products. The core of the sport product is an athletic event where the consumer is either a participant or spectator. Other sport product forms are no less important, but are dependent on the core product for their survival. The sport form model in Figure 6-2 indicates how the forms interconnect. The athletic event, the core product, is part of a group of primary products. These primary products also include athletes, teams, leagues, and clubs, which all depend on the athletic event for their existence. For example,

---

[14] Taylor, J. (1988) A nation in mourning. *Sports Illustrated*, August 22: 94.

[15] Mullin, B. (2000) Characteristics of sport marketing.

[16] ibid.

Chapter 6: The Sport Product

if no actual hockey games were played: the National Hockey League would have no reason for existence; the Montreal Canadiens would have no purpose; and the hockey players would have nothing to do. The second group of product forms, the derivative products, include merchandise, skilled services, facilities, and media. The derivative products are an expansion of the primary products: They are no less important, as they also support the primary products. For example, sport-specific media are an expansion of events, leagues, athletes, and teams: *The Hockey News* could not exist without the NHL, its teams, and its athletes, as it would have nothing to report on. However, in return, they offer the products exposure and a direct communication channel to their consumers, the fans. To provide a better understanding of the collective sport product, the rest of this section will discuss each product form with examples from Canadian sport.

FIGURE 6-2

Sport Product Model

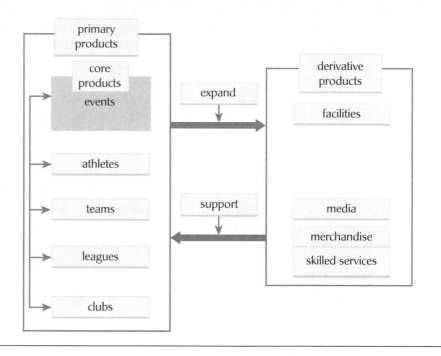

Events

The sporting event is the core sport product form: It stimulates and drives production of all other sport products. The athletes, leagues, teams, clubs, facilities, merchandise, skilled services, and media all exist as a result of the events. Although the first association made with the sport event product is professional sport, an event can actually represent a wide variety of competition levels, including professional games, the Olympics, national championships, intercollegiate athletics, minor sport, and recreational activities. For example, an organized minor soccer game influences the production of a league; and within that league, there must be teams. It also requires the completion of a soccer pitch (facility) and the production of equipment like balls, cleats, nets, and shin pads. On the other end of the scale, the Olympics stimulate the mass production of facilities, merchandise, and equipment, and provide the media with countless hours of programming and inches of newspaper and magazine column space. Events offer consumers various benefits, including the entertainment experience, the vicarious thrill of victory or agony of defeat, and, for some fans particularly in baseball, the numbers of the game, percentages and stats, can be exciting.

Athletes

Athletes are "participants who engage in organized training to develop skills in particular sports[17]." This definition applies to both amateur and professional athletes, both a form of sport product. The benefits offered by the athlete product form can be two-fold: Highly successful athletes not only aid the production of another product (the event), but also provide their image as a marketing tool for their team, league, or sport, as well as outside companies through endorsement deals. A prime example of this is Sidney Crosby, a rising hockey superstar who has been in the limelight since he was touted by experts to be the "new Wayne Gretzky." His rise to stardom in the NHL has benefited not only his team and the fans but also the league as a whole. Before he had played a single game in the NHL, he was already a household name and had been on the *Tonight Show* with Jay Leno, as well as in *GQ* magazine as the new face of the NHL[18]. The 2004–2005 lockout put the NHL into the back of some fans minds, and so the NHL and corporate sponsors used Crosby to try to re-establish their product. In 2005, endorsement deals with Reebok and Gatorade meant that Crosby made more money from his image than his $850 000 annual salary from the NHL[19].

athletes: participants who engage in organized training to develop skills in particular sports.

Teams

Teams are a collective product, comprising a group of athletes who not only work together to create the on-field performance but also represent a brand that can be sold to consumers. While specific athletes may come and go and success may be fleeting, the team product usually remains the same and is best represented by its name and logo. While the Toronto Raptors have seen numerous star players like Vince Carter and Tracy McGrady come to Toronto and than leave, the entity of team product has remained. The Toronto Raptors

team: a collective product comprising a group of athletes who work together to create the on-field performance and represent a brand that can be sold to consumers.

---

[17] Shank, M.D. (2005) *Sports Marketing: A Strategic Perspective*, 3rd ed. Pearson Prentice Hall: 17.

[18] Spencer, D. (2005) The selling of Sid: Crosby already helping boost league in the US. *Calgary Herald*, September 16: E1.

[29] ibid.

team still goes out and competes each year, no matter who fills the jerseys. The team product can be shaped by many elements, including the current players and the team's former players, along with such factors as the history of the team, ownership, and marketing. It is the marketing professional's responsibility to recognize those aspects of the team product that will be the most beneficial in selling the team and exploiting them to their fullest advantage. What works for one team may not work for another, so a detailed examination of the team product is required when putting together a marketing strategy. For instance, while a hockey team like the Toronto Maple Leafs or Montreal Canadiens may be able to use their history as an aspect of their marketing, a newer sports team like the Toronto Raptors must focus on something else as history is not a strength of their team product.

Leagues

league: a group of teams; a service that provides the framework for sport competition; a sellable brand that can be sold as merchandise, is best represented by a logo and official name, and offers other benefits to the consumer, such as pride and nostalgia.

The league product form is very similar to that of the team product. While a team is made up of a group of athletes, the league is made up of a group of teams. The **league** is a service that provides the framework for sport competition. It is also a sellable brand that, like teams, can be sold as merchandise and is best represented by a logo and official name. However, the league product can offer other benefits to the consumer, such as pride and nostalgia. The Canadian Football League (CFL) is a league product that offers its consumers many benefits. First and foremost is a sense of "Canadian-ness." The CFL is the only major professional league made up of only Canadian teams. Fans feel a sense of pride about the Canadian nature of the league: The threat to this from possible expansion into the US was met with resistance, as fans felt that they were losing an integral part of the league product[20]. Once again, like the team product, it is the responsibility of the marketing professional to identify the elements of the league product that are of most value to current and potential consumers. The service of organizing the competition itself will always be an aspect of the league product, but it is the images associated with the league that can provide the best marketing potential.

Clubs

club: a service that offers consumers a chance to get involved with sport as a participant and that provides a social venue.

The **club** form product is a service that offers consumers a chance to get involved with sport as a participant rather than just a spectator and fan. All across the country are gymnastics clubs, figure skating clubs, curling clubs, golf clubs, and more. Each of these can provide the consumer with the opportunity, infrastructure, and coaching needed to participate in a sport. They also provide a social venue. Many people see socializing as a benefit of sport participation, and clubs (especially in golf clubs) offer an opportunity to get together and socialize with fellow participants. Some clubs are private, and only those who fulfill certain criteria and obligations can gain membership.

---

[20] Nauright, J. & P. White (2002) Mediated nostalgia, community and nation: The CFL in crisis and the demise of the Ottawa Rough Riders 1986–1996. *Sport History Review*, 33: 121–37.

Sometimes members may feel that the club membership offers them the opportunity to not only socialize but also make business contacts, all while getting in a great round of golf.

Facilities

The **facility** product form has seen many changes over the past 30 years, as "there have been improvements in facility construction, technology and design. Before these changes, sport took place in a basic facility designed only for enveloping the court, arena, or field. This meant the spectators comfort and other needs were not considered[21]." Not only has the facility product become an extension of the event product, but it also is a destination itself. Facilities now offer visitors more than just a place to sit when they attend a game; they offer a full entertainment service. The Rogers Centre in Toronto is an excellent example of a facility that offers more than just the basics: Its website[22] declares that the "Rogers Centre is recognized as one of the world's premier entertainment centres." While the facility is home to the Toronto Blue Jays and the Toronto Argonauts and offers its product as a place to watch their competitions, it is also home to numerous other features: 95 luxury suites, 4 major restaurants, a retractable roof, one of the world's largest video boards at 110 feet by 33 feet, a hotel, a fitness centre, and about $5 million worth of specially commissioned artwork[23]. These features have made the Rogers Centre not only a home for sports teams and fans but also one of the top three tourist attractions in Toronto[24]. Facilities have become such a product of their own that many authors argue that a new facility alone can significantly increase attendance with what they call the "stadium novelty effect[25]." Howard and Crompton[26] noted a significant increase in attendance in the first year a facility was open, and despite the substantial decline in attendance after the first year, later attendance was still better than it was before the new facility opened.

facility: an extension of the event product and a destination itself, often offering visitors not only a place to sit when they attend a game but also a full entertainment service.

Skilled Services

The **skilled services** product represents those aspects of the sport product form that involve a skilled professional providing a sport-related service to consumers that "influences the level of sport or fitness performance[27]." This can include fitness trainers, massage therapists, nutritionists, and athletic therapists. Statistics Canada announced that fitness and recreation centres

skilled services: those aspects of the sport product form that involve a skilled professional providing a sport-related service to consumers that influences the level of sport or fitness performance.

---

[21] Pitts, B.G., L.W. Fielding, & L.K. Miller (1994) Industry segmentation theory and the sport industry: Developing a sport industry segment model. *Sport Marketing Quarterly*, 3(1): 15–24.

[22] Rogers Centre (2006) About Rogers Centre: Rogers Centre history. Retrieved November 27, 2006 from http://www.rogerscentre.com/about/history/index.html.

[23] ibid.

[24] ibid.

[25] Howard, D.R. & J.L. Compton (2003) An empirical review of the stadium novelty effect. *Sport Marketing Quarterly*, 12(2): 111–6.

[26] ibid.

[27] Pitts, B.G., L.W. Fielding, & L.K. Miller (1994) Industry segmentation theory and the sport industry.

in Canada reported revenue of $1.5 billion in 2004, an increase of almost 21 percent over the previous year[28]. Recent trends toward more healthy active lifestyles have led to an increased demand for skilled sport product services.

In addition to fitness and health-related services, the skilled services product form includes coaching or instructional services. For instance, tennis professionals who give lessons are providing a service to their students in order to enhance the sport performance levels of their students. This product form can also include the provision of legal services. For example, professional sport agents look after their athlete-clients' interests in negotiating with clubs, leagues, schools, and sponsors.

Finally, sport agents and sport marketing agencies provide services to athletes, coaches, and sport properties. For example, the International Management Group (IMG), created in the 1960s by the late Mark McCormack, provides a bundle of services to their clients, including Canadian golfer Mike Weir. The agency may manage Weir's appearances at various events (sports and charities), sponsorship deals (Bell), and media tours and offer financial services as well.

Media

media: sport product form that depends on the production of sport events, athletes, leagues, and teams to provide the information they need to produce their own sport product.

Another sport product form is the sport specific **media** form. Numerous all-sport television stations, radio stations, newspapers, and magazines depend of the production of sport events, athletes, leagues, and teams to provide them with the information they need to produce their own sport product. The last 20 years have seen a boom in the number of sport media products, and this boom is "continually experiencing growth both in term of products and audience[29]." In Canada, the first sport-specific television channel was The Sports Network (TSN) launched in 1984. When it was getting started, people questioned how TSN would fill 24 hours of each day with sports. However, despite initial doubters and a rocky start, the channel broke even in its third year and saw profits peak in 1999 at about $35 million[30]. Although the increasing number of specialty channels as well as direct competition from other all-sport networks, SportNet and The Score, have led to a slight decline in profits in recent years, TSN is still the most watched and most profitable specialty channel in Canada[31]. Another newer form of sport media product is the Internet, increasingly popular as it can offer the sport fan a lot of information in one place. Not only do sports websites offer all the stats, scores, interviews, news articles, and pundits' opinions one can find in a newspaper, but they also offer live streaming video of games not broadcast on television. For example, for about $90 a year, fans can subscribe to Manchester United's official television station MUTV online so they do not miss a minute of the

---

[28] Canadian Press (2006) Fitness fuels bonanza for spas, golf courses and recreation centres. Canadian Press NewsWire, May 8.

[29] Shank, M.D. (2005) *Sports Marketing*: 21.

[30] Zelkovich, C. & G. Colbourn (2004) TSN bucked the odds. *Toronto Star*, September 1: C03.

[31] ibid.

action even though soccer is not covered in North America in the same way as baseball, football, hockey, or basketball[32]. At the very least, most sport websites now offer live scoring services with running commentary so sport fans can follow along as it updates and reloads every 30 seconds.

Merchandise

This section has classified many types of items under the heading of merchandise, including sport, fitness, and recreation equipment; sport and fitness apparel; and collectibles and memorabilia. All of these represent tangible goods that are "manufactured, distributed and marketed within the sport industry[33]." Sport, fitness, and recreation equipment as well as some of the sport and fitness apparel is then used in the production of the core sport product (a sport event), which further classifies them as an industrial good. For example, a curling broom is produced in a factory and is a tangible product; however, its purpose is to be used in the production of a game of curling. The merchandise sport product form is also tied significantly to the idea that sport is an entity that inspires emotions and creates a deep sense of personal attachment by the fan to the sport, league, or team. Burton explains that "the most visible method for reflecting the teams glory [is] for the fan to purchase and wear licensed clothing in public. In doing so, the fan moves one step closer to perceived team membership[34]."

The nine sport product forms discussed in this section are distinct yet interconnected. To get a full and complete understanding of the sport product, we must understand each form individually and the collective group. Sport marketers must be able to define what they are selling and understand the unique aspects of the product.

merchandise: tangible good that is manufactured, distributed, and marketed within the sport industry.

Sport Brands

The importance of branding is becoming increasing apparent in the field of sport marketing. While many professional teams and sporting good products have put significant time and money into branding for many years, it is only recently that everyone—from individual athletes to national sport organizations and university athletic departments in Canada—has begun to see branding as essential to their marketing plan. Shank[35] defines branding as a "name, design, symbol, or any combination that a sports organization uses to help differentiate its products from the competition," hopefully to have a positive impact on the behaviours of the targeted consumers[36]—an increase in attendance, more merchandise sales, or increased athlete recruiting opportunities, among other things. In most cases, an organization's **brand** involves

brand: the name, logo, and other outward symbols that distinguish a product or service from others in its category.

---

[32] Manchester United (2006) MUTV. Retrieved November 27, 2006 from http://www.manutd.com/default .sps?pagegid={E4451CDB-9ED3-4508-B3A4-8C21D482D430}.

[33] Shank, M.D. (2005) *Sports Marketing*: 18.

[34] Burton, R. (2004) Teams as brands: A review of the sport licensing concept. In Kahle, L.R. & C. Riley (eds) *Sport Marketing and the Psychology of Marketing Communication*. Lawrence Erlbaum: 260.

[35] Shank, M.D. (2005) *Sports Marketing*.

[36] ibid: 228.

a brand name, brand mark, and trademark. While it is not imperative that all three are present for a brand to exist, they each serve a specific function. Shank[37] defines a brand name as "the element of the brand that can be vocalized." For example, the BC Lions, Spalding, or the Calgary Stampede are all brand names. A brand name is the form of branding that is most often used and recognized[38]. In some cases, it is the only element in the marketing mix that cannot be copied and reproduced by a competitor[39]. Therefore, it is important for a brand name to conjure up a positive and memorable image in the consumers' mind[40]. A brand mark is the opposite to a brand name: It is the element of a brand that cannot be spoken. The flaming C of the Calgary Flames is a brand mark. Whether the brand name and brand mark are used in combination or separately, they should reflect the image the product is trying to sell. For example, in 2003, the Toronto Blue Jays were looking to revitalize their brand and so redesigned their logo to make it better reflect their current realities. The old logo was a "soft cartoon-like image," which the club did not think represented their new no-nonsense approach to the game[41]. Also the team had a second-season manager and many young players, so the Jays wanted to new logo to reflect the "young and hip" qualities of the team[42]. The third important branding concept is the trademark, which "identifies that a sports organization has legally registered its brand name or brand mark and thus prevents others from using it[43]." The money made from licensing official merchandise makes this an essential element of many brands as counterfeit merchandise can offer a severe threat to a company who has not protected its brand with a trademark.

One of the most important elements of building a brand is creating an emotional attachment between the consumer and the product. Richelieu[44] argues that this is so because if a product is able to capitalize on such an emotional attachment, it can trigger trust and loyalty toward the brand. In this area, many sport products have an advantage. Sport has the ability to create strong emotional ties between the fan and sport product forms like teams, leagues, and athletes. Both the team and its league are typically represented by a brand name and a brand mark. This means that, in many cases, the positive attachment associated with the team can be transferred to the brand name or mark, which should have a positive impact on brand equity[45].

---

[37] ibid: 225.

[38] Solomon, M.R., E.W. Stuart, A. Carson, & J.B. Smith (2003) *Marketing*.

[39] Shapiro, S.J., W.D. Perreault, & E.J. MacCarthy (1999). *Basic Marketing*.

[40] Solomon, M.R., E.W. Stuart, A. Carson, & J.B. Smith (2003) *Marketing*.

[41] Holloway, A. (2003) Brand new. *Canadian Business*, 76(18): 79.

[42] ibid.

[43] Shank, M.D. (2005) *Sports Marketing*: 227.

[44] Richelieu, A. (2004) *Sharing Best Practices in Sport Marketing*. Fitness Information Technology.

[45] Gladden, J.M. & G.R. Milne (1999) Examining the importance of brand equity in professional sport. *Sport Marketing Quarterly*, 8(1): 21–9.

Brand Equity

Aaker[46] defines brand equity as "a set of liabilities and assets linked to a brand, its name and symbol, that add to or subtract from the value provided by a product or service to a firm and/or to that firms customers," while Shank[47] defines it in economic terms as "the difference in value between a branded product and its generic equivalent." A study by Gladden and Milne[48] found that brand equity had a positive impact on merchandise sales and was more important in the sale of National Hockey League and Major League Baseball merchandise. In addition, the development of brand equity provides numerous other benefits for the sport product, which include increasing the probability of brand choice, consumer retention, profit margins, willingness to pay premium prices, marketing effectiveness, licensing opportunities, positive word of mouth, and potential for brand extensions[49]. The ability of brand equity to increase licensing opportunities as well as the potential for brand extensions are two important benefits for the sport product.

Licensing

Licensing is a vital aspect of the sport product brand. Shank[50] defines it as "a contractual agreement whereby a company [licensee] may use another company's trademark [licensor] in exchange for a royalty or fee. A branding strategy through licensing allows the organization to authorize the use of brand, brand name, brand mark, [or] trademark in conjunction with a good, service or promotion in return for royalties."

Licensing is seen everywhere one looks, with people dressed in Montreal Canadiens caps or Toronto Maple Leafs socks or carrying an Edmonton Oilers travel mug. In 2003, the Sporting Goods Manufacturers Association reported that licensing accounted for US$10.5 billion or about 5.4 percent of the total US sports industry sales. Of that amount, the NFL and NCAA each claimed US$2.5 billion, Major League Baseball US$2.3 billion, NASCAR US$1.2, National Basketball Association US$1 billion, National Hockey League US$900 million, and other leagues US$100 million[51]. While almost anything has been licensed, traditional sport products are apparel, collectibles, and sports equipment. New technologies, however, are leading a new generation of licensed products to the forefront, the most popular being video games. In 2001, the NHL attributed a 7 percent growth in licensed product sales primarily to the video game category[52]. Licensing offers many benefits to both licensor and licensee. For the licensee, benefits include a positive association with a

---

[46] Aaker, D.A. (1991) *Managing Brand Equity: Capitalizing on the Value of a Brand Name.* Free Press: 15.

[47] Shank, M.D. (2005) *Sports Marketing.*

[48] Gladden, J.M. & G.R. Milne (1999) Examining the importance of brand equity in professional sport.

[49] Ross, S.D. (2006) A conceptual framework for understanding spectator-based brand equity. *Journal of Sport Management,* 20(1): 22–38.

[50] Shank, M.D. (2005) *Sports Marketing*: 235.

[51] Sporting Goods Manufacturers Association (2002) Licensing revenue by league or governing body. *Sports Business Journal,* March 11–17.

[52] Bernstein, A. (2002) Licensed product sales up 7%, NHL says. *Sports Business Journal,* August 12–18: 5.

sport entity, greater brand awareness, and the ability to charge higher prices. For the licensor, it may allow them to experience new market penetration and to increase brand awareness[53]. However, there can also be disadvantages for both parties. The licensee is taking a risk that an athlete or team might do something that would damage to their brand. The licensor is running the risk of being associated with a product over which it has little control. For example, if the Canadian Football League signs a licensing agreement with a company that is going to produce footballs with the CFL brand mark on them, the league may not be able to ensure the quality of the finished product: A poor product could negatively affect the CFL brand.

Brand Extensions

This chapter has noted a unique characteristic of the sport product: It makes more sense for marketers to focus on product extensions rather than the core product, because the latter is usually an athletic event not under the control of the marketer. The coach will decide the team and the tactics, and it is up to the players to provide the win, with the marketing professional having no say. While it is not always possible for the marketer to have a say in the brand extensions either, it is more likely. Solomon and colleagues[54] define **brand extension** as "a new product sold with the same brand name as a strong existing brand," while Aaker[55] describes it as "the use of a brand name established in one product class to enter another product class." The common elements in these two definitions are the use of an already established brand and the loan of a brand from one entity to another. For example, LeafsTV is a specialty cable pay channel owned and operated by Maple Leaf Sports and Entertainment Ltd. It offers viewers exclusive Toronto Maple Leaf programming 24/7. In this case, the channel has taken the popularity of the Maple Leafs brand and used it to enter the media marketplace. Other examples of brand extensions are mascots and cheerleaders, team publications, youth leagues, merchandise stores, and sport camps and clinics[56]. Apostolopoulou[57] further identified six keys to successful brand extensions:

- the strength of the parent brand
- the perceived fit between the club and the extension
- the promotional support offered by the sport organization to the extension
- the quality of the extension product
- the distribution strategy
- the management of the extension

brand extension: the use of an already established brand and the loan of a brand from one entity to another.

---

[53] Mullin, B., S. Hardy, & W. Sutton (2000) *Sport Marketing*, 2nd ed. Human Kinetics.

[54] Solomon, M.R., E.W. Stuart, A. Carson, & J.B. Smith (2003) *Marketing* : 273.

[55] Aaker, D.A. (1991) *Managing Brand Equity*: 208.

[56] Apostolopoulou, A. (2002) Brand extensions by US professional sport teams: Motivations and keys to success. *Sport Marketing Quarterly*, 11(4): 205–14.

[57] ibid.

Within these strategies, the marketer can look for ways to help control the product and thus market the extension. For example, while the marketer may not be able to control the on-field performance, they will stand a better chance of ensuring that a proper fit is found between the club and the extension.

Sport Packaging

Throughout this chapter, we have discussed the idea of the sport product being made up of a collective group of product forms. This feature of the sport product makes it ideal for promotion as a package. Since each element of the sport product is interrelated, it is easy to combine the elements to make a full entertainment, or participant, sport package. Mullin and colleagues[58] state that, for the most part, the individual sport forms are but a small portion of the total entertainment package. When fans go to the baseball park, they no longer expect just to sit, watch the game and be entertained by what is happening on the field. At the Rogers Centre, for example, fans know there are numerous additions to, and distractions from, the core product that can hold their attention. The entertainment package may get under way even before the game does. With a hotel on the premises, fans may arrive the night before to get an early start on their fan experience. For those not staying in the hotel, there are still ways to start their night out before the first pitch is thrown. In fact, one of the restaurants at the Rogers Centre uses the slogan "the game starts here[59]." During the game, numerous products are being produced and consumed simultaneously. The video board shows replays, birthdays, and out-of-town highlights; and people often find they are watching the game on the big screen rather than on the field. There are also bands, cheerleaders, and mascots, which all create an atmosphere of excitement and involvement among the crowd so that they can feel engaged even during the most boring games. The concourse is also filled with things to do and see: In addition to numerous concession stands and merchandise outlets, there are usually games for children, draws, and promotional offers for adults. All of this leads to the creation of a total sport entertainment package. In some cases, fans could even go to the game and entertain themselves all night without ever watching a pitch thrown or a bat swung.

Other elements of the sport product can also be packaged. Many gyms and training centres bring in skilled professionals to meet the needs of their clients all under one roof. For example, a gym may offer fitness training, massage therapy, nutrition counselling, athletic therapy, and sports psychology to its members, along with the standard fitness classes and exercise equipment. They may also have a juice bar and a tanning salon, just to add that little bit extra to the experience.

---

[58] Mullin, B., S. Hardy, & W. Sutton (2000) *Sport Marketing.*

[59] Rogers Centre (2006) About Rogers Centre: Rogers Centre history.

Case: 2005 Mount Everest Expedition

The Beginning

On September 1, 2001, Dr. Sean Egan sat quietly in his office at the University of Ottawa. Although a renowned proponent of a positive outlook on life, he was having trouble smiling today: His dream of reaching the world's highest point on Mount Everest seemed in doubt. This didn't stem from his fitness, drive, or motivation, but from his inability to acquire the resources necessary to fund such an endeavour. As a professor and lifelong practitioner of health, Sean had rarely thought of things from a business strategy point of view and he was struggling. In his 1998 and 2000 trips to Everest, he'd gone as a researcher and been able to use funds from related grants and projects to cover his costs. Of course, those trips costs $10 000 and this one was looking to be over $100 000. Reaching the summit of the world's highest peak is not inexpensive.

In addition to being a recognized expert in health, Sean was an accomplished athlete, fundraiser, and proponent of a healthy lifestyle. He had led many groups on similar (but smaller) expeditions, including fundraising marathon walks and charity events. He had been a champion boxer, top marathon runner, accomplished ultra-marathon walker (e.g., he had walked from Toronto to Los Angeles), and cyclist (he had crisscrossed North America numerous times). And he was a natural leader. Organizing and detail were not his strengths; charisma and vision were. He was the kind of person who could walk into a room of strangers and engage everyone, and, by the end of the night, all would be gathered around him listening to his stories. People followed his teachings and changed their lifestyles because of him. His books were widely read and his following worldwide.

Sean wanted to reach the summit in the spring of 2004. His dream would see him become the second oldest man, and oldest Canadian, ever to climb Everest.

Over the summer, Sean had talked to all the key groups at the university, including deans, vice-president of development, and research directors, about funding. All had the same answer: Small grants for research projects were possible, but a large grant to support such an endeavour was not possible without external partners or support of a major granting agency. Both of these solutions were challenging, with the achievement of a major research grant bordering on impossible given that achieving the summit was Sean's primary goal. One positive response among the many negative was the pledge of the university advancement office to support the search for resources as part of their overall university fundraising. At first, that was a positive prospect; however, following a few meetings with the assigned officer, Sean was skeptical if anything would come of it, given the many priorities for funding.

Bottom line, he was on his own and knew he had to look for support. Having just turned 60 years old and with his final sabbatical slotted for 2004 or 2005, he knew time was not on his side. Was funding possible? What could he do? His dream was on the line.

Crunch Time

On September 1, 2003, Dr. Egan was once again sitting quietly in his office. He was reflecting on a few key achievements accomplished over the two years since he first dreamt of his climb to the summit of Everest. First, he asked his former teaching assistant and good friend, Norm O'Reilly, to develop a comprehensive business plan for the expedition. Norm, a sport business professor was tasked with the challenging job of raising the necessary resources for the project. At first, Norm focused on business planning aspect of the expedition but he soon became interested in the expedition itself—the trek to the mountain. Norm was an accomplished coach, business consultant, sport administrator, and athlete. He had competed internationally as a triathlete and been the captain of his university swim team but was still a novice mountain climber. Second, with some success and many failures, Sean approached others to become involved with his team, including local event planners, researchers, suppliers, and Canadian and international climbers. Third, Sean improved his own physical training and preparation significantly, spending many hours working on his technical climbing skills and endurance with major bicycle trips (e.g., Oregon to Ottawa), stair-climbing sessions (e.g., five-hour climb with 50 pounds on his back), weight training, and long walks (e.g., walk of 80 km), and a daily regimen of nutrition and fitness.

On the business side of the proposed trek, Sean had been working with Norm for over 18 months with some energy but limited success. Now was the critical moment, and he was excited about his trip the following week to Toronto to meet with Norm and his friend Harold Mah from the City of Toronto. Harold was an experienced and savvy event manager and marketer who was highly connected in the event industry in Toronto and recommended by Norm. Harold knew how things worked and how to get them done. He was an experienced athlete (triathlete and runner) and an amateur climber. If they were to go in the spring 2005, they needed to find some financial support soon. Otherwise, the dream would be put off further or given up entirely. Given the huge investment of time and energy by both Sean and Norm, this was not an appealing option.

Sean's focus on his physical training remained paramount, and he had plans to bicycle across Canada in the summer of 2004 (which he did) and to climb the highest mountain in South America, Aconcagua in Argentina in January 2005 (which he also accomplished) in preparation for his summit bid. Despite the success of his training, the generation of resources to support the climb was an ongoing challenge. Specifically, sponsorship remained a frustration, as he had made over 200 pitches with very little success. Communications were improving, with a functional website and decent media coverage in the Ottawa area.

The Meeting

Just a few weeks later in mid-September 2003, Sean, Norm, and Harold were at their three-day planning retreat in Toronto. Following some terrific team bonding, a review of progress to date, and a forecast of the potential for success, the group of three decided unanimously and strongly to forge ahead to make the trek a reality, acting as volunteers and committing to put in the hours necessary. They outlined a detailed plan for generating sponsorship interest and resources and put together a strategy and implementation plan. Implementation was to begin immediately: Another delay and the expedition would be unlikely to ever occur. Key aspects of the plan included:

1. A clearly defined product "research expedition to Mount Everest" with the theme "fitness and aging." The group reviewed many options and felt strongly that Sean and what he stood for—healthy living at an advanced age and high-quality research—were the key differentiating factors to success. Since Everest has been done before, this expedition had to be different in some respect.
2. The brand that would be promoted was based clearly on the first point—Sean, then research.
3. A recruitment plan to build a team of climbers, researchers, trekkers, and supporters developed to create a team that would be of value to sponsors and media.
4. A communications plan to build awareness of the team in the third point once built.

The team left with a positive feeling and confidence that only an achievable plan could provide. In the weeks that followed, a key sleep researcher from the University of Ottawa, researchers from throughout Europe, climbers worldwide, and various interest groups all expressed interest in joining the expedition. Although many would not join in the end, the energy was there, and the buzz led to a well-sponsored team of 20 heading to Everest in late winter 2005. The expedition ended up as the "Kanatek Expedition to Mount Everest 2005" with Kanatek Technologies, an Ottawa-based systems integrator, as title sponsor after originally turning down the opportunity in 2002. Interestingly, they supported the expedition as a business decision to promote their organization and achieve very specific objectives. Other sponsors included Hewlett-Packard, Energizer, and Urban Voyageur.

The Climb

In March 2005, a group of 20 left from Canada (Ottawa, Toronto, and Montreal), Australia, and the United States to embark on an adventure of a lifetime. They included the expedition leader planning to summit (Sean), the base camp manager (Harold), 10 researchers, and 8 trekkers. One additional researcher accompanied the team to Kathmandu but did not go up the mountain. The 10-day trek to base camp was a resounding success. All 20 members made it without major issue or health problems. The training had been worthwhile, and, even better, the team bonded exceptionally well. Friends were made on the trail, fun was had, and an experience to last a lifetime unfolded. In addition to the ongoing research activities, a number of media activities took place, including nightly connection via satellite to the Internet and sending blog messages and photos to a website that had nearly 100 000 readers by the end of the trek. Sean made special calls to elementary schools in the wee hours of the morning and backed up data (PDA to laptop to Ottawa via satellite) vital to the success of the researchers.

Arrival at base camp was a celebration followed by a week of camaraderie, continued research, and climbing preparations. The world's highest hockey game took place on day 3 and research wrapped up on day 5. However, this was little consolation for the difficult life at base camp. Ice, snow, desolation, and boredom hit many of the team, and they were happy to be out of there after the week. Only Sean, Harold, and a couple of researchers remained after the week.

A few days later, once acclimatized, Sean, Harold, and their Sherpas began preparations and training to build towards Sean's summit attempt. They scaled to Camp 1 and back down. Then Sean and a couple of the Sherpas got sick, some kind of bug that they couldn't shake. During his run to Camp 2, Sean was forced to turn back. He visited a doctor at base camp who said he had a cold. He knew better: Something was wrong, and he began to head down for a second opinion. Only a few hours' walk from the closest hospital, he was forced to stop. He called a helicopter but died awaiting its arrival. Final reports confirmed a combination of factors including a lung infection caused Sean's death.

Post-Climb: Reality Bites

Many of the team had difficulty with Sean's passing, both personally and professionally. Many mourned and made life changes. Almost all sponsorship and promotional plans post-climb were cancelled. A few of the research projects were completed and published although many never came to fruition. Sean's planned outputs (a book and a few articles) were never realized. Team members channeled their grief by rallying around a fund-raising effort- the Ad Astra campaign- to build a school at a Nepalese orphanage in Sean's honor. A number of initiatives (golf tournament, fundraising banquets, Nepal-theme dinners, etc.) raised $150,000 to build the school. It took the group approximately 2 years to raise this amount.

In the year following Sean's death, it was widely assumed that his vision would be lost. However, quietly and devotedly, Elia Saikaly- one of the documentary filmmakers on the expedition- had other plans. During 2005, he had spent countless hours with Sean late at night in his tent filming Sean's deepest thoughts and visions. Just chatting and sharing. Like hundreds of students before him, Elia was captured by Sean and, upon Sean's death, took it up on himself to take up the torch, change his life and carry on with the vision. This was exemplified by his "Finding Life" (www.findinglife.ca) vision which was how he encapsulated how Sean viewed the world.

Case Questions

1. Define the sport product of this case.
2. Why might defining the product be the most important marketing decision that made the expedition possible?
3. Why were they successful in raising sponsorship dollars?
4. In your opinion, what went wrong? What could have been done differently to create a positive outcome?
5. With respect to their goal of building a team, what marketing approaches would you recommend to Sean, Norm, and Harold in 2003 to encourage sponsors, trekkers, climbers, and researchers to join the trek?
6. Using sport product theory, what other marketing approaches could the expedition have used?

Chapter Summary

This chapter discusses the well-developed marketing concept of a product as a bundle of attributes that satisfy a particular market need and then presents the first element of the sport marketing mix—the sport product. The uniqueness of the sport product is emphasized throughout the chapter, as it takes on one of the four product forms (tangible good, service, behaviour, idea). Examples include a running shoe (tangible good), coaching (service), anti-doping (behaviour), and believing in sport participation as a solution to childhood obesity (idea). We introduce strategic elements of sport product marketing, including the product life cycle, brands, licensing, and packaging, as well as the nine specific sport product forms are also introduced—events, athletes, teams, leagues, clubs, facilities, skilled services, media, and merchandise.

Test Your Knowledge

1. What must a marketer do before defining their sport product?
2. What is a sport product?
3. Is a sport product different from other products? Explain.
4. List the nine forms of sport products provided in the chapter and give an example of each?
5. An additional sport product form is presented in the chapter case. Can you think of any others?
6. Why is a skilled service a sport product?
7. What is the difference between merchandising and licensing?

 For more review questions, go to http://www.sportmarketing.nelson.com.

Key Terms

athletes

brand

brand extension

club

event

facility

league

media

merchandise

packaging

skilled services

sport product

team

A full glossary of key term definitions is located at http://www.sportmarketing.nelson.com.

Internet Resources

Callaway Golf, http://www.callawaygolf.com/ca.html

SportsNet, http://www.sportsnet.ca/

TSN, http://www.tsn.ca/

Toronto Maple Leafs, http://www.mapleleafs.com/

Mount Everest, http://www.mounteverest.net/

Nike Bauer, http://www.nikebauer.com/

**Upper Deck trading cards,
http://sports.upperdeck.com/collectorszone/cardsethome.aspx?sid=45373**

MLB shop, http://shop.mlb.com/home/index.jsp

NHL auction network, http://auction.nhl.com/

Chapter 7

Branding in Sport

Source: Jeff Vinnick/Stringer / Getty Images

Learning Objectives

- To appreciate the role of branding in sport
- To understand and apply the concept of brand equity in the sport settings
- To understand the role of brand management in sport
- To appreciate the consequences of strong brand equity

Introduction

A brand is our most important intangible asset

The concept of **brand** is one that has been studied widely across the marketing industry. Marketing scholars such as David Aaker[1], Kevin Keller[2], and Jean-Noel Kapferer[3] all suggest that a brand is a company's greatest asset. The study of brand concepts in the sport settings remains relatively new. However, few domains generate as much passion from its customers as sport[4]. Capitalizing on the consumers' (i.e., the fans) emotional attachment to a team, club, or sport, sports marketing fosters an associative symbolism that can trigger trust and loyalty toward a sport brand[5]. This loyalty can help

brand: the name, logo, or other outward symbol that distinguishes a product or service from others in its category.

---

[1] Aaker, D.A. (1992) The value of brand equity. *Journal of Business Strategy*, 13(4): 27–32.

[2] Keller, K.L. (2003) *Strategic Brand Management*, 2nd ed. Prentice Hall.

[3] Kapferer, J.-N. (1998) *Les marques, capital de l'entreprise: Créer et développer des marques fortes*, 3rd ed. Éditions d'Organisation.

[4] Séguin, B., A. Richelieu, & N. O'Reilly (2008) Leveraging the Olympic Brand through the reconciliation of corporate and consumers' brand perceptions. *International Journal of Sport Management and Marketing*.

[5] Richelieu, A. (2004) A new brand world for sports teams. In *Sharing Best Practices in Sport Marketing: The Sport Marketing Association's Inaugural Book of Papers*: 3–20.

the sports team generate additional revenues through the sale of a variety of goods and services, within and beyond the sports arena[6]. Think of strong sport brands like Hockey Canada or the Toronto Maple Leafs. They are able to make the customers live through their brands at many different levels in their daily lives (e.g., wearing the jersey of Matt Sundin with his name and number proudly displayed on the back) with unwavering loyalty. This has been seen in professional sport franchises and could similarly be applied to other Olympic sport organizations (e.g., Skate Canada, Rowing Canada).

A strong brand enables a company to differentiate itself from its competitors and create close relationships with consumers. This is especially true in sports where the connections between the brand and consumers usually happen in a highly charged emotional environment. A well-established brand is usually one that consumers is aware of and is associated with trust, quality, and perceived value. Consider brands like the Olympics, Montreal Canadiens, the X-Games, and, for baby boom generation skiers, the Crazy Canucks. Just mentioning their names invoke, in the minds of consumers, a certain image, a memory, associated attributes, and other related products and services. The value of a brand to a sport organization can outlast its equipment, its employees and even its products. This chapter introduces the concept of a brand, clarifying what branding is, and the concept of brand equity and how to manage it.

EXECUTIVE PERSPECTIVE

Scott Smith, Senior Executive Vice-President, Hockey Canada

The Hockey Canada Brand—A Source of Revenue and Inspiration

Since the early 1990s, Hockey Canada has adopted a brand strategy whose success is off the charts. In fact, our merchandising has gone from minimal levels to nearly $55 million in revenue (retail values) in 2005. Next to the NHL teams, our brand is the most valued sport property in Canada. One agency has estimated that Hockey Canada holds 15% of the sport merchandising market in Canada.

How did it all begin? The mid-1990s was a time of great on-ice performance by our teams. The National Junior Men's Team won five World Championships in a row, and our National Women's Team won all four Women's World Championships between 1990 and 1997. With the merger that created Hockey Canada in 1994, we decided to create a brand that would be instantly recognizable as hockey and Canada. Additionally, senior management made the decision that all of Hockey Canada's

teams would start playing in the same uniform with one look and one brand. This was a major change as up until then, all teams (e.g., men, women, junior, under-18) had played in their own distinct jerseys. After considerable discussion and deliberation, we requested proposals for a new brand that would achieve this goal. Of the many proposals submitted, we selected three for further consideration. The suggestion determined to be best for Hockey Canada was a proposal that asked only for a small percentage of future merchandise sales. However, our negotiators, determining the brand would be a revenue-generating success, said no and offered a lump sum so we'd be free of any future takes on revenues. That turned out to be a very wise decision.

And, how did it become a success? Clearly, we didn't do it alone. We focused on activation and pushing our sponsors and co-sponsors to activate with us. This means that our partners used our brand in their own communications programs giving us great brand visibility and, in

---

[6] Gustafson, A. (2001) Advertising's impact on morality in society: Influencing habits and desires of consumers. *Business and Society Review*, 106(3): 201–23.

turn, maximized the impact of the sponsorships. As our brand increased in value, so did the desire of our sponsors (*and* non-sponsors) to link to our brand as well. Partners like Esso, Bauer, Telus, RBC, and TSN have all leveraged their investments in Hockey Canada significantly, and their promotions of hockey in their marketing programs further build the Hockey Canada brand. Brand building is a long-term process, and we have made a few changes along the way. For example, the humorous message in a series of television commercials of one of our partners during the 2002 Olympic Winter Games caused some negative consumer reaction toward the sponsors and our brand. In fact, after a few broadcasts of that commercial, complaints arrived from all over the country with people upset at the way the promotions were referring to the other nations. Later, we decided that the presentation of our brand would always be in a positive light. This policy, I believe, has had an enormous effect on the continually increasing value of our brand and its presentation.

What else happened to develop our brand. First, the incredible growth in fan interest, media coverage, and youth participation in the women's game—a ten-fold increase since the mid-1990s—has really created a property of value with a significant following. Second, the steady and rapid growth of the World Junior Championships (men) has really played into the growth of the brand, as this event emphasizes Canadian pride as future top stars are playing for their country prior to playing in the NHL. Third, the inclusion of ice hockey on the program of the Olympic Games in 1998 where the top players in the world were wearing our mark was a tremendous step forward.

If I had to summarize the key factors of our brand, I'd say that:

1. Canadian pride—a vital component of our success, a huge value to our brand, and important to the Canadian marketplace.

2. Hockey success on the ice.

3. Playing in a healthy, quality way.

Today, we protect our brand with diligence. Our law firm in Calgary handles trademark protection. This entire process is known as brand protection, or basically countering the ambush marketing that damages our brand equity. Here, our efforts include a variety of activities designed to enhance the equity of our brand and to protect the interests of all our stakeholders, including working with external partners to proactively deal with the key issues of the day like ambush marketing and anti-doping.

What's next? We want to continue to our efforts to support Hockey Canada's core mandate, the game on the ice, and to follow the lead of great sport marketers like the NBA to take our brand international.

Scott Smith was named senior executive vice-president in 2006 and is currently in his eleventh year with Hockey Canada with a leadership role in the business related responsibilities of the national sport organization.

Branding Defined

Upshaw[7] defines brand as "the name, logo, and other outward symbols that distinguish a product or service from others in its category." Aaker[8] suggests that a brand points to the source of the product and also serves to protect the customer and the producer from the competitors who attempt to provide products that appear to be identical. The latter is important, especially in light of ambush marketing, which we discuss in Chapter 13.

---

[7] Upshaw, L.B. (1995) *Building Brand Identity: A Strategy for Success in a Hostile Marketplace.* John Wiley & Sons: 11.

[8] Aaker, D.A. (1991) *Managing Brand Equity: Capitalizing on the Value of a Brand Name.* The Free Press.

The sport industry has grown tremendously in the past few decades. There are more spectators at events (on-site and television), more media covering and specializing in sport, more jobs, more sport merchandise being sold[9]. This has created a highly cluttered environment, which has made it extremely difficult for sport organizations to attract and maintain consumers' attention and, more importantly, loyalty. Sport organizations have to appeal to a variety of consumers, including spectators who observe sporting events (on-site or on television), participants who take part in sporting events, and sponsors who exchange money or product for the right to be associated with a sport.

The need to break through the clutter has led many sport organizations to adapt business principles to the management of their products. An increasingly popular business technique sporting bodies use is **branding**. The purpose of branding a product, such as an event, is to allow the organization to distinguish and differentiate itself from all others in the marketplace[10]. A brand can enable differentiation via product-related effects (i.e., perceived quality in consumers' minds), price-related factors (i.e., a stronger brand reduces the number of customers lost following a price increase), messaging effects (i.e., a strong brand results in better promotional effects), distribution channel factors (i.e., retailers are keen to include well-known brands on their shelves), and purchase decision process effects (i.e., strong brands are more likely selected when consumers scan the alterative choices available to them). For example, the Toronto Maple Leaf brand with a very rich history is well known across the country. Even though sport marketers have little control over the core product (i.e., the team's performance), its product extensions have been of high quality (e.g., Air Canada Centre, entertainment, promotions). This is reflected in the price of tickets, which has traditionally been higher than for other NHL teams: Few tickets are available game in and game out. In addition, television ratings, merchandising sales, and sponsorship dollars have skyrocketed. These are all signs of a very strong brand.

Consumers know a brand, first by its brand name, which can be one or more words (Winnipeg Blue Bombers), logo or trademark (Nike swoosh), or sound representative of the brand name (rally song or motto of a sport team), since the brand can be communicated physically and emotionally. Often accompanying the brand name is a slogan, such as Nike's "just do it" or NHL's "Hockey the fastest game on earth." In selecting brand names, marketers must consider a number of important aspects or risks affecting the long-term viability of the brand and the equity it could generate. Brand name selection must recognize both the semantics and the phonetics of the name itself and how easy the name is to read, say, and memorize. A difficult name to pronounce may affect brand development. Further, cultural and linguistic differences must be accounted for, specifically in a country like Canada where a majority of the Quebec population speaks French. Hence, a company interested in creating a brand must consider the language and cultural differences. Similarly, the marketer must be aware of differences when engaged in international business where the brand name must function in different countries: A name with another negative meaning

---

[9] Shank, M.D. (2002) *Sports Marketing: A Strategic Perspective*, 2nd ed. Prentice Hall.
[10] ibid.

in another country can hinder the brand's performance there. Well-planned and selected brand names and slogans help build consumer brand awareness, increase the brand's perceived quality, create the associations consumers make with the brand, and support consumer loyalty.

When a brand is known to have high level of awareness, is perceived as a quality product (including extensions and entertainment), has strong associations and high level of loyalty (sell out, merchandise sales, ratings), it is known to have high brand equity.

Brand Equity

Brand equity is "a set of assets and liabilities linked to a brand, its name and symbol, that adds to or subtracts from the value provided by its product or service to a firm and/or to that firm's customers[11]." These assets and liabilities differ from context to context. As marketers strive to build equity in their brands, they need to benchmark their successes by measuring brand equity at different times. For example, measures before and after a marketing campaign, a new product launch, or a specified period of time (e.g., quarter, year) will reveal—controlling for external influences—the changes in brand equity. Another important concept for building brand equity is brand identity, "a unique set of brand associations that the brand strategists aspire to create or maintain. These associations represent what the brand stands for and imply a promise to customers from the organization members. Brand identity should help establish a relationship between the brand and the customer by generating a value proposition involving functional, emotional, or self-expressive benefits[12]."

While relatively new to sports, brand concepts have increased in importance over the past few years, especially in relation to professional team sports (e.g., Manchester United, New York Yankees, Toronto Maple Leafs). As a result, a number of academics have begun to study brand concepts in sport. A leading scholar of **brand management** in sport is Dr. Jay Gladden, a sport marketing professor at the University of Massachusetts Amherst. His extensive work on brand equity in intercollegiate athletics and professional teams has provided a framework to study a number of brand concepts (e.g., image, loyalty, associations) in the context of team sports. Gladden and colleagues[13] have developed a model of assessing brand equity for sport teams by extending the previous work of Aaker,[14] who suggested four components that contribute to brand equity: brand awareness, perceived quality, brand associations, and brand loyalty.

Brand Awareness

Building the first component of brand equity, brand awareness—the likelihood with which a brand name will be recalled or recognized—is getting your potential market(s) to know about you and your products. For a local triathlon club such as the North Shore Triathlon Club, brand awareness can

brand equity: set of assets and liabilities linked to a brand, its name, and symbol, that adds to or subtracts from the value provided by its product or service to a firm and/or to that firm's customers.

brand management: strategic implementation of all aspects of the brand, aligning all of the brand's attributes for maximum effectiveness and ensuring that no organization action compromises the brand.

---

[11] Aaker, D.A. (1991) *Managing Brand Equity*: 12.

[12] Keller, K.L. (2003) *Strategic Brand Management*, 2nd ed. Prentice Hall: 763.

[13] Gladden, J.M. & G.R. Milne (1999) Examining the importance of brand equity in professional sport. *Sport Marketing Quarterly*, 8(1): 21–9.

[14] Aaker, D.A. (1991) *Managing Brand Equity*.

Chapter 7: Branding in Sport

refer to the familiarity of the residents of North Shore and surrounding areas with its name and logo. The club may be competing for attention against other triathlon clubs and clubs from other sports. Therefore, a high level of awareness can help it get some attention. The marketer of the club should pay close attention to the quality of services/programs it offers since quality is closely related to awareness: Consumers often assume that a familiar brand is probably reliable and of reasonable quality. For the North Shore Triathlon Club, quality can be measured in many ways, such as: certification level of coaches in the club, number of athletes competing for the club, performance results at competition, quality and number of educational programs, social benefits of being a member, quality and number of events organized. Awareness is important when measuring brand equity for these reasons[15]:

1. Awareness increases the likelihood that a brand will be considered by consumers.
2. Awareness can affect the decisions about brands in the product category or consideration set.
3. Awareness influences the development and depth of brand associations.

Research indicates that the Olympic symbol, the five interlocking rings, is the most recognized symbol in the world. A 2006 study conducted in 11 countries found that the Olympic Games have over 94 percent recognition, ahead of the brand symbols of such multinational corporations as Shell, McDonald's, and Mercedes and such other well-known organization as Red Cross and United Nations[16].

By attaining a high level of awareness, a company can benefit from having something with which other associations can be attached. For example, the Montreal Canadiens hockey club has a long-standing reputation of success and a fan base that reaches far beyond Montreal; and this attracts the interest of corporate sponsors (e.g., Bell, Molson) that seek a similar reputation. Brand awareness creates liking or familiarity with the brand and signals substance/commitment of the firm over a long period of time. This sends a message to consumers that the brand is worth considering[17].

Perceived Quality

The second component of brand equity, perceived quality is "the customer's perception of the overall quality or superiority of a product or service with respect to its intended purpose, relative to alternatives[18]." The sport marketer focuses on building the quality of their brand, as consumers perceive it: The higher the perceived quality of one's brand, the more likely consumers are to build strong associations with it and become loyal customers. Perceived quality is measured by recall, a market research technique that also enables a marketer

---

[15] Keller, K.L. (1993) Conceptualizing, measuring, and managing customer–based brand equity. *Journal of Marketing*, 57(1): 1–22.

[16] International Olympic Committee (2006) *2006 Global Brand and Consumer Research: The Power of the Olympic Brand*. IOC Television and Marketing Services, IOC.

[17] Aaker, D.A. (1991) *Managing Brand Equity*.

[18] ibid: 85.

to discover if potential consumers remember the product and its associations. Note that perceived quality is a perception by customers, an intangible, overall feeling about a brand. Since perceived quality is linked to purchase decisions, it can make all elements of the marketing program more effective.

Gladden and colleagues[19] describe the perceived quality of sport as consumers' perceptions of a team's success. However, the quality of product extensions also plays a role in building associations. The concept of perceived value can be extended beyond the notion of a team to other sport products such as a sporting event. For example, the perceived quality of the Olympic brand refers to the importance consumers place on the benefits and attributes associated with the Olympics. These will be discussed in detail in Chapter 17.

Consumer perception of high quality benefits a brand in numerous ways:

- It gives consumers faced with numerous choices a reason to buy the product.
- It can be used to differentiate a product and position it against other similar ones. For example, a sport marketer may be better equipped to use a premium pricing strategy.
- It encourages the distribution channel to treat the brand better.
- It makes it easier for sport marketers to build brand extensions.

Brand Association and Brand Image

A **brand association** is anything linked in memory to a brand[20]. It is an intangible set of associations that can be categorized as experiential (what it feels like to use the product) and symbolic (benefits that satisfy underlying needs for social approval and personal expression)[21]. For example, a local curling club can link a number of associations to its brand. Consumers may associate the club with fun, togetherness, friendship, community, competitions, health, and more. The marketer who knows what consumers associate with the club can develop outreach programs and communication strategies to reinforce those associations between the club and consumers. This is important since a link to a brand will be stronger when it is based on many experiences or exposures to communications[22].

Brand association is closely related to **brand image**. An association and an image both represent perceptions that may or may not reflect reality. Positioning is closely related to association and image concepts except that it implies a term of reference, the reference point usually the competition. A well-positioned brand has a competitively attractive position supported by strong associations. A brand position does reflect how people perceive a brand; however, positioning can reflect how a firm is trying to be perceived.

The underlying value of a brand name often is its set of associations—its meaning to people. In the case of sport, brand associations refer to the intangible attributes of a brand, the experiential and symbolic attributes offered by

brand association: anything linked in memory to a brand; an intangible set of associations that can be categorized into experiential and symbolic.

brand image: the impression a brand conveys to consumers.

---

[19] Gladden, J. M., G.R. Milne, & W.A. Sutton (1998) A conceptual framework for evaluating brand equity in Division I college athletics. *Journal of Sport Management*, 12(1): 1–19.

[20] Aaker, D.A. (1991) *Managing Brand Equity.*

[21] Milne, G.R. & M.A. McDonald (1999) *Sport Marketing: Managing the Exchange Process.* Jones and Bartlett.

[22] Aaker, D.A. (1991) *Managing Brand Equity.*

an athletic team, sport event, or league. Milne and McDonald[23] suggest that "both the emotional identification with a particular team and the exhilaration derived from attending a sporting event would be considered brand association." It is critical that sport organizations/events begin to understand the attributes associated with their sports/events. Ultimately, some combination of tangible and intangible attributes creates a brand identity.

The Olympic brand has its own set of expectations and associations; and the public, the Olympic family, and its commercial partners all perceive these in different ways. Over the years, the Olympics have developed strong sets of associations with consumers all over the world.

Aaker[24] suggests that having clear brand associations helps the consumer process and retrieve information on the brand. In addition, it is easier to differentiate between brands and position them using various attributes. It gives consumers reasons to buy the product (want to benefit form the associations of the brand) and may result in positive attitudes and feelings towards it[25].

Brand Loyalty

The brand loyalty of the customer base is often at the core of a brand's equity. Thus, if customers pay little attention to brand features, price, and convenience and to the brand name, it is unlikely that they would equate much equity in that brand. If, on the other hand, they continue to purchase the brand, even in the face of competitors with superior features, price, and convenience, substantial value exists in the brand and possibly its symbol and slogan. Brand loyalty, long a central construct in marketing, is a measure of the attachment a customer has to a brand[26].

There are four proven ways to build or sustain brand loyalty[27]:

1. Make sure that the brand lives up to customers' expectations (brand promise).
2. Build innovation into current products/services and introduce innovative new entries as often as possible.
3. Design loyalty-building programs into marketing activities.
4. Invest in marketing support to strengthen the brand identity.

Loyal customers are great assets to a firm. They are familiar with the brand, they have developed associations with it, and they know what to expect from it. As a result, marketers don't need to invest as much in marketing communications programs, thus reducing marketing costs[28]. For some firms, loyal customers provide opportunities to leverage the trade. For example, the Vancouver Canucks may be able to leverage their relationship with the local television networks to increase broadcast rights and/or the number of televised games as a result of high television ratings. Another benefit of having loyal customers

---

[23] Milne, G.R. & M.A. McDonald (1999) *Sport Marketing*: 46.

[24] Aaker, D.A. (1991) *Managing Brand Equity*.

[25] ibid.

[26] ibid.

[27] Upshaw, L.B. (1995) *Building Brand Identity: A Strategy for Success in a Hostile Marketplace.* John Wiley & Sons.

[28] Aaker, D.A. (1991) *Managing Brand Equity*.

is the potential to attract new ones through word-of-mouth communication as a result of increased awareness and by reassuring potential customers that the brand is of high quality. Finally, having loyal customers provides a firm with time to respond to competitive threats or in times of crisis as the loyal customers will stay with the firm's products longer than would non-loyal customers[29].

Aaker[30] suggests that a high level of brand equity adds value to both the customers and the firm (Figure 7-1). However, managing the components of brand equity will result in consequences for customers and the firm that will increase the overall brand equity.

FIGURE 7-1

Brand Equity Model

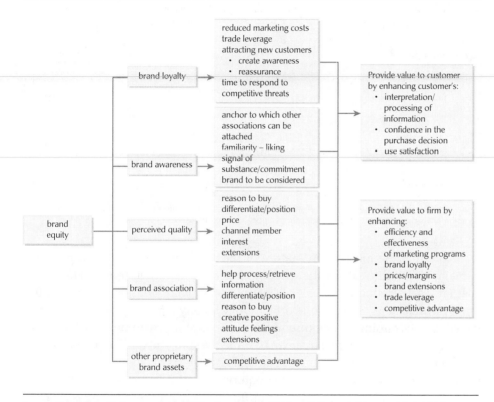

Source: Reprinted with the permission of The Free Press, a Division of Simon & Schuster dult Publishing Group, from MANAGING BRAND EQUITY: Capitalizing on the Value of a Brand Name by David A. Aaker. Copyright © 1991 by David A. Aaker. All rights reserved..

Conceptual Framework of Team Sport Brand Equity

The conceptual framework of team sport brand equity developed by Gladden and colleagues in 1998[31] suggests that prior to reaching brand equity, all of these must be in place—a team (success and head coach), an organization (tradition,

---

[29] ibid.

[30] ibid.

[31] Gladden, J. M., G.R. Milne, & W.A. Sutton (1998) A conceptual framework for evaluating brand equity in Division I college athletics.

conference, and logo), and a market (media coverage and geographic location). These three antecedents will contribute to brand equity, which will then lead to six forms of marketplace consequences: national media exposure, merchandise sales, individual donations, corporate support, atmosphere, and ticket sales.

FIGURE 7-2

Conceptual Framework of Team Sport Brand Equity

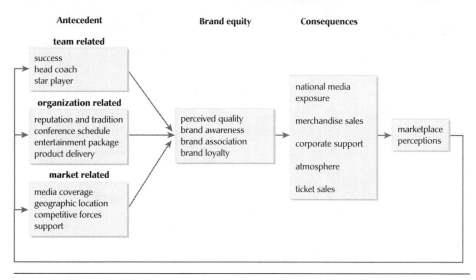

Source: Gladden, J.M., Milne,G.R., & Sutton,W.A.(1998) A conceptual framework for evaluating brand equity in Division 1 college athletics, Journal of Sport Management, 12(1),1-19

Note that the inconsistent nature of the sport product (e.g., competition, game) makes it difficult for the sport marketer to retain customers[32]. Therefore, customer satisfaction must be emphasized as the main reinforcement tool for repeat purchasing. Since the sport product largely provides only intangible benefits, determining the requirements for generating customer satisfaction is more difficult than in mainstream marketing. Despite the challenges, customer loyalty is critical to building brand equity as it protects against aggressive competitors who could undermine brand equity. In addition, it provides the assurance of a predictable level of sales in difficult times, such as a losing season.

The Olympic brand has been the target of numerous ambush marketing cases since 1984. Companies use this aggressive behaviour to achieve such objectives as gaining some of the benefits of an official sponsor or weakening the benefits that official sponsors, mostly competitors, gain from such an association. In the long term, this could have serious negative impact on the brand equity of the Olympics. By establishing strong brand loyalty, the Olympic movement may be in a better position to protect its own brand and the brand of its sponsors.

---

[32] ibid.

The Branding Process

In striving to achieve a unique brand that gives their organization an advantage over the competition, sport marketers follow a process to develop that brand. At the same time, the marketers have to develop the brand and understand the target market(s). The secret to success in branding is creating a brand with an image that perfectly matches the image that the target market(s) seek association with. Figure 7-3 outlines the branding process and emphasizes how it takes place in the minds of consumers.

FIGURE 7-3

Branding Process

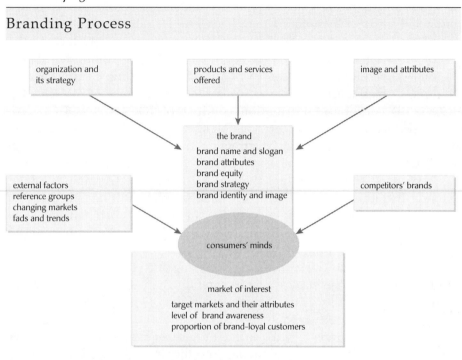

The importance of brands and their management has led to the common practice of the brand audit. This involves assessing each element of Figure 7-3 by adopting various principles of market research to examine how all aspects of the organization relate to its brand. The objective is to identify any element(s) that are not supporting the brand and alter them so that they do. A good marketing manager always plans marketing-related activities to align with their brand.

Real-Life Brand Management

So What Does This All Mean?

Throughout this chapter, we've outlined many of the key aspects of branding theory and provided a diagram of the sponsorship process, which clearly demonstrates how and where it works. But what does this mean? How does one use it?

Whether a marketer is working in a multinational organization or running their own local company, the noted branding concepts will enhance their success. As the identity by which their business will be known to consumers and other stakeholders, the brand is essential to its long-term survival. An organization benefits from managing its brand and not letting it develop on its own. It is the job of the marketer to do this and to strategize and implement all aspects of the brand, aligning all of its attributes for maximum effectiveness, ensuring that all actions made by the organization do not compromise the brand.

Brand Management—The Case of Olympic Brand

Using his determinants of corporate image and the results of a major study conducted on the Olympics[33] (quantitative and qualitative), we adopted Keller's corporate image model to identify factors.: i) the product, ii) the corporate social conduct of the International Olympic Committee (IOC), National Olympic Committees (NOC), and Organizing Committees of Olympic Games (OCOG), corporate employees conduct of IOC/NOC/OCOG, iii) corporate contribution conduct of IOC/NOC/OCOG, iv) company business conduct of IOC/NOC/OCOG, v) communications, vi) marketing/brand teams, vii) distribution channels, viii) price, ix) service, and x) support. Figure 7-4 outlines the Olympic brand management system.

Product(s): The athletes are the key feature to the Olympic product. Through the athletes, such Olympic ideals as excellence, fair play, ethics, friendship, and respect are brought to life. In addition, their achievements provide a high level of entertainment, thus attracting a wide audience. The Olympic product has been durable and consistent over the years making it a reliable product. However, incidents of doping and cheating, which are in direct opposition to the ideals, must be carefully managed and controlled to ensure long-term quality. The sport program of the Olympic Games (competitions) will have to be relevant to the consumers. In addition, the entertainment component will continue to grow in importance as television and sponsors continue to invest large sums of money into the Olympic Games. Attention must be given to product extensions (host cities, facilities at Games, merchandising, promotions), which can have an impact on brand.

Corporate employee conduct: This is a challenging task for the IOC, which has been blamed for laxity in this area for a number of years. The corporate culture has led to abuse of power, scandals, and other questionable behaviour on the part of IOC members in recent years. The corporate culture and the brand culture must be aligned if brand equity is to be achieved. Thus, the creation of an ethics commission was an important step taken by the IOC in

---

[33] Séguin, B. (2003) Représentations d'acteurs sociaux sur la relation entre le marketing et les Jeux olympiques. Unpublished doctoral thesis, Université Marc Bloch, Strasbourg, France.

creating a code of conduct that all members and employees involved in the Olympic organization will have to respect. Employees must stay true to the brand essence (values and ethics of the brand).

Corporate social conduct: The Olympic movement has made great progress in recent years dealing with environmental and peace initiatives (Olympic Truce). In addition, the work done through Olympic solidarity in helping developing nations with sport facilities, equipments, educations, and so on should be enhanced and communicated to the public.

Corporate contributions' conduct: Olympic solidarity is a program that many of the Olympic Partners identified as vital to the Olympic image. Several million dollars have been donated for a variety of causes. Once again, these programs should be developed further and integrated into a strategic public relations program. The Olympic organization has been involved in education projects with schools, universities, the International Olympic Academy, and a number of national Olympic academies.

Company business conduct: This was another area identified as a brand liability. The lack of marketing expertise in a majority of NOCs created problems in creating consistency with the Olympic brand. In addition, many indicated that the IOC was not investing enough in brand-related programs. The lack of true understanding of brand management within the entire organization was also of concern. Other issues were related to community rather than the company managing the brand, the lack of innovation with the brand/ product, the threat of losing a generation of Olympic fans, and the restructuring of the Olympic Movement. The inability to protect exclusive rights for partners was also identified as a key issue.

Communications: Communications/public relations programs were suggested as vital to reaching a high level of brand equity. Experts interviewed in this study identified the lack of a strategic public relations program integrated within a marketing and communications program as an urgent need. Other concerns were related to sponsor recognition program. On the other hand, it was suggested that the Olympic movement fully leverage its media partner. Programs such as Celebrate Humanity were said to be a step in the right direction, but they must be integrated into an overall marketing communications program. Corporate communications programs should be headed by IOC and integrated within NOCs.

Marketing brand team: Much work has yet to be done especially at the NOC level to reach a level of competency and professionalism needed to deliver value to partners and consumers.

Support: This is an area where the IOC has accomplished much work. A number of educational programs are available through Olympic solidarity, Olympic research Center, NOCs, and others. In addition, the marketing department has created a number of manuals and reports related to Olympic marketing (e.g., ambush prevention guidelines, hospitality guidelines, Olympic marketing report, NOC marketing guidelines). Perhaps the IOC could establish stronger relationship with academics, especially in marketing, in the implementation and dissemination of scientific research.

Service: The interviews with experts suggested that service to sponsors was appropriate at the IOC level but needed improvement at the NOC level. One area that seemed to be lacking was added-value programs for sponsors. The hospitality programs were mentioned to be the best in the industry.

Price: Price seemed to be a major concern for partners. Most believed that property was overvalued. The property needed more value-added programs and better integration at all levels. In addition, the lack of integration between sponsors' rights and broadcasters' rights was believed to increase the price to sponsors significantly. In addition, ticket prices at Games are a concern, especially during preliminary rounds.

Distribution channels: The distribution channels consist of NOCs and OCOG. As identified earlier, there is a need for additional marketing skills at the NOC level. Great use is made of the Internet and other media in creating merchandise programs during the Games. Brand strategies and marketing communications programs must be communicated and understood throughout the distribution channels.

FIGURE 7-4

Olympic Brand Management System

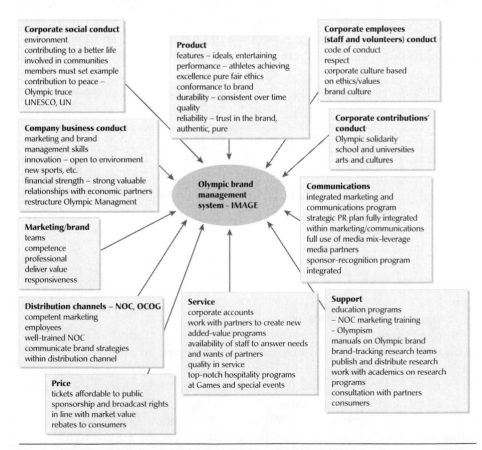

Source: Adapted from Keller, Kevin Lane, Strategic Brand Management 2nd ed., ©2003. Electronically reproduced by permission of Pearson Education Inc. Upper Saddle River, New Jersey.

Case: Montreal Alouettes – Rebuilding the Brand[34]

Background

The Montreal Alouettes (aka "the Als") is a professional football club and a member of the Canadian Football League (CFL). The city of Montreal has a long history with the sport of football. The first recorded game ever played in North America was on the downtown cricket grounds on October 10, 1868. The original Montreal Foot Ball Club was created in 1872, and the Als were born in 1946. The 1970s was a glorious decade for the Als including Grey Cup triumph, but trouble came in the early 1980s. The Als became the Concordes in 1983, and finally, burdened by mounting financial problems, the franchise ceased operations on the eve of the 1987 regular season.

The Rebirth of the Alouettes

The Als returned to Montreal following the failure of the CFL's expansion in the United States. The winners of the 1995 Grey Cup, the Baltimore Stallions, relocated to Montreal in 1996. The decision to bring CFL football back to Montreal at the Olympic stadium (aka "the Big O") was a gamble as the public perceived the Big O as an unfriendly place for pro sports. For years, the Montreal Expos lobbied the various levels of government for a new, friendlier stadium in downtown Montreal. In 1997, Larry Smith was hired as president of the football club. Smith had been an all-star player in the Als' glorious years in the 1970s and commissioner of the CFL in the mid-1990s. Despite having a winning team, the Als were playing at the Big O, and the old problems persisted. The crowds were small, media coverage was spotty, and the city's support of the team was cool at best. Average crowds the first couple of years were about 8000 spectators per game. In the wake of the old franchise folding and claiming bankruptcy in 1987, many unpaid bills from the media, corporate partners, and other creditors were left. Hence, convincing the media, business community, and public that a new franchise was "serious" in offering a quality product was difficult; getting their support was even more challenging as the CFL in general also lacked credibility. In 1996, only two media assigned a journalist to cover the "new" Als—RDS (French-language sport network, sister station of TSN) and *Le Journal de Montréal*. In addition, the Als had not identified TV or radio broadcasting as a top priority since the franchise had to pay production costs.

Despite the negative factors surrounding the team, a strategy based on the following priorities was developed:

1. Position the Als as a quality product at an affordable price.
2. Offer an entertaining product and respect the fans who are coming to see you, understanding that they are giving you their time and appreciate the sport of football.

---

[34] Séguin, B. (2006) *Canadian Sport Sponsorship: Case Studies Report*. Institute of Sport Marketing.

3. Develop a transparent organization.
4. Develop a "community" strategy by bringing the Alouettes to the community and developing the fan base "one at a time" through getting the fans to "feel, touch, and smell" the product. The thrust of the community strategy was to reach a young clientele. "Kids remember forever when they first met a professional athlete in person." While this was a long-term strategy, this was also the way to ensure the future of the franchise. Ticket price and promotions was determined with this niche in mind.

Once the strategy was developed, Larry Smith embarked on a public relations campaign, making his presence felt at numerous business luncheons, speaking at the chamber of commerce, frequenting business cocktails, presenting at business conferences, and pursuing other business-related activities. He made the commitment to welcome fans into the Big O by standing at the gates and then walking into the stands during games. Finally, he called every single season ticket holder who cancelled their ticket at the end of the year to determine why they chose to cancel.

Despite the lack of interest at first, the new Als were a winning team and "God knows people in Montreal and in Quebec love a winning team, they have been spoiled with the Montreal Canadiens for years.... We knew that if we kept winning, interest in the team would increase." (Montreal Alouettes Vice-President Marketing) Thus, having a winning team was an important part of the strategy in the Montreal and Quebec markets. The team made the playoffs every year after its rebirth, reaching the Grey Cup in 2000, 2002, 2005, and 2006 and winning the Grey Cup in 2002. The incredible success currently enjoyed by the Als may have been the result not of the success of the team and its community program but of a scheduling conflict. A concert by musical rock band U2 was booked at the Big O when the Als were scheduled to play in a playoff game. The decision to host the Eastern semi-finals at the rundown Percival Molson Stadium at McGill University in downtown Montreal created such a buzz within the community that the Alouettes have called the Percival Molson Stadium home ever since. The city's love affair with the team and the CFL has been rekindled. The move back to Molson came 51 years after the club's creation, a decade after the franchise's demise in the late-1980s, and 18 months after its rebirth. It is a great success story. According to the Als' vice-president of marketing, Claude Rochon, "Everything about Percival stadium indicated that it was doomed to fail":

- no public transportation access;
- only two entries into the stadium creating long waits;
- a stadium in "ruins" (e.g., a 20-foot tree was growing in the south stands);
- unusable washrooms: the Als having to initially bring in some temporary toilets creating very long waits, a problem exacerbated by beer drinking at football games;
- few concessions in bad shape also leading to long waits;
- wooden seats breaking as people were sitting on them;
- no outlets to sell merchandise products so they had to be created; and
- no parking facilities adjacent to the stadium.

But, there was an upside, namely:

- The stadium overlooks the Montreal skyline from atop Mount Royal and, as such, Percival Molson Stadium remains one of the most scenic places in Canada to watch a sporting event.
- November 7, 1998 was a beautiful fall day.
- 14 000 spectators came to the game.
- Surveys conducted during the game indicated that 96 percent of spectators preferred the Percival Molson Stadium to the Big O.
- The spectators loved the closeness to the players, to the action—they could hear the players collide, hear the quarterback make calls, feel the action.
- The atmosphere was electrifying, and the word quickly spread.
- In the week following the game, over 400 new season tickets were sold on the condition that the Als played the following season at Percival Molson Stadium.

While faced with huge logistical problems and having to invest large sums of money to renovate the stadium, the Als moved into Percival Molson Stadium the next year, and the love affair between the city and the Als has been rekindled. It appears that listening to the fans worked.

Today, things are looking very good for the Als:

- Heading into the 2007 Season, the Als have been sold out for six straight years in Percival Molson Stadium.
- They've been a winning team since 1996.
- Als' games are broadcast on television and on radio for a rights fee.
- Als' games are sponsored for all 10 home games.
- In-stadium advertising (e.g., signage, game day promotions) is sold out.
- A strategic community relations program using players, cheerleaders, mascots, and senior executives exists to "deepen" the fan–team relationship and provide opportunities to "feel-touch-smell" the product.
- The total budget is nearly $15 million, with about $4 million in sponsorship.
- 17 500 season tickets have been sold out for five years (waiting list of more than 3000).
- Within two weeks of the launch of the season, all remaining tickets are usually sold out.
- Tickets for games have a "value" because they are not readily available.
- Much effort is placed on entertainment.
- The popularity of the Als has led to the commercialization of three distinct subproducts: players, cheerleaders, and mascots.
- Tailgate parties before home games have become well-attended events.
- The stadium has gone through numerous renovations; the latest one increasing seat capacity to almost 25 000 including luxury boxes.
- The Als are very involved in the community running programs in these intervention sectors: stay in school program, literacy, healthy eating, physical activity.
- Programs for youth include Adopt an Alouette (175 schools, 50 000 young people).

Chapter 7: Branding in Sport

- Basketball team made up of Als players tours the province and visits schools (35 schools).
- Provincial tour of junior camps, where young football players get the chance to learn from Als coaches and players.
- Their special booklet, *Jouez Gagnant*, has sold 100 000 copies.

Sponsorship

As the Als VP marketing suggests, sponsorship is like "candy" for the organization: "we would need another 25 metres of field to place A-frames (signage) for all our sponsors." The team's major sponsors receive on-field logo (painted) and/or board signage within TV range, program advertising, players appearances at corporate functions, 30-second spots during broadcast of cames on TV/radio, press conference signage, logo on official game jersey (Molson) and practice jersey (RONA), in-game promotions, sampling opportunities, hospitality, Internet presence, logo on team posters, and tickets. Each TOP sponsor is the presenting sponsor for one game during the season. During that game, the sponsor becomes the "star"—sponsoring a coin toss, sampling opportunities, thunder sticks, raffle, and so on—as representatives of the team run the event while promoting the sponsor. Presenting sponsors are in control of the game from a promotion standpoint, and the Als provide the necessary logistic support. According to the VP marketing, the Als have created more value for games sponsors because they believe the audience is more "captive/receptive" to sponsors:

- No jumbotron (large screen) means no replays, which means more attention is paid by fans to what is happening on the field of play which leads to fans being more receptive to signage.
- They seek alternative ways to get spectators engaged in all aspects of the game, to create a fun experience, and to be entertained. Thus, the importance of "quality of cheerleaders, music and promotions" is underlined and, as suggested by the VP marketing, "there is never a dull moment, no dead time, so the spectators must pay attention to what goes on the field at all times."

The case revealed that the challenge for the Als marketing team is to develop alternatives for sponsors through new community programs, product extensions, and unique leveraging opportunities. This is one such community program.

Community Properties That Support the Brand

CN Adopt an Alouette Program

Created to combat high-school dropout rates among French and English students across Quebec, the program targets Grade 7 to 9 students in the province. This player-driven in-school mentorship program reaches an average of 60 000 adolescents in Quebec high schools annually. The Als hired a leading clinical psychologist to train players on issues of adolescent development.

Those taking part in the program learn how to approach more complex topics like drugs, alcohol, and gangs. They can adapt their own personal stories using proper communications, language, messages, and so on. A total of 20 players typically take part in the program, visiting 90 to120 schools during the off-season. Each school "adopts a player" with whom it develops a special relationship through follow-up visits, e-mail, tickets for games, posters of Alouettes, and so on. A tracking system has been developed to provide information about each school visited, messages delivered, and feedback from students/teachers. When players return to a school, they know the message that was delivered during previous visit(s) and are able to build upon it.

CN is title sponsor of the Als community program, which helps make communities better places to live and work. Pfizer is a presenting sponsor for the program. Adopt an Alouette is also an opportunity for CN to provide information to thousands of students about railroad safety. CN's name appears on posters, flyers, signage in TV range, special promotions, and other places. This program is very successful and has led to other opportunities:

- Alouettes school is cool basketball jam, where a team of players from the Alouettes face local primary school representatives in friendly basketball games across Quebec.
- Players spend about four hours at each school, talking with children, signing autographs, playing basketball, and eating lunch in school cafeteria. This creates a great sense of belonging between the young people and the Als players. This 'feel-touch-smell' plan is part of the sub-branding strategy.
- The Montreal *Gazette* created a special section called "Playbook for success," a six-step game plan aimed at inspiring students across the province to think about all they can be. Over 100,000 tabloids were distributed.
- A number of politicians are invited for speaking engagement throughout the friendly competitions.

Als' Cheerleaders

The cheerleaders are an integral part of marketing strategy. It is "the glamorous, exotic, fun, attractive, and sexy" side of football. For the past six years, the Als have invested in the cheerleaders' team by providing superior training opportunities. Each year, the team goes to Las Vegas to work with well-known choreographers to learn the newest trends in dancing to become the best at what they do. According to the VP marketing, the cheerleaders are an important element of the "fan experience" at the game. The increased popularity of the cheerleaders has led to new revenue-generating opportunities:

- 15 000 special swimsuit calendars (developed in a manner similar to the *Sports Illustrated* swimsuit issue) are produced and sold annually.
- A television production, *Gentille Alouettes*, about making the swimsuit calendar was broadcast by RDS/TQS and captured almost one million viewers.
- The cheerleaders make over 200 appearances a year at promotional and charity events at schools, hospitals, and amateur sports events, as well as

participating in numerous fundraising activities, conferences, commercial events, and festivals. The cheerleaders also attend a number of community events, where demand for their participation is very high.

- The cheerleaders are sponsored by Sports Experts and MexxSport.
- The cheerleaders' team is managed by a full-time employee.

Source: Institute for Sport Marketing Case Studies. Laurentian University 2003-2005

Case Questions

1. Do you think the Als have built a brand with a high level of equity? Explain.
2. Using this case, what are some key success factors to building a strong brand?
3. What is the role of community relations in brand building?

Chapter Summary

Sport marketers pay attention to the role of brands in building successful sport organizations/teams. The goal of brand building is to create brand equity: a high level of awareness, perceived quality, strong brand association, and loyalty for your product. This can be achieved through long-term investment. To develop brand equity, a brand must be consistent and coherent over time. The outcome of brand equity can benefit a sport organization with: a high level of support from the community, increase in sponsorship dollars, higher attendance at events, strong media following, strong television ratings, or additional revenue from merchandise programs.

Test Your Knowledge

1. Define brand.
2. What constitutes a strong brand?
3. Why is brand management important to a sport organization? A sport team?
4. What are the four key elements of brand equity?
5. What are the consequences of brand equity for a sport team?

For more review questions, go to http://www.sportmarketing.nelson.com.

Key Terms

brand	brand equity
branding	brand image
brand association	brand management

A full glossary of key term definitions is located at
http://www.sportmarketing.nelson.com.

Internet Resources

Nike, http://www.nike.com

Why is Branding so Important?,
http://www.fiba.com/asp_includes/download.asp?file_id=406

Branding, Sponsorship and Commerce in Football,
http://www.le.ac.uk/so/css/resources/factsheets/fs11.html

Branding Professional Sports,
http://www.brandchannel.com/features_effect.asp?pf_id=264

Sport Brands get a Reality Check,
http://www.brandrepublic.com/bulletins/design/article/605929/mark-
ritson-branding-sport-brands-15-realitycheck/

Brand it like Beckham,
http://knowledge.wharton.upenn.edu/createpdf.cfm?articleid=1642&CFID
=4759786&CFTOKEN=99574462

Company Fans, http://www.westernstandard.ca/website/

Pricing in Sport Marketing

Source: Gualberto Becerra / Shutterstock

Learning Objectives

- To understand the importance of price for a product and identify price-setting strategies
- To understand the importance of value in setting a price
- To identify the steps in setting the price for a product
- To recognize key issues that can affect pricing in sports

Introduction

You traded my favourite player. Why should I buy a ticket?

Although it may seem mundane at first, pricing is actually fascinating, affected by many factors and a very powerful strategic tool of business. Some even call price a marketer's best friend. It is the one strategic element that can be changed immediately (or within a few minutes) to move product (i.e., encourage immediate sales). The economic concept of **supply** and demand explains how this works: If a team is struggling to attract fans, its management can drop the price of tickets immediately to increase attendance. Although profitability is a challenge, the immediate effect of the action is clear. None of the other 4 Ps is able to achieve this kind of immediate return.

supply: availability of a product to satisfy a given demand.

This chapter looks at the different aspects of pricing in sports marketing. It provides the basic theory and concepts of pricing and applies them in the sport context. It shows how the issue of pricing is not simple but rather calls on concepts from marketing, economics, management accounting, and business strategy.

Price: What Is It?

Price takes many forms. Some pay tuition to attend school or rent to have a place to live. Others pay a fare to ride a bus or a toll to drive across a bridge. Anyone with an overdue credit card bill pays interest. Firms pay lawyers a retainer to have them at the ready, salaries to their managers, commissions to their salespeople, and wages to their staff. Each form of price differs in its application and is affected by different factors.

But pricing is strategy, as this example illustrates. Following continued financial problems, a local high-school basketball team recently repriced its tickets to improve attendance at their games. All tickets used to cost $5, but now there is a more elaborate pricing scheme: Adults pay $9, students $4 in advance or $7 at the door, seniors $5, and groups of eight or more pay $3 per student or senior and $5 per adult. Will this make a difference? The answer is yes. The team has taken a marketing approach to pricing and sought to understand the needs of each target group. The adults are typically parents of the players. What parent is not going to come to their child's game over a few dollars? Students are fickle and often change plans at the last minute, so the upfront pricing schema is appropriate. Seniors (either grandparents of the players or interested local boosters) are a growing market for the team but one that is price sensitive. Group pricing also makes sense as it encourages groups of students to find a few more friends to come to lower their price, or perhaps it will bring the entire family of a player to a game.

Defining Price

The Oxford dictionary[1] defines price as the amount of money or goods for which a thing is bought or sold. It is determined by not only what a firm chooses to charge for the item but also what a consumer is willing to pay for it. The actual price is based on several factors. Consumers are introduced to price early in life, establishing references in their minds of how various products should be priced. This price reference point permits or limits consumption patterns and can affect social standing. For some, price can even become part of a "sport/hobby," as shopping for the best price becomes an important activity for them.

Price is one of the four main components of the marketing mix—the 4 Ps. However, understanding how a price is determined is not easy. To explain, this chapter examines several important pricing factors including value, the pricing window, ethics of pricing, and break-even points.

Nagle and Holden[2] note: "It is widely agreed that price plays a slightly different role than the other three Ps. The purpose of pricing is different from the other elements of the marketing mix. Pricing should be designed to capture the value that has been created by the other elements of product, place and promotion." Price has historically been the little sister of the 4 Ps,

---

[1] Oxford University Press (1995) *The Concise Oxford Dictionary of Current English*, 9th ed.: 1084.
[2] Nagle, T. & R. Holden (1995) *The Strategy Tactics of Pricing*, 2nd ed. Prentice Hall.

receiving limited attention from both academics and practitioners, despite the fact that it clearly is the P that can most directly and readily be altered by a marketer[3].

The Pricing Window

Many marketers use the idea of the pricing window when setting price. At the bottom of the window is the lowest price possible (for the marketer to set), which is determined by the total costs or the minimum return demanded by investors. At the top of the window is the maximum price possible, which would be defined (theoretically) as the price that could be charged where one unit of the product would still be sold. Within these boundaries is the window in which pricing can be set.

Price in Marketing

Price and the 4 Ps

To build a strategy, marketers often use the marketing mix comprising the 4 Ps—product, place, promotion, and price. Marketers can target their product to a certain segment of the population by properly combining these elements. Specific to the price component, the marketer must consider and establish what the target group is able and willing to pay to receive the product. Thus, to determine the price, the marketer must consider all the decisions that precede offering the product, such as the costs of manufacturing, the customer's first reaction, perceived value, any additional costs the customer may incur, and finally the discounts and allowances[4]. The total impact of these factors allows the marketer to determine a price that will meet both the customers' needs and the company's need to make a profit.

Price provides firms with different strategy options to present their product to consumers. The particular pricing strategy for their product(s) will be determined by whether they want to introduce a new product, maintain market share, or become the market leader. Wong and colleagues[5] identified these pricing strategies:

- *Cost-oriented price setting* (cost-plus pricing) involves calculating the estimated costs (variable and fixed) and adding a markup suitable for the firm to achieve a profit.

  Example: It costs Canadian Tire $35.50 (fixed plus variable costs) per Sidney Crosby hockey stick to get each stick on the rack ready for sale. In seeking a 10% margin, the sticks are retailed for $39.05 (cost plus 10%).

- *Experience curve price setting* is a variation of the cost-oriented price setting that involves adding future average costs to the calculation. It assumes that future costs will decrease due to efficiency and volume.

---

[3] O'Reilly, N. (2003) Industrial pricing: A review of price in B2B technology markets. Working Paper.

[4] Nagle, T. & R. Holden (1995) *The Strategy Tactics of Pricing*.

[5] Wong, K.B., S.J. Shapiro, W.d. Perreault, & E.J. McCarthy (2005) *Basic Marketing: A Global-Managerial Approach*, 11th ed. McGraw-Hill Ryerson: 508–9.

Example: ABC Inc., a manufacturer of tennis balls, has forecasted that its future cost to manufacture each ball will go from 11.5 cents today to 4.5 cents in five years' time. Thus, they've established a price of 9 cents per ball to attract business today, enable price stability for the medium term, and generate profits in the short term.

- *Target-return price setting* is another variation cost-oriented pricing where the markup is a specific percentage return or dollar amount.

Example: Canadian Tire has reconsidered its cost-plus-10% strategy and has set a target return price of $39.99 per stick, which results in a 13% (approximate) margin.

- *Leader and bait price setting* (loss leader pricing) involves retailers setting their price for a particular item very low to attract consumers into the store where they will purchase additional products at regular prices.

Example: A new driving range opens its doors in St. John's. To encourage people to try the range, it offers the first bucket of balls free of charge, with additional buckets costing $2.50 each.

- *Psychological price setting* involves setting the price of items at specific points that appeal to specific consumers to encourage higher-volume purchases.

Example: A Junior C Hockey team in northern British Columbia offers tickets at various price points to appeal to certain markets: adults $19, students $12, seniors $10, children under 5 free, ages 6 to 12 $5, ages 12-17 $10, groups of 8 or more $9 each.

- *Odd-even price setting* involves retailers using a particular number to end their prices to give the impression of lower prices.

Example, Wal-Mart often prices items at $19.97 or $18.99 rather than $19.00 or $20.00.

- *Price lining* sets the price of all products at a series of specific prices.

Example: Nike prices products in its line of running shoes from about $50 to about $250, based on various factors.

- *Demand-backward price setting* sets the final price of the product and working backward to determine the amount available for markup and cost for a particular item.

Example: NB Inc., a start-up sport marketing consultancy in Saskatoon, has found a market for full marketing plans for sport events priced at $5000. The organization works backwards from there to determine expense line items.

- *Prestige price setting* involves retailers setting a higher than average price to give the impression of superior quality and class. Interestingly, if the price of the product goes below an acceptable point, demand from consumers will decrease.

Example: During the 2007 Stanley Cup playoffs, the Ottawa Senators increased their ticket prices significantly to reflect the prestige of the events.

Example: Red Bull, the well-known energy drink, is typically priced 50% higher than its competitors, signalling a prestige product.

- *Full-line price setting* is used when many different models of one type of product must be priced to indicate the added values and features of each item.

Example: Calloway offers a line of golf balls with an escalating price based on their quality, features, flight, and durability.

- *Complementary product price setting* involves adjusting the price of items that are used together since future sales of a complementary item will increase profits.

Example: Ink-jet printers are inexpensive; replacement ink cartridges are not. Thus, a consumer may be enticed to purchase the inexpensive printer (often the manufacturer takes a loss) while later paying a premium for ink cartridges where the manufacturer recoups its losses and accumulates profit.

- *Product-bundling price setting* involves selling a group of items or services for one price that is lower than the sum of the individual prices.

Example: The Montreal Canadiens offer fans flex-packs of tickets for multiple games at a from the regular prices of tickets purchased individually.

Price and Value

The price decision for any particular product always has a "value" element. A marketer must consider how value is created, particularly through the promotion of the intangible benefits that its product offers. This process of creating value can best be described when a firm's marketing mix and the costs associated with the product effectively meet consumer's needs[6]. This will depend on the customer's perception of the product based on its brand image, availability (or lack thereof), and quality. In other words, if a firm can effectively determine the needs of consumers in a particular segment and then create a marketing strategy that communicates the benefits of their product to meet those needs, consumers will recognize the added value as they consider which product to purchase. The added value of a product allows firms to charge consumers higher prices.

Value is easily described in two equations[7]:

$$value = benefits / price$$

or

$$value = quality\ received / expectations.$$

---

[6] ibid: 506–7.

[7] Wikipedia (2006) Marketing Value. Retrieved December 5, 2006 from http://en.wikipedia.org/wiki/Value_%28marketing%29.

The amount customers are able and willing to spend on a product will largely be influenced by what they will receive for their money and what they expect at that price. If you have exceeded their expectations, you have succeeded in giving additional value from your product. Value will typically be different in each consumer segment for the product. For example, a radically decorated piece of sports equipment at a premium price may add value for the segment of the market that prefers items that reflect their individuality and prestige. However, the same item may be considered garish and overpriced by an individual looking for a less expensive standard item.

Ethics and Pricing

An interesting issue in pricing concerns companies' ethics. In Canada, consumers are protected by the Competition Bureau, which enforces *The Competition Act*[8], "a federal law governing most business conduct in Canada. It contains both criminal and civil provisions aimed at preventing anti-competitive practices in the marketplace." Its overall mission is to "maintain and encourage competition" in business in Canada as a means to foster economic development domestically and globally, and to achieve competitive prices and product choice for Canadian consumers[9].

Wong and colleagues[10] outline three practices of unethical pricing:

- *Price fixing* occurs when competitors in a geographical area collude to set market prices for a product above the average price point where high margins are achieved to achieve higher profits.
- *Price discrimination* occurs when manufacturers charge different prices to different consumer segments for reasons not associated with differences in cost[11].
- *Predatory pricing* occurs when a firm in an industry prices its product much lower than the regular market price to reduce competition. This forces competing companies to abandon the market and discourages new competitors from entering. The firm then raises its prices to regain lost profits.

Setting Price

Estimating Demand

demand: the need for a given product in a specific market.

One of the first steps marketers take in pricing is to estimate the consumer **demand**. The information required to determine consumer demand can often be acquired from such sources as the company's historical data (e.g., how many units the company sold last year of a similar product) or it may require

---

[8] Competition Bureau Canada (2005) About the acts. Retrieved December 10, 2006 from http://www.competitionbureau.gc.ca/internet/index.cfm?itemID=148&lg=e.

[9] ibid.

[10] Wong, K.B., S.J. Shapiro, W.d. Perreault, & E.J. McCarthy (2005) *Basic Marketing*: 508–9.

[11] Ragan, C.T.S. & R.G. Lipsey (2005) *Economics*, 11th Cdn ed. Pearson Addison Wesley: 51.

intensive market research (e.g., how many units of the new product can be sold in this particular market at this particular price). The better the forecast, the better the decisions the marketer can make.

Figure 8-1 shows the inverse relationship between price and quantity sold, a well-known economics principle. Thus, as the price of an item increases, fewer consumers are willing to purchase the item, and demand drops. And as the price of the item drops, more consumers are now willing to buy, and demand increases. Consumer demand can be influenced by many factors, including the price of the product, competitive offerings, current economic situation of the consumer, consumer's lifestyle, consumer trends, and availability of substitute products[12].

FIGURE 8-1

Price–Demand Curve

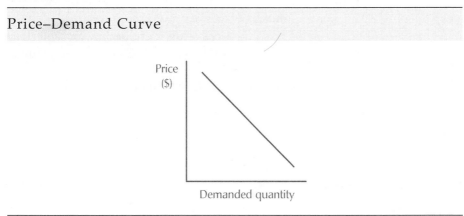

Identifying Restrictions

There are two caveats to note before using the price–demand curve in determining price. First, the **elasticity** of demand of a given product must be considered: With products having a more elastic demand, changes in price have a greater impact on quantity sold. Second, the ends of the curve are neither reliable nor valid for forecasting: It is difficult and unreliable to forecast demand at very low or very high prices.

elasticity: the change in demand for a product following a change in price—an elastic market is very sensitive to changes in price, while an inelastic market is not.

Estimating Cost, Volume, and Profit

After determining demand, the marketer must estimate the costs that will be incurred, volume to produce, and profits to be made. To produce a product or service, a company incurs **costs**, which can be estimated by management and production staff. They include costs for the components of the item and equipment and tools for production, and wages for the employees to build the item. The firm, however, must not stop there but must identify every cost that

costs: expenditures to produce a product or service and then take it to market.

---

[12] Horngren, C.T., G.L. Sundem, W.O. Stratton, & H.D. Teall (2002) *Management Accounting*, 4th Cdn ed. Prentice Hall: 44–8.

is associated with the product. Considering two distinct categories of costs (variable costs and fixed costs) is a useful method to organize and analyze expenditures.

variable cost: added cost to build just one more item.

A *variable* **cost** is the firm's added cost to build just one more item. For example, the individual parts that make up the item are variable costs: If you make six items, you incur the cost for the parts of those six items. Shipping costs and the cost of labour to manufacture are also considered variable. Variable costs are usually stated per unit: labour $5.00 per unit, shipping $3.45 per unit, and parts $7.75 per unit.

Fixed costs are those for such items as the heat, electricity, and taxes for the building, wages for management and administrative personnel (these wages are incurred regardless of number of items made), and promotional and marketing costs. These costs are usually identified by a fixed amount over a unit of time. For example, a company may incur heating costs of $3500 per year, telephone $100 per month, and wages of $90 000 per year.

Once the item's variable and fixed costs are identified, a marketer can focus on performing a cost-volume-profit analysis (CVP)[13]. Cost-volume-profit analysis is the study of the effects of output volume on revenue (sales), expenses (costs), and net income (net profits). The most practical analysis is the break-even.

Break-Even Analysis

break-even point: point where expected total revenue is zero once all the costs are paid.

The break-even analysis is a calculation that focuses on determining the minimum quantity of products that must be sold to break even, so that the expected total revenue is actually zero once all the costs are paid. The break-even point becomes an indispensable tool that management can use to make production decisions[14].

To determine the break-even point, we must first determine the contribution margin (marginal income) from each unit. The contribution margin, the amount of money that the item will contribute to the firm to defray the fixed cost expenses, is calculated by subtracting the variable costs from the selling price:

contribution margin=selling price–variable costs

Second, we divide the fixed costs of the firm by the contribution margin to determine the number of units required to reach the break-even point:

number of units to break-even=fixed costs/contribution margin

This example will help clarify the break-even analysis process. O&S Manufacturing in Montreal has designed a premium baseball glove. Based on last year's sales' results and secondary research, the firm believes it can easily sell 2500 gloves at a retail price of $150 per glove. We know the following:

- Variable costs: $98.50/glove (includes leather, padding, and thread; labour to cut the leather, stuff the glove, and sew it together)

---

[13] ibid.

[14] Thompson, A.A. & A. Strickland (2007) *Crafting & Executing Strategy: A Case Study: Dell Inc. in 2006: Can Rivals Beat Its Strategy?* McGraw-Hill Irwin: C-89.

- Fixed costs: $150 000 (sales and marketing costs, new sewing machines, cutting tools, and wages for salesperson, manager, and, secretary)

We solve the first equation as follows:

selling price – variable costs = contribution margin

$$\$150.00 - \$98.50 = \$51.50$$

The item contributes $51.50 to the fixed costs (then profits) of the firm. Thus, to calculate the unit sales the firm needs to break even and pay for all their fixed costs, we solve:

fixed costs / contribution margin = number of units required to break even

$$\$150\ 000\ /\ \$51.50 = 2912.6 \text{ or } 2913 \text{ baseball gloves}$$

Thus, at the retail price of $150, the firm must sell 2913 baseball gloves to pay all the fixed costs incurred and break even. This calculation is easily repeated to gather data on the number of gloves required to break even at different retail prices. For example, if we maintain variable and fixed costs, the firm would have to sell:

- 1961 gloves at $175 (contribution margin of each glove is now $76.50)
- 5661 gloves at $125 (contribution margin of each glove is now $26.50)

Controlling Costs

As markets increasingly become global, competition becomes fiercer. Firms looking to increase their market share or even maintain their current position quickly learn that failure to control costs decreases their competitiveness in an ever-changing global marketplace. Firms operating in regions with lower production costs and fewer regulations often gain a critical competitive advantage over local firms. Therefore, to stay competitive, local firms must continuously scrutinize every aspect of operation and production to reduce operating costs.

Local firms have been creative in competing against lower production costs in other countries by gaining competitive advantages in other areas. Dell, for example, maintains its competitiveness by providing its computers directly to the consumer by focusing on Internet and telephone sales[15]. This eliminates the need for intermediate distributors (increases Dell's contribution margin) or its own salesforce in retail stores (reduces fixed costs). But Dell has not stopped there. It has also gained a competitive advantage from its just-in-time production, where the individual parts for a computer are received after an order is placed. By having the parts shipped from the manufacturer to Dell's production facility and assembled within days or even hours, the company reduces carrying costs of spare parts. Dell's extensive integration with suppliers has given it a competitive advantage[16].

---

[15] ibid.
[16] Wong, K.B., S.J. Shapiro, W.d. Perreault, & E.J. McCarthy (2005) *Basic Marketing*: 501–5.

We consider again the O&S Manufacturing case. At the retail price of $150 per baseball glove, the firm will have to sell 2913 gloves to break even. However, the estimated consumer demand is only 2500 gloves for next year, and the failure to sell the 2913 baseball gloves will cause the firm to incur a loss. Therefore, the firm must scrutinize every facet of its operation and production to find additional ways to cut costs. O&S manufacturing could potentially decrease its variable costs for the glove by:

- switching to new suppliers of raw material offering lower costs;
- outsourcing selected activities that can be done by others for less; or
- using manufacturing process innovations to increase efficiency and reduce labour costs (which may increase the company's fixed costs from the purchase of new technology and equipment but may reduce labour time per glove sufficiently to bring about a savings).

O&S Manufacturing may also find ways to decrease the company's fixed costs by negotiating better rates for telephone services or outsourcing such clerical tasks as bookkeeping and payroll.

Taking the example of O&S Manufacturing further, we can better demonstrate the variable–fixed cost relationship. Due to recent changes at O&S Manufacturing, the firm now has the following cost structure:

- Variable costs: $79.75/glove (includes leather, padding, and thread; labour to cut the leather, stuff, and sew it together)
- Fixed costs: $140 000 (sales and marketing costs, new sewing machines, cutting tools, and wages for salesperson, manager, and secretary)

We can solve:

selling price – variable costs = contribution margin

$150.00 - $79.75 = $70.25

This item now contributes $70.25 to the fixed costs (then profit) of the firm. Thus, to break even and pay for all their fixed costs, we calculate:

fixed costs / contribution margin = number of units required to break even

$140 000 / $70.25 = 1992.9 or 1993 baseball gloves

Thus, at the retail price of $150, the firm must sell 1993 baseball gloves to pay all the fixed costs incurred. The company still anticipates selling 2500 gloves, giving an additional contribution from 507 gloves worth $35 616.75 in profits.

This articulates the point that profits are not encountered until a firm has met its break-even point and has paid off the fixed costs. Any additional sales over the break-even point will begin to accumulate profit for the firm; sales below the break-even point will result in a loss.

Key Pricing Issues

Discounts and Allowances

Discounts and allowances are both *decisions* that involve adjusting the existing price of an item. In marketing, the seller gives discounts to the consumers to shift some of the marketing function from the retailer to the consumer. Wong and colleagues[17] list these types of discounts:

- *Quantity discounts* are given to consumers who purchase large quantities; however, in doing so, they choose to inventory the product. For example, big-box sporting goods retailer SportCheck does this with running shoes, workout clothes, and golf balls.
- *Seasonal discounts* are given when consumers choose to purchase an item off-season, such as a discount offered by snow machine retailers in March. The consumer once again chooses to inventory the item.
- *Payment term discounts* are often seen when a business sells to another business. They are given to encourage early payment. For example, many companies offer a 2 percent in 10 or net 30: The buyer can deduct 2 percent from the total of his invoice if it is paid within 10 days; otherwise the net amount of the invoice is due within 30 days. This shifts the economic burden to the buyer more quickly to improve the seller's cash flow. For example, the wholesaler that supplies Sherwood the wood for its hockey sticks gives Shewood with a 1.5 percent discount if it pays within 30 days of receiving the invoice.
- *Trade and functional discounts* are passed down to retailers to compensate them for additional services they must perform. For example, sport drink manufacturer Gatorade could provide a 10 percent discount to a chain of grocery stores in return for product placement in an ideal shelf location.
- *Chain discounts* are passed down by the manufacturer to the different members of the distribution network, such as wholesalers and retailers. For example, a logging company, lumberyard, canoe maker, wholesaler of outdoor equipment, and chain of retailers form an alliance and share discounts in return for a chemical lab, fibreglass manufacturer, and builder of tennis racquets
- *Sale price discounts* are temporary savings featured by the retailer to consumers to meet certain marketing strategies. Sale price discounts could serve to persuade consumers to try a new product or even reduce overstock. For example, Speedo could offer women's swimsuits for 50 percent off to reduce stock before launching new designs for the next season.

---

[17] Ragan, C.T.S. & R.G. Lipsey (2005) *Economics*: 246.

In marketing, an allowance is given for having accomplished something. These allowances are common in marketing practice.

- *Advertising allowances* are granted to retailers based on a percentage of total sales; this allowance rewards the retailer and permits additional advertising of the product.
- *Stocking allowances* are typically seen in supermarkets where manufacturers pay a fee to promote their new products on the supermarket shelves.
- *Spiffs or push money allowances* are targeted to retail salespeople to encourage them to push a particular product.
- *Trade-in allowances* are often used in the automotive industry, where a consumer can receive a cash value for their older vehicle that must be applied to the new purchase. An example in the sports industry would be the Play-It-Again Sports chain which buys and re-sells used ski or hockey equipment.

Discounts and allowances allow retailers, wholesalers, and manufacturers to adjust the price of an item on a temporary basis without changing the regular retail price. This enables them to achieve specific marketing goals on a short-term basis without compromising the brand or company image.

Price versus Cost

Cost is the broader construct of price that includes all costs incurred by a consumer. For example, the price of a new driver for a young golfer might be $349, but the cost is that price plus all other costs incurred (e.g., gas to drive to the store, taxes, upgraded handle, cover to protect the driver, pack of balls purchased with it). Thus, although the price may be $349, the cost is closer to $500.

Sport consumers are faced with many different costs—above and beyond the price—when attending or participating in an event. This becomes apparent when we consider that the cost of attendance to a sporting event often includes:

- tickets
- transportation
- parking
- food
- beverages
- memorabilia

A sport marketer must be aware of these costs and must price their product properly relative to the total cost of attendance, as the consumer views the exchange based on cost, not price. This type of thinking led to the fan cost index[18].

---

[18] Team Marketing Report (2006) Index. Retrieved December 5, 2006 from http://www.teammarketing.com/index.cfm.

Fan Cost Index

The **fan cost index** (FCI) is a survey prepared by Team Marketing Report[19] (TMR), a market research firm that specializes in sports. They have prepared a yearly series of surveys covering the prices of items for a consumer attending NHL, MLB, NFL, NBA, and Minor League Baseball games. The costs for a consumer attending the game include:

fan cost index: Team Marketing Report survey of total costs to attend professional sport games.

- four average-price tickets
- four small soft drinks
- two small beers
- four hot dogs
- two game programs
- parking
- two adult-size caps.

Table 8-1 gives the fan cost index values for all the NHL teams, including the six Canadian franchises, for the 2006–2007 season. Note that the prices are in US dollars and that average ticket prices are based on a weighted average of season ticket prices for general and club-level seats, determined by factoring the tickets in each price range as a percentage of the total number of seats in each stadium[19].

TABLE 8-1

Fan Cost Index in the National Hockey League, 2006–2007 Season

Team	Avg. Ticket	% Change	Prem. Avg. Ticket	Ticket Rank	Beer	(oz.)	Soda	(oz.)	Hot Dog	Parking	Program	Cap	FCI	% Change
Montreal	$56.82	5.6	$99.74	2	$4.94	16	$3.16	14	$2.96	$18.02	$3.83	$22.48	$332.27	5.6
Boston	$56.44	6.4	$77.50	3	$6.00	16	$3.00	14	$4.00	$18.00	$4.00	$18.00	$327.77	6.0
New Jersey	$54.67	0	$0.00	5	$7.00	16	$3.50	16	$3.75	$10.00	$5.00	$23.00	$327.66	5.8
Vancouver	$58.96	3.9	$120.00	1	$6.31	16	$3.60	20	$3.38	$18.02	$2.70	$12.61	$325.00	2.8
Philadelphia	$55.66	5.5	$169.80	4	$5.75	12	$3.75	24	$3.75	$10.00	$5.00	$16.00	$314.15	4.0
Minnesota	$51.37	2.5	$90.00	7	$5.75	20	$3.50	20	$3.25	$10.00	$2.00	$18.00	$293.98	3.9
New York Rangers	$45.83	2.7	$141.67	12	$5.75	20	$3.00	24	$3.50	$20.00	$10.00	$12.00	$284.83	1.7
Edmonton	$51.76	12.4	$118.33	6	$5.86	16	$2.98	16	$3.38	$4.51	$3.60	$13.52	$283.65	8.7
Calgary	$47.35	9.2	$102.56	9	$6.08	20	$3.15	20	$3.60	$9.01	$4.51	$18.01	$282.60	8.1
Los Angeles	$45.98	4.9	$105.24	10	$7.25	16	$3.50	16	$3.75	$10.00	$5.00	$12.00	$271.42	3.3
Florida	$44.28	29.1	$105.17	13	$6.50	20	$4.00	20	$4.25	$12.00	n/a	$18.00	$271.12	20.6
Toronto	$49.23	–0.8	$154.59	8	$4.51	14	$2.25	20	$2.48	$13.52	$2.25	$13.52	$271.07	–0.6
Ottawa	$45.95	5.1	$89.78	11	$4.66	14	$3.16	20	$2.96	$7.90	n/a	$20.72	$266.93	3.7
Atlanta	$43.54	4.5	$93.42	17	$5.75	20	$2.00	14	$3.75	$10.00	$8.00	$15.99	$266.64	2.9
Tampa Bay	$44.27	0	$81.90	14	$6.00	12	$3.50	12	$4.00	$10.00	n/a	$18.00	$265.09	0
Detroit	$43.13	0	$58.58	18	$5.00	16	$2.00	12	$3.00	$15.00	$7.00	$15.00	$261.51	0
League Average	$43.13	3.7	$95.59	—	$5.55	17	$3.04	17	$3.42	$11.06	$3.36	$15.43	$258.08	3.2

[19] Team Marketing Report (2006) TMR's fan cost index. National Hockey League 2006–2007. Retrieved December 5, 2006 from http://www.teammarketing.com/fci.cfm?page=fci_nhl_06-07.cfm.

New York Islanders	$44.01	0	$97.92	16	$5.50	20	$3.00	14	$5.00	$6.75	n/a	$15.00	$255.77	0
Columbus	$44.08	4.9	$93.27	15	$6.00	20	$3.00	16	$3.00	$7.00	n/a	$12.00	$243.31	4.6
Nashville	$40.78	9.2	$86.47	19	$5.25	16	$3.00	16	$4.25	$10.00	n/a	$15.00	$242.63	7.9
Colorado	$38.48	0	$112.45	20	$6.00	16	$3.75	16	$3.75	$10.00	$5.00	$9.99	$235.91	0
Dallas	$36.36	6.2	$106.13	24	$4.00	16	$2.75	15	$4.00	$12.00	$5.00	$14.99	$232.41	4.2
Washington	$38.15	0	$94.82	21	$4.50	16	$2.50	16	$2.50	$15.00	$5.00	$12.00	$230.61	0
Chicago	$34.88	0	$71.72	25	$5.00	16	$3.00	16	$3.00	$16.00	$5.00	$13.00	$225.52	0
San Jose	$33.00	0	$76.92	26	$4.50	16	$2.50	16	$3.75	$13.00	$5.00	$15.00	$219.02	0
Carolina	$37.91	45.0	$81.34	22	$5.00	16	$2.75	20	$3.00	$7.00	$1.00	$12.00	$217.62	27.6
Pittsburgh	$36.61	0	$100.99	23	$5.25	21	$2.50	16	$2.50	$10.00	n/a	$15.00	$216.96	0
Anaheim	$30.32	0	$88.34	27	$6.25	16	$3.50	16	$3.50	$12.00	n/a	$18.00	$210.77	2.4
St. Louis	$28.23	−29.3	$96.58	29	$5.25	14	$3.50	12	$3.50	$10.00	$5.00	$12.99	$197.39	−16.8
Buffalo	$30.07	1.3	$65.05	28	$5.00	22	$2.00	12	$2.00	$7.00	$5.00	$12.00	$187.29	0
Phoenix	$25.41	−7.2	$87.54	30	$6.00	16	$3.00	16	$3.00	n/a	$2.00	$20.00	$181.62	−8.5

Source: Team Marketing Report Web-site. Retrieved 5 December 2006 from http://www.teammarketing.com/fci.cfm?page=fci_nhl_06-07.cfm

The TMR's fan cost index permits consumers and promoters to compare the cost of attending a NBA game in Toronto in 2004–2005 (FCI=$229.08) with the cost of attending an NHL game in Toronto 2006–2007 (FCI=$271.07). It allows individual teams to compare the price of their product offering against the league average and specific teams in their league throughout North America. In addition, it is possible to investigate the change in prices from year to year.

To review an example of a marketing plan, go to http://www.sportmarketing.nelson.com.

Case: Pricing in Practice

Background

To stress the importance of break-even analysis in sport marketing, we provide an example followed by a set of related questions.

Siu & Marlene's Sport Fashion Company wants to manufacture for this Christmas season a new yoga short—the YY-100—specifically designed for women. A salesperson will personally sell to the retailers and will receive a $32 000 base salary with 10 percent commission on every short sold (on the manufacturer's selling price). The cost of the overhead (e.g., building rent, hydro) for manufacturing is $20 000. The retailers will pay $10 for each short. The cost of producing each short is $2.50.

How many shorts does Siu & Marlene's Sport and Fashion Company need to sell to break even?

profit = total revenue – total costs

$$P = (P \times Q) - [FC + (VC \times Q)]$$

where P = price, Q = quantity, FC = fixed cost, VC = variable cost.

Solution

1. Let profit = 0
2. Determine which are the fixed costs and variable costs

$$FC = \$32\,000, \$20\,000$$

$$VC = \$10, \$2.50, \$1\,(10\% \times \$10)$$

$$\text{Selling price} = \$10$$

3. Plug in the numbers and rearrange the formula to work it out

$$0 = (10 \times Q) - ([32\,000 + 20\,000] + [2.50 + (0.10 \times 10) \times Q])$$

$$0 = 10Q - [52\,000 + 3.50Q]$$

$$0 = 10Q - 52\,000 - 3.50Q$$

$$52\,000 = 10Q - 3.50Q$$

$$52\,000 = 6.50Q$$

$$52\,000 / 6.50 = Q$$

$$8000 = Q$$

Therefore, Siu & Marlene's company needs to sell 8000 *YY-100* shorts to break even.

Chapter Summary

Pricing is a very useful and quick-responding tactic that the sport marketer needs to understand as it has a direct impact on sales revenue and profits. Price is used to capture the value of all other elements of a product, place, and promotions. This can be illustrated with the price of a ticket to a Toronto Maple Leafs game: While the price may be considered high, it represents the highest quality of hockey in the area (product), delivered in a first-class sport entertainment facility (place), with upscale promotions before and during the games. In addition, the games are sold out every year, making the demand for the product high. Specific to the sport industry, a number of important tools are available for determining price, including break-even analysis for the manufacture of sport products and the fan cost index for those working in spectator sport.

Test Your Knowledge

1. What two issues affect price?
2. Name two ways to estimate demand.
3. How do you calculate the break-even point for a product?

4. What effect will reducing variable costs have for a manufacturer? What about reducing fixed costs?

5. Name two types of pricing discounts and two types of pricing allowances.

6. What is the difference between price and cost?

7. The break-even point is the quantity at which total _____ and total _____ are equal and beyond which _____ occurs.

8. State what each item stands for in this equation:

$$Profit = (P \times Q) - [FC + (VC \times Q)]$$

   a. P
   b. Q
   c. FC
   d. VC

9. Circle the correct choice for each of the two pairs of options in the definition below:

Elastic demand is when a (small/large) percentage price change results in a (small/large) percentage demand change.

10. Marie has started her own business that makes custom wetsuits for tri-athletes. The total cost of materials and her time is $4500/wetsuit. Last year, she had expenses of rent $12 000 annually, equipment of $60 000 (total), and monthly utilities of $200. Assuming that fixed costs remain the same, how many designer wetsuits does she have to sell at $7500 each to break even for the year?

11. Following their Grey Cup win in 2006, the BC Lions entered the music industry with their renowned Grey Cup Shuffle. In producing a new CD of Christmas songs for Christmas 2006, a major recording company had to pay the band (The Lions) $20 000 plus 15 percent royalties (on manufacturer's selling price) to make a recording of six songs. The actual cost of manufacturing each CD is $1.80 and retailers pay the manufacturer $8 for the CD. The cost of producing (i.e., recording) the CD is $15 000. How many CDs must the recording company sell to break even? Show all of your work.

 For more review questions, go to http://www.sportmarketing.nelson.com.

Key Terms

break-even point

costs

demand

elasticity

fan cost index

supply

variable cost

 A full glossary of key term definitions is located at http://www.sportmarketing.nelson.com.

STP and The Canadian Sport Marketing Mix

Internet Resources

Team Marketing Report, http://www.teammarketing.com/index.cfm

2006 Fan Cost Index,
http://www.teammarketing.com/fci.cfm?page=fci_mlb2006.cfm

Lethbridge Hurricanes 2006-2007 regular season ticket prices,
http://lethbridgehurricanes.com/

Source: CP PHOTO / Halifax Daily
News / Jeff Harper

Chapter 9

Sport Promotion

Learning Objectives

- To understand the tools available in the promotion mix
- To appreciate the link between promotional mix and communications mix
- To put together a promotion plan for a sport organization

Introduction

So you've got a neat product. Now, does anyone know it even exists?

Sport promotion is one of the most dynamic and exciting areas of sport marketing. You will probably work in promotion at some time during your career, possibly on an event like your local 10-kilometre Run for the Cure fundraiser. A few months before the race, you create a plan to attract participants, volunteers, and businesses that will support your event. You create a pamphlet that communicates information about the event: its cause, when and where it will take place, prizes to be won and drawn, and sponsors that are supporting it. You print 200 pamphlets and distribute them around town to raise awareness of your event and garner public support. The spokesperson for the event, a well-known person in the community, conducts media interviews and meets with key business contacts to sell sponsorship packages. The event is promoted by your local IGA, the official food and beverages supplier, and the Running Room, official sponsor, through a number of special events leading up to the race. The grand prize, donated by a travel agency, is a one-week trip for two to Whistler, BC. During the race, a number of local stores set up tents on-site to sell merchandise, offer interactive displays, and so on. All of these activities are promotion activities. They serve a multitude of purposes, from raising awareness for your product to enhancing participants' experience at the event. This chapter examines the various forms of promotions (promotional mix) and the execution of a promotion. A case study will illustrate the importance of promotion in sport.

EXECUTIVE PERSPECTIVE

Blaine Smith, Vice-President of Hockey Operations, Sudbury Wolves Hockey Club

Sport Promotions: A Sudbury Saturday Night

The Stompin' Tom Connors hit song rings loud as thousands of Sudbury Wolves' fans walk into the aging Sudbury Arena to participate in the *Sudbury Saturday Night* promotion sponsored by Inco, which is referred to in this popular hockey song with the phrase: "... and we think no more of Inco on a Sudbury Saturday night." Despite the unflattering words to this song, Inco has pursued this promotion with great vigour.

The event features three of Sudbury's greatest passions—mining, hockey, and charity. Inco is one of the world's largest nickel producers, and the Sudbury Wolves have been a member of the Ontario Hockey League since 1972. Every fan attending the game is asked to bring a food item to donate to the local food bank. All fans who contribute are eligible to win a pair of season tickets. Easter Seals spokespeople, Timmy and Tammy, are invited to participate in a pre-game ceremony. All proceeds from the 50-50 draw will be donated to the local chapter of Easter Seals.

For this event, Inco purchases all available seats for the game and provides them to their employees through internal lucky ballots. Some of the tickets are distributed to the general public through phone-in contests on local radio stations and lucky ballots in local newspapers. Inco provides every fan attending with complimentary Wolves' tattoos and cheer-sticks featuring the Wolves and Inco logos. Talented Inco employees provide musical entertainment by singing the national anthem and performing Stompin' Tom songs at centre ice during the intermission. The second intermission features a minor hockey shootout where youngsters from the local minor hockey association compete. The winning team donates $500 to the charity of their choice, while the losing team donates $250 to the charity of their choice. Funds are provided by Inco.

Inco concludes the game by presenting the game's three star awards. Our organization recaps the event by presenting all photos and video to Inco with a sincere letter of thanks.

What Sudbury Saturday Night Means to the Wolves

Sudbury Saturday Night has become our flagship promotion because it combines many elements that are critical to a successful sport promotion. From the team's standpoint, the promotion reaches every objective we strive to attain with our game promotions, including:

- incremental ticket revenue
- incremental sponsorship revenue
- increased consumer satisfaction/entertainment
- community benefit element

From the sponsor's standpoint, the promotion provides them with a number of benefits:

- enhanced corporate profile in the community
- employee participation
- recognition for key executives
- charitable donation

Normally, we would include "increased sales or revenues" as a benefit to a prospective sponsor; but in this case, there is no retail element. One of the keys for this promotion and for any other promotion is the ability to "promote the event in advance." There is little advantage to be gained from organizing a promotion unless there is a reasonable amount of time to communicate the benefits of the promotion to the community and consumers.

We use contra agreements with our local newspapers, radio, and television to advertise upcoming home game promotional details to the general public. We also use in-arena signage, PA announcements, message-board commercials, and the Internet to promote our upcoming games and events. We avoid the tendency to conduct promotions that only serve to give products away and entertain the fans. We do not lose sight of our primary promotional objective—increase event revenues.

Group sales are an important source of promotional revenues. All of our tyke minigames at intermission are sponsored by Tim Hortons. The sponsor purchases the tickets for the team members, and we offer group rates to the parents and family friends. Retail sales are another promotional opportunity. We often organize silent auctions and special game-night promotions to stimulate sales of retail items.

Businesses often offer us products to give away to our fans. Some will not expect to pay for this promotion since they are providing us with 'X' dollars in value. It has been important to our marketing program that we apply a fee to this type of product sampling as we are providing businesses with a sales benefit. This policy also assists in controlling the number of products that we give away to our fans each game. Revenues are vital to every sport organization. Junior team revenues are restricted to ticket sales, sponsorship, advertising, and retail sales. It is important to maximize these revenues and refrain from giving event tickets and advertising products away.

We do provide complimentary Wolves' tickets to local elementary schools to increase our "walkup" sales. The Reaching for the Stars program is sponsored by a local Toyota dealership, and our players visit the schools to talk to youngsters about the importance of education and goal setting. Youngsters bring the complimentary ticket vouchers home and indicate that their school is invited to attend a Wolves' game. Many parents will purchase a ticket and attend the game with their youngsters.

We pack as many items as we can into our Event Night game program, including Go Wolves Go bracelets, team poster calendars, schedule magnets, statistic packages, action shots of our players, prize contests, all with the objective of increasing our program sales and providing added exposure for our program advertisers.

Intermission sponsors provide promotional revenues to the team, but we also want to ensure that on-ice promotions provide good entertainment for the fans. Shootouts for vehicles (cars or trucks) have been totally eliminated because the chance at winning is zero. The majority of our promotions include: T-shirt toss, tyke minigames, musical chairs, and go-cart races, where there is always a winner and/or entertainment value. Fan recognition is another important element of our event promotions. We want to recognize our season ticket buyers first and foremost, but we also want to recognize the fans who show up to our games from game-to-game.

Therefore we have inserted a number of fan promotions into the actual game experience, including:

- free pizza to a lucky row of fans
- free products to a lucky row of fans from the game sponsor
- Fan of the Period prize (winner selected by lucky seat ticket draw)
- Fan of the Game prize (winner selected from lucky season ticket holder names)
- Lady of the Game prize (flowers presented directly to their seat)

All of these promotions are sponsored and provide sponsorship revenues to the team. Team mascots have become an important part of the game experience. Howler is often surrounded by youngsters seeking hugs and autographs. Mascots should be an integral part of a game night experience. Therefore, a team mascot's role should not be restricted by an awkward costume design that can prevent climbing stairs, walking on the ice, or performing other movement.

One of the best mascot designs that I have seen is that of the AHL's Chicago Wolves' mascot who performs a figure-skating demonstration during the intermissions while the ice is being resurfaced. Sports promotions and game night entertainment have become a vital aspect of the overall presentation of sporting events. Player introduction ceremonies, laser lights, musical performances, video-scoreboards have become the norm rather than the exception.

Despite the emphasis and importance of sports promotions, spectators do not attend events to see "promotions," unless they are exceptional. Consumers primarily attend sporting events to cheer on the home team and watch the athletes perform. Promotions should be perceived as an important extension of the event and should not interfere with the actual game.

In summary, it is very important to continue to upgrade your knowledge base of sports promotions, modernize promotional activities, and find new and effective ways of reaching your consumers.

Blaine is a graduate of Laurentian University's sports administration program. His work experience includes *such positions as executive director of the Sudbury Minor Hockey Association and marketing director for the Sudbury Wolves. Smith is currently overseeing the renovation and expansion of the Sudbury arena.*

Promotion

promotion: communicating information to the consumers to influence them to buy a product and/ or service.

Promotion plays a key role in the marketing mix. Once decisions on product, price, and place have been made, the marketer must plan the most effective way to communicate critical information about them to the various publics. The recent proliferation of media outlets provides the marketer with effective and efficient means to reach very specific targets with very little waste. Preparing and executing a promotion require support from a number of employees in a sport organization. A successful promotion is one that makes the consumer aware of the product or service, generates interest in it, creates desire, and ultimately leads to action, a purchase: This promotion model is known as AIDA. The ultimate goal of promotion is to get consumers to try the product or service and build loyalty over the long term. One should realize that promotion does not work in isolation, it is an integral part of the marketing plan and must be consistent with the organization's objectives.

Promotional Mix

Promotion is a specialized form of communication designed to provide information to the consumers and persuade them to buy a product or service. A number of promotional tools are available to marketers in the promotional, or communications, mix. Since the marketplace is extremely competitive, sport marketers must be creative to make their promotions break through the clutter and attract people's attention to their product or service. Every promotional idea does not have to be a new one; it can be borrowed from many sources and changed to suit individual needs. For example, golf's skins game concept can be modified to suit the sport of curling or a bowling confrontation. These events focus on entertainment, and the rules of the sport can be altered for the specific promotional event. The number of variations evolving from these starting points is limited only by one's imagination.

Essentially the promotional mix consists of:

- advertising
- publicity

- personal sales
- sales promotions
- public relations
- sponsorship

Advertising

Despite a fragmented and cluttered environment, advertising remains an important marketing tool to marketers. Essentially, **advertising** is used to create brand awareness and brand loyalty[1]. Since advertising is paid for by the organization, the sport marketer controls the content (message) to be communicated to consumers as well as creative aspects, choice of media, and timing. The available advertising budget will dictate the quality of the production and the choice of media. For example, a local sport club with a limited budget can be successful in creating an in-house video promoting the various summer clinics on the local television station. Since television stations run a limited number of public service announcements (PSA), the club may be able to get its announcement run free of charge. On the other hand, Nike is notorious for creating powerful advertising campaigns that connects its products to the strong emotional appeal of certain athletes. Nike pays millions of dollars to such athletes as Tiger Woods to build advertising campaign around certain products (e.g., golf shoes). If Nike wants to buy advertising time during the Super Bowl, it will pay US$2–2.5 million for a 30-second commercial.

Shank suggests a five-step approach to developing an advertising campaign. Decisions have to be made at each step about[2]:

1. the development of clear objectives for the ad campaign
2. the amount of money available for the entire ad campaign
3. the content/creative of the ad
4. the media strategy (e.g., television, print, Internet)
5. the evaluation of the advertising campaign

An ad campaign should support and reinforce brand positioning and overall corporate strategies. The media choices include: print (e.g., magazines, newspaper, direct mail), electronic (e.g., radio, television, Internet), posters, billboards, signage at events, brochures, balloons, and athlete bibs. The choice of media largely depends on the available budget. Again, a key distinction between advertising and another form of promotion such as publicity is that advertising is paid for by the marketers who then keeps total control over what is said, where and when it is said, and to whom.

Publicity

Publicity is an important component of the promotional mix for sport marketers. Unlike with advertising, marketers do not pay (directly) for publicity. The opportunities to get one's sport into the media are numerous, whether at

advertising: promotional activity to communicate information on a product or create brand awareness and brand loyalty by using paid announcement in various media.

publicity: an important component of promotion that sport marketers do not pay (directly) for.

---

[1] Shank, M.D. (2005) *Sports Marketing: A Strategic Perspective*, 3rd ed. Prentice Hall.
[2] ibid.

local, regional, provincial, or national levels. Every day, hundreds of reports on sporting events, athletes, and other types of sport information are given by numerous media outlets nationwide (e.g., television, newspaper, radio, Internet). While a majority of the space and airtime is devoted to professional sports, the opportunity to get your story in the media depends mainly on your media relations plan. Effective media relations usually take years to implement and may include news releases, PSAs, demonstrations of product or service, press conferences, media days, interviews, and newspaper photographs. An important component of any media relations strategy is the relationship that a marketer, coach, athlete, or spokesperson develops with journalists. Since publicity is what a third party decides to say about your organization, this often adds credibility to your sport. Therefore, getting one's story in the media can provide excellent public relations benefits to an organization. In addition, good consistent media coverage is closely tied to sponsorship opportunities: One key benefit sought by companies involved in sponsorship is media coverage. While it is true that an organization has less control over timing and content of publicity than advertising, it remains an interesting and essential promotional platform.

Personal Sales

personal selling: a form of promotion in which individuals representing a company provide information on the product/ service to potential buyer through direct dialogue.

A key characteristic of **personal selling**, another form of marketing communications used by sport organizations, is its approach—targeted and personal rather than broad and impersonal. Personal sales can take numerous forms: A varsity basketball player visits local schools to share personal experiences; a swimming coach lobbies community groups for the construction of a new pool; a volunteer calls potential donors for a local soccer tournament; a 10-year-old hockey player goes door-to-door selling chocolate bars to subsidize the travel cost to the provincial championships. Key to personal sales is a dialogue created between the organization offering a product or service and targeted publics. For example, the marketing director of a university athletic program meets with representatives of a student association (e.g., human kinetics) to sell group tickets to a football game.

Selling sponsorship is also a form of personal selling. For example, the director of corporate partnerships of Alpine Canada may tailor a sponsorship program to meet the needs and objectives of a specific organization (e.g., CIBC). Prior to making a formal presentation, Alpine Canada invites key senior executives of marketing of CIBC to a World Cup event (hospitality), which happens to be at a beautiful resort in Whistler. The environment, hospitality, and special events may strengthen relationships and, in the end, create a favourable atmosphere when the pitch is finally made.

Since personal selling is about creating human contacts, a key to its success is developing long-term personal relationships. In fact, this relationship marketing—creating, maintaining, and enhancing strong, value-laden relationships with customers and other stakeholders—is critical to sport marketers.

Sales Promotion

The aim of **sales promotion** is to stimulate immediate demand for a product or service. It can also create consumer goodwill and/or reinforce the relationship between consumers and a company. Sales promotions can take the form of price-oriented or non-price-oriented tactics[3]. For example, a skiing resort that offers 2-for-1 tickets on Tuesday night uses a price-oriented strategy, while a sales promotion that gives a team calendar to the first 10 000 spectators to arrive for a hockey game uses a non-price-oriented strategy. In the price-oriented promotion, sport marketers must decide if their promotions should be keyed to current weaknesses (e.g., weekdays are slow sales days, low ranking teams are coming to town) or to strengths (e.g., Sidney Crosby and the Pittsburg Penguins are in town). Whatever strategy is used by the marketer, it is important that loyal customers do not feel alienated by the promotion. For example, a sport marketer looking at selling tickets at half price needs to carefully assess the potential impact of short-term revenue versus long-term alienation of season ticket holders who are loyal to the team.

Sales promotions take a multitude of forms, including **premiums**, contests and **sweepstakes**, sampling, point-of-purchase displays, and coupons[4]. The decision on which form to choose depends on the objectives of the sport organization.

sales promotion: marketing promotion to stimulate immediate demand for a product or service, create consumer goodwill, and/or reinforce the relationship between consumers and a company.

Premiums

These include give-aways that are tied with a sponsor's product as part of the sales promotion. For example, spectators purchasing a ticket to an outdoor diving event are given a bottle of Ombrelle sunscreen. This kind of promotion is popular among sponsors as it gets their products into the hands of a targeted audience.

premiums: give-aways that are tied with a sponsor's product as part of the sales promotion.

sweepstakes: form of promotion that offers consumers the chance of winning a prize.

Contests and Sweepstakes

This form of promotions offers consumers the chance of winning a prize. For example, during the 2006 Canadian Figure Skating Championships, MasterCard set up several booths in the arena where the company offered spectators who signed up for a MasterCard a chance to win a trip for two to the world figure skating championships: The trip including airfare, tickets to all events, and a number special hospitality events such as back stage passes to meet athletes, luxury box seats, and dinner with a skating star (e.g., Kurt Browning, Elvis Stojko).

To successfully promote the organization, premiums or prizes offered in a contest or sweepstakes must have wide consumer appeal, be new, or be tantalizingly unavailable (e.g. an all expenses paid trip to the Olympic Games or an exotic sports car) to an average person. Cash, trips, and cars are often the hooks, proven to be powerful attractions to enter a contest.

---

[3] Mullin, B., S. Hardy, & W. Sutton (2000) *Sport Marketing*, 2nd ed. Human Kinetics.
[4] Shank, M.D. (2005) *Sports Marketing*.

Sampling

A company introducing a new product can get participants and/or spectators to try it by offering samples. For example, a company specializing in skin care products may use its sponsorship of a beach volleyball tournament to distribute sunscreen products to athletes and/or spectators on site. Or the company may decide to install a tent and have a representative giving information on the importance of sunscreen product and giving out samples.

Point-of-Purchase

point-of-purchase: retail promotion that enhances sport's image connection with the trade and consumer by featuring a sport, a team, or an athlete.

The **point-of-purchase**, or POP, display is a popular form of promotion in retail. For example, General Mills partnered with several grocery chains where it developed an Olympic theme promotion for its Cheerios brand and positioned displays in key locations. On occasions, the POP promotion may be supported by the presence of well-known athletes and a contest or sweepstakes. In general, the objectives of POP programs are to:

- enhance sport's image connection with the trade and consumer
- generate consumer awareness, interest, involvement, and traffic
- encourage trade support over a longer than normal period
- maximize in-store display, feature price, and advertising support
- provide strong incentives for the trade to feature the products.

Public Relations

Public relations is everyone's business, from top to bottom of an organization. Every athlete, coach, volunteer, and administrator must be conscious of the public relations aspect of every major decision that an organization makes and of every contact with the public. Since sport organizations connect with the public in many ways, the essence of public relations is to plan for and manage those connections. It is an essential aspect of brand management, and it is no coincidence that, for most professional teams, community relations is an important aspect of a public relations strategy. When the president of the Regina Roughriders is invited to speak at the Rotary Club, plays at a golf tournament, addresses the media during a major game or trade, or speaks at a business school or any other public or private function, he is on stage: He is representing the brand every time he interacts with the public. Similarly, when players have speaking engagement in schools, visit a children's hospital, or take part in a charity event, they are engaged in public relations activities.

A positive attitude is essential to public relations. Because the public establishes its opinion of an organization through personal contact with individuals in the organization, it is necessary to develop a positive internal and external perception of the organization. Public relations is important not only for athletes but also for the entire organization. As suggested by Dr. Bob Wanzel, professor emeritus in sport management, public relations is the business of the entire organization and should be an essential component of an integrative sport management (ISM) system. In other words, public relations strategy should be integrated throughout the entire organization.

Public Relations and Integrative Sport Management

Sport organizations make decisions all the time. What may be considered a minor decision at the time may have future consequences that lead to a public relations fiasco. Naturally, it is best to have the time to thoroughly think through a decision, take the correct action, and report on that action. But in reality, this does not always happen. Since the ISM system provides a broader understanding of issues, everyone can play a public relations role in an organization. For example, coaches do not just coach; they are salespeople to athletes, organizational members, sponsors, governments, and the public. Therefore, media training is essential to enable coaches to shape a positive public image of the organization. When a coach or other representative of an organization stays silent when given the opportunity to speak to the media, they are basically inviting the media to shape the public image of the organization. And this is risky.

Progressive organizations have a communication plan as part of their business strategy. Such a plan should identify publics, the messages to be sent, and the communication vehicles to be used. If a concern arises, the integration of corporate image into corporate strategy leads to less criticism by a special interest group. An image communication program must identify sources and channels through which the image is conveyed, making sure relevant concerns are addressed. The organization must establish an image of itself that it wishes to communicate to its publics.

A foundation for solid public relations can be built through an ISM system. Role players gain a better understanding of management philosophy that is eventually expressed in organizational policy. Therefore, positive actions are initiated from sound policies, reducing likelihood of policies causing public outcry. These external reactions, coupled with internal conflicts, result in harmful public relations for an organization.

Since public relations programs have a direct impact on organizational image, people with good public relations and communication skills usually gain personal influence within a sport organization. The involvement of sponsors, media, and governments in sports has encouraged sport organizations to develop public relations policies. Professional sport teams and leagues have been more efficient than Olympic sport organizations in this regard. While public relations programs are often developed for external publics, sport marketers must also consider internal publics (staff and volunteers) as they also develop beliefs and assumptions about the organization. Because all decisions will ultimately affect the members of the organization, integration is a valuable policy to develop.

Effective public relations is recognized very quickly. Regardless of size, every organization must depend on public support for its continued existence. It is critical for a small organization to be perceived favourably. This image becomes a valuable informal public relations tool. A small organization has the advantage of face-to-face internal communications. An ISM system makes it a matter of policy for the board to explain issues to personnel. The system can work in the reverse as well, where issues can be explained from a grassroots point-of-view to the board.

A sport organization's public perception should be assessed continually, internally with members and externally with various publics, including government, suppliers, sponsors, and media. One might also find it valuable to survey people or corporations that have no present dealings with the organization. A poor perception may affect external business relations: If a policy or action is misunderstood, it clearly pays to explain one's position to the public.

Thus, it is extremely important for an organization to operate in a favourable public relations climate, which is conducive to gaining support and allows the organization to withstand unfavourable publicity. People who respect an organization because of its reputation will be less inclined to believe public statements that contradict their personal experience. Public relations is also an integral part of brand management.

Sponsorship

sponsorship: a promotional approach in which an organization or individual offers resources (e.g., financial) and/or services to support a sport organization's event, program, or product offering.

Sponsorship is a promotional practice that has moved from its roots as a tool for corporate donations[5] to a highly developed course of action in which both the sponsor, or investor, and the sponsee, or property, benefit in a marketing relationship[6]. Its rapid adoption into practice by organizations is reflected by the huge growth of worldwide sponsorship investment that went from US$500 000 in 1984 to more than an estimated US$3[7] billion in 2007. The position of sponsorship in marketing's traditional promotional mix ranges from no inclusion at all (e.g., the vast majority of marketing and marketing communications texts) to recognition that it is an integral part of the communications mix, alongside advertising, publicity, personal selling, and sales promotion[8]. This is supported by a number of studies suggesting that sponsorship plays an important role in enabling an organization to attainment its communications objectives (e.g., awareness, reach target markets).

Tripodi argues that sponsorship has become one of the top promotional tools[9]. A well-planned and coordinated approach to communications is essential if sponsorship is to be effectively integrated into other marketing activities. Keller suggests that event sponsorship provides an interesting communication option for a company, as the brand becomes engage during a "special and relevant moment in consumers' lives[10]." For example, RBC's involvement with Special Olympics events (athlete with an intellectual disability) is an opportunity for the company to connect with thousands of Canadians (athletes, parents and volunteers) who have deep feelings for this

---

[5] Wilkinson, D.G. (1993) *Sponsorship Marketing: A Practical Reference Guide for Corporations in the 1990s.* The Wilkinson Group.

[6] Polonsky, M.J. & R. Speed (2001) Linking sponsorship and cause related marketing. *European Journal of Marketing*, 35(11/12): 1361–85.

[7] IEG (2006) 2006 sponsorship spending. *IEG Sponsorship Report*: 25.

[8] Meenaghan, T. (2001) Understanding sponsorship effects. *Psychology and Marketing*, 18(2): 95–122.

[9] Tripodi, J. (2001) Sponsorship—a confirmed weapon in the promotional armoury. *International Journal of Sports Marketing and Sponsorship*, Mar/Apr: 1–20.

[10] Keller, K.L. (2003) *Strategic Brand Management: Building, Measuring, and Managing Brand Equity* (2nd ed). Prentice Hall: 375.

cause. A key challenge for sponsorship is to provide evidence that it is more effective than advertising or sales promotion[11]. On the one hand, advertising seeks to exploit emotion; on the other, sponsorship strives to connect with the emotion inherent in the property (e.g., sport)[12]. The association between the two parties, sponsor and sponsee, is often considered key differentiating sponsorship from advertising as it enhances the relationship beyond a basic cash purchase of promotional value. In this sense, firms should employ an integrated approach and use sponsorship with other elements of the communications mix (publicity, advertising, sales promotion, personal sales). A synergetic effect will not only maximize communications effectiveness but also contribute to building brand equity.

For example, well-known Canadian sport marketer Keith McIntyre of K.Mac & Associates helped General Mills develop its strategy to fully leverage its sponsorship of the Canadian Olympic team[13]: "We worked closely at developing relationships with key accounts at the retail, making sure they understood that we held the authentic association with the Olympic rings, the Games and the athletes, we owned the space!" The General Mills approach to Olympic sponsorship was fully integrated into its marketing and promotional mix. This included product packaging (integrating rings and athletes profile on boxes), pricing (special pricing leading up to and during Olympics), distribution (working with key retail accounts, developing in-store positioning), and promotional mix (developing sales promotion campaigns, athlete appearances, personal selling programs, advertising, publicity). The promotional campaign provided something meaningful to consumers and received tremendous publicity. This approach to sponsorship enabled consumers' associations with General Mills to be linked to emotions and passion rather than signage or rink boards.

Chapters 11 and 12 will cover sponsorship in more detail.

Executional Elements of Promotions

Preliminary

When deciding to use a promotion, you must have a sound knowledge of the total operation of the organization so that the promotion and organization complement each other. It is crucial to know both the product and the aim of the promotion. Will the promotion be seen as a natural extension of the product and/or marketing concept? It is necessary to know your audience and the demographics that one plans to reach with promotion. For example, a 1960s nostalgia-day promotion may not be suitable if the audience consists of teenagers.

---

[11] Brooks, C.M. (1994) *Sports Marketing: Competitive Business Strategies for Sports*. Prentice Hall.

[12] Meenaghan, T. (2001) *Understanding sponsorship effects.*

[13] Keith McIntyre, personal communication, January 26, 2005.

Timing

Although a crucial element of preparation, timing is not well researched by all promoters, a mistake that can harm an otherwise good promotional idea. For example, many organizations force the promotion into the wrong time of year for a segment of their target market. A promotion on a Jewish holiday, when the potential audience is 40 percent Jewish and unable to attend, does not constitute strategic planning. Consider the day of the week and the time of the event. Are there any obstacles to the smooth operation of the promotion?

Do not forget to research what other events are scheduled in the same city for the proposed promotion day. This research must be coupled with sufficient lead time to book space, activities, and entertainment for the promotion. Even during the off-season, don't assume you can postpone concluding arrangements and bookings. You may discover that the Shriners World Convention had booked space a year ago. A chamber of commerce or hotel association can provide helpful information on potential conflicting events. This knowledge saves embarrassment and allows promoters to entice visiting convention delegates to their game or other event.

Ideas

Use brainstorming or similar techniques to get creative input from as many sources as possible. In initial group discussions, don't allow negative opinions; rather, discuss each idea until all present agree it is not acceptable. The most promising ideas should then be assessed against the organization's objectives. As well, strive to secure opinions from sources outside your group. For example, one enterprising promoter discussed various ideas with taxi drivers, who often discuss sport events with the public.

Next, develop a mock situation that allows an outsider to play the devil's advocate when promotional ideas are presented. Thorough preparation results in greater promotional success.

Follow-up

This ensures that all the elements of a promotion fit together. It must have the proper lead time, not only for the staff/members, but also for the commercial and community sectors. Everyone must execute assignments within the specified period of time. The idea must be checked against both promotional and budget requirements. A good promoter attempts to secure the necessary equipment or personalities at minimal cost. A successful promoter must be aware of people and resources in the community and then negotiate contra deals. For example, if an upscale hotel suite is required for a visiting personality, you could offer the hotel prominent publicity in exchange for the suite at no cost.

Another example of follow-up is the coordination of advertising to support the promotion. A newspaper could begin a home subscription drive by offering a season ticket as the prize to the carrier signing the most new subscribers. In exchange for the season ticket, the newspaper would provide free advertisements for the promotion day.

Essential to proper promotional execution is an itemized list detailing what has to be done, by whom and when, as well as what could go wrong and how the situation could be rectified. For example, to prevent a disaster if special microphones are required for the promotion, have those present learn how to check power source and microphone trouble spots. Arrange for a standby back-up unit and technician in case of emergency.

Day of Promotion

Personnel must check their individual lists to ensure all elements are operative. Every promotional element must be rechecked on the day of the event. As well, a group meeting should be held to delineate staff responsibilities so that an error in assignment can be corrected before the event begins. No promotion is too small for this kind of commitment to detail. Remember, the promotion reflects upon the professionalism of your organization.

Preparation cannot guarantee a trouble-free event, but it can provide contingency plans that turn problems into positive outcomes. For example, if the facility heating system fails, perhaps the concessionaire could be convinced to provide free coffee, tea, or hot chocolate during the event. Purchases in addition to the free item may actually increase revenue. An enterprising promoter should discuss this possibility with the concession owner prior to the season. A mutually beneficial arrangement would characterize sound planning.

Whatever is offered during the promotion must be delivered, even if a situation results in additional cost to the promoter. To do otherwise, regardless of the reason, alienates the public and affects the success of future promotions.

As a final promotional assessment, you should carefully consider hidden promotional costs, especially important for a volunteer association. For instance, if advertising costs are $1000 and the expected net profit is $3000, you might feel the promotion is worth the effort. However, generating the net profit will entail the time, energy, and talents of many volunteers to develop promotion kits and posters, make community contacts, and distribute printed material. Personnel will also be required to contact the media before and after the event and work at the event. This legwork could represent 150 person-hours. Salaries calculated at only $3.00 an hour decreases the actual net profit to $1550. This may still be an acceptable profit to an organization, but at what cost? Since the volunteers gave 150 hours to make the promotion a reality, it may be unrealistic to expect similar service more frequently than once each season. Overloading association volunteers risks losing the human resources of that organization. Using different volunteers for each promotion entails additional person-hours involved in training or explaining tasks on each occasion. As well, changing the personnel dealing with individual community contacts prevents the establishment of a long-term cooperative relationship throughout the season.

Case: Sponsorship in the Trenches

Case Study Evidence of Its Legitimate Place in the Promotional Mix

Given that the initial sponsorship investment buys only the rights to an association, many academics and practitioners in sport marketing have suggested that sponsors leverage it by spending resources in additional communications or promotional activities. This can be achieved through a variety of marketing communications elements. By supporting sponsorship with other marketing components such as advertising, sales promotion, point-of-purchase, on-pack signage, and production of merchandise, a corporation may be in a better position to claim its space in an increasingly cluttered sponsorship environment. Abratt and Grobler[14], Witcher, *et al.*[15], and Shanklin and Kuzma[16] have all suggested that the sums required for successful **leveraging** may be up to three to five times the initial expenditure. Such an approach to sponsorship was found to be embraced in practice by Keith MacIntyre (K.Mac): "Sponsorship is not a money grab.... It is about business, selling product. I work in the trenches and that is where it is."

Given sponsorship's roots in philanthropy and advertising, it is interesting to note that according to K.Mac sponsorship is still misunderstood within corporate Canada, especially within the advertising industry. For many, sponsorship is no different than advertising and, in fact, is treated as advertising: "I've got clients that disagree, one says 'If I want footsteps in my store, I'll put my most popular product on sale.' This is not helpful except for awareness building. We are interested in affecting consumer behaviour. What is the incremental [sales] volume? That is what we want ... to drive business."

While more research is needed to identify the reasons for this lack of differentiation between sponsorship and advertising, K.Mac suggests that large advertising agencies understand advertising and public relations but not necessarily the role of sponsorship. As a result, "they may fail to see that sponsorship meets the needs of sponsor and sponsee driven by the passion of both the property and the consumer, as opposed to an advertising deal which is one directional."

"I look at sponsorship as part of the promotional mix—and as one of the four or five components of how you build a communications program. Signage [advertising] used to be a big deal but that is now just wallpaper. Sponsorship

leveraging: supporting a sponsorship program by many or all of the other elements of the communications mix, thus incurring additional costs.

---

[14] Abratt, R. & P.S. Grobler (1989) The evaluation of sports sponsorship. *International Journal of Advertising*, 8: 351–62.

[15] Witcher, B., J.G. Craigen, D. Culligan, & A. Harvey (1991) The links between objectives and function in organizational sponsorship. *International Journal of Advertising*, 10: 13–33.

[16] Shanklin, W.L. & J.R. Kuzma (1992) Buying that sporting image. *Marketing Management*, Spring: 59–65.

now is about defining your consumer (demographics plus psychographics, what makes them tick). Then you know what they want and can identify a sponsorship that meets those criteria. Then, you build that link by telling them why it is important to them [consumer]. You also need to tell them [consumer] on their own terms. Get them excited and meet their needs and wants. It has to get really deep these days to really actually make it work."

Clearly, such an approach makes sponsorship, like advertising, as valid a promotional tool as any other member of the promotional mix. In fact, evidence shows that, in some cases, it may be a superior communications choice when the objective is to drive sales. In this regard, K.Mac points out: "Our litmus test is [to ask] what will sponsorship do to effect consumer behaviour? What will it do to meet the client's pillars [objectives] of evaluation?" The case of K.Mac provides additional support for sponsorship as a legitimate member of the promotional mix. First, as suggested in the literature, a key benefit associated with sponsorship is the ability to target specific markets. This is supported in this case as K.Mac suggests "Sponsorship is very target driven ... corporations want to communicate with their core target."

Second, K.Mac highlights sponsorship's ability to focus on the exact objectives of the sponsor. "Companies do not care about what is going on behind the scenes. They are very sophisticated. Signage ... is not enough. Brand managers' careers are on the line, they do not take big risks and throw up signs; they want return." Thus, sponsorship's ability to achieve specific objectives is an efficient way to differentiate a sponsor from its competitors.

Third, K.Mac stresses the ability to build a promotional campaign around a sponsorship was highlighted and the need to leverage a sponsorship strategically: "A major threat to my business is when a sponsor occupies a [sponsorship] category but does not leverage [that sponsorship]." He added that "my rule of thumb is that you must leverage at least 2:1. Tylenol [sponsor of Rowing Canada and Canadian Olympic Committee] leveraged 6:1 as a minimum, maybe even 8:1 with TV."

Finally, K.Mac suggested that future trends in the advertising industry may increase sponsorship's effectiveness as compared to advertising: "Think about the playing field for a minute. TV is powerful, 700 channels. Mass advertising moves awareness of new products but it does not do the trick for sales. People can easily avoid commercials ... so unless there is an inherent interest or association [in the product that] people have, it [the promotion] doesn't work."

Source: Institute for Sport Marketing Case Studies. Laurentian University 2003-2005.

Case Questions

1. Do you agree that sponsorship is part of the communications mix? Support your position.
2. How do leveraging activities support the integration of sponsorship into the promotional mix?

Chapter Summary

This chapter provided an overview of the importance of promotion within the marketing mix. The promotional mix comprises five components: advertising, publicity, personal selling, sales promotion, and sponsorship. While the place of sponsorship within the marketing mix has been questioned, it is a form of communications that has attained tremendous popularity among marketers because of its ability to connect with emotions. The promotional mix is used to communicate information about the product or service and is interchangeable with the communications mix. The chapter also includes some advice on how to plan and execute a promotional strategy.

Test Your Knowledge

1. Explain the relationship between promotion and each of the other Ps of the marketing mix. Give an example.
2. What makes a promotion successful?
3. Describe an experience where you have seen all elements of the promotional mix in action.
4. Visit a sport retailer in town and describe how it uses sales promotion. What tactics do you believe to be most effective in reaching consumers and why?
5. When is personal selling used by sports marketers? What are some key elements to personal selling?
6. Describe the elements of the promotional mix.

 For more review questions, go to http://www.sportmarketing.nelson.com.

Key Terms

advertising	promotion
leveraging	publicity
personal selling	sales promotion
point-of-purchase	sponsorship
premium	sweepstakes

 A full glossary of key term definitions is located at http://www.sportmarketing.nelson.com.

Internet Resources

The Sponsorship Report, http://www.sponsorship.ca/

Key word mapping—Marketing, http://www.kwmap.com/

Canadian Marketing Council—Sponsorship of Canadian athletes, http://www.the-cma.org/council/athletesponsorship.cfm

Sports promotion products, http://www.motivators.com/Promotional-SportsShapes-Products-10.html

Price and non-price promotions in Minor League Baseball, http://www.thesportjournal.org/2005Journal/Vol8-No4/hixson1.asp

Promotions and attendance in Minor League Baseball, http://www.middlebury.edu/services/econ/repec/mdl/ancoec/0510.pdf

Fan attendance crucial to sports today, http://newsarchives.tamu.edu/stories/00/020400-8.html

Sport Kingston—Sport funding and promotion, http://www.sportkingston.ca/promotion.asp

NHL teams with IBM to promote and enhance hockey through new alliance, http://www.encyclopedia.com/doc/1G1-18651230.html

Source: provided courtesy of Diving Canada

Chapter 10

Media and Distribution in Sport

Learning Objectives

- To understand the importance of the media in any marketing activity
- To learn tools and tactics to obtain media coverage
- To know how the media can determine the effectiveness of an event or promotion
- To understand and be able to apply distribution concepts in sport marketing situations
- To define channels and understand distribution of sport products
- To understand the distribution process in relation to the media, facilities, and retailing

Introduction

How do I get my hands on a ticket for the main event?

This chapter presents the strategic concept of distribution—"place" in the marketing mix—combined with the vital distribution channel of the media. We emphasize the importance of the media and their technologies in distributing sport products.

The media play a key role in the distribution of sport to consumers. Effective **media relations** depends on relationships between the sport organization and media representatives that are built over time. Media outlets provide sport organizations with the opportunity to reach large number of consumers at minimal cost. Hence, understanding the inner workings of media is an important aspect of a sport marketing strategy.

media relations: solid understanding of media and relationships built over time between the sport organization and media representatives.

Why Is Media Relations Important?

With the increased attention devoted to sport, the media can be a great source of promotion for a sport organization. However, if used poorly, media relations can damage the sport. Often, marketers and managers in sport organizations find themselves in the eye of a media storm, either as the central figure or as the spokesperson for an athlete, their sport, the organization, or a government. Therefore, all sport organization personnel must be prepared to weather the storm: In a crisis, interaction—rather than reaction—with the media holds the greatest potential for defusing a problem and creating a positive interpretation of a situation. Proactive beats reactive every time. One must attempt to create positive attention for their sport organization and, in the process, gain respect from the media.

Building long-term relationships with the media can be a great asset to your sport organization. As a partner, it is your role as the sport marketer to service the media by providing information that is timely, professional, and accessible, in good times and bad. Having good relations with the media is an integral part of any sport marketing strategy. A newspaper can provide such information on your events as the price, product (information on individuals/teams participating), and place (where to get tickets, where the event is taking place), and it can promote the event (interesting stories, things to watch for)—all at no or little cost to your sport organization.

EXECUTIVE PERSPECTIVE

Claire Carver-Dias, Marketing Director and Communications, Bobsleigh Canada , President AthletesCAN

It's Your Story. Own It.

I'd step out of the pool, exhausted and out of breath from having just completed a gruelling synchronized swimming routine and find a camera and microphone thrust in my face. Whether at the World Cup, World Championships, Commonwealth Games, or Olympic Games, the scenario was always pretty much the same: Plunked between me and a warm shower was a media scrum, waiting to ask me a dozen questions about my performance.

It wasn't long into my career as a national team athlete that I began to see media interviews as an opportunity to promote my own story, my team's new sponsorship, or any important issues and ideas, rather than just a hassle I had to survive to get to my towel. Media relations became a part of the performance. Every moment in front of a tape recorder or camera was a chance to tell the story I wanted to tell.

Tasty Bites

One of the frustrations I experienced as an athlete was when a 30-minute interview was cut down to a 10-second sound bite. It seemed like such a waste of my time—until I realized that the journalist was simply wading through a series of questions to get the short sound bite they needed from me. So I learned how to create tasty sound bites.

Since the competition for airtime is fierce, having the tastiest sound bites helps move your story above others that happened on the same day. To maximize the effectiveness of a sound bite, you must prepare. It's important to rehearse the sound bite so that you are able to deliver it succinctly but as naturally as possible.

Ideally, you want an interview to be conducted on your terms, so that you can enforce your own key messages. When an interview begins to veer away from your chosen story, do your best to steer it back to the subject area you would like to discuss.

Story Time

Now in my role at Bobsleigh Canada Skeleton, I encourage the athletes, coaches, and staff members to be as prepared as possible for their media encounters. Prior to every major event, I create and distribute basic key messages to help focus their thinking on a few issues. Not only does this prime them for their media encounters, it provides our organization with the ideal opportunity to build a cohesive team voice among our key stakeholders and reinforce our vision and strategic plans by embedding them in the messaging.

Advice

The temptation for any media relations professional working with a client is to script and control every aspect of their client's media encounters with the media. Beyond ensuring that the key messages are well researched and that the client is well briefed and prepared, the real trick behind effective media relations is ensuring that the client's unique voice comes through in the message delivery. To accomplish this, the media relations professional must get to know their client and nurture the aspects of their personal story and/or voice that will make their message stand out from others.

Claire Carver-Dias is a 2000 Olympic medalist in synchronized swimming and former Canadian Olympic Committee program manager. She is currently the director of marketing and communications at Bobsleigh Canada Skeleton and president of AthletesCAN.

The Role of the Media

There are two main categories of media: print and electronic. Print media include newspapers, magazines, and special publications; electronic media are all forms of radio, television broadcasting, and the Internet.

While the print media have historically been more concerned with the technical aspects of a game (e.g., tempos, tactics, and style), the electronic media (especially television) have played a large role in the glorification of individual athletes and coaches and the popularity of sports. With the recent attention given to the business side of sports—salary spirals, collective bargaining processes, sponsorship and television rights, lifestyle issues such as doping and gambling, lawsuits, facility questions, race and discrimination concerns—sport reporting now closely resembles news reporting as stories about sport are investigative in nature, like their criminal and political counterparts.

The electronic media, especially television, are far more effective than print in creating sports fans and sports stars. Indeed, both electronic journalists and ex-athletes have become media stars, generating substantial personal income from this recognition. Think of tennis star Anna Kournikova who never won a major tournament but has gained celebrity status thanks to the media. This has led to numerous lucrative endorsement contracts, music videos, and many other opportunities. This kind of media attention also provides sports with additional exposure. The majority of events covered on television today continues to be such professional sports as hockey, football, and basketball, or such popular "amateur" sports as skiing, curling, and figure skating. However, emerging sports like snowboarding, speed skating, freestyle skiing, BMX, and beach volleyball are getting their share of airtime. In addition, the creation of specialized sport networks (The Sport Network, Réseau des sports, Sportsnet) offer new opportunities for smaller sports to get on television. Hence the importance of understanding the various options offered to sport marketers and the inner works of the broadcasting industry.

It is essential for sport organization personnel to understand the people and the environment of the media system. First, one must appreciate the influence that print and electronic sport journalists have on the public. Sport journalists attain recognition and power because they possess a commodity (theoretically, the inside sport story) that the public craves. Since sport journalists have the power to shape the image and reputation of athletes, teams, leagues, coaches, and owners, a number of amateur sport organizations are now training athletes, coaches, and key staff in media relations.

However, the journalist's role is associated not only with power and influence but also with stress and pressure. The employer expects the journalist to contribute to increasing readership, thereby selling more papers and/or increasing advertising revenue. Leagues, teams, and sport managers, by virtue of their control of dressing room and/or athlete access, also put pressure on the journalist. Athletes may be encouraged to alienate a journalist considered to be reporting negatively. Athletes and the public have been known to threaten or physically abuse specific journalists for their reporting of a situation.

Ways to Get Media Coverage

The media can be a great source of distribution to sport organizations. There are a number of ways that a sport organization can get its events, athletes, or coaches in the media. Key factors are the development of relationships and the quality of the servicing: The journalist and sport marketer must develop a relationship based on trust and understanding; news release, press conferences, and interviews are the most often used methods to service the media.

News Releases

News releases are among the most common forms of communications between sport marketers and the media, used by all levels of sports from major league sports to the little league soccer team competing in a city tournament. Ideally, the press release is written in a style that conforms to the needs of the media. It should include not only basic information but also quotes and/or pictures when available. With fierce competition to get space in the media, one needs to provide a news release that will be newsworthy, timely, and interesting to the media audience. It is important to know that every sport event represents three major news opportunities, when the press is legitimately interested in timely information: pre-event, event, post-event.

Helitzer[1] states that press releases must be of high quality if they are to make it into the news. He notes that the basic structure of a press release has been fairly consistent over the last 50 years and prescribes[2]:

1. Write the press release on 8½ × 11 paper if it is part of a package or sent by fax. This is not an issue if the sport organization uses e-mail and/or PDF files.
2. Leave space for journalists to take notes—two inches at top and bottom, and one inch to either side.
3. Use official letterhead with information on the sport organization. If you use electronic format, scan the letterhead and send the press release as an attachment to an e-mail. It is essential to have a contact name and number and best time to call on the press release.
4. Mark the release with "immediate release," indicating that media can use the press release as soon as they wish to, depending on their own schedule.
5. Write a meaningful headline to catch the attention of the media sport editor. The first paragraph, or the lead, should be two to three lines below the headline, with the first word of each paragraph indented 8 to 10 spaces. The lead should include the 5 Ws: who, what, when, where, and why.
6. In the body, write the facts to support the lead. The general rule is to use the inverted pyramid: The lead is most important paragraph and each succeeding paragraph contains less important information.
7. Use short sentences and short paragraphs, as they are easier to read.
8. Put a page number at the top and bottom of release. Indicate the end of release with "30" or "end" centred on the last line.

To maximize coverage, make sure you know the deadlines of the media so you can send the news release on time: Deadlines for print media are different than for electronic media. Don't forget to send your news release to a wire service (e.g., Canadian Press) when appropriate: Smaller newspapers and radio and television stations depend heavily on the wire services for information, and you want to ensure your voice is heard.

A sport event broadcast may be controlled by leagues, teams, owners, or networks, thus dictating what the public hears or sees. The transmitted information naturally serves the interests of each particular group. This is more prevalent in connection with professional sport, but can also occur with amateur sport events. Sport organization personnel should consider this if they seek a broadcasting contract for an event. For example, more amateur sport organizations hire a producer to broadcast their events on a private sport cable network like TSN. By paying for the production, the sport organization has usually more control over the content and creative of the broadcast. For example, you may want to consider an interview with a key sponsor representative,

---

[1] Helitzer, M. (1992) *The Dream Job: Sports Publicity, Promotion and Public Relations*, 3rd ed. University Sports Press.

[2] ibid: 97–101.

place the signage in the right television spots, and develop a special vignette. Sport organizations are also often given advertising inventory to share with a broadcaster (e.g., 30-second spots, opening/closing billboards, in-program graphics). The value of such advertising should be acquired ahead of time. Finally, understanding event broadcasting is critical when negotiating a fee with potential production companies. Consider:

- number and types of cameras required to provide a quality broadcast
- number of technicians needed to produce the broadcast
- commentators
- lights and equipment
- production crew and truck

Press Conference

press conference: an invited media covered news release for which journalists ask questions about the newly publicized announcement.

The sport marketer must assess the value of a **press conference** and whether it is needed. Media representatives are busy people and do not like to be called in for something of little or no value to them. In addition, especially in big cities, the competition for getting the media's attention is fierce. Too often, sport organizations believe they have something newsworthy when, in fact, it is not the case. Can a press release be issued instead? This is usually where previous relationships with the media can pay dividends. Prior to sending an invitation, it may be wise to check with a few prominent media representatives to find out their availability for the event[3]. If you decide to go ahead with a press conference, send out invitations with information for an RSVP on it.

Make sure that everything is ready on site, from staff and volunteers to equipment including: media kits, parking spaces, podium and microphone if needed, key personalities confirmed (athletes, coaches, administrators), master of ceremonies, refreshments, projector, multimedia projector (if needed), and lighting. Bring a media list to confirm which media attended. Usually, a press conference will be held late morning (11:00 a.m.) or mid-afternoon to get the maximum electronic coverage—news broadcast at noon, repeat coverage in evening, and late-night news. Once again, it is essential that the reason(s) for the press conference be newsworthy.

Provide media with opportunities to come into the training facility to capture some videos of athletes in action and to get brief clips for television news.

Media Kit

media kit: press kit which includes schedule of events, athlete bios, stats, selection process, interview request form, accreditations, fact sheet, technical information, history of sport, sponsor list, and action shots; given out to journalists at a press conference, in a media room, or delivered directly to the media.

Whether at a press conference, in a media room, or delivered directly to the media, a press kit should be provided to the journalists. This kit should include:

- schedule of events
- biographies of national team athletes, players, and coaches
- previous statistics (e.g., results, records)

---

[3] Pitts, B. & D. Stotlar (1996) *Fundamentals of Sport Marketing*. Fitness Information Technology.

- selection process in the case of a selection for a major event (Olympic Games)
- interview request form
- accreditations
- fact sheet on sport
- technical information
- history of the sport
- names of sponsors
- action shot photos

Action shot photos can be of great value if a journalist does not have a camera or cannot come to the event. In addition, for very technical sports such as diving, it may be an opportunity to provide the media with quality pictures from the right angles and with the sponsor logos placed appropriately. A good picture with a well-written press release can increase the chances of getting your information into the newspaper.

Media Training

The media training of athletes, coaches, administrators, and volunteer boards is essential for a successful media relations strategy. The athletes and coaches in particular are most likely to be sought after for interviews. Some may be asked to face the media on a frequent basis (e.g., professional hockey players and coaches). Others may only get the opportunity to be on television once every four years during the Olympic Games. Either way, athletes and coaches are sports' best ambassadors, and good preparation can contribute to building awareness and interest for a sport organization.

While a sport organization may wish to get as many athletes as possible in the media under normal circumstances, there are times when only one spokesperson should be speaking on behalf of an organization (e.g., doping infraction, harassment cases, selection criteria for teams). Selecting a single spokesperson has merit as long as other personnel within the organization are informed of the facts. Reporters will seek multiple opinions for a story, and you must not leave a news coverage opportunity to chance. The possibility for misrepresentation is decreased if the reporter cannot uncover conflicting opinions. This is critical especially in time of crisis. Preparation is essential when dealing with the media.

A briefing session (or press conference) in time of crisis is a useful tool because a planned response reduces the chance of harm the organization. The briefing session allows personnel to obtain correct information on many topics. Key messages should be developed and distributed to the individuals who may be speaking to the media. Preparing answers to questions that are most likely to be asked by the media is also an effective way to get ready for a media interview. The key messages and the Q&A (question and answer) documents must not be disseminated to a few individuals on a "need to know basis" but rather to all personnel when contact with the media is possible. Remember that opinion makers are not limited to media personnel.

Completely briefed personnel increase the chance for positive reporting in general. The idea is to eliminate the "I don't know but I think …" response and replace it with facts delivered in a positive manner. This type of planned media strategy will position the sport organization as a leader in the eyes of many opinion makers, especially with the media themselves.

Media Relations and Crisis Management

A good media relations strategy usually includes a crisis management plan. A crisis is a turning point for better or for worse, and the way a sport organization deals with a crisis can be a deciding moment. Crises are usually brought on by an issue or event that has potential for widespread, long-lasting impact. Crises require the attention of senior executives. Take the example of the figure skating scandal at the 2002 Winter Olympic Games in Salt Lake City when a judge's cheating denied Canadian skaters Sale and Pelletier an Olympic gold medal. This brought not only Figure Skating Canada into a crisis, but also the Canadian Olympic Committee, Salt Lake City Organizing Committee, International Skating Union, and the International Olympic Committee. In fact, this crisis had most likely damaged the "figure skating brand" as well as the Olympic brand. Communications and making sure the Canadian team's message was clear were key to creating a unified message in the media.

Sport managers should be prepared to deal with crisis with the 3 Ps of crisis management:

- prepare
  on the field (e.g., injuries, brawls, unsportsmanlike behaviour)
  off the field (e.g., strikes, sexual harassment, layoffs, lawsuits, key controversial decisions)
- predict
  potential problems, crises, controversies
- *prevent*
  with sufficient security; proper policies; anticipating labour problems; educating athletes, coaches, officials, volunteers

A proper crisis plan should minimize the impact on the organization's objectives and priorities: ticket price, fan support, player enthusiasm, support for management, recruiting, image, community support (financial and political), and brand management.

Distribution in Sport

You have a cool product, a nice price, great media, and wicked promotions. But how do you deliver the product?

The final strategic marketing element is distribution, connecting with our customers. Distribution, the "place" in the 4 Ps, involves the management of channels, or the chain or organizations that a product flows through from its origin to the end-user.

Distribution is the process of how a product or a service gets from the producer to the consumer[4]. If we consider a tangible good (snowboard), this process of moving the snowboard to a consumer is important in many ways, not just geographic (i.e., from location of manufacture to location of purchase) but also by time. In other words, it is not enough to provide Christine with a store to buy a Burton's snowboard, but the board must be available when she wants it—just in time to hit the slopes. It is also important for Christine to gain possession of the product in the form that she wants—proper design, colors, style, and so on. In summary, Christine gets 'the' Burton snowboard she wants, where she wants, and when she wants.

The same distribution concepts apply to services such as sporting events. For example, the fans for curling's most prestigious event, the Brier, may prefer to have games played during the week in the evenings in a facility that offers top-notch amenities (concessions, jumbotron, parking, public transportation) and broadcast on a major network (CBC). They may also want easy ticket access (Internet) and have the choice to buy tournament passes and choose their seat locations.

As demonstrated in the examples above, the marketing function of enabling consumers to access products conveniently and when they want is considered one of the most important strategic tactics that sport marketers implement. This can range from making sure local tennis players can get your rackets or that the televised product of your team is available to fans nationally or even globally. In accomplishing such goals, "distribution" refers to getting the product to the end-users and "channels" to the route the product takes to get to them, with each organization along the way known as a channel member. The form of the channels, or delivery systems, depends on the nature of the sport product being distributed. For example, telecasting a National Hockey League game is very different from selling hockey sticks.

In terms of the function that distribution channels provide to organizations, consider the efficiencies in the interactions between producers and consumers that they provide. Specifically, it is important to note that some large sporting goods stores sell as many as 5000 different items. If the manufacturer of each of those items needs to have a way of accessing the consumer directly, the number of outlets required would be unmanageable. However, the department store—as a channel member—allows for the producer of each of those 5000 products to access many customers in a very efficient way[5].

Channel Management in Sport

Sport marketers can manage **distribution channel**s, or the set of companies and individuals who participate in getting the product from the producer to the consumer, in a variety of ways. First, there are direct and indirect channels. In a direct channel, the end-user deals directly with the manufacturer or producer of the sport product. For example, a national team cyclist works directly with

distribution: the process of moving a product or a service from the producer to the consumer through one or many channels of distribution.

distribution channel: the set of companies and individuals that participate in getting the product from the producer to the consumer; includes wholesalers, retailers, dealers, distributors, brokers, franchises, and agents.

[4] Shank, M.D. (2005) *Sports Marketing: A Strategic Perspective*, 3rd ed. Prentice Hall.
[5] Dewan, T., K.B. Jensen, C. Farrell, & N. O'Reilly (2005) *Marketing: What Is It Good For?* Copley Publishers.

a bicycle manufacturer to have a custom bike made for racing and training. In an indirect channel, at least one channel intermediary exists between the producer and the end-user, often more. These channel intermediaries, often called middlemen or middlepersons, can be wholesalers, who purchase the product and resell it to another channel intermediary, or retailers, who sell the product to end-users. Examples in sport include the person scalping tickets to a professional sport event and a large wholesaler who buys hockey cards and resells them to a local wholesaler. Intermediaries provide these functions:

- taking ownership (and therefore risk) of the product
- managing the physical storage of the product (risks associated with stocking the product)
- gathering, sorting, and delivering the product
- providing information about the product
- facilitating purchase including financing of the product.

Each of the channel members—wholesalers, retailers, dealers, distributors, brokers, franchises, and agents—is influenced by key factors that affect the distribution in most industries.

Key Influencers on the Distribution Process

Not all channels have the same number of channel members. For example, the Toronto Blue Jays do not sell their game tickets to each customer in the same way. They may sell directly on the Internet or through a sales agent such as TicketMaster, a sponsor (grocery chains), or at the gate. Shorter channels, those with fewer levels, exist when there are fewer consumers (e.g., business consumers) and higher service needs, the product is complex or perishable, and the producer has the resources and ability to reach the consumers directly and requires a high degree of control over the process. Longer channels are required when the consumers are highly dispersed, products are standardized and inexpensive, producer does not have expertise in distribution, and the need for control is low.

Case: The Sudbury Wolves Hockey Club

The Sudbury Wolves Hockey Club is a team that plays in the Canadian Hockey League, the Major Junior A League that remains the primary source of young talent to the National Hockey League. Part of the Sudbury community for 33 years, the Wolves—members of the Ontario Hockey League (OHL)—are the most important sport property in the city of Sudbury. The team employs three people full time and dozens of others on a part-time basis.

The team is a success story. Games are popular and often sell out, with Friday Night in Sudbury games being the hottest ticket in town. Through effective marketing over many years, the Wolves have built a very strong brand equity in the Sudbury area, have stable ownership, enjoy a close relationship

STP and The Canadian Sport Marketing Mix

with the city of Sudbury, and play in front of an average of 4500 (one of the OHL's highest). The club has enjoyed many high-profile players over the years, including a number who went on to the NHL. Currently, the team has a high-profile coach in former NHL player Mike Foligno and some well-known players including Foligno's son, Nick, and two of the Staal brothers, Marc and Jared. Blaine Smith, VP of marketing for the club, and his staff have built an effective and award-winning marketing strategy. Over time, they have established strong relationships with sponsors, and today 50 percent of revenue for the team comes from marketing activities linked to their sponsors while the other 50 percent comes from ticket sales. One aspect of that strategy involves engaging the local media in their efforts. The media provide an important benefit to the Wolves as they promote the team, its players, and its games, and they allow for added value to be provided to the team's sponsors.

For promotion, the Wolves identify media relations as one of their key success factors and have a detailed plan of activities to keep themselves in the media. To keep the media interested, they focus on: on-ice success, community involvement of players, professionalism, entertainment value, and delivering on their promises. The Wolves understand that this attention to detail and the media creates a reputation within the city, and people expect a high level of service.

For distribution, the Wolves have several channels to get the games to their fans. First, they offer a number of season ticket packages tailored to the needs of consumers. Their partners also help in distributing tickets to consumers through various promotional activities. Tickets are also available on the team's websites and at the arena. Fans can follow the team on the local radio, on Rogers cable, and, for select games, on Sportsnet. To reach fans that are either on the road or have relocated to other regions, the Wolves recently added webcasts to their distribution strategy. Now fans can access a Wolves' game from anywhere in the world.

To provide value added to its sponsors, the Wolves marketing team keeps track of everything related to sponsorship to build a strong year-end report (e.g., media clippings), focus on promoting the Wolves as the best form of entertainment in the area, and protect and build the Wolves brand through messaging to the media (local TV station MCTV, newspapers including *The Sudbury Star*, and radio.) Their Sponsor of the Game promotion is provided in exchange for a quarter-page ad in *The Sudbury Star*, all rights for promotion of that game, the opportunity to drop the opening faceoff, and an allocation of 50 tickets. An example of a Wolves' sponsor using the media is Laking Toyota, a Sudbury car dealership, which builds its communications mix around a major advertising spend on radio and newspapers, with a small amount of television. Through the media, the dealership reminds everyone that it has a tradition of giving back to the community through a variety of donations and sponsorship of sports and non-sport activities.

Source: Institute for Sport Marketing Case Studies. Laurentian University 2003-2005

Case Questions

1. If you were vice president of marketing for a sport property in a mid-size city, what would you do to engage the media in your activities?
2. How do media relations help support the Wolves' sponsorships?
3. How does media relations fit into the Wolves' promotional mix? Their marketing mix?
4. Why do the Wolves have very limited use of television? Could this change?
5. What distribution channels are used by the Sudbury Wolves?
6. What other distribution strategies could the Wolves consider in the future?

Chapter Summary

This chapter introduces the fields of media relations and public relations. Given the tremendous coverage of sport by the media, a solid understanding of its importance and the value of public relations to a sport marketer are the key objectives of this chapter. The two media categories available to sport marketers are print (e.g., newspapers, magazines) and electronic (e.g., television, Internet) media. News releases, press conferences, and media kits are effective ways to provide information to the media. The media can also be an important channel for the distribution of sport products as it provides a means to get the product (sporting event) from the producer (NHL) to the consumers (fans). While the media provides an indirect channel of distribution, a direct channel is one in which the end-user deals directly with a manufacturer.

Test Your Knowledge

1. If you were tasked with getting media coverage for a local 10 km run, what would you do? Outline all the steps.
2. Why are the media important?
3. Why would media print a specific article?
4. Define public relations.
5. Define media relations.
6. Hundreds of people work for public relations firms in Canada. What do they do?

 For more review questions, go to http://www.sportmarketing.nelson.com.

Key Terms

distribution

distribution channel

media kit

media relations

press conference

A full glossary of key term definitions is located at
http://www.sportmarketing.nelson.com.

Internet Resources

NHLPA board places Saskin and Kim on paid leave of absence,
http://nhlpa.com/MediaReleases/ReleaseDetails.asp?mediaReleaseDisplay
Id={7B6B3EE1-A8EF-432D-8FE1-F569971D2BD6}

VANOC partners with Air Canada,
http://www.aroundtherings.com/Default.aspx?articleid=29127

NHL and STATS announce data partnership,
http://biz.stats.com/releases/index.asp?page=nhl

27 hours of scouting combine coverage on NFL network,
http://www.nflcombine.net/files/pdf/nic_news_rel_07.pdf

Hurricanes, RYHA to hold press conference Thursday,
http://hurricanes.nhl.com/team/app?articleid=292487&page=NewsPage&se
rvice=page

2007 NHL all-star celebration to feature week-long events for fans,
http://www.americanairlinescenter.com/index.cfm/FuseAction/Page/
PageID/73/ArticleID/183

Rogers Sportsnet hits a homerun with 116 Blue Jays games,
http://www.sportsnet.ca/pressroom/release
.jsp?news=20070323_113659_4916

CN8 (Comcast) to broadcast Holyfield-Maddalone on March 17,
http://www.mainevents.com/pressreleases.php?id=34

2007 Soccer Hall of Fame inductees,
http://www.itsportsnet.com/leagues/1000/documents/
teamofdistinction07.pdf

Best Canada Games to date draws to a close,
http://www.2007canadagames.ca/en/media/documents/ENGClosing_
Release.pdf

Source: Litwin Photography / Shutterstock

Chapter 11

Sport Sponsorship

Learning Objectives

- To appreciate the history of sponsorship and its use in sports today
- To understand the place of sponsorship in the promotions mix
- To know the differences between sponsorship and advertising
- To be able to integrate a sponsorship strategy within a sport organization
- To understand the corporate objectives associated with sport sponsorship

Introduction

Sponsorship is not charity

Sport sponsorship is big business. How big a business? According to International Event Group (IEG), sponsorship spending worldwide was expected to reach US$30 billion in 2006. While there is no base figure for sponsorship spending in Canada, there have been signs of tremendous growth here as well. With the Olympic Games set to take place in Vancouver in 2010, the tier one sponsors comprising six Canadian companies have pledged in excess of $650 million over the next six years. This does not include the investment made by non-Olympic sponsors to such national sport organizations as Hockey Canada, Speed Skating Canada, or Alpine Canada. In addition, sponsorship of professional sport leagues such as the National Hockey League has flourished in the last few years. Millions are invested in naming rights for arenas (Bell Centre, Scotiabank Place, General Motors Place) as well as other forms of sponsorship. Companies invest in sport sponsorship because sport brings value.

Jean R. Dupré, Director General, Speed Skating Canada

The Relentless Pursuit of Excellence

This perspective is about Speed Skating Canada (SSC), the most successful national sport organization in Canada in the past decade.

In amateur sport, success does not come easy. Canada is competing on the international scene against countries whose teams have access to considerably more resources. In 1998, SSC set the ambitious goal of making Canada the number one nation in speed skating by 2002. To achieve this goal, a comprehensive high-performance plan was crafted by the best technical minds in our sport. Its purpose was to identify everything needed to get our athletes on the Olympic podium. While there would certainly be financial implications, we first wanted to know what we needed to get there: training needs (e.g., staff, facilities, assessment camps, coaching, technology, sports sciences), competition needs (e.g., support team travelling with athletes, select sites of competitions, parents' opportunities to join team at key competitions), and administrative needs (e.g., office, management).

Once the organization had completed the high-performance plan and identified the financial support required, it needed to develop a financial strategy that would ultimately provide the necessary funding for the plan to unfold. A key component of this financial strategy was a successful team sponsorship program. For the plan to succeed, we needed to generate $1 million annually in sponsorship revenue. Needless to say, this was an important mindset shift for the organization but our board of directors was fully committed to making this work.

Following a comprehensive audit of our marketing properties, we determined that we needed to change various aspects of our marketing approach. For example, athletes' racing attire was identified as one of the key areas where potential sponsors could gain significant benefits by associating with our national team property. However, sport-specific regulations dictated by our international federation (IF) allowed very little corporate visibility on racing attire. Hence, we needed to play a leadership role at the IF level through lobbying efforts and by presenting innovative changes to the sponsorship regulations. Our efforts paid off and a number of changes were made to the regulations that yielded increased sponsorship opportunities. Our next challenge was making sure that our properties were clearly defined with a specific value attached to each.

In our quest to raise sponsorship dollars, we believed that corporate sponsors support amateur sports for various reasons, the most important of which was a return on investment. Therefore, to attract corporate partners, we needed to know our product and our audience and present the information in a manner that would be attractive to the sponsor. We conducted numerous market research projects with the goal of gaining a much better understanding of our membership, spectators, and television. We devoted much effort to improving the presentation of our events to make them look appealing, professional, consistent, and exciting for athletes, spectators, and television.

As we were getting ready to approach potential partners, we knew our proposed partnership had to be based on a natural fit between our brand and the sponsor's brand. We also wanted a company that shared interest in a fast-growing amateur sport at the grassroots level and a mutual goal of excelling and helping Canadian athletes achieve their dreams of reaching the World Cup and Olympic podiums. We thought that if we succeeded in getting the sponsors to believe in our sport and in our pursuit to excellence, we would touch on an important aspect of sport sponsorship—emotions (pride, joy of winning, sharing success). However, we were very much aware of sponsors' bottom line: Companies are interested in achieving numerous objectives through sponsorship whether be it awareness, image, hospitality, sales, or something else. More important, our proposal had to demonstrate how a potential sponsor's market share objective could be reached.

The decision of our board of directors to commit to excellence and to make Canada the number 1 nation in speed skating was bold and ambitious. Given the environment at that time, finding $1 million dollars in corporate sponsorship was a challenging proposition for a national sport organization. Simply put, we rolled up our sleeves and made it our "relentless pursuit of excellence."

Jean Dupré is director general for Speed Skating Canada. He has 20 years of experience in sport management, marketing, project planning, and organizational management. Jean is also vice president of the Canadian Olympic Committee and has been a member of the Canadian Olympic Committee board for the past 15 years.

History of Sponsorship

The sponsorship of sports organizations is not a new phenomenon. In fact, it can be traced back to the ancient Olympic Games (dating back 3000 years), when wealthy patrons helped athletes in their training and supplied them with proper equipment, including chariots and horses[1]. In return for their contributions to the Olympic Games, these wealthy Greek men gained not only goodwill and enhanced civic standing in the community and the state but also a variety of privileges including the rights to special seats.

The origins of sponsorship as we know it today may be more recent, dating to the nineteenth century. Brooks[2] and Irwin[3] note that transportation industry companies in the United Sates were the first businesses to be associated with sponsorship. As early as 1852, the New England railroad transported rowing teams from Yale and Harvard to a competition and used various promotional strategies to communicate their involvement to the public. The growing popularity of baseball in the US in the late nineteenth century provided companies like Spalding a great platform to reach and influence a burgeoning consumer population to purchase its products and services. The first modern Olympic Games were funded by such marketing activities as commemorative medals and stamps, ticket sales, program advertising, and private donations. In 1896, companies like Kodak purchased advertising in the first official Olympic program. In 1928, Coca-Cola recognized the value of

---

[1] McMahon, E.A. (1996) The evolution of Olympic commercial partnerships. *Olympic Message—Sources of Financing Sports*, 3: 14–8.

[2] Brooks, C.M. (1994) *Sports Marketing: Competitive Business Strategies for Sports.* Prentice Hall.

[3] Irwin, R.D. (1993) In search of sponsors. *Athletic Management:* 11–6.

association with the Olympics by donating 1000 cases of soft drinks to the US Olympic team in Amsterdam, enabling it to claim the title of official Olympic supplier[4].

The most important factor in the development of sport sponsorship was the progress in communications technology in the 1950s and 1960s, setting the stage for future radical changes in the world of sport. Technical progress and growing prosperity accelerated the spread of television, which was to "become the catalyst in the marketing of sport.... In the second half of the 'fifties, the sale of television sets took off to such an extent that the phenomenon has been described as 'contagious commercialism'[5]." The symbiosis between television and sport influenced the development of one another. One result was the acceleration of the commercialization and professionalization of sport. "The spiraling effect of media exposure, popularization and commercialization had been set in motion: the popularity of sport increased, and, with it, financial interest in the sport as a commodity; this in turn intensified its media exposure which ultimately helped to promote sport itself[6]."

Commercial sponsorship is mainly a phenomenon of the last 30 to 35 years[7]. Until the early 1970s, corporate sponsorship of sporting events, clubs, and athletes was done first and foremost for philanthropic reasons[8]. In this way, corporate decisions to sponsor sports were not necessarily made as a business decision but as ones that could generate public goodwill. This corporate attitude greatly shifted in the 1980s, as companies started devoting substantial resources to sponsorship.

Technological changes, especially in television, had the most profound effect on making sport an attractive commercial commodity. Howard and Crompton[9] credit the US *Television Act*, which prohibited tobacco companies from advertising on television, as having a great impact on the growth of sport sponsorship. Otker[10] and Meenaghan[11] both suggest that sponsorship grew in popularity due to the increased cost and the cluttering of traditional media. The increase in television channels and radio stations resulted in advertisers competing for the consumer's attention and made it difficult for any particular advertisement to make an impact. Sponsorship was therefore seen as a cost-effective way to break through the **clutter** and reach specific target audiences. According to Mullin, et al.[12] sponsorship also offers a unique opportunity for lifestyle marketing, a means of communicating with a specific target market through leisure and lifestyle activities.

clutter: advertising and/ or sponsoring messages vying to get the attention of fans, spectators, and potential consumers, which may cause confusion in the marketplace.

---

[4] Howard, D.R. & J.L. Crompton (1995) *Financing Sport*. Fitness Information Technology.

[5] Schantz, O. (1995) La présidence d'Avery Brundage (1952-1972). And Lennartz, K. & O. Schantz (1995) La présidence de S. Edstrom et la présidence de A. Brundage. In Gafner, R. & N. Muller (eds), *Un siècle du Comité International Olympique*, Vol. 2. IOC: 72–200.

[6] ibid: 151.

[7] Sandler, D.M. & D. Shani (1993) Sponsorship and the Olympic Games: The consumer perspective. *Sport Marketing Quarterly*, 2(3): 38–43.

[8] Sleight, S. (1989) *Sponsorship: What It Is and How to Use It*. McGraw-Hill.

[9] Howard, D.R. & J.L. Crompton (1995) *Financing Sport*.

[10] Otker, T. (1988) Exploitation: The key to sponsorship success. *Marketing and Research Today*, 16(2): 77–86.

[11] Meenaghan, T. (1991) The role of sponsorship in the communications and marketing mix. *International Journal of Advertising*, 10(1): 35–47.

[12] Mullin, B., S. Hardy, & W. Sutton (2000) *Sport Marketing*, 2nd ed. Human Kinetics.

Combined with the IOC's decision to open the door to commercialization in the early 1980s, the 1984 Olympic Games played a key role in the growth of sponsorship. The great success of the LA Games and subsequently the IOC's Olympic marketing program may have contributed to legitimizing the commercialization of sport by the sport governing bodies. Irwin & Sutton[13] believe that the Games served as the catalyst for the phenomenal growth in American sport sponsorship. Prior to the 1984 Games, financing had primarily come from government funding, lotteries, and donations. According to Meenaghan[14], the hunger to associate with desirable positioning values through clean, exclusive, and cost-efficient access has always been the key driver in the development of sponsorship as a medium of promotion. However, the clutter resulting from multilevel deals negotiated by such sponsees as the Olympics and the effects of ambush marketing may inevitably wreck the purity of the transfer of values between event and sponsor.

Relationship of Sponsorship to Marketing

The rapid growth of sport sponsorship has led to the misuse of the term "sponsorship." People often use the term interchangeably with other terms like marketing, sport marketing, and promotions, thus saying "marketing" when referring to sponsorship. While sponsorship is part of the promotional mix, it cannot be used to describe marketing. Although sponsorship is now considered a legitimate element of a company's communications mix, it is important to understand its place within the broader concept of the marketing mix. The process of marketing begins with the identification of the needs and wants of consumers: A consumer-oriented organization tries to understand consumers' requirements and satisfy them in ways that are beneficial to both consumer and the organization. This is usually achieved through the marketing mix (4 Ps)—product, price, promotion, and place—discussed in previous chapters. A transaction occurs when equitable terms of exchange are agreed upon by the two parties[15]. In the realm of sports, consumers have demonstrated an intense want for sport, which has translated into demand, since these wants were backed up with purchasing power.

Sport promotion plays a significant role in the marketing mix. While the term "promotion" is often used synonymously with advertising[16], it is much more than that, since it involves all form of communications to the consumers. This is why contemporary marketing theorists often refer to the **promotion mix** as the "communications mix." The role of the communications mix is to inform and persuade consumers and thus influence their purchase decisions.

promotion mix: tools used to communicate information about a product—its function, characteristics, price, place, and so on—to inform and persuade consumers and thus influence their purchase decisions.

---

[13] Irwin, R. & W. Sutton (1994) Sport sponsorship objectives: An analysis of their relative importance for major corporate sponsors. *European Journal of Sport Management,* 1(2): 93–101.

[14] Meenaghan, T. (1998) Current developments and future directions in sponsorship. *International Journal of Advertising:* 3–28.

[15] McCarville, R.E. & R.P. Copeland (1994) Understanding sport sponsorship through exchange theory. *Journal of Sport Management,* 8: 102–14.

[16] Shank, M. (2005) *Sport Marketing: A Strategic Perspective,* 3rd ed. Prentice Hall.

For a growing number of organizations, sport has become an effective and efficient way to communicate to current and potential target markets. An increasingly popular method used by corporations to market their brands through sport has been sponsorship.

Since corporations typically use sponsorship to achieve a number of objectives[17], many sport properties have offered fully a "integrated marketing communications program[18]." This concept consists of carefully integrating and coordinating the promotional mix elements to deliver a unified message and take full advantage of the synergy between its elements. For example, an integrated marketing communications program for Canada's Olympic women's hockey team may include the rights to athlete images, corporate hospitality, media advertising, sponsor recognition programs, and sales promotions. A sponsor may choose to leverage its investment by using a variety of communications tools: Leveraging, or activation of rights, refers to incurring additional costs to support a sponsorship program by many or all of the other elements of the communications mix[19]. For example, RONA's sponsorship of the Canadian Football League (CFL) may only provide the company with the right to associate with CFL and its eight teams. RONA will have to spend additional money to activate its rights through such promotional mix elements as advertising during TSN's broadcast on CFL Friday night games, getting players from each of the eight teams to come to local RONA stores for signing sessions, creating in-store incentive programs for customers and/ or employees, providing key clients/accounts with hospitality at the Grey Cup, special events before or during games, sales promotions, or most likely a combination of all of these tools. On average, companies spend about five times the original investment in leveraging[20].

Legitimizing sponsorship as an important element of the communications mix has contributed to making sports "big business." Worldwide expenditure on sponsorship has grown from about US$500 million in 1982[21] to an estimated $37 billion in 2007[22]. These figures support the argument that sponsorship is an integral part of the marketing communications mix alongside advertising, public relations, sales promotions, and selling, in that its basic function lies in achieving communications objectives[23].

---

[17] Berrett, T. (1993) The sponsorship of amateur sport—Government, national sport organization, and corporate perspectives. *Society and Leisure.* 16(2): 323–45.

[18] ibid: 18.

[19] Tripodi, J. (2001) Sponsorship—A confirmed weapon in the promotional armoury. *International Journal of Sports Marketing and Sponsorship.* Mar/Apr: 1–20.

[20] Eisenhart, T. (1988) Sporting changes zap competitors. *Business Marketing:* 92–7.

[21] Shanklin, W. & J. Kuzma (1992) Buying that sporting image: What senior executives need to know about corporate sports sponsorship. *Marketing Management,* Spring: 59–64.

[22] IEG Sponsorship Report (2006) 2006 sponsorship spending. *IEG Sponsorship Report:* 25.

[23] Tripodi, J. (2001) Sponsorship—A confirmed weapon in the promotional armoury.

Sponsorship and Philanthropy

Kuzma and Shanklin[24] suggest that sponsorship's foundation is philanthropic giving. In the last few years, the lines between pure philanthropy and sponsorship have been blurred. According to Arthur, et al.[25], this has made it difficult for other researchers to agree on a precise definition of sponsorship. This lack of a precise definition confuses consumers and businesses alike about the delineation of sponsorship, charitable donation, and patronage[26]. While both sponsorship and philanthropy offer funds, resources, and in-kind services to sport organizations, they differ in the nature of what they expect in return[27]. Pure philanthropic donations, where the individual or corporation donates funds for altruistic benefit, and charity, where an individual or corporation makes a donation and publicizes the fact, are different from sponsorship primarily because a commercial orientation is absent[28]. According to Wilkinson[29], the shift in attitude regarding sponsorship and philanthropy occurred when corporations began the search to receive a return on their donations to various associations. This resulted in substantial increases in the resources devoted to sponsorship. Sponsorship became not so much a form of social corporate behaviour but rather an important promotional tool and business expense that had to be justified[30].

In essence, financial support of a philanthropic nature should not be part of sponsorship since a firm making a donation should not expect any benefits in return. It may be possible to place various forms of corporate giving along a continuum defined by the extent to which giving is linked to corporate marketing objectives[31]. On one end would be pure philanthropy—no direct link to marketing objectives; on the other end would be sponsorship marketing—explicitly tied to sales of the sponsoring companies. Meenaghan's definition[32] "... sponsorship can be regarded as the provision of assistance either financial or in-kind to an activity by a commercial organization for the purpose of achieving commercial objectives" falls somewhere in the middle of the spectrum depending on the specific objectives of the program.

---

[24] Kuzma, J. & W. Shanklin (1994) *Corporate Sponsorship: A Framework for Analysis*. Brown & Benchmark.

[25] Arthur, D., D. Scott, & T. Woods (1997) A conceptual model of the corporate decision-making process of sport sponsorship acquisition. *Journal of Sport Management*, 11: 223–33.

[26] ibid: 8.

[27] Howard, D.R. & J.L. Crompton (1995) *Financing Sport*.

[28] Gross, A.C., M.B. Traylor, & P.J. Shuman (1987). Corporate sponsorship of art and sports events in North America. *Marketing and Research Today*, 15(4): S9–S14.

[29] Wilkinson, D.G. (1993). *Sponsorship Marketing: A Practical Reference Guide for Corporations in the 1990s.* The Wilkinson Group.

[30] Sandler, D.M. & D. Shani (1989) Olympic sponsorship vs ambush marketing: Who gets the gold? *Journal of Advertising Research*, Aug/Sept: 9–14.

[31] Becker-Olsen, K. (1998) Corporate Sponsorship: A Look at the Moderating Effects of Fit and Reach on Image and Purchase Intentions. Lehigh University.

[32] Meenaghan, T. (1983) Commercial sponsorship. *European Journal of Marketing,* Special issue: 93.

Sponsorship and Advertising

Despite its roots in corporate philanthropy, sponsorship fits within the promotional mix; however, contemporary marketing scholars do not agree on *how* it fits. While some authors consider sponsorship as part of advertising[33], others position it as different from advertising and as a promotional strategy unique in its application and benefits[34]. In fact, as suggested in the RONA case, sponsorship fits quite naturally alongside advertising, public relations, sales promotion, and selling as an element of the marketing communications mix, in that its basic function lies in achieving communications objectives. While the debate goes on, sponsorship is now widely believed to be different from advertising[35]. Table 11-1 details Bloxam's[36] three key points of difference between sponsorship and advertising.

TABLE 11-1

Sponsorship's Distinction from Advertising

DISTINCTION	MEANING	EXAMPLE
Sponsors are viewed as part of the program.	Due to the association effect, consumers perceive a sponsor as more involved with the sponsee than an advertiser who lacks the association.	The Nike Run TO event in Toronto (sponsor) versus a Nike TV commercial (advertising) during CBC Sports weekend.
Advertising and sponsorship function differently.	The process by which the communication takes place differs: In sponsorship, the message is coded, delivered, and decoded in collaboration with the sponsee; in advertising, the process occurs independently.	Leading up to and during the Olympic Games, the IOC and its TOP sponsors work together on all promotions, while Ford purchasing an advertisement in *The Globe and Mail* develops the promotion on its own.
Sponsorship is widely believed to benefit a wider audience.	Consumers often believe that supporting a sponsor has greater benefit than supporting an advertiser, as they perceive that the sponsee also will benefit. This is particularly important in the sponsorship of causes (e.g., amateur sport, charity).	The CIBC Run for the Cure.

Source: Bloxam, M.(1998). Brand Affinity and television programme sponsorship. International Journal of Advertising 17 (1). 89-98.

[33] Cornwell, T.B. & I. Maignan (1998) An international review of sponsorship research. *Journal of Advertising Provo,* 27(1): 1–21.

[34] Meenaghan, T. (1998) Current developments and future directions in sponsorship.

[35] Tripodi, J. (2001) Sponsorship—A confirmed weapon in the promotional armoury.

[36] Bloxam, M. (1998) Brand affinity and television progamme sponsorship. *International Journal of Advertising,* 17(1): 89–98.

As Table 11-1 outlines, what differentiates sponsorship from advertising is the association between the two parties (sponsor and sponsee), which enhances the relationship beyond a basic cash purchase of promotional value (advertising). Javalgi, et al.[37] describe sponsorship as a form of promotion, but clarify that it differs from advertising in that the medium and created messaging are not as tightly controlled by the sponsor as they would be by an advertiser.

An additional important difference between sponsorship and advertising lies in how each works to persuade customers. Advertising exploits the construct of emotion, and sponsorship seeks to connect with the emotion inherent in sport or the arts or the charity (depending on the sponsee of interest)[38]. Other authors describe sponsorship as fundamentally different from advertising as it persuades consumers indirectly[39]. This is based on the association that exists and the fact that consumers are influenced by the sponsee, the association, and the sponsor, not just the last. If a firm is seen to support a sponsee (e.g., team, charity, event, athlete), the sponsor's expectation is that the consumer, who is interested to some extent in the sponsee, will view the sponsor positively provided that there is a good fit between the image of the sponsor, the sponsee, and the association. Sponsorship may also be differentiated as it offers an interaction with consumers unlike advertising, which only talks to them. This, in theory, allows sponsorship to create a bond with consumers via the values they both share by association with the sponsee of interest[40]. For example, Coca-Cola's sponsorship of the Olympic Games allows for the transfer of attributes from the sponsee's image (e.g., performance, international) to the sponsor's product's image via the promotion of the association between the two.

A brief analysis of the objectives sought by advertising and sponsorship reveals the similarities and differences between the two promotional tools. Like advertising, sponsorship may sometimes be employed to enhance public awareness of a sponsor or to improve or change a previously established image[41]. Also similar to advertising, sponsorship may seek to increase sales or increase media exposure[42]. However, a sponsorship can achieve more diverse objectives than an advertisement, including increased awareness, change in image of a brand, or the enhanced ability to improve business relationships with customers[43]. Cornwell, et al.[44] point out two additional objectives that differentiate sponsorship from advertising: achieving corporate hospitality

---

[37] Javalgi, R.G., M.B. Traylor, A.C. Gross, & E. Lampman (1994) Awareness of sponsorship and corporate image: An empirical investigation. *Journal of Advertising*, 23(4): 47–58.

[38] Meenaghan, T. (2001) Understanding sponsorship effects. *Psychology and Marketing*, 18(2): 95–122.

[39] Crimmins, J. & M. Horn (1996) Sponsorship: From management ego trip to marketing success. *Journal of Advertising Research*, 36(4): 11–21.

[40] Kover, A.J. (2001) Editorial: The sponsorship issue. *Journal of Advertising Research*, 41(Jan–Feb): 5.

[41] Cornwell, T.B., D.P. Roy, & E.A. Steinard II (2001) Exploring managers' perceptions of the impact of sponsorship on brand equity. *Journal of Advertising*, 30(2): 41–51.

[42] ibid.

[43] Meenaghan, T. & D. Shipley (1999) Media effect in commercial sponsorship. *European Journal of Marketing*, 33(3/4): 328–47.

[44] Cornwell, T.B., D.P. Roy, & E.A. Steinard II (2001) Exploring managers' perceptions of the impact of sponsorship on brand equity.

and advancing the personal agendas and interests of senior executives, both of which are enabled by the ability to leverage a sponsorship, which more readily allows for associated events and activities.

Corporate Objectives and Sponsorship

ROI: return on investment, usually measured in monetary and/or media forms.

During the 1970s, sponsorship often served the personal interests of top executives or was used as a vehicle for charitable contributions. However, as the economic fortunes of companies changed, the need to prioritize spending and justify expenditures increased in importance[45]. In other words, since companies are looking for a return on investment (**ROI**), they must allocate sponsorship dollars wisely. In this context, sponsorship is considered less a form of social corporate behaviour and more an important element of the marketing mix. As a result, research on sponsorship has largely focused on the sponsoring company perspective on such issues as identifying its objectives[46]. Corporate objectives that support image and goodwill seem to be most popular for corporations. Sandler and Shani[47] identify three main groups of objectives associated with sponsoring sports:

1. broad corporate objectives (image based)
2. marketing objectives (brand promotion, sales increase)
3. media objectives (cost effectiveness, reaching target markets

One advantage of sponsorship is that it can achieve a number of objectives simultaneously[48]. In the literature, the most often cited objectives for corporate involvement in sport sponsorship are:

- increasing public *awareness* of the company, brand, or both
- altering or reinforcing public perception, or *image*, of the company, brand, or both
- identifying the company with particular *market segments*
- generating *media benefits*
- achieving *sales* objectives
- creating a competitive advantage through *exclusivity*
- gaining opportunities in terms of *hospitality* and entertainment

Each objective provides sponsors with an ROI that might be in monetary form but could also be in media exposure (number of impressions), the ability to exclude competitors, and so on.

Awareness

Awareness is widely accepted by practitioners and academics alike as a mechanism through which sponsorship is likely to function. Exposure to an object leads to positive affect towards it; and, as a result, the consumer may

[45] Mullin, B., S. Hardy, & W. Sutton (2000) *Sport marketing.*

[46] Lee, M.S., D.M. Sandler, & D. Shani (1997) Attitudinal constructs towards sponsorship. *International Marketing Review,* 14(3): 159–69.

[47] Sandler, D.M. & D. Shani (1993) Sponsorship and the Olympic Games.

[48] Berrett, T. T. & Slack (1999) An analysis of the influence of competitive and institutional pressures on corporate sponsorship decisions. *Journal of SportManagement,* 13: 114–38.

feel better about the brand or the company[49]. This good feeling can provide numerous benefits to the brand and/or corporate image. For example, consumers may pay greater attention to subsequent commercial communications and may be more likely to include the sponsor's product in their consideration sets. If a local grocery store is actively involved in supporting the activities of children year in and year out, parents may become more sensitive to future communications by the store. Meenaghan[50] suggests that awareness is created at events, where sponsors intrude on the consciousness of event audiences. In such a case, awareness is closely linked to image objectives since a sponsor's image may be enhanced by the association of the sponsor with the event, thus transferring values from the event to the sponsor[51].

The importance of increasing consumer level of awareness is significant in light of ambush marketing battles. Meenaghan[52] describes **ambush marketing** as "a practice whereby another company, often a competitor, intrudes upon public attention surrounding the event, thereby deflecting attention to themselves and away from the sponsor." A number of studies in this area demonstrate that consumers with relatively low levels of awareness of sponsors are easy to fool[53] and strong consumer identification of sponsorship requires both knowledge of the event and an emotional link to the activity/event or sponsor[54]. As a result, event organizers use an integrated approach to sponsorship communications, which may include strategic use of signage, rights in naming events and/or stadiums, jumbotron advertising, in-stadium promotions, and/or sales promotion. These methods are a way to highly targeted segments.

ambush marketing: a practice whereby another company, often a competitor, intrudes upon public attention surrounding the event, thereby deflecting attention to themselves and away from the sponsor.

Note that recall and recognition of sponsors is key to achieving many other objectives such as image and sales. If consumers do not remember the Tim Hortons affiliation with the week-long Brier, there will be little if any impact on the company's image, sales, or market share, thus resulting in a low ROI.

Image

Firms have long attempted to enhance their corporate image by creating awareness of their "good deeds" in the hope of ultimately increasing sales and profitability. Even when they refrain from explicitly promoting their altruistic efforts, they expect to generate goodwill, enhance their image, and ultimately increase sales. The opportunity to capitalize on image association/transfer makes sponsorship attractive to businesses as a communications tool.

[49] Pracejus, J. (1998) An inference-based model of building brand equity through sponsorship. PhD Dissertation, University of Florida.

[50] Meenaghan, T. (1998) Current developments and future directions in sponsorship.

[51] Meenaghan, T. (1983). Commercial sponsorship. *European Journal of Marketing,* Special issue, 1–73.

[52] Meenaghan, T. (1996) Ambush marketing: A threat to corporate sponsorship? *Sloan Management Review,* 38(1): 103–13.

[53] Seguin, B., M. Lyberger, N. O'Reilly, & L. McCarthy (2005) Internationalizing ambush marketing: The Olympic brand and country of origin. *International Journal of Sport Sponsorship and Marketing,* 6(4).

[54] Meenaghan, T. (1998) Current developments and future directions in sponsorship.

This possible impact of sport sponsorship on corporate image has been the focus of many researchers, who agree that a majority of companies involved in sponsoring are attempting to meet an image objective.

Image is the sum of beliefs, ideas, and impressions a person has of a business or its products[55]. Image benefits are most frequently sought by companies that are striving to create interest and a favourable attitude toward their products by "borrowing" the image of a sport to enhance the product's image with its target audience[56]. Ferrand and Pages[57] suggest that the image of a sporting object or phenomenon is a social representation and propose that sporting organization, as a social object or phenomenon, embodies a stock of image capital.

Sponsorship involvement in special events provides both a range of emotion and a perceived image[58]. By transferring the positive image of sport, a sponsoring company pursues the purpose of distinguishing itself from other organizations and, thereby, achieving a competitive advantage. The choice of a sport or event with particular attributes can help a company achieve a desired image that will reinforce or change consumers' perceptions of the company and its products[59]. There are numerous examples of companies that use sport sponsorship as a means to borrow images of sport. For example, Canada Post has traditionally been perceived as a somewhat boring government corporation; hence its reason for sponsoring freestyle skiing, a sport that connotes images that are audacious and innovative. Canada Post believes that through sponsorship of speed skating, the fastest sport on ice, it can transfer the image of speed to its delivery of mail and parcels. In addition, the company wants to maintain and improve its brand image and maintain a strong presence in the Canadian community. "Everybody understands that it is important to support amateur sports and their athletes that do not have much support. Image is everything: Canada Post wants to be perceived as a good corporate citizen[60]."

Three factors can affect one's perception of a particular event: event type, event characteristics, and individual factors[61]. For example, such characteristics as event size (2005 World Aquatics Championships in Montreal), professional status of participants (top swimmers in world), tradition/history associated with the event (one-off event, no tradition), venue (on island with Montreal

[55] Kotler, P. & A. Andreasan (1995) In Howard, D.R. & J.L. Crompton *Financing Sport*. Fitness Information Technology.

[56] Howard, D.R. & J.L. Crompton (1995) *Financing Sport*.

[57] Ferrand, A. & M. Pages (1996) Image sponsoring: A methodology to match event and sponsor. *Journal of Sport Management*, 10: 278–91.

[58] Ludwig, S. & J.D. Karabetsos (1999) Objectives and evaluation processes utilized by sponsors of the 1996 Olympic Games. *Sport Marketing Quarterly*, 8(1): 11–9.

[59] Howard, D.R. & J.L. Crompton (1995) *Financing Sport*.

[60] Seguin, B. (2006) *Canadian Sport Sponsorship: Case Studies Report*. Institute of Sport Marketing.

[61] Gwinner, K. (1997) A model of image creation and image transfer in event sponsorship. *International Marketing Review*, 14(3): 145–58.

skyline as backdrop), and promotional appearance of the event (look and feel) all influence consumers' perceptions of the image related to that event. Hence, sponsorship potential will be at its maximum when there is an association between the target group of the company and the target group of the sport or event, between the desired image of the company and the image of the sport or event, or between the product characteristics promoted and the credibility of the sport entity helping to promote the product[62].

The degree of similarity between the event and the sponsors may be a key factor in the image transfer process. A product can have either functional or image-related similarity with the event[63]. Functional similarity means a sponsoring product is actually used by participants during the event. For example, Speedo sponsors the Canadian swimming team. Image-related similarity means the image of the event is related to the image of the brand. For example, Mountain Dew sponsors the X Games, where youth, excitement, and cool orientation of both the extreme sports and the product offer similarity. Thus, companies should consider not only the potential customers their sponsorship signage will reach but also the image of the event, as this may become associated with the brand.

Reaching the Target Market

Corporations searching for an optimal event or team to sponsor need to find a link between the their product and the event. While Speedo has a direct link to aquatic sports and Nike an evident one to basketball, the link between Pizza Pizza and the Edmonton Eskimos football team may not be as obvious. However, through marketing research, the marketing director of the Eskimos may have found a great fit between the audience and the "typical" Pizza Pizza's desire target. Similarly, Tim Hortons may not have a direct link to curling, but its sponsorship of Canadian curling events reinforces its presence at events important to its target market. In other words, prior to selecting a sponsee, corporations should have a clear understanding of their target market. On the flip side, the sport marketer should also have a good understanding of its consumer base. Companies evaluate their potential consumers and produce a product that best adheres to the needs and wants of their own particular target market. A company using target market strategies is looking at entering segments of the market where it can offer superior value and gain an advantage over competitors[64].

With the proliferation of advertising outlets (television, print, Internet, radio), sponsorship provides the ability to break through the clutter and reach specific target markets. Marketing managers have used sponsorship to present their message to consumers in a more relaxed atmosphere and to support their

---

[62] Mullin, B., S. Hardy, & W. Sutton (2000) *Sport Marketing.*

[63] Gwinner, K. (1997) A model of image creation and image transfer in event sponsorship.

[64] ibid.

other marketing efforts[65]. As marketing and advertising have become more cluttered, sport organizations must concentrate on sponsorship opportunities that deliver specific segments within the market. For example, RONA's sponsorship of the CFL and its eight teams coincided with the opening of stores in the western provinces.

Certain events can help companies reach specific segments, such as heavy users, shareholders, and investors, or specific groups that have been demographically, psychographically, or geographically segmented. For example, RBC decided to streamline its marketing strategy and signed multiyear sponsorship with the Canadian Olympic Team, Hockey Canada, and Canadian University Sports after research indicated that participants in and followers of these events were typical users of financial services. On the other hand, RONA's intention to become "national in scope" led to its sponsorship of the CFL, which provides opportunities for the company to solidify its presence outside of the province of Quebec. The location and size of communities where CFL franchises exists across the country fits in well with RONA's expansion plans nationwide. Hence, the activation of the sponsorship in Regina (Saskatchewan Roughriders) coincided with the opening of a store in that city. RONA's sponsorship of the 2010 Winter Olympic Games in Vancouver also supports the company's national growth strategy.

A company can use sponsorship to reach its target consumers by targeting their lifestyles. Lifestyle marketing is "a strategy for seizing the concept of a market according to its most meaningful recurring patterns of attitudes and activities, and then tailoring products and their promotional strategies to fit these patterns[66]." The rationale behind this kind of sponsorship is that certain types of leisure activities (e.g., outdoor lifestyle like mountain biking, mountaineering, trail running) appeal to individuals who share similar lifestyles, values, and behaviours. Hence, the consumers in this target group may be more receptive to a sales message from a company that shares those values. In other words, lifestyle sponsorship creates opportunities to reach consumers who partake in similar activities and who possess similar interests and opinions. The association of the company or product with the event is also important since sporting events are well accepted by the public and often have a strong fan following. For example, sponsors have attempted to reach new and sometimes difficult to capture audiences: The X Games represent a perfect opportunity to reach generation Xers, a target market that is "difficult to reach through traditional media[67]."

Media Benefits

Media exposure/coverage has been identified as a key benefit sought from sponsorship as well as a key objective of sponsorship programs. Early studies even found that media objectives were the first priority for sponsoring

---

[65] Pitts, B. & D. Stotlar (1996) *Fundamentals of Sport Marketing.* Fitness Information Technology.

[66] Hanen, M. (2000) In Mullin, B., S. Hardy, & W. Sutton *Sport Marketing*, 2nd ed. Human Kinetics: 261.

[67] Shank, M.D. (2005) *Sports Marketing.*

companies[68]. According to Howard and Crompton[69], a central issue in negotiations between a sponsor and a sports manager is likely to be the probable extent of the event's media coverage. In addition to extending the audience, coverage of events by the media has a second important dimension—it takes the form of publicity or news. Furthermore, since sport events often get tremendous media coverage, this may provide company with cost-effective media coverage and help in reaching specific target markets more effectively[70].

Media benefits include advertising and publicity related to the promotional efforts surrounding the product or event. Media benefits are usually equated with ROI and measured in the numbers of impressions generated and the source of those impressions. The ability of an event to achieve media coverage and exposure for its sponsor is often presented as the key valuation criterion for a sponsorship[71].

A sponsor can achieve media related objectives in many ways. Shank[72] identifies alternative forms of advertising, from conventional stadium signage to the most creative media. For example, an advertising message may be an actual advertisement during a specific event. During the 2004 Grey Cup, Pfizer developed an advertising campaign that used a number of complementary media to promote one of its products. The in-stadium spectators were exposed to a specially designed vignettes aired on the jumbotron, while a 30-second commercial was aired during the broadcast of the event. The spectators and viewers were also exposed to in-stadium signage throughout the game. Sponsor signage is often prominent in a newspaper photographs, too. The various forms of advertising provide a number of impressions for the sponsor. Impressions are the number of viewers (television), readers (all print forms), and listeners (radio) exposed to the advertising message. However, more importantly, the source of these impressions will also be of importance to the sponsor. A photograph in a national newspaper (e.g., *The Globe and Mail*) is much more powerful in terms of impressions than one in a local newspaper because of the subscription base, the online value, and the national distribution of the paper. The same applies for television exposure (e.g., signage, interviews) in a national broadcaster such as CBC versus a cable specialty channel such as TSN. These are reasons that media benefits involving a variety of outlets or an association with an established entity may be the crucial element for some sponsors in determining whether to become involved as a sponsor: Thus the importance of a good media relations program.

Unfortunately for some sponsors, there are times when they are promised the benefits of sponsorship (e.g., recognition, percentage of reach in target market, sales), but, for some reason (possibly ambush marketing), those benefits fail to materialize.

---

[68] Abratt, R., B.C. Clayton, & L.F. Pitt (1987) Corporate objectives in sports sponsorship. *International Journal of Advertising*, 6: 299–311.

[69] Howard, D.R. & J.L. Crompton (1995) *Financing Sport.*

[70] Sandler, D.M. & D. Shani (1993) Sponsorship and the Olympic Games.

[71] Crowley, M.G. (1991) Prioritizing the sponsorship audience. *European Journal of Marketing*, 25: 11–21.

[72] Shank, M.D. (2005) *Sports Marketing: A Strategic Perspective.*

Sales

Companies use sponsorship to fulfill the primary marketing communications objectives of creating brand awareness, enhancing image, and reaching target markets. However, they sometimes explicitly seek and achieve bottom-line sales results[73]. Shank[74] suggests that, although there may be an indirect route to sales (i.e., the hierarchy of effects model of promotional objectives, which states that awareness must come before action or sales), the major objective of sponsorship is to improve the bottom line. When integrated with other elements of the promotional mix, sponsorship can influence the buyer to purchase[75]. After all, it is unreasonable to believe that organizations would spend millions of dollars to lend their names to stadiums or to events such as the Olympic Games if they did not feel comfortable about the ROI. Recent studies have shown that increasing sales and market share are the primary motives of sponsorship[76]. In Canada, Copeland and Frisby[77] found that 46.2 percent of the companies surveyed cited sales as one of the three most important indicators of sponsorship success.

Corporate sponsorship has often been classified as a type of sales promotion[78]. It offers opportunities for companies to address various short-term objectives, provide product sampling, and develop point-of-sale merchandising. Regardless of the short duration of a sponsorship or a promotion, residual long-term effects may be accrued through the continued use of a memorabilia, premiums, and/or special programs. For example, Petro-Canada's sponsorship of the torch relay for the 1988 Calgary Olympic Winter Games provided a promotional platform that still lives on 18 years later in the form of the Petro-Canada Olympic Torch Scholarship Fund. Since the program's inception in 1988, scholarships valued at a total of about $3.5 million have been awarded to 115 coaches and to over 1500 athletes.

Sales objectives can also relate to product use as a benefit of a sponsorship/licensing agreement. Sponsorship agreements with an event, venue, and even an entire university campus may require the exclusive use of a product at all events, functions, or facilities. For example, Coca-Cola's strategy is to sign sponsorship/licensing agreements that ensure product exclusivity and utilization: The morality of such deals on university campuses has created a lively debate in many postsecondary institutions. VISA also has used sponsorship to increase sales. Its experience with the Olympics since 1986 has shown that such activities significantly increase card use, help retain existing cardholder accounts, and generate significant numbers of new accounts. VISA is the only card accepted to buy Olympic tickets and merchandise on-site at Olympic Games. In fact, VISA credits its sport sponsorship programs, particularly the Olympics, as having significantly influenced sales.

---

[73] Meenaghan, T. (1996) Ambush marketing.

[74] Shank, M.D. (2005) *Sports Marketing: A Strategic Perspective.*

[75] Mullin, B., S. Hardy, & W. Sutton (2000) *Sport marketing.*

[76] Shank, M.D. (2005) *Sports Marketing: A Strategic Perspective.*

[77] Copeland, R. and Frisby, W. (1996). Understanding the sport sponsorship process from a corporate perspective. *Journal of Sport Management, (10),* 32–48.

[78] Copeland, R. & W. Frisby (1996) Understanding the sport sponsorship process from a corporate perspective. *Journal of Sport Management,* 10: 32–48.

Although the desired result of sponsorship may be increase in sales, sponsors are not necessarily identifying increased visibility and image enhancement as the vehicle to achieve this objective. The director of corporate sponsorship and events at the Eastman Kodak Company stated[79]: "As a sponsor, I look to the promoter to come to us with ideas on how the property can, in our case, sell film. Like most other companies today, we are no longer satisfied with enhanced image; give us opportunities for on-site sales, well-developed hospitality packages, dealer tie-ins, etc., and we'll listen."

Exclusivity

"If they are going to devote their marketing resources to a particular event, they do not want their competitor undertaking a similar promotional program[80]." In fact, **exclusivity** and/or blocking the competition are key requirements for all major sponsors of sports. In the case of Olympic sponsorship, TOP sponsors pay in excess of $70 million for their sponsorship rights fees. In return, these corporations are guaranteed exclusivity in their product category, exclusive rights to use the five ring logo worldwide marketing campaigns, and many other benefits. Ludwig and Karabetsos[81] report that the most important objective for sponsors of the 1996 Olympic Games was having exclusive sponsorship rights in their product categories. The respondents emphasized their concerns about exclusivity with comments pertaining to the anti-ambush marketing campaign of the International Olympic Committee and the Atlanta Committee of the Olympic Games. They also pointed out their own proactive measures to prevent any opportunities for competitors becoming involved in an ambush marketing strategy.

According to Townley, et al.[82], whatever the sponsor is looking to get out of a sponsorship, its investment or continuing investment is ultimately determined by the ability to deliver exclusive rights. Exclusivity provides an opportunity for sales-driven use of the sponsorship agreement while prohibiting competitors from using the event, venue, product, or activity to transmit a message to the audience[83]. This limitation of communication avenues can improve the ability of the marketing message to increase sales, and may affect the profitability of both the sponsor and the competitor. In light of the strong, emotional attachment and following that sport inspires, exclusivity allows the marketer to position brands or products as supporting an event or the efforts of a particular team, while implying that a competitor's product does not, thereby encouraging consumer support where it counts.

exclusivity: an opportunity for sales-driven use of the sponsorship agreement that prohibits competitors from using the event, venue, product, or activity to transmit a message to the audience.

---

[79] Kuzma, J. & W. Shanklin (1994) *Corporate Sponsorship: A Framework for Analysis.*

[80] Diggelman, R. In Howard, D.R. & J.L. Crompton (1995) *Financing Sport.* Fitness Information Technology: 242.

[81] Townleys Sports Lawyers, M. Payne, & D. Marshall, D. (1992) *Ambush/Parasitic Marketing and Sport.* Professional Direction: 1–24.

[82] Ludwig, S. & J.D. Karabetsos (1999) Objectives and evaluation processes utilized by sponsors of the 1996 Olympic Games. *Sport Marketing Quarterly,* 8(1): 11–9.

[83] Townleys Sports Lawyers, M. Payne, & D. Marshall, D. (1992) *Ambush/Parasitic Marketing and Sport.*

In their study on Canadian sponsorship, Berrett and Slack[84] report that exclusivity was important to all companies interviewed. Exclusivity was also found to be the most important criterion associated with sport sponsorship by Copeland and Frisby[85]. More recently, a study published by the Canadian-based Institute of Sport Marketing[86] found that exclusivity remains a key component to any sponsorship activity. A company may also choose to sponsor an event that offers exclusivity to prevent the competition from accessing it; however, this strategy may not be in the best interest of the sponsee since the sponsor is unlikely to activate its investment and removes the sponsee's opportunity to get additional benefits from a relationship. Nevertheless, when leveraged properly, a sponsorship can certainly be used to gain a competitive advantage over one's competitors. Finally, to be successful, a sponsorship should be exclusive—not available to competitors—and not easily copied[87], and its benefits should not be easily obtained by competitors through ambush marketing[88].

Hospitality

Hospitality and entertainment play a critical role in the packaging of sponsorship and promotional licensing programs. They both enable the sponsor to construct certain benefits and opportunities that are often unique and unavailable in the marketplace. Such opportunities may include winning trips to prestigious events such as the Stanley Cup finals or curling's Briers with special treatment through on-site hospitality and special events. Hospitality opportunities have become an integral part of sponsorship agreements for professional and Olympic sport organizations, which may package hard-to-obtain tickets in prime locations along with tents, catering, and other amenities. There are similar hospitality programs on the professional golf tours and throughout professional football, often forming the basis for the sale of luxury boxes in sporting venues worldwide. The key to successful use of hospitality is to ensure it is not available except as part of a comprehensive sponsorship or promotional licensing agreement. Corporate partners use hospitality benefits to reward their own personnel or, in the majority of cases, to induce their own clients to increase product consumption or renew agreements or sign new ones. This is done through entertaining. Hospitality is now an integral part of Canadian sponsorship programs.

In the context of the Olympic Games, sponsors and broadcasters use their hospitality resources to maintain or increase revenues, influence potential customers, reward existing customers, and even reward key employees. One of the major benefits of the Olympic partnership is the right to entertain these guests and customers in a manner exclusive to marketing partners: The access

[84] Mullin, B., S. Hardy, & W. Sutton (2000) *Sport Marketing.*

[85] Berrett, T. & T. Slack (2001) A framework for the analysis of strategic approaches employed by non-profit sport organisations in seeking corporate sponsorship. *Sport Management Review,* 4: 21–45.

[86] Copeland, R. & W. Frisby (1996) Understanding the sport sponsorship process from a corporate perspective.

[87] Amis, J. & Slack, T. (1999). Sport Sponsorship as a Distinctive Competence. *European Journal of Marketing.* 33 (3/4), 250-272.

[88] Seguin, B. (2006) *Canadian Sport Sponsorship.*

to exclusive hotel rooms, tickets, transportation, and accreditation creates an unprecedented forum to help make their partnership investments worthwhile. An Olympic marketing program comprises two distinct segments: development and on-site operations. In the Olympic Games, hospitality management encompasses a wide spectrum of services and responsibilities. It may take a partner over two years before the opening ceremonies to plan a hospitality and entertainment program.

Entertainment and corporate hospitality opportunities are important motives for most forms of sport sponsorship. One does not have to be involved with major sport properties to provide unique and interesting hospitality opportunities. For example, in its sponsorship of Swimming Canada, Maritime Life identified hospitality as the best strategy by which to achieve the objective of strengthening relationships with distributors, brokers, consultants, and employees[89]. In implementing this, one of the key elements of the leveraging plan was to promote and educate each of the company's divisions about the various hospitality opportunities. Despite some upfront apprehension, Swimming Canada worked closely with Maritime Life and committed the necessary human and financial resources to ensure that the proper environment was obtained for the various hospitality events. This included site selection and working in collaboration with a number of partners, including the event organizing committees, national team athletes and coaches, Olympic gold medalists, and Maritime Life. In all, 10 successful hospitality nights were organized in conjunction with the two major swimming competitions. This strategy proved to be a success, with a 22 percent increase in the attendance at hospitality nights over the previous year's hospitality program at the national championships.

Hospitality opportunities may be used either to interest targeted individuals in a product or to strengthen bonds with existing customers and reinforce their commitment to the company and/or its products. It can also be used to support other strategic areas of a company. For example, relationship marketing is concerned about "attracting, developing, and retaining customer relationships[90]." Berry and Parasuraman[91] state that "its central tenet is the creation of 'true customers'—customers who are glad they selected a firm who perceived they are receiving value and feel valued, who are likely to buy additional services from the firm, and who are unlikely to defect to a competitor." Thus, offering hospitality at a sporting event to existing or prospective customers may not be about conducting business then, but rather to use a relaxed informal context outside the normal business environment to create a personal interactive chemistry that will be conducive to doing business later. When hospitality opportunities are not exclusive to sponsors, companies that have paid the more expensive fee to be a sponsor see their presence ambushed or diluted by hospitality buyers. These must be controlled and protected by

---

[89] Seguin, B., Teed, K. and O'Reilly (2005). National sport organizations and sponsorship: an identification of best practices. International Journal of Sport Management and Sponsorship. 1 (1/2), 69-92.

[90] Berrett, T. & T. Slack (2001) A framework for the analysis of strategic approaches employed by non-profit sport organisations in seeking corporate sponsorship.

[91] Berry, L. & A. Parasuraman (1991) *Marketing Services.* The Free Press.

the property owner. In addition to fostering closer links with customers, hospitality opportunities can be used to perform the same function with other important publics.

Case: Rouge et Or Football

Background

Université Laval (UL) is located in Quebec City, a city of about 700 000 people. Canada's oldest university, UL has a student population of 36 000. Sport and physical activity has played an important role at UL as demonstrated by its tremendous sport facilities located in the pavilion known as the PEPS. The football stadium seats 12 000 spectators. The sport services department offers a number of services including recreational and intramural opportunities. A number of years ago, the university launched a sport excellence program, Rouge et Or (R&O), a co-management program where each of the 13 clubs is registered as a nonprofit corporation.

Sponsorship

The sponsorship program for R&O operates at two levels: philanthropic and commercial based. The first is associated mostly with companies making cash donations or in-kind contributions. In return, sport services provide visibility through communications messages that are positioned as philanthropy. "We find it challenging to provide these sponsors [donors] with a visibility program that equates the amount of dollars donated." The other strategy is more commercially driven, leveraged with the R&O media partners, including radio, newspapers, and television networks. In this case, the ROI is much greater, especially with the football club. The R&O can count on two major philanthropic sponsors associated with the R&O fund at $50 000 each. These two partners are associated with all of the sport clubs and receive visibility at games, special events (e.g., award dinner, golf tournament), and in each venue. However, they do not receive exclusivity status. Sponsor category exclusivity is offered only on a club-by-club basis. For example, Pepsi is a sponsor of the soccer team, while Coca-Cola is a sponsor of the football team. In 2005, the total sponsorship revenue for R&O was about $600 000 or 35 percent of its total budget.

Rouge et Or Football

Varsity football, was introduced at UL in 1995 as a result of a community initiative led by businessman Jacques Tanguay (owner of Entreprises Tanguay) whose support of sport teams and events in the Quebec community is well known. Entreprises Tanguay owns part of the Quebec Remparts (Major Junior hockey), a midget AAA hockey team, and a semiprofessional baseball franchise. The revival of football at UL in 1995 coincided with the loss of the NHL franchise Quebec Nordiques the same year. While the loss of the Nordiques was a huge blow to the community, it created an opportunity for UL football, which became one of the highest-level competitive sports being played in the city. Thus, businesses that had invested in the Nordiques were looking for new investment opportunities. The football club adopted an "entrepreneurial" strategy. From a business standpoint, Tanguay has been the driving force behind the club since its beginning in 1995. In fact, Entreprises Tanguay created its own sponsorship department, with a full-time employee responsible for seeking sponsorship for all of its properties including the R&O football club. This entrepreneurial approach to university sports created some challenges. "The university and the private sector cultures are quite different and understanding and respecting each others' cultures are important factors in the successful implementation of this model. The R&O strategic positioning is social responsibility and that is what we sell." In such a model, corporate support is on athlete development, "the pursuit of academic and sport excellence. Corporations invest in education and in the development of youth first while winning [or losing] on the field of play comes second." The club president (Tanguay) has been a "strong advocate" of this philosophy in the business community. The same corporate partners have continued to invest $10 000 a year since 1995 to be associated with the football club. This select 'sponsor club' consists of 24 partners, which sign deals for three years at a time. In addition, sport services negotiated a number of contra deals with media partners, including radio, television, and newspapers. Media partners play a key role in a variety of promotional campaigns, ticket sales, and sponsor recognition programs. As a result, each sponsor is guaranteed a certain amount of visibility; nearly $17 000 worth of visibility in the media. Additional publicity for sponsors comes from the university's media relations efforts and related special events. Sponsors receive signage in the football stadium—exposure to an average of 15 000 spectators a game.

The popularity of R&O football in the Quebec City region has led to the television broadcast of two away games a year. The decision to only broadcast away games initially was to protect ticket sales for home games. The production cost was paid by the university. In return, it received a percentage of advertising inventory—advertising spots, billboards, in-program graphics— from French sports network RDS, which televised the games. This allowed the university to break even at first and eventually to generate a small profit. It also provided team sponsors with additional exposure through signage and enhanced value for their sponsorship investment.

The creation of football programs at the University of Montreal and the University of Sherbrooke heightened the interest in university football in the province of Quebec and created (or revived) new (old) "rivalries" between the schools. The success of R&O's television coverage led to the creation of a television package with RDS, which is now controlled by the league (Quebec University League). The package on RDS includes the broadcast of 12 games.

The production cost of $16 000 per game is guaranteed by the two universities playing ($8000 each). While the league sells sponsorship for the television broadcast, signage at the venues remains the property and responsibility of each university, thus providing added exposure for team sponsors at no extra cost. The popularity of the football team among the student population and the general public has led to the creation of a number of additional fundraising activities. These activities have also been used by sponsors to leverage involvement with the team. For example, special game day promotions are integral to all football games. Special events that have evolved over the years include:

- A banquet recognizing the achievements of the various clubs and a golf tournament.
- A "mega" Super Bowl party created by the football club to leverage the growing popularity of football within the student population. The success of this event—a "happening" a "must attend" event within the community—has exceeded all expectations. R&O football players are involved in all aspects of the event including promotions with media and corporate partners. Other than sponsorship, this event is the most important revenue generation activity for the football club, generating about $50 000 a year in profit.
- The R&O brand has reached a high level of equity in the Quebec region. That is to say that the R&O brand has reached high level of awareness, fan loyalty and positive associations with its team. As a result, corporate partners have increased their leveraging activities thus creating more visibility. For example:
- McDonalds has created a special meal at the beginning of the football season called the Rouge et Or Trio.
- Labatt created point-of-purchase promotions at retailers around the city for the Budweiser brand. In addition, Budweiser is highly involved in promoting the Super Bowl party at the university.
- A number of corporate partners are taking advantage of a new "tailgating" tradition before and after football games by installing corporate tents and entertaining customers and clients.
- Tailgating is also open to anyone in the community. For example, a local law firm invited 300 to 400 guests to a game and provided hospitality opportunities during the tailgate.

Compared to other sport properties in the Quebec region, the Rouge et Or garner much goodwill from the general public and corporations ("capital de sympathie"). According to the director of sports services, this is a "key point of difference" with other properties. This is the result of the positioning of university sports against professional sports: "the public and corporations perceive university sports differently from professional sports. The young people that are on the playing field are not there for the money, they are there for the love of sport, for the passion. In addition to giving heart and soul to their sport, they are committed to getting an education and receiving a university degree. This is what turns into high level of sympathy from the public." In many ways, the loss of the Nordiques (due in part to the increase in professional players' salaries) is believed to have contributed to the success of R&O and to the sympathy effect.

Source: Institute for Sport Marketing Case Studies. Laurentian University 2003-2005

Case Questions

1. What do you consider the key success factors in this case?
2. Why would companies sponsor Rouge et Or? Identify key objectives for such a sponsorship.
3. How could a sponsor leverage its investment? Give examples.
4. Can such a model be applied to other sport properties? How?

Chapter Summary

Sponsorship has experienced phenomenal growth over the past 30 years. From its modest roots as a form of philanthropic giving, sponsorship is now a $30 billion plus industry worldwide. Progress in communications technology had a great impact on sponsorship by being the catalyst that moved sports into the "entertainment" industry. Another factor that led corporations to sponsorship was the cost combined with the cluttering of the traditional media. Many corporations were looking for new avenues to communicate with consumers, and sports appeared to be an effective and efficient way to reach them. Finally, as corporations poured more money into sports, the decision to sponsor sports became a business decision with an expected return on investment. Sponsorship is recognized as a legitimate part of a corporation's promotions mix alongside advertising, sales promotion, personal selling, and publicity. Sponsorship programs are developed to meet a variety of corporate objectives. Those identified most often in the literature are: increasing awareness, changing/enhancing corporate image, reaching specific market segments, generating media benefits, achieving sales, creating hospitality opportunities, and gaining competitive advantage through exclusivity.

Test Your Knowledge

1. What is sponsorship?
2. What are the key differences between sponsorship and philanthropy?
3. Why do corporations invest large sums of money in sponsorship? Explain.

4. Explain the place of sponsorship within the promotional mix.
5. Explain how sponsorship is not advertising.
6. What is leveraging/activating? Give an example.
7. Give an example of a company that uses an integrated approach to sponsorship.

 For more review questions, go to http://www.sportmarketing.nelson.com.

Key Terms

ambush marketing   promotion mix
clutter   ROI
exclusivity   sponsorship

 A full glossary of key term definitions is located at
http://www.sportmarketing.nelson.com.

Internet Resources

Sponsorship marketing, http://www.sponsorshipmarketing.ca/

Australian Sponsorship Marketing Association, http://www.asma.com.au/

**International Journal of Sports Marketing and Sponsorship,
http://www.imrpublications.com/JSMS/**

**Sport sponsorship (UK),
http://www.sports-sponsorship.co.uk/sponsorship.htm**

**Bell rides west,
http://www.sponsorship.ca/p-happening.html#sports**

**Reality check on sports sponsorship in Canada,
http://www.sportdecision.com/modules/news/article.php?storyid=444**

**The future of sports sponsorship?,
http://www.superbrands.com/newsletters/pdfs/65.pdf**

Source: provided courtesy of Norm O'Reilly

Chapter **12**

Building Successful Sport Sponsorships

Learning Objectives

- To learn the steps in the sport sponsorship process
- To know the various elements of a sport property
- To understand the benefits of sponsorship to a potential company
- To appreciate the resources an organization must commit to implement a successful sponsorship program
- To understand the place of sponsorship in the marketing/communications mix
- To understand conceptually the complexities involved in activating a sponsorship
- To understand the key success factors to sponsorship in Canada
- To identify best sponsorship practices

Introduction

"I suggest that investing into a sport property without any kind of 'activating' poses a threat to sponsorship"—Marketing Director, IOC

Academics and practitioners in the business of sport have recognized the need to compete with all forms of entertainment for their share of participants, spectators, consumers, and sponsors[1]. Finding and developing successful partnerships with corporate sponsors is, and will continue to be, a challenge for professional and amateur sport organizations of all sizes.

---

[1] Mullin, B., S. Hardy, & W. Sutton (2000) *Sport Marketing,* 2nd ed. Human Kinetics.

property: an entity that can provide value to a potential sponsor.

sponsee: organization being sponsored.

sponsor: organization that provides the financial support or services to a sponsee.

activating: integrating a sponsorship into its promotional mix, usually in the form of advertising, sales promotions, or personal sales (e.g., hospitality).

The decision to sponsor a sport **property** (e.g., athlete, sport organization, national team, event) by a company is usually made following an evaluation of the property's value and the ability to reach corporate objectives. Some companies have sophisticated evaluation criteria, while others may just look to gain some goodwill by supporting a local event. Whatever the reasons, once an agreement is reached, the **sponsee** and the **sponsor** will most likely work together to maximize the benefits from the relationship. This will involve some kind of **activating** from the sponsor. For example, in 1994, Maritime Life, an insurance and investment firm headquartered in Halifax, realized that it had access to the Olympic rings through its parent company (John Hancock), a TOP sponsor[2]. Until then, Maritime Life had never been involved in sport sponsorship. Its main marketing tactic was promotional and communication materials aimed at developing long-term relationships with agents, distributors, and employees. The firm rarely conducted mass media advertising campaigns and had no television or print advertising. Maritime Life soon realized that using the Olympic trademark by itself was insufficient to achieve corporative objectives. Therefore, it contracted a third party to search for a national sport organization (NSO) for a partner. Following a national search, Maritime life signed a long-term sponsorship agreement with Swimming Canada, which included title sponsorship of three national events including the Olympic trials. The company entered into this deal with very little knowledge about sport, let alone sport sponsorship; no previous relationships with Swimming Canada; very limited experience with the promotional mix (no television); no previous experience in sport sponsorship. However, Maritime Life was committed to making this sponsorship work. Senior management was fully supportive and set money aside for the sponsorship cost and for leveraging. Because of its lack of experience in sponsorship, the company hired a sport marketing consulting firm, worked closely with Swimming Canada, developed a plan, leveraged the sponsorship extensively, conducted extensive research, and, following a complete evaluation, made the decision to sign a long-term sponsorship deal with Swimming Canada.

The purpose of this chapter is to take you through the process Maritime Life went through to gain a positive experience with sport sponsorship. A four-step approach to sponsorship will be presented along with a list of key success factors and best practices in Canadian sport sponsorships.

EXECUTIVE PERSPECTIVE

Jean R. Dupré, Director-General, Speed Skating Canada

In the previous chapter, which introduced sport sponsorship, I discussed Speed Skating Canada's (SSC) goal to make Canada the number one nation in speed skating. To accomplish this goal, we determined that we needed to raise $1 million in sponsorship revenue. And we did. Our strategy has been to provide a potential sponsor with a turnkey, integrated speed skating sponsorship package

---

[2] Seguin, B., K. Teed, & N. O'Reilly (2005) National sport organizations and sponsorship: An identification of best practices. *International Journal of Sport Management and Marketing,* 1(2), 69–92.

Important Strategic Elements of Sport Marketing in Canada

designed to meet the company's marketing and corporate needs and objectives, including:

- nationwide visibility and exposure
- store involvement and opportunities for sales
- market diversification and accessibility
- an ability to create a unique consumer experience (most important)

When implementing sponsorship programs, it is important to identify any external opportunities that may influence your ability to sell sponsorship. For example, we are currently capitalizing on the fact that Vancouver will be hosting the 2010 Olympic Winter Games. This gives us a unique opportunity because the Olympics represent the best multisport event in the world. Yet it is also critical to understand the sport and commercial landscape to demonstrate that companies must associate with your product to take advantage of the benefits the Games will bring. Hence, one must first understand the ways a company can create an official association with the 2010 Vancouver Olympic Winter Games. These include:

- International Olympic Committee sponsorship
    TOP sponsor (worldwide exclusivity rights)
    Olympic Spirit
    torch relay
- Vancouver Organizing Committee (VANOC) sponsorship
- International Sport Federation sponsorship
- National Sport Federation sponsorship
    events
    athletes (national teams)
    grassroots programs
- official broadcaster media buy
- individual athlete endorsements

One of the most cost-effective ways for corporations to build and sustain a marketing and communications program around the 2010 Games is to "own" specific sports via the sponsorship of a national sport federation (NSF). In our case, with the upcoming Games in 2010 and the performance potential of Canada's speed skating team, we feel strongly that the potential sponsor will consider investing in athletes through a partnership with SSC. Why?

- The 2010 Vancouver Olympic Winter Games will be the most important sporting event to take place in Canada since the 1988 Calgary Olympic Games.

The Games themselves will resonate highly among Canadians, and sponsors will be able to leverage their involvement to capitalize on the associated emotion.

- Various blue-chip companies have recently announced their partnership with VANOC 2010, meaning that the potential speed skating sponsor can position itself as the foremost supporter of winter amateur sport in Canada by supporting the most successful Canadian winter Olympic sport.
- To combat other manufacturers' positioning as a VANOC or winter sport sponsor, the potential sponsor must determine ways to strengthen its amateur sport portfolio.
- Speed Skating Canada can deliver the unique consumer experience in all parts of the country in both official languages.

Once the rationale for associating with your product has been articulated by the sport organization (i.e., SSC), the next step is to clearly demonstrate what we can bring to the potential partner—the $1000 question: What is the return on investment? Based on our understanding of the potential sponsor's business and its objectives, we believe that an amateur sport sponsorship would be highly desirable for the company if it included these key elements:

- Association with a successful, prominent, high-profile Canadian sport organization with matching brand attributes
- A leadership role/position within the sport
- A national, coast-to-coast presence
- Grassroots programming
    to be recognized as giving something back to the community
    to be seen as helping develop/grow the sport at the grassroots level
    to be seen as a catalyst in taking grassroots athletes and turning them into podium successes at the elite level
- Hosting/hospitality
- Ability to use current and/or former athletes as spokespeople to create the unique consumer experience
- B2B networking and cross-promotional opportunities
- Broadcast opportunities
- Rights to athlete imagery and association marks
- Category exclusivity

Chapter 12: Building Successful Sport Sponsorships

Source: Simon Pichette.

The next step is to explain in detail each component of your proposal demonstrating the fit between the properties and the product. In our case, we have to demonstrate the fit between the potential sponsor's attributes and SSC. The potential sponsor can effectively use speed skating as a metaphor to reinforce various brand characteristics that the company desires to communicate in the marketplace. These might include teamwork, dedication, excellence, cutting-edge technology, leadership, success, determination, pride, speed, national presence, performance, competitiveness. The potential sponsor can use these shared attributes as a platform for marketing and communication initiatives, reinforcing its positioning relative to its competitors.

The National Team

By becoming a major sponsor of our national teams, a sponsor creates an association with our country's most elite speed skaters. Canada's National Speed Skating teams are a group of young Canadians the entire nation can take pride in. This translates directly into brand association for the consumers. Our athletes have won more Olympic medals than Canadian athletes in any other sport, and our skaters have the greatest potential to bring home a record number of medals from 2010 Vancouver Olympic Winter Games. Canadian speed skaters also win more World Cup and World Championship medals each year than athletes in all Canadian winter sports combined. Canada is considered to have the best speed skating team in the world. As a result of our national teams' success, our skaters receive a tremendous volume of national and international media

attention. There are numerous ways companies can be associated with the teams:

- Major sponsors are given category exclusivity.
- Suppliers of national training centres and athletes receive nationwide visibility.
- Display and use of product constantly deliver the message that our sport and athletes are endorsing the potential sponsor's products.
- The potential sponsor will have access to national team imagery to use for promotion.
- The company will have rights to all marks and logos of Speed Skating Canada for promotion.
- Logo visibility to the potential sponsor on the racing and training wear, outer wear, and podium wear is a key component. The value of the logo space depends on the position and the size of the marking.

The Athletes

- We offer the potential sponsor the opportunity to become associated with some of Canada's most recognized and successful Olympic athletes.
- Athletes could be used to promote the company's involvement in various speed skating programs (e.g., grassroots programs, charitable initiatives).
- Major sponsors of the National Speed Skating teams have access to athletes for five appearances a year.
- A unique aspect of an SSC sponsorship is the association with athletes representing various demographic groups, for example, English speaking (from the west), French speaking (from the east), women, and Aboriginals. The potential sponsor can use the athletes appropriate to the nature of their public relations initiatives.

Grassroots Programming

Should there be an interest in getting involved in this aspect of our sport, the potential sponsor could be given the choice to sponsor one of SSC's grassroots programs, each with the ability to help the potential sponsor achieve a different marketing/communications goal. In general terms, the potential sponsor has the choice of being seen as:

- Helping the growth of the sport in Canada, introducing children to the sport (in-school curriculum program)
- Helping young speed skaters improve and master their speed skating skills (cutting-edge pin program)

- Providing funding directly to amateur speed skaters to aid in their development (dealers' scholarship program)

Hospitality

SSC offers the potential sponsor a hosting program that the company can use to achieve its hospitality goals.
- The unique consumer experience can be delivered in all parts of the country in both official languages.
- The hosting program can be national, permitting a potential sponsor to host guests at events across the country (e.g., Vancouver, Calgary, Montreal).
- The potential sponsor could use these opportunities to develop and strengthen relationships with key internal and external stakeholders.
- The potential sponsor could use the VIP hosting opportunities for consumer promotions or employee incentives.
- SSC is prepared to work with a potential sponsor as a partner to further develop the hosting program to ensure the experience meets the company's hospitality needs.

The Events

- SSC offers a potential sponsor excellent brand exposure via on-site signage at national- and international-level events held in Canada
- SSC offers additional exposure at all national-level speed skating events and will include exposure at major international events.
- National and international television coverage ensures extensive logo visibility.

- Should the potential sponsor wish to purchase television inventory for televised events, the company can purchase spots through SSC at about $1500 each.

A potential sponsor would also be provided with:
- Visibility on Speed Skating Canada's official website, including a special section featuring the athletes' testimonials about the sponsor.
- Special SSC branding of all vehicles supplied for our national training centres and for the 2010 Games.
- Opportunity to include corporate literature as part of SSC's membership mailings.
- Invitation to participate in SSC's annual general meeting.
- Invitation to take part in any team or organization fundraising activities.
- Annual report of press clippings that include the potential sponsor's logo visibility (SSC uses the services of Bowdens to collect such data).
- Opportunity to work with other SSC partners to create various co-promotions for Canadian consumers.

Jean is director general for Speed Skating Canada. He has 20 years of experience in sport management, marketing, project planning, and organizational management. Jean is also vice president of the Canadian Olympic Committee and has been a member of the Canadian Olympic Committee board for the past 15 years.

Introducing Sponsorship

The sponsor (e.g., Coke, Adidas, RBC, General Motors, Government of Canada) is the investor who provides resources and in return seeks promotional value and fulfillment of other objectives from the association. The sponsee (e.g., Alpine Canada, Alexandre Despatie, Skate Canada's National Team, a fundraising dinner, Atom AA hockey team) is the property (or sponsee) that receives resources and most often seeks to achieve its own objectives from the association. Affiliated entities are intermediaries that support the sponsor–sponsee relationship, such as a benefiting charity, a sponsorship sales agent, an event manager, or a facility provider. Sponsorship is attractive to these stakeholders for several reasons. First, faced with the challenge of a cluttered marketplace, most organizations can no longer promote themselves through advertising alone. Sponsorship can provide an efficient way by which to differentiate a company from its competitors[3]. Second, anecdotal evidence of the attractiveness of sponsorship relative to other promotional tools is supported by sponsors who have bolstered their initial sponsorship investment with additional funds to leverage it[4]. Leveraging, used in this context, refers to strategies that the sponsor funds and implements to increase the effectiveness of the sponsorship, such as the title sponsor of a televised event developing commercials and paying for their broadcast leading up to, during, and following the event.

In an increasingly competitive climate, Olympic and Paralympic sport properties (also known as amateur sport) are seeking alternative strategies to financially support their athletes, programs, and events. On the international stage, international sport federations (IF) such as FINA (aquatic sports), IIHF (hockey), and IAAF (athletics), look to non-institutional sources of funding by taking control of their properties and leveraging them for sponsorship in the form of cash contributions and in-kind product. At the national level, national sport organizations (NSO) seek alternative sources of funding in sponsorship opportunities. At the provincial/territorial, municipal, and individual levels, the pursuit of sponsorship is carried out by provincial/territorial sport organizations, municipalities, facilities, coaches, athletes, clubs, teams, and others.

Corporations often use sponsorship to achieve multiple objectives[5]—involvement with the local community, increase in general public awareness of the company, enhanced company image, changed public perception, trade relations, enhanced employee relations and motivation, competition blocking, increased sales and/or market share, reaching target market[6]. Sponsorship success is often tied to a sponsor's effective use of leveraging their sponsorship, by investing at least three times the initial investment into additional activities[7]. This enables the sponsor to exploit its upfront investment in the sponsorship through such marketing communications elements as sales promotions, packaging, and merchandising[8]. Evaluating the impacts of a sponsorship and its leveraging activities on achieving corporate objectives is another important aspect of a sponsorship program. While the need for sponsorship evaluation has increased in recent years, researchers have yet to develop a theoretical evaluation model for sponsorship. This points

[3] Amis, J., T. Slack, & T. Berrett (1999) Sport sponsorship as distinctive competence. *European Journal of Marketing*, 33(4): 250–72.

[4] Berrett, T. & T. Slack (2001) A framework for the analysis of strategic approaches employed by non-profit sport organisations in seeking corporate sponsorship. *Sport Management Review*, 4: 21–45.

[5] Berrett, T. (1993) The sponsorship of amateur sport: Government, national sport organization, and the corporate perspectives. *Leisure and Society*, 16: 323–46.

[6] Irwin, R. & W. Sutton (1994) Sport sponsorship objectives: An analysis of their relative importance for major corporate sponsors. *European Journal of Sport* Management, 1(2): 93–101.

[7] Eisenhart, T. (1988). Sporting changes zap competitors. *Business Marketing*, 6, 92–97.

[8] Meenaghan, T. (1991). The role of sponsorship in the communications and marketing mix. *International Journal of Advertising*, 10(1): 35–47.

Important Strategic Elements of Sport Marketing in Canada

out to the complicated and difficult nature of sponsorship evaluation due to multiple objectives and varied leveraging techniques. In the practitioner's context, most firms do not have formal evaluation programs in place.

Sponsorship in Canada—A Model for Sport Sponsorship Success

Sport properties are found in all four facets of Canadian sport—professional (Ottawa Senators), Olympic (Canadian Cycling Association), university/college (CIS women's championships), and grassroots (little league baseball). Within each, events are omnipresent at the local, regional, provincial, national, and international levels. However, the strategic use of sponsorship varies greatly within the Canadian sport industry. While most professional sport organizations (e.g., Blue Jays, Edmonton Oilers) and "big" NSOs (e.g., Alpine Canada, Hockey Canada) rely on professional marketing staff and/or sport marketing consulting firms to develop sponsorship programs, it is common for smaller sport organizations—many NSOs, PSOs, and clubs in Canada—to have volunteers direct the sponsorship function. In fact, the lack of resources committed by sport organizations to marketing was identified as an issue by Berrett and Slack[9] and the Institute of Sport Marketing (ISM)[10]. The issue is not that volunteers are involved in the sponsorship process but the fact that a large number of volunteers have no training in this area. This is most likely the result of having technical experts running these types of organizations. While marketing may be identified as important area for most organizations, the lack of expertise within these sports results in a lack of true commitment. For example, a volunteer vice-president of marketing typically has many responsibilities, including public relations, event management, and administration, not to mention the overall operations of the organization. On occasion, the volunteer may enjoy the support of a staff, albeit limited. Nevertheless, the majority of sport organizations today seek some forms of support from government and/or sponsors; hence, the importance of acquiring some knowledge in the area of sponsorship development and activation is fundamental.

Following an extensive review of successful sport sponsorships in Canada, we present a four-step approach for sponsees to developing successful sponsorship partnerships. The chapter will conclude with some key success factors along with some best practices in sport sponsorship in Canada. The four-step approach to successful sponsorship includes:

- Step 1: *Pre-sponsorship practices.* Developing product, building organizational capacity, building long-term relationships, and planning.
- Step 2: *Negotiation.* Finding the right fit, terms of contract, and commitment to leveraging.

---

[9] Berrett, T. & T. Slack (1995) Approaches to corporate sponsorship in Canada's national sport organizations. A report submitted to Sport Canada by Faculty of Physical Education and Recreation, University of Alberta.

[10] Seguin, B. (2006) *Canadian Sport Sponsorship: Case Studies Report.* Institute of Sport Marketing.

- Step 3: *Sponsorship life.* Organizational support, joint planning, implementing leveraging tools (activation), and developing an evaluation framework.
- Step 4: *Sponsorship termination.* Collaborative succession planning, gradual decrease of involvement, and termination.

Pre-Sponsorship Practices

The first step, pre-sponsorship practices, involves establishing the prerequisites for future success—developing the sport organization's properties, along with associated hospitality events, to a point where they can provide value to a potential sponsor. While a number of sport organizations believe they have nothing of value to attract the corporate sector, it is worth mentioning that the ones that are successful 'invest' resources (e.g., human resources expertise, advertising, PR, leveraging) in their properties to increase marketability[11]. This was also reported by Berrett & Slack[12], who noted that "some other NSOs had extended extensive effort over a relatively long period of time in order [to] change the image of their sport and make it more marketable and attractive to television audiences." Hence, long-term relationships with potential sponsors (identified through comprehensive market research) and, in some cases, with the media must be developed and maintained. The organization of the sport organization, whether volunteer or professional, must adopt sponsorship as a priority and develop the expertise required to manage events and hospitality functions. Finally, a comprehensive sponsorship plan and budget must be developed in collaboration with legal experts. Once the antecedents are in place, a sport organization will be better positioned to seek corporate sponsors.

Organizational Capacity

To develop and implement a sponsorship program, a sport organization must first assess its capacity. As suggested above, it must assess the level of expertise, commitment, and resources (human and financial) needed to build a sport property. Most professional sport organizations (e.g., Saskatchewan Roughriders, Toronto Raptors), major sporting events (Formula One Grand Prix, FIFA U-20 World Cup, Brier), and large NSOs (e.g., Hockey Canada, Soccer Canada) are fully committed and rely on professional marketing staff and/or sport marketing consulting firms to develop sponsorship programs; however, smaller sport organizations usually have volunteers direct the sponsorship function. Building organizational capacity is essential for potential sponsors as well. Some companies have a lot of experience and have developed sophisticated sport sponsorship programs (e.g., Bell Canada, RBC, Telus, Esso, General Mills, Roots); however, many large, medium, and small companies have little to no experience in sport sponsorship. Hence, the commitment of both sponsee and sponsor organizations to marketing/sponsorship

---

[11] ibid.

[12] Berrett, T. & T. Slack (1995) Approaches to corporate sponsorship in Canada's national sport organizations: 24.

Important Strategic Elements of Sport Marketing in Canada

is essential for the success of the program. The necessary time, energy, and money must not be underestimated. Sport organizations that are successful in sport sponsorship invest in their properties. The same is true for corporations: They invest in the sport properties by integrating the sponsorship into their marketing/communications mix and activating their rights. Some have even taken steps to make their sport more attractive (e.g., for television, spectators) by changing rules or ways that events are presented[13]. Some examples are the 24-second clock in basketball, the dropping of compulsory figures in figure skating, and the draft legal cycling portions in triathlon. These were done to make the sport television friendly. While sometimes risky, the ultimate goal of investing in a property is to increase marketability. Table 12-1 summarizes the stages of organizational capacity.

TABLE 12-1

Building Capacity for Sponsorship Development and Acquisition

STAGE	QUESTIONS
Organizational capacity	Do we have the expertise internally? Staff, volunteer, or both?
	Is the organization committed to marketing and sponsorship? If yes, is the commitment short term or long term?
	How much money is available?
Background research	Do we know our members? Demographics? Psychographics?
	If sport is on television, what are the ratings? Profile of audience?
	How many events do we have? How many spectators come to the events?
	Why do they come?
	Do we know our product(s)? What do we have to offer?
Planning stage	What are our sponsorship objectives?
	What are the product categories available?
	What are the team the policies regarding sponsorship? Any restrictions?
	League policies?
	Who are some potential sponsors?
	Where is the fit?
	What are the company objectives of sponsee?
Building relationships	Do we have contacts with potential sponsors?
	How can we establish contact?
	What events, conferences, and so on should we attend?
	Do we know anyone within our organization with contacts?

Source: Berrett,T.& Slack,T. (1995) Approaches to corporate sponsorship in Canada's national sport organizations. A report submitted to Sport Canada. Faculty of Physical Education and Recreation, University of Alberta, Alberta, Canada p.24.

[13] ibid.

Research

Chapter 3 stated that research is a fundamental component of sport marketing. While the types of research may vary, it is always essential for building a sport property. The extent of the research depends on resources available. It is unfortunate that research seems to be overlooked by a number of sport organizations, even though it has been shown that sport organizations that are successful in sponsorship do their homework. Research typically involves the following:

- Information on the sport

    description of the sport (mission, values, strategic objectives, etc.)
    programs offered (grassroots, national team, events, coaching, etc.)
    number of participants (athletes, coaches, officials, volunteers)
    demographic information on participants (age, gender, education, income, etc.)
    other

- Information on spectators/viewers

    number of spectators at events
    profile of spectators (demographic information, reasons for attending, etc.)
    if televised, information/profile of audience (ratings, demographic profile, etc.)
    attitudes and behaviours (research on consumer attitudes and behaviours)

- Information on media coverage

    interest of media in the sport (athletes, events, etc.)
    coverage of sport by the media (television, newspaper, radio, etc.)
    value of publicity in media

- Information on competitors

    who are the competitors?
    what kind of sponsors do they have?
    what kind of attendance/ratings?
    others

- Restrictions from sport organizations/leagues/governments

    restrictions in terms of sponsorship (e.g., no tobacco sponsors, no alcoholic beverages sponsors, etc.)
    policies about finder's fee (percentage of sponsorship fee to the staff/volunteer who finds sponsorship)
    restrictions in terms of conflicting sponsors (e.g., a national team athlete cannot have a sponsor conflicting with NSO)

Planning

The organization of a sport, whether volunteer or professional, must adopt sponsorship as a priority and develop the expertise required to manage the available properties (e.g., events and hospitality functions). A comprehensive

Important Strategic Elements of Sport Marketing in Canada

sponsorship plan must be developed prior to approaching potential sponsors. Hence, the organization must have a clear understanding of its needs (e.g., financial, human resources, products) and stablish clear sponsorship objectives.

The sponsorship plan consists of the identification of properties available within the sport organization, the categories of sponsorship offered, and a sponsorship budget. A property is any entity that can provide value to a potential sponsor. Examples of properties are an individual athlete (Sidney Crosby), team (national triathlon team), event (national synchronized swimming championships), organization (Canadian Olympic Committee), program (learn to skate), league (NHL), or club (Ottawa sailing club). For example, Alpine Canada Alpin (http://www.canski.org) properties include.

- *Programs*

  Development programs (Farham Project, Grade 2 Funpass, Husky's Snow Stars program, Development of Young Elite Skiers)
  National teams (Canadian Alpine Ski Teams—men and women; Development Teams—men and women; Alpine Disabled Ski Team—men & women)
  Coaching programs (education, clinics, coaching association)
  Official programs (clinics, manuals)

- *Events*

  World Cup (Bombardier Lake Louise Winterstart)
  National championships (NorAm Cup, Pontiac GMC Cup, Mars Canadian Juvenile Championships, Junior National Championships, Masters Races)
  Fundraising events (golf tournament, auctions, etc.)
  Special events (Tour of Champions, challenge, etc.)
  Made-for-television events (Stars on Ice)
  Promotional events
  Media events (press conferences, demonstration, announcements)
  Hospitality

- *Merchandising*

  Accessories
  Apparel
  Bags
  Educational videos
  Headwear

The next step in the sponsorship plan is to determine the sponsorship categories that may be available. Wilkinson[14] identifies these categories:

- *Title sponsor:* A sponsor whose name is part of the property—a specific program (e.g., Sears I Can Swim Program), event (Bell Tennis Challenge), team (BMW racing team), or facility (Scotiabank Place).

---

[14] Wilkinson, D.G. (1993) *Sponsorship Marketing: A Practical Reference Guide for Corporations in the 1990s.* The Wilkinson Group.

- *Major sponsor:* A corporation recognized as a major contributor to the property through its financial commitment and supporting activity (e.g., Bell's sponsorship of Speed Skating Canada).
- *Co-sponsor:* One of two or more corporations involved in the event at the same level of contribution.
- *Presenting sponsor:* A corporation recognized as making the program available but not named in the program title (e.g., 2007 Bianco's Audiotronic SPAD Hockey Tournament presented by The Doghouse).
- *Sub-sponsor:* A corporation with minor involvement in the event and minor financial commitment relative to other levels of sponsorship.
- *Supplier:* A corporation that supplies product (usually at no cost). In return, it may make the public aware of its contribution (e.g., Official ski supplier of the Canadian Alpine Ski Team).

Sponsorship Budget

The sponsorship budget requires pricing the various properties to be offered to sponsors. According to Stotlar[15], when pricing sponsorship, the sponsee should know that companies really don't care about how much money a sponsee needs. As suggested in the previous chapter, sponsorship is different from advertising and cannot be priced the same way. While some advertising may be involved (e.g., 30-second ad during a broadcast of an event), there remains many intangibles associated with the sponsorship (e.g., image transfer, brand benefits). Sport organizations should carefully price their properties. In fact, the Institute of Sport Marketing (ISM) reports that one barrier to sponsorship involvement by corporations was the overpricing of properties by sport organizations[16]. Hence, sport marketers must be realistic when putting a dollar value to their properties.

First, it is important to know the expenses the sponsee will incur in providing the sponsorship package[17]. For example, Maritime Life's sponsorship of Swimming Canada in the 1996 Olympic trials included a full hospitality program with the participation of 1992 Olympic gold medalist, Mark Tewksbury. Sponsorship expenses included the cost of tickets, catering (food and drinks), rental of room, Tewksbury's appearance fee, posters of event, invitation flyers, staff time, and so on. Once all of the expenses have been calculated, the sponsee can add the desired profit. This cost-plus pricing method was described in Chapter 8.

Another method for determining the price of a sponsorship is by knowing what the competitors are offering. This may be difficult to obtain; however, information may be available from such sources as trade publications and/or conferences. In Canada, the Canadian Sponsorship Forum, Sponsorship Marketing Council of Canada, *The Sponsorship Report*, Selling Sponsorship Strategies for Success, and *Marketing* magazine are all good sources of information. In the US, the *IEG Sponsorship Report* is an industry leader. It is essential that the sport marketer keep up to date.

---

[15] Stotlar, D. (2005) *Developing Successful Sponsorship Plans*, 2nd ed. Fitness Information Technology.

[16] Seguin, B. (2006) *Canadian Sport Sponsorship*.

[17] Brooks, C.M. (1994) *Sports Marketing: Competitive Business Strategies for Sports*. Prentice Hall.

Research of Potential Sponsors

While this step may involve tedious work, it is a key to sponsorship success. The sport marketer must do the appropriate research on all potential sponsors, which will enable the organization to tailor the sponsorship to each company's needs. An annual report is an excellent source of information, as it includes the company's mission, vision, and strategic objectives. The website is another source of information on a company's products, marketing orientation, its brand, and distribution processes. Information on sponsorship and other properties supported by a company may also be available on the website. Other sources include business magazines, newspapers, Statistics Canada (http://www.statscan.ca), and conferences. The purpose of gathering this information is for the sport marketer to understand the business of potential sponsors, as well as the sponsor's organization. There is little value in pursuing a sponsorship without understanding the potential sponsor, its business, and its industry. Your background research should include a potential sponsor's:

- mission, values, corporate philosophy, history, culture
- product or service
- marketing approaches
- promotion/communications mix (advertising, personal sales, sales promotions, sponsorship)
- customers—who they are and how they are reached
- place of distribution
- partners in cross promotions (e.g., Pepsi, Wendy's, and Frito-Lay)
- selling process—how the product(s) gets to customers
- annual donations—participation in the Imagine campaign
- current and past sponsorship
- annual advertising budget
- person responsible for making sponsorship decisions

Relationships

Building strong relationships is a necessity for any business and is a "key success factor" for most sponsorship programs[18], where emphasis should be on building meaningful and long-term relationships with more than one person in the sponsoring organization. This can be accomplished by keeping regular contact, implementing hospitality opportunities, and effectively servicing all aspects of the sponsorship. While relationships help make an existing sponsorship stronger, they are also invaluable for acquiring sponsorship. Results of a recent study conducted by the ISM[19] suggest that most sponsorship deals are the result of existing relationships between individuals within the partnering organizations. Therefore, we recommend that the sport marketer first determine if someone from within the organization (staff or volunteer)

---

[18] Seguin, B. (2006) *Canadian Sport Sponsorship.*
[19] ibid.

Chapter 12: Building Successful Sport Sponsorships

already has a relationship with the potential partner(s). If so, a strategy to leverage the relationship should be developed. Otherwise, conferences are a great place to meet business executives and exchange personal information. Long-term relationships with television broadcasters and potential sponsors (identified through comprehensive market research) are also integral parts of a sport marketer's job.

Negotiation

Once the pre-sponsorship practices (antecedents) are in place, a sport organization will be in a better position to seek corporate sponsors. Negotiation, the phase of contacting and attempting to sign a sponsorship agreement, addresses three main areas. First, there must be a fit between the sponsor's and sponsee's objectives and brands, even if the negotiation stemmed from CEO interest[20]. Prior to signing any agreement, the sponsee should ensure that the sponsor has both the resources and motivation to leverage the sponsorship with an investment at least three times the size of the sponsorship value. This includes integrating the sponsorship into the company's overall marketing mix, part of which may be sharing in TV production costs to ensure the events receive national television media coverage. Finally, during the negotiations, the sport organization should prioritize a long-term contract over higher sponsorship dollars and use legal expertise throughout the entire process.

Fit

The fit between the potential partners will be an important consideration in the negotiation stage. Whether it is through image, associations, or objectives, the fit must be clear to both parties. Consider the example of Canada Post and its sponsorship of freestyle skiing and speed skating, where both image (fast space, audacious, innovative) and corporate objectives (good corporate citizen) are illustrated[21]:

> Canada Post has traditionally been perceived as a conservative government corporation, kind of boring. Its sponsorship of 'Freestyle skiing' brings images that are audacious and innovative. Its sponsorship of the 'fastest sport on ice' (speed skating) fits well for Canada Post products such as parcel delivery service Purolator. Canada Post believes that it can transfer these types of images to its delivery of mail and parcels. In addition, the company wants to maintain and improve their brand image to keep their presence in the Canadian community. Sponsorship is also the opportunity for Canada Post to be perceived as a good corporate citizen. "Everybody understands that it is important to support amateur sports and their athletes that do not have much support. Image is everything: Canada Post wants to be perceived as a good corporate citizen."

[20] Seguin, B., K. Teed, & N. O'Reilly (2005) National sport organizations and sponsorship.
[21] Seguin, B. (2006) Canadian Sport Sponsorship.

Source: Simon Pichette

Leveraging Commitment

Leveraging activities (activation) are marketing or promotional tactics implemented by the sponsor to promote the sponsee or association with the sponsee. The initial investment only buys the rights to an association; there is still a need to exploit this further by investing additional sums. The association can then be promoted and leveraged by the sponsor using such marketing communications elements as advertising, sales promotion, point-of-purchase, packaging, and production of merchandise. By leveraging its association, a corporation may be in a better position to claim its space in an increasingly cluttered sponsorship environment[22]. In addition, leveraging by corporations can greatly benefit sport organizations. For example, the sponsorship of Diving Canada by Ombrelle, a sunscreen product, before the 2004 Olympic Games provided great value for the sport. In activating its sponsorship, Ombrelle used the images of the National Diving Team in: television advertising; point-of-purchase displays in drugstores nationally (Shoppers Drug Mart, Jean Coutu); a website and a diving game to encourage consumers to make donations to the national diving team; print advertising including pictures of the team; and a public relations campaign with key accounts (national team appearances at stores). The promotional value and exposure created by this campaign was considered to be exceptional for the sport.

Leveraging must be part of the discussion and not just from the point of view of the sponsor. As Chapter 11 discussed, companies employ sponsorship for such reasons as achieving competitive advantage, generating revenue, and having an impact on consumer-oriented objectives, such as increasing brand awareness, brand image, and purchase intentions. By leveraging a sponsorship and the accompanying association, a sponsor will more likely reach its objectives[23]. The sponsee must also take on a leveraging and involvement role to enhance the value of the association, build their own brand, and combat ambush marketing. While leveraging activities will happen later on, the

[22] Seguin, B., K. Teed, & N. O'Reilly (2005) National sport organizations and sponsorship.
[23] ibid.

discussions should take place in the negotiation stage. In fact, this is where the sport marketer's homework will most likely pay off. By offering ways by which a company can benefit from the leveraging of an association demonstrates knowledge and understanding of the business.

Terms of the Sponsorship Contract

The intent of a sponsorship contract is to anticipate every eventuality and determine how the various parties might be affected[24]. Depending on the extent of the sponsorship (e.g., price, television) and the experience of the sport marketer in drafting the contract, a lawyer with experience in entertainment/event law could be contacted by the sport organization to draw up a detailed contract to protect both parties. Wilkinson[25] suggests that both sponsee and sponsor use this sponsorship contract checklist:

1. Status of sponsor (exclusivity, category, etc.)
2. Event signage (how many, where, who pays)
3. Advertising credits (where—on stationery, event name, program cover/ad)
4. Sponsorship fee (how paid, when paid)
5. Merchandising rights (Can sponsor sell T-shirts, mugs, or other souvenirs? Can sponsor manufacture its own souvenirs or buy from the promoter at cost? Who gets profit?)
6. Ownership of television rights (who owns and controls, rights of refusal for advertising spots, opening and closing billboards, rights to use footage of event)
7. Public relations and personal appearances (athletes as spokespersons, mention of sponsor's name in media interviews, ticket availability, hospitality)
8. Future options (right of renewal)
9. Trademarks (ownership and usage of special logo, sponsor quality control, promoter's quality control)
10. Liabilities (to observers, participants, site; infringement of trademarks; event cancellation)

Sponsorship Life

After successful negotiation, the sport organization (or sponsee) will be fortunate to have a sponsorship partnership ready to implement. This is not the time to celebrate, relax, and lose focus. It is at this step, sponsorship life, where the benefits of the sponsorship are maximized by both the sponsor and sponsee. First, the sponsee must dedicate a volunteer director and/or a staff member to service the sponsorship and develop the relationship with the sponsor. Second, the sponsee must collaborate with the sponsor(s) to put in place a variety of leveraging tactics during an event. For example, the presence of

---

[24] Wilkinson, D.G. (1993) *Sponsorship Marketing.*
[25] ibid.

high-profile athletes (both active and retired) at hospitality functions are usually popular. In addition, the presence of television (national networks) is an important factor for sponsors. An internal marketing plan through which the sport organization leverages the sponsorship within its organization needs to be launched. Non-intrusive leveraging tools (e.g., a charity foundation) should be explored. Strategic alliances with media, additional sponsors, and events should be developed. Third, an evaluation plan measuring the effectiveness of the sponsorship must be implemented, including monitoring the sponsor's commitment to the 3:1 leveraging ratio. This plan must allow for improvements to be made to the sponsorship. The sponsee should work with the sponsor in its planning. The sport organization's marketing plans should consider the interests of the sponsor's customers as well as its own. The two organizations need to work together to integrate the sponsorship both vertically and horizontally. Should additional sponsors be involved, all organizations should work together to enable collaboration and cross-promotion.

Organizational Support

A dedicated staff member or volunteer should be responsible for servicing the sponsorship. However, all members of the organization (staff and volunteer) must understand the sponsorship to support the efforts of the sponsor in leveraging it. Many sport organizations have special sessions with athletes and coaches to educate them on the value of sponsorship and the need to service it. For example, sponsor representatives (vice-presidents and directors) may bring some clients to a resort setting such as Whistler for the weekend of a freestyle skiing competition. Athletes may participate in hospitality functions and special events or even go down the slopes with the sponsor representatives. The objective here is to develop a program that will create unique experiences for your sponsor, which is part of supporting or servicing a sponsor.

Servicing a sponsorship includes: keeping regular communications on activities of the sport (e.g., press releases, telephone calls, visiting in person), making sure that all materials needed from the sponsor for a specific event are in place (e.g., signage, sample material, ad in programs), inviting the sponsor to special events (e.g., press conferences, visits with athletes, shows, competitions), knowing sponsor's objectives so you can create innovative promotions, keeping track of all the things you do for a sponsor (log), working with media to ensure your sponsor gets publicity, ensuring the sponsor's logo specs are respected in all collateral materials (e.g., posters, signs, advertisers), providing added-value benefits to sponsor without asking for more money—people enjoy getting a deal.

Deliver, deliver, deliver: there are a number of failure stories associated with sponsorship. Too often a sport organization signs a sponsorship deal with a company, promises a number of benefits, and then fails to deliver on its promises. This will not only ruin your reputation as a sport organization but also hurt others in the industry. The key in servicing is to keep your sponsor happy. Take every opportunity to make your contact a "star" in their own organization. Providing added value is also looked on favourably by sponsors.

It is essential that the sponsor support the sponsorship. The sponsee should know who is responsible for managing the sponsorship from the sponsor's side, as well as other people in the sponsoring organization. While one person may be identified as the champion from the sponsor's side, it is important that other executives support the sponsorship. In this way, if the key sponsor contact is no longer responsible for the sponsorship, others will support it.

Developing an Evaluation Framework

Evaluating sponsorship programs may be one of the greatest challenges facing the sponsorship industry. A major difficulty stems from the many objectives that sponsors seek with sponsorship programs. Brooks[26] notes that the fundamental problem in sponsorship evaluation lies in demonstrating that it worked better, relatively, than more traditional methods of promotion (e.g., advertising or sales promotion). The measurement of any sponsorship program is a difficult task, especially if the only criterion for measurement is sales. According to the marketing representative of a major Canadian sponsor[27], "it takes time, and repeated exposures, for a communications plan to register upon one's target audiences (both internal and external) and for them to fully understand all that the sponsoring company is trying to accomplish." For a number of companies, "gut feeling" is the tool used to evaluate sponsorship programs as suggested by this quote from a sponsor[28]: "It is my belief that no other program undertaken by the company has had the positive effect on furthering relationship with customers and consumers as the sponsorship of Freestyle. Also, the company's support of Canadian heroes has greatly contributed in building employees pride and motivation. The sponsorship has, in my opinion, greatly exceeded expectations. At the start we didn't know what to expect but what we got was something that positively affected the company's relationship with all of its stakeholders."

Measuring Return on Investment

It is the responsibility of the sport organization to demonstrate the value received by the sponsor[29]. The saying "what gets measured gets done" holds true in the evaluation of sponsorship[30]. Hence, the importance of establishing clear, measurable objectives associated with sponsorship. Some flexibility should be built into an evaluation program since sponsorship is not as easily quantifiable compared to other business activities[31]. In fact, a sponsorship offers a number of tangible and intangible benefits.

---

[26] Brooks, C.M. (1994) *Sports Marketing*.

[27] Seguin, B., K. Teed, & N. O'Reilly (2005) National sport organizations and sponsorship: 79.

[28] ibid: 80.

[29] Stotlar, D. (2005) *Developing Successful Sponsorship Plans*.

[30] Wilkinson, D.G. (1993) *Sponsorship Marketing*: 287.

[31] Stotlar, D. (2005) *Developing Successful Sponsorship Plans*.

Tangible benefits: These are the quantifiable assets in a sponsorship package. They may include activities that take place in or around an event: signage, public service announcements, collateral materials produced by the sponsee or sponsor (e.g., posters, flyers), website, sampling/coupons, and hospitality. The sport marketer must be able to track the number of spectators or people that can be reached through these activities. It is also important that sport marketers keep track of sponsor identification through broadcast of an event and the media coverage (publicity) resulting from it.

Intangible benefits: These are the qualitative assets that a sponsee delivers, such as borrowed imagery and audience loyalty. These are much more difficult to measure than the tangible benefits.

According to the International Event Group (IEG)[32], sponsorship can be measured in three different ways:

- measuring awareness levels achieved or attitudes changed
- quantifying sponsorship in terms of sales results
- comparing the value of sponsorship-generated media coverage to the cost of equivalent advertising space or time

Note that a pre-sponsorship benchmark will be needed to assess any changes in attitudes or in sales. In addition, if a company is involved in a number of promotions at the same time, it may be difficult to determine if an increase in sales is the result of the sponsorship rather than other promotions.

Wilkinson[33] suggests four types of measurement to assess ROI of sponsorship:

1. *Activity*, in terms of event, includes:

    event signage
    event attendance
    merchandise sold
    programs sold
    numbers reached through sampling
    total number of impressions generated through paid media
    impressions created through unpaid media coverage (publicity, PR)
    impressions created though consumer/customer communication channels (packaging)
    impressions created through sales promotions and cross-promotions (point-of-purchase displays)
    documenting "extensions" to other areas of business (e.g., hosting by the salesforce)

2. Attitudinal research
    sponsorship fit
    tracking: Involves quantitative surveys targeted at audience and implemented through on-site intercepts, telephone surveys, surveys of employees, customers. Topics can include knowledge of sponsorship,

---

[32] International Event Group (1995) *IEG'S Complete Guide to Sponsorship*. IEG One.

[33] Wilkinson, D.G. (1993) *Sponsorship Marketing*: 287.

sponsor recall, attitudes toward sponsors, and behavioural changes resulting from a sponsorship.

image transfer: More difficult to assess, will depend on the strength of the sponsee's brand and the amount of leveraging on the part of the sponsor. These benefits are usually the result of long-term investment in a property.

3. Benchmarking sponsorship program

sponsorship positioning
rights fees
communications support
business extensions
marketing integration

4. Sponsorship efficiency

ROI of sponsorship versus other communications options
cost of awareness
cost of favourability
cost of trial

The bottom line, or sales objective, is also critical to sponsors. As suggested in Chapter 8, it is unreasonable to believe that organizations would be spending large amounts of money to a sponsee if they did not feel comfortable about the return on investment. According to Shank[34], recent studies have shown that "increasing sales and market share are the primary motives of sponsorship." In Canada, Copeland and Frisby[35] found that 46.2 percent of the companies surveyed cited sales as one of the three most important indicators of sponsorship success. Hence, sport marketers must find ways to measure increases in sales. IEG[36] suggests using this method to measure sales:

Track sales objectives, including a sponsorship's ability to:

- increase sales of a product or a service to consumers
- drive sales to business customers
- increase distribution outlets
- generate product display at point of sale
- produce targeted new leads
- improve efficiencies of this and other promotions
- lock in heavy users
- boost retail traffic

Measure sales gains through:

- sales for the two- to three-month period surrounding the sponsorship to the same period in previous years
- sales in the immediate event area versus national sales

---

[34] Shank, M.D. (2005) *Sports Marketing: A Strategic Perspective* (3rd ed). Prentice Hall: 383.

[35] Copeland, R. & W. Frisby (1996) Understanding the sport sponsorship process from a corporate perspective. *Journal of Sport Management*: 10: 32–48.

[36] International Event Group (1995) *IEG'S Complete Guide to Sponsorship*: 26.

- sales tied directly to the sponsored event (e.g., ticket discount with proof of purchase, then tracking redemptions)
- number of outlets carrying product
- customer brand preference
- number of retailers/dealers participating in the program
- incremental sales to retailers—additional case orders, display penetration, shipments, features, and price reduction

Media Coverage

Media coverage and its related value is a tangible asset that must be measured. The sport marketer must be able to answer these questions:

- What is the value of a sign/banner placed within television range?
- What is the value of a 30-second ad on television? Newspaper advertising?
- How much coverage did the event get from the media (publicity)? What is the value of this coverage?

Sport marketers must get CD/DVD copies of televised events to, among other things, measure the value of signage. They should also request information on the audience (e.g., ratings, share of audience, demographic information on audience). A media monitoring system should be developed to keep track of media coverage. A number of companies specializing in media monitoring can provide detailed summaries of newspaper, radio, television, and Internet coverage through a tracking device. A monitoring system is also essential for measuring the success of your media/public relations efforts (e.g., press conferences, press releases).

The metrics used to calculate the value of sponsor identification through signage do not represent an exact science; however, industry-accepted methods provide ballpark figures. The first method is calculating the amount of time a sponsor is clearly identified in television range. For example, a one-hour broadcast of a diving event on CBC may provide Speedo with 15 minutes of clear identification. Given that the value of a 30-second commercial for that specific time period is at $1000, the estimated value of signage would be at $30 000. Another method is by counting the number of signage impression a sponsor gets during the coverage, the number of times the signage appears in camera view. In this case, every three clear impressions are estimated to equate to a 30-second commercial. In the Speedo example, a total of 30 impressions would be valued at $10 000. Finally, the amount of exposure can be estimated at five to ten percent of rate card value. In the case of Speedo, 15 minutes of signage exposure would be valued at $1000 to $3000. The same calculation would be used to determine the value of sponsor identification in other media (e.g., newspaper, radio).

Encouraging Joint Planning

Planning a sponsorship involves the collaboration of all partners (sponsee and sponsor) from the beginning. Once the parties are clear on the details of the contract, they should develop a detailed plan with the goal of maximizing—for both sponsor and sponsee—the opportunities/benefits associated with the sponsorship. Therefore, clear objectives must be set and supported by a leveraging plan. For example, how will the sponsor integrate the sponsorship within its communications mix? Through advertising? Sales promotion? Point-of-purchase programs? Production of merchandise? Any of these activity takes time; thus the importance of beginning the planning stage early (usually 8 to 12 months before execution). The sponsee is encouraged to provide support and ideas to the sponsor. Oftentimes, sport marketing consultants are involved in facilitating the process (e.g., TrojanOne Marketing, K.Mac. & Associates).

According to sport marketing consultant Keith McIntyre[37]: "sponsorship is the only way to have 'authentic' association and sponsors must be strategic in providing promotional programs that take advantage of this authenticity." This strategy was used by General Mills during the 2000, 2002, and 2004 Olympic Games. As a Canadian Olympic Committee sponsor, General Mills had numerous objectives tied to its sponsorship, including creating brand association with the Olympics, increasing the awareness of the Cheerios brand, enhancing employee morale through support of Olympic team, connecting with consumers, and increasing sales. In fact, General Mills was looking for ways to activate its Olympic rights to create opportunities and benefits to its business partners (retail), consumers, and employees: thus the need to integrate the sponsorship within its marketing/communications mix. The company launched a program—Team Cheerios—featuring profiles of selected athletes on the Cheerios boxes distributed over three months prior to the Olympics. Each athlete in the program was profiled (alone) on a Cheerios box, with a picture, bio, and personal story. The profiled athletes received tremendous exposure; and this was an excellent way for consumers to discover the athletes and "connect" with them on a personal level. While competitor Kellogg's cereal brand Victor secured television advertising rights during the Games, General Mills's strategy focused on the grocery chains. "We worked closely at developing relationships with key accounts at the retail, making sure they understood that we held the authentic association with the Olympic rings, the Games and the athletes, we owned the space!" The General Mills Olympic sponsorship was fully integrated into its marketing and promotional mix, including product packaging (integrating rings and athletes' profiles on boxes), pricing (special pricing leading up to and during Olympics), distribution (working with key retail accounts, in-store positioning), and promotional mix (sales promotion campaigns, athletes appearances, personal selling programs, advertising, publicity). The promotional campaign provided something meaningful to consumers and received tremendous publicity. This approach to sponsorship enables associations linked to emotions and passion,

[37] Seguin, B. & N. O'Reilly (2007) Sponsorship in the trenches: Case study evidence of its legitimate place in the promotional mix. *The Sport Journal:* 10(1).

Important Strategic Elements of Sport Marketing in Canada

unlike signage or rink boards. However, it needs tremendous planning and collaboration from all parties. To get this program off the ground, General Mills needed to:

- determine which athletes would fit with the brand
- contact athletes and / or agents identified
- sign a contract with athletes
- get information on each athlete (bio, stories) and get any necessary rights to pictures
- determine the number of boxes produced for each athlete
- produce the boxes
- develop promotional / communications to support the program (point-of-purchase plan, signage, photos, advertising, sales support material)
- train employees (e.g., salesforce) on all elements of the program from getting the retail involved to executing and evaluating the program
- plan athletes' appearances

Clearly, leveraging a sponsorship requires proper planning, timing and execution.

1. *Review the details of the contract and ensure that both parties are clear on their roles and responsibilities:* status of sponsor, event signage, merchandising, etc.
2. *Set clear sponsorship objectives:* sales, image, hospitality
3. *Develop leveraging strategies:* athletes / teams at POP, incentive programs for trade, consumer contests, sponsee brand in collateral materials, cross-promotions with other sponsors, etc.
4. *Develop sponsorship/activation plan:* timelines
5. *Evaluate:* research analysis, broadcast analysis, value of sponsorship

POP: point-of-purchase displays include merchandising of all sorts—kiosks, cardboard cutouts, signage—targeted at consumers at the location of the purchase decision.

Implementing Leveraging Tools

Having a sponsorship plan, it is time to implement leveraging tools. Sponsorship can be leveraged in a number of ways. For example, General Mills used athletes in activating its sponsorship, a common practice. Table 12-2 lists popular leveraging tactics.

TABLE 12-2

Leveraging Tactics

TACTIC	EXAMPLE
Sponsor name used as official team name	Team RONA (cycling team)
Official sponsee poster	Bombardier Lake Louise Winterstart
Website title and weblink	2007 Esso Women's Nationals (women's hockey) http://www.hockeycanada.ca

Sponsor/sponsee signage at track	end zone signage at CFL game
Front cover of event program	photo of Mats Sundin drinking Pepsi on front of Leafs' program
Related publications (e.g., newsletter)	Sony's magazine about CFL football (but really promoting their products)
Sponsor logo on equipment and/or team uniform	Canada Post on National Speed Skating Team uniform
Mailing lists (use of)	Endurosport (Ontario bike store) sponsors the Ontario Association of Triathletes to access their mailing lists
On-site product sampling	PowerBar samples distributed at a PowerBar-sponsored running event
Right to use trademarks, logos, and slogans in advertising, packaging, and promotions	FINA awarded Montreal with the 2005 World Aquatic Championships allowing the local organizing committee to use the FINA logo on all messaging
Prestige of sponsee	any Olympic sponsor
Awareness and association with sponsee	Consumer opinion of association including image transfer and awareness
Category exclusivity (no other) product or service in same category allowed to sponsor the sponsee	Bell Grand Prix (Bell Canada, official telecommunications provider for Swimming Canada) means no similar firm can have sponsorship status with Swimming Canada Grand Prix events
Level of audience interest/loyalty	television ratings
Cross-promotional benefits with sponsor	shared production of a joint TV commercial or co-branding program
Limited degree of sponsor clutter	Guaranteed exclusivity and number of sponsor categories by the sponsee
Inability to ambush sponsee	Guaranteed exclusivity and number of sponsor categories by the sponsee
Networking opportunities	associated hospitality events and VIP invite list(s)
Newsworthiness	publicity achieved

To assess the effectiveness of these tactics, the sport marketer can apply various metrics in these general areas of evaluation:

- *Measuring awareness and attitude of consumers:* prior/during/after sponsorship
- *Measuring media coverage:* ratings, signage, 30-second spots, etc.
- *Measuring sales:* compared with past sales for same period, coupon redemption.
- *Image:* consumers' perceptions (pre and post)

- *Motivation of employees of sponsor:* through internal surveys, focus groups, etc. on loyalty to firm, confidence in firm, etc.
- *Hospitality effectiveness:* attraction of key contacts to event, satisfaction of attendees, etc.

Sponsorship Termination

The final step of the sponsorship process is termination, when the agreement comes to an end. If the previous stages of sponsorship were well executed, then termination can actually be rewarding for both parties[38]: If the relationship developed with the sponsor was positive throughout the life of the sponsorship (e.g., good communications, well-executed programs, sponsorship objectives achieved, value-added benefits provided, professional), the outgoing sponsor can actually act as the property's best "salesperson." Well in advance of the termination date, the sponsee should know whether the sponsor wishes to renew the deal. To maximize the sponsorship benefits at this stage, the sponsor and sponsee need to work collaboratively to develop a succession plan to find a new sponsor and respect the original sponsorship. In an ideal situation, the sponsorship is terminated slowly over a number of years.

An example of a close sponsor–sponsee relationship is the partnership between Owens Corning and the Canadian Freestyle Skiing Association (CFSA). The support of Owens Corning over the life of the sponsorship agreement far exceeded the financial commitment to CFSA. In fact, Owens Corning was instrumental in raising the profile of the sport nationally and internationally. The company's deep involvement in the sport included the presence of its marketing director on the CFSA board of directors, a rare type of occurrence in amateur sport management. Throughout the years, Owens Corning made extensive use of all elements of the promotion/communications mix, including media advertising (television, print, radio, Internet), collateral materials (e.g., company annual report, magazines), television coverage of World Cup events (assumed cost), title sponsorship of events, sponsorship of individual athletes, signage (on-site, bobs on athletes), incentive programs for the trade (e.g., athlete appearances, POP promotions, contests), and extensive use of hospitality at events (Whistler, Mont Tremblant). The company also assisted CFSA in developing marketing/communications strategies. For example, Owens Corning covered the cost of a full-time communications employee; provided media training for athletes; and assisted in the production of events. As CFSA's properties continued to rise in value, Owens Corning employed a long-term leveraging strategy to continue to garner benefit from the sponsorship while controlling its associated costs. After helping build to freestyle skiing into one of the most dynamic, most popular, and most watched Olympic sports in the world, Owens Corning's decision to diminish its involvement and eventually terminate its sponsorship was motivated by a major restructuring of the company worldwide. However, the company did play a key role in helping the CFSA sign a major sponsor, one of its major clients, as successor[39].

---

[38] Seguin, B., K. Teed, & N. O'Reilly (2005) National sport organizations and sponsorship.
[39] ibid.

The involvement of Owens Corning in succession planning was extensive; however, other ways to get outgoing sponsors to help in the succession planning can be as simple as including a testimonial or a letter of reference or acting as a reference when the sponsee is actively pursuing a replacement.

Best Practices in Canadian Sport Sponsorship

Chapter 11 suggested the growth of sport sponsorship worldwide has been phenomenal. In Canada, the hosting of the 2010 Olympic Winter Games has prompted Canadian companies to spend an unprecedented amount for the rights to be associated with the Vancouver Olympic Organizing Committee (VANOC). Bell Canada reports that its VANOC sponsorship amounts to an overall commitment of $200 million; of which $90 million is in cash[40]. Petro-Canada, RBC, General Motors, Hudson Bay Company, and RONA have each committed over $65 million. While there is little doubt that having the Olympic Games in Canada has sparked the interest of many Canadian companies in sport (especially winter sports), sport sponsorship remains at an early stage of development, especially as in the amateur sport sector. A recent ISM study[41] reports that 43 percent of NSO revenue comes from the federal government, only 14 percent from sponsorship. However, the lack of data makes it difficult to have a valid representation of the current state of sponsorship in Canada: There are numerous examples of successful corporate partnerships with sport but detailed information and the trends for the Canadian sport marketing/sponsorship industry require further research. A major study undertaken by the ISM in 2003–2006 analyzed more than 70 case studies related to sport sponsorship. Information for these case studies came from primary data from in-depth interviews and secondary data from sponsorship marketing materials, company policies, internal business plans, corporate sponsorship plans, and Internet materials. Both the sport properties and the private sector identified a number of key success factors.

- Building relationships: This is identified as a *must*, a key success factor for most sponsorship programs. Emphasis should be on building meaningful and long-term relationships with more than one individual within the sponsoring organization. This can be accomplished through keeping regular contact, hospitality at events, and servicing all aspects of the sponsorship. A number of sport properties said they devoted much effort to that one key contact within corporate sponsor's organization—the "champion" for the sponsorship.
- Understanding each other's needs and objectives: To provide value, individuals working for sport properties must understand the business of its sponsors and its brands. However, ISM's 2006 *Case Study Report* identified that a number of properties do not know their sponsors' objectives and vice versa.

---

[40] Bell Canada Enterprises (2004) Vancouver 2010 selects Bell Canada as premier national partner. Retrieved on January 21, 2007 from http://www.bce.ca/en/news/releases/bce/2004/10/18/71721.html.

[41] Institute of Sport Marketing was created in 2003 by Laurentian University's School of Sport Administration program. Its main goal is to conduct research in sport marketing.

- Professionalism: Corporate sponsors have high expectations that sport property will deal with them in a professional and business-like fashion. This goes for the entire sponsorship management process, from acquisition to servicing to evaluation. Follow-up appreciation letters, progress reports, invitations to events are all important. If involved with events, attention to details, to the look of the event and its execution are all important factors that create a professional impression for sponsors.
- Community involvement: Many corporations look for opportunities to leverage involvement sponsorship deals with the consumers.
- Quality of product/success: Having a successful team helps attract interest from fans and the media.
- Innovation and creativity: A number of case studies showed the importance of being creative—suggesting new promotional ideas, new ways to leverage sponsorship.
- Sponsorship evaluation: Property owners must evaluate all aspects of the sponsorship, both tangible and intangibles assets.
- Deliver more than expected: Provide sponsors with added value—people want to get a deal.
- Television/media support: Essential for successful sponsorship programs, sponsors and sponsees should spend time forging solid relationships with media.

Table 12-3 lists best practices that complement the key success factors.

TABLE 12-3

Best Practices

Fit	Ensure a good fit between the partners, whether through image, associations, or objectives.
Exclusivity	Know that most companies demand exclusivity in their product category.
Leveraging	Understand that companies seek sport organizations who offer and create leveraging opportunities for their sponsorship.
Relationship building	Build good relationships and networks with sponsors. Consider offering sponsors the opportunity to network with each other.
Market expansion	Understand that many companies use sponsorship to break into new markets and create brand awareness.
Community/Cause	Consider that many organizations want to be seen as a good corporate citizens that support the community. They often see sport sponsorships as a way to give back to the community.

Employee motivation/education	Know that many companies see sport sponsorships as an opportunity to get their employees involved and motivated toward the company's goals.
Know both parties objectives	Understands what both parties are trying to gain through the sponsorship agreement to make it easier to reach those objectives:

Source: Seguin, B. (May 2006). Canadian Sport Sponsorship case studies report. Institute of Sport Marketing. Prepared for Canadian Sport Summit and Sport Canada. 110 pages.

Model

The model in Figure 12-1 summarizes the four steps to successful sponsorship presented in this chapter. Clearly, numerous external variables could hamper the effectiveness of this model; however, based on the review of the literature and numerous sport sponsorship cases, adherence to the steps will enhance the likelihood of finding success in the pursuit of sponsorship.

FIGURE 12-1

A Model for Sponsorship Success

Step 1: Presponsorship Practices

Product Development
- national team, events and hospitality functions
- support achievement of Olympic success

Build Long-term Relationships
- with major television broadcasters
- with potential sponsors internally (not via party)

Build Organizational Capacity
- event/hospitality HR expertise: volunteer and staff
- organization-wide commitment to sponsorship
- solid non-sponsorship funding base

Planning
- detailed market research on potential sponsors
- clear sponsorship plan, including legal contracts
- realistic resource ($$ and HR) sponsorship budget

Step 2: Negotiation Stage

Be Certain of "FIT"
- sponsor an sponsee objectives
- consider both brands
- CEO contact needs fit

Leveraging Commitment
- sponsor intention to 3:1 leverage ratio
- integration into sponsor's marketing mix
- include TV production/service expectations

Terms of Contract
- require legal approval
- prioritize long-term over higher dollar value

Step 3: Sponsorship Life

Develop Evaluation Frameworks
- formal evaluation of sponsorship effectiveness
- monitor leveraging activity by sponsor (at least 3:1)
- mechanism to alter sponsorship based on evaluation

Implement Leveraging Tools
- own leveraging plan (internal)
- strategic alliances with media/events/sponsors
- involve star athletes, retired Olympic champions, national TV and hospitality at all events
- explore nonintrusive leveraging tools

Encourage Joint Planning
- consider sponsor's customers
- jointly work to integrate sponsorship
- collaboratively seek associate sponsors

Organizational Support
- dedicated staff member to service sponsorship

Step 4: Sponsorship Termination

Collaborative Succession Plan

Gradual Decrease of Involvement

Case: Direct Energy

Background

Direct Energy was founded in 1985 as a producer-owned wholesale natural gas marketing company. Since 2000, Direct Energy has been part of the well-capitalized Centrica, a company with 31 million customers worldwide and an operating profit of £1058 million. Direct Energy focuses on providing superior service to consumers. Its offices in Calgary, Edmonton, Vancouver, and Toronto employ over 2600 people. Direct Energy Marketing is the leading retail energy and services provider in North America, serving 2.5 million customers in Canada alone. In Alberta, 1.3 million households use Direct Energy regulated services.

Quick Marketing Facts

Direct Energy operates under two brand names in Alberta:

- Direct Energy Essential Services: Serves residential and small business customers province wide.
- Direct Energy Business Services: Serves medium and large commercial customers in BC and Alberta.

Direct Energy faces some marketing challenges in Alberta:

- nonexistent unaided brand awareness
- limited awareness of competitive energy services as a category of retail energy
- negative brand perception

Direct Energy's target markets are:

- large families that are very family focused
- lower- to middle-class families
- people whose community is important to them
- those most apt to switch to other gas and electrical providers

Direct Energy has identified its consumers as:

- active in their children's lives
- brand loyal
- into healthy lifestyles
- striving to instill confidence and values in their children
- involved in their communities
- appreciating simple but fun activities

Sponsorship

Direct Energy is deeply committed to grassroots event marketing. While numerous challenges are associated with grassroots marketing and sponsorship (Table 12-4), the company feels that it is an excellent vehicle to communicate their brand message. Direct Energy's sponsorship strategy is to complement a mass media campaign with involvement in community-level sponsorship in Calgary and Edmonton to create brand awareness. The company wishes to extend its brand promise of "fresh thinking" to families in their communities.

TABLE 12-4

Benefits and Challenges of Grassroots Marketing and Sponsorship

BENEFITS	CHALLENGES
Engages stakeholders	Perceived inability to evaluate
Involves all aspects of marketing mix	Most labour-intensive marketing vehicle
Opportunity to make the brand the 'hero'	Short-term commitment by brand owners
Puts local events on national scene	Uncertainly about how to enter the arena
Community involvement	Costly sponsorship that doesn't deliver
Good corporate citizen	Outdoor activities subject to factors beyond the organizer's control (weather)

Kid Power Soccer

Kid Power (KP) Soccer[42] is one of the largest community soccer commitments in Canada. The mission of Kid Power is to "assist and support the commitment of parents and community volunteers who invest endless time and energy into our community's children." Calgary and Edmonton help make up the 1100 teams for the program and the 15 000 participants, who are all under the age of eight. "Kid Power is about strengthening families and communities by providing them support to tap into the energy and passion of their children." The program properties include KP Indoor Soccer, KP Outdoor Soccer, and KP Zone, an activity area for local events of key children. To maximize the controlled branding opportunities, Direct Energy manages the branding of team and coach jerseys, soccer goal posts, team and individual photos and soccer balls, ball bags, and water bottles. The company sees this program as "Investing in the energy of Alberta's children." To promote its investment, Direct Energy purchased media for bus wraps, community print, soccer publications, and a television series *Soccer Tips*. In addition to all the PR investment, Direct Energy puts on Kid Power Coaches Clinics: Over 1000 coaches participate in over 60 clinics each year. The company believes the Kid Power program has contributed to the 18 percent increase in brand awareness since the launch in Alberta.

---

[42] Compiled from the Direct Energy website (http://www.directenergy.com) and presentation by Barbara Conkie at Canadian Sponsorship Forum 2005.

Keys to Success

- Define priorities: Clearly identify segments of the target market you wish to reach, review your marketing mix, and identify the role you want your sponsorship to fill.
- Set objectives.
- Understand your consumers: Understand what is important to them, identify their interests and motivations, and make the sponsorship relevant to them.
- Measure success: Analyze the property and its effect on your company.
- Leverage volunteers: Harness them to drive your ROI.
- Train front-line staff: Hire and train your staff in all relevant business aspects and select staff that fit your brand.
- Ensure and coordinate brand consistency.
- Drive impressions.

Source: Institute for Sport Marketing Case Studies. Laurentian University 2003–2005

Case Questions

1. How committed is Direct Energy to sponsorship? Explain.
2. Can the model sponsorship success be applied in this case? Why or why not?
3. What are some possible objectives associated with this sponsorship?
4. As a sponsor, how would you leverage this property?
5. What would you do different if you were Direct Energy?

Chapter Summary

This chapter provides practical instructions for building a successful sponsorship. The four-step approach—pre-sponsorship practices, negotiation, sponsorship life, and sponsorship termination—gives the necessary building blocks for successful sponsorship programs. The commitment of the sport organization to sponsorship is a key component of a successful program. While short-term success may be gained from some sponsorship programs, the emphasis should be long term, which must be understood by the decision makers (board of directors). Resources (time, staff, financial) will have to be invested throughout the sponsorship process. The sport organization should develop a strong relationship with its partners. Sponsors should be encouraged to activate their sponsorship by integrating some or all aspects of the sponsorship within their communications mix. Best practices in sport sponsorship include fit, exclusivity, relationships building, market expansion, community, employee motivation, and understanding objectives.

Test Your Knowledge

1. What is leveraging? Explain with an example.
2. Explain the pre-sponsorship practices? Why are they critical in the sport sponsorship process?
3. What are five benefits usually sought by sponsors?
4. You have been asked to research a potential sponsor for your sport. Where do you start? What information will you look for?
5. How can you create your own property?
6. Explain how the four-step approach presented in this chapter could help your local soccer organization to get sponsorship.

 For more review questions, go to http://www.sportmarketing.nelson.com.

Key Terms

activating	sponsee
POP	sponsor
property	sponsorship

 A full glossary of key term definitions is located at http://www.sportmarketing.nelson.com.

Internet Resources

Maximising the value of sponsorship, http://www.sportbusinessassociates .com/sports_reports/value_sponsorship.pdf

NCAA sponsorship was slam dunk for Coca-Cola, http://publications.mediapost.com/index.cfm?fuseaction=Articles .showArticleHomePage&art_aid=58033

Sponsorship in sport, http://www.britishjudo.org.uk/pdf/SponsorshipinSport-Summarydocument_000.pdf

Sports sponsorship vs. advertising, http://www.ameinfo.com/61816.html

Sports sponsorship linked marketing and public relations, http://www .buseco.monash.edu.au/gsb/mbr/assets/issue-two/sport-sponsorship.pdf

Sport sponsorship is about more than just winning, http://www.biz-community.com/Article/196/48/7006.html

Know the score, http://www.sbnonline.com/National/Article/170/1503/Know_the_score.aspx

Sponsorship executive summary,
http://www.srsa.gov.za/ClientFiles/SQ_sponsorsh.PDF

A theoretical evaluation of selective sport sponsorship research frameworks, http://upetd.up.ac.za/thesis/available/etd-11072001-165433/unrestricted/06chapter5.pdf

Successful sponsorship,
http://www.ausport.gov.au/fulltext/1999/cjsm/v3n3/cheng&stotlar33.htm

Chapter 13

Ambush Marketing

Source: AP Photo/Luca Bruno.

Learning Objectives

- To recognize ambush marketing and its place in sponsorship
- To understand the objectives of ambush marketing
- To be familiar with the strategies of ambush marketing
- To be able to develop strategies to prevent ambush marketing and protect your property
- To explore the ethics of ambush marketing
- To appreciate the relationship between ambush marketing and clutter
- To understand the role of brand management in controlling ambush marketing

Introduction

"Ambushers [are like] thieves, knowingly stealing something that does not belong to them. A form of parasite, feeding off the goodwill and value of the organization, they are trying to deceive the public into believing they support. Like leeches, they suck the lifeblood and goodwill out of the institution"—Michael Payne, Former Marketing Director, International Olympic Committee[1]

The words of an international sport business expert like Michael Payne clearly show the incredible stakes in sponsorship today. With sometimes millions of dollars on the line, it becomes evident that event organizers and their sponsors

---

[1] Payne M. (1991) Ambush marketing: Immoral or imaginative practice. Presented at Sponsorship Europe '91, Barcelona: 24.

are not amused by what some may consider a game. In fact, sport sponsorship is serious business, and the demands on sport marketers are increasingly challenging. Faced with a marketplace that is ever more cluttered with official sponsors and ambush marketers, sport marketers have to build and manage brands that will provide value to their partners while creating meaningful relationships with consumers.

EXECUTIVE PERSPECTIVE

Martin Benson, Director of Strategic Partnerships, National Basketball Association (NBA) in China

The Business Impact of Ambush Marketing

Companies that imply a false association with or make unauthorized use of a sports organization's intellectual property pose a serious threat to the industry. In marketing speak, they are referred to as cheaters, fakes, pirates, or parasites—companies conducting ambush marketing, a practice that can have severe business repercussions on properties.

Many properties rely on revenues generated from the sale of marketing rights (e.g., broadcast, sponsorship, licensing) to subsist. Companies pay fees, in cash or goods and services, to governing bodies or event organizers in exchange for the right to use an event or a property's intellectual assets such as logos, terminology, images, or video footage. Thanks to these revenues, sport properties can finance the staging of events, pay appearance fees or prize money, contribute to the development of the athletes, and build structures to help the sport grow as well as prepare the next generation of champions.

Unfortunately, a number of companies conduct marketing campaigns around a given event or property without paying rights fees. This not only misleads consumers into believing that they are a sponsor of the event, but also ambushes the rights of companies that have paid fees that entitle them to an association with the event. This behaviour fails to contribute any resources to the staging of the event or the development of the sport.

As a Sport Business Manager, Why Should You Care?

Ambush marketing can have significant financial consequences for a property. Beyond the obvious costs incurred in the case of legal action by a sponsor against a property/organizer or in the case of a property/organizer against an ambusher, ambush marketers spend significant dollars that never reach the property. Additionally, in many cases, properties have made contractual promises to their sponsors to prevent and fight ambush marketing, and they need to be upheld.

The Olympic Effort

In the Olympic Movement, the International Olympic Committee (IOC) is at the forefront of the fight against ambush marketing. The IOC strives to generate billions of dollars to distribute to organizers of the Olympic Games, 203 national Olympic committees (NOCs), such as the Canadian Olympic Committee, and international federations (governing bodies for a given sport at the international level). To protect its revenue base and the rights that it sells to sponsors, the IOC develops extensive ambush prevention and education initiatives and, when required to do so, takes measures against ambushers.

What Does Ambush Marketing Look Like?

Ambush activities can take many forms. At the 2005 Torino Olympic Winter Games, Samsung and Panasonic were the official worldwide partners in the categories of wireless communications equipment and audio-video equipment, respectively. Organizers faced a challenging situation with an outdoor billboard campaign by one of their sponsors' major competitors. This company purchased billboards that were strategically located at the base of the Olympic mountain venues, where all spectators would transit. While the Olympics are one of the few major events that secures outdoor advertising space to prevent such types of advertisements, the company had managed to buy inventory that was viewed by hundreds of thousands of spectators every day and caused confusion in the marketplace as to who was really supporting the Games.

In the lead-up to the 2004 Athens Olympic Games, a potato chip company—not an Olympic sponsor—conducted a television campaign that mocked the delayed construction of the Olympic stadium. By imitating the sound of the starting pistol for a race and using actors as athletes and construction workers in the stadium, the company connected with viewers through sight and sound. All the more challenging was that this company openly used a visual disclaimer at the end of its commercial, stating that: "Obviously, this company is not a sponsor."

Around the time of the 2000 Sydney Olympic Games, a leading Australian airline—not a Sydney 2000 sponsor—used one of Australia's most recognizable athletes in its advertising campaigns. Through this athlete's participation in the Olympics, the company was able to gain an association with the Olympics, thereby undermining the investment made by Ansett, the official airline sponsor of the Games.

What Can Be Done?

The complexity of the problem is significant. How do you prevent unauthorized companies from associating with or implying an association with one of the world's most widely recognized brands?

Prevention is key. To effectively combat ambush marketing, sport properties need a well-stocked tool box. Extensive trademark and copyright registration as well as other legal instruments are essential for developing a legally robust intellectual property inventory for the modern-day property; however, legal tools are insufficient to deal with ambush marketing. Today's sophisticated marketers craft creative campaigns that steer clear of registered trademarks, yet manage to create a connection with consumers. As such, laws often need to be supplemented or, in many cases, created to specifically address ambush marketing. This gives law-enforcement bodies the legislative grounds to take action, should the need arise. Legislation is an effective strategy but must be complemented by communication campaigns and operational plans designed to ensure compliance and enforcement of rules and laws.

Increasing awareness of those companies that are legitimately supporting and financing the property can be one angle used in a communication campaign. The advertising campaigns, commonly paid for by the property are designed to recognize—and often thank—its sponsors. In doing so, they enhance consumers' awareness levels of the "real supporters" of the event/property.

In most recent Olympic Games, the organizing committees have developed integrated communication campaigns to recognize their sponsors and condemn ambush marketers. In major markets, certain NOCs have undertaken similar strategies. In the lead-up to the Athens and Torino Olympic Games, the IOC took unprecedented steps to create a significant, multinational advertising campaign.

These preventive measures culminate in an impressive deployment of resources in the weeks leading up to and during the Olympic Games. Organizers, volunteers, law enforcement, and other supporting agencies unite forces to monitor and enforce regulations, laws, and contractual commitments inside and around the venues, throughout the city as well as in television, Internet, and print media. In the Olympic system, this is the result of more than seven years of work.

Conclusion

Ambush marketers are becoming increasingly sophisticated, often indirectly leveraging investments made by true event/property supporters. In most cases, ambushers will not use any registered trademarks or copyrighted materials. Their ability to operate in a grey zone makes enforcement all the more challenging since legal recourse is not always an effective means to resolution.

The threat is real. The consequences are significant. Understanding the stakes and the means to counter ambush will better serve you, your organization, and your sponsors.

Martin Benson began his career as a player agent, representing professional ice hockey and volleyball players in North America and Europe. After eight years working in the marketing department of the IOC, Martin is now director of strategic partnerships with the National Basketball Association (NBA) in China.

Ambush Marketing: An Alternative to Traditional Sponsorship Strategies?

As previous chapters have demonstrated, the continued growth in sponsorship expenditure suggests that sponsorship remains an effective form of corporate communications. Both global sport properties (e.g., Olympic Games) and national properties (e.g., Hockey Canada) have maximized revenue by offering exclusive sponsorship opportunities. In turn, they have become commodities sought after by potential sponsors. This has resulted in a fantastic growth in the investment needed to be associated with such properties[2]. Given the desirability of these sponsees, in conjunction with the increase in rights fees necessary to become officially associated with them, there has been a growth in companies wishing to reap the benefits of sponsorship but without paying the fee. Such activities are considered ambush marketing.

The pioneers of ambush marketing research, Dennis Sandler and David Shani[3], define ambush marketing as "a planned effort (campaign) by an organization to associate itself indirectly with an event in order to gain at least one of the recognition and benefit that are associated with being an official sponsor." This definition suggests that ambush marketing is similar to sponsorship since strategies are put in place to gain specific benefits associated with a specific sponsee.

The subject of ambush marketing first gained major media attention following the 1984 Los Angeles Olympics, when Kodak successfully ambushed official Olympic sponsor Fuji. Since then, ambush marketing has grown both in the number of occurrences and in the number of sport properties that have been subject to it. The use of ambush marketing by some companies is now common practice in the sport world. It has become a strategic alternative to formal association through the purchase of legitimate sponsorship rights. And the long-term effect of this practice has yet to be determined. Many believe that ambush marketing can be detrimental to sport because it diminishes the value of sport properties and increases an already cluttered sporting environment.

Official sponsors and owners of events deplore the tactic of ambush marketing. Companies that engage in it argue that "to expect non-sponsors to treat event sponsorship differently than any other commercial battleground is unrealistic"[4] and thus feel justified in their activities. To some, marketers that are successful at creating effective ambush marketing campaigns may appear to be 'intelligent' marketers, since they are able to neutralize the competitive advantage by confusing the consumer as to who the legitimate sponsor of an event really is: They consider such behaviour to be legitimate competitive marketing. For others (especially sponsees), ambush marketing is a form of

---

[2] McCarthy, L. & M. Lyberger (2001) An assessment of consumer knowledge of, interest in, and perceptions of ambush marketing strategies. *Sport Marketing Quarterly*, 10(4): 130–7.

[3] Sandler, D. & D. Shani (1989) Olympic sponsorship vs ambush marketing: Who gets the gold? *Journal of Advertising Research*, 9(14): 9–14.

[4] Shani, D. & D. Sandler (1998) Ambush marketing: Is confusion to blame for the flickering of the flame? *Psychology & Marketing*, 15(4): 367–83.

cheating since no authority to associate with the event has been provided. The notion of exchange between a sponsor and an event organizer is violated through the use of ambush marketing, since "a third party is seeking to benefit from an exchange without making a proportional contribution to that exchange[5]." As a result, the sport entity is threatened by ambush marketing because it diminishes the corporation's dependence on the sport group: The existence of ambush marketing suggests that the sponsor may be able to enjoy comparable benefits without contributing to the sport group[6]. Regardless of one's opinion on the matter, it is the responsibility of the event organizers to develop programs that will both enhance and protect their sponsors. Educating the consumers about the meaning of an official sponsor may be an effective way to diminish the effectiveness of ambush marketing campaigns. This is the responsibility of both the sponsor and the sponsee[7].

Ambush Marketing Research

The attention given to ambush marketing has led to an increase in the number of academic studies of the phenomenon. Longitudinal studies by Sandler and Shani[8] and Shani and Sandler[9] have consistently reported that the level of consumer confusion is high and that companies active in ambush marketing usually perform better than companies that choose not to. Others[10] have critiqued the effectiveness of recall studies, suggesting that a brand's popularity rather than its associations is most likely to be recalled. Nevertheless, Lyberger and McCarthy[11], Seguin, et al.[12], and others have also found high levels of confusion regarding sponsorship. Most of these studies suggest that consumers do not empathize with sponsors and do not feel concerned with issues like ambush marketing. The emphasis on maximizing revenue rather than creating value to sponsors may have contributed to an increasingly cluttered environment resulting in a confused marketplace. In turn, there has been increased emphasis on managing sponsorship programs as part of an integrated brand management system. We will come back to this concept later on in this chapter.

The rest of the literature on ambush marketing focuses on the success or failure of ambush marketers and official sponsors to incite a high level of recall or recognition. While some have argued that the practice of ambush marketing may be ethically questionable, others believe that there is nothing

---

[5] McCarville, R.E. & R.P. Copeland (1994) Understanding sport sponsorship through exchange theory. *Journal of Sport Management*, 8: 102–14.

[6] ibid.

[7] Sandler, D. & D. Shani (1993) Sponsorship and the Olympic Games: The consumer perspective. *Sport Marketing Quarterly*, 2(3): 38–43.

[8] Sandler, D. & D. Shani (1989) Olympic sponsorship vs ambush marketing.

[9] Shani, D. & D. Sandler (1998) Ambush marketing.

[10] Crompton, J.L. (2004) Sponsorship ambushing in sport. *Managing Leisure*, 9: 1–12.

[11] McCarthy, L. & M. Lyberger (2001) An assessment of consumer knowledge of, interest in, and perceptions of ambush marketing strategies.

[12] Seguin, B., M. Lyberger, N. O'Reilly, & L. McCarthy (2005) Internationalizing ambush marketing: The Olympic brand and country of origin. *International Journal of Sport Sponsorship and Marketing*, 6(4).

wrong with such behaviour. The conflicting views of this issue clearly indicate that there remains considerable vagueness about the concept of ambush marketing[13]. As suggested earlier, discussions about ambush marketing include what are arguably known as normal competitive practices[14]. While there may be disagreement on the views of consumers on this issue, it is clear that practitioners believe that ambush marketing works[15].

Canadian Research on Ambush Marketing

While research on ambush marketing in Canada has been sparse, two notable consumer-based studies were carried out in four countries (including Canada) around the 2000[16] and 2004 Olympic Games. The findings support previous studies conducted in the United States and suggest that most respondents were not aware of any attempt by a company to represent itself as an Olympic sponsor when it was not. However, respondents pointed out that: they were slightly opposed to the practice; they felt that ambush marketing was unethical, unfair, and inappropriate; non-sponsors should not lead consumers to believe that they are sponsors of the Olympic Games; and it was not fair for companies to associate themselves with the Olympics without being an Olympic sponsor.

It is interesting to note that in both the 2000 and 2004 studies, Canadians were most disposed to view the practice of ambush marketing as unethical. In fact, across each of the statements related to ambush marketing, Canadians were more opposed to ambushing than Americans, Germans, and French[17]. Such findings reveal significant differences between countries in attitudes toward ambushing. This is of particular interest for the Olympic Games since they may need to develop specific strategies country by country. In this regard, it is likely that Canadians would be more responsive to communications strategies that would position ambush marketing as unethical practice. This was successfully used by the VANOC just a few months prior to the 2006 Olympic Games in Turino. As a long-term partner of Hockey Canada, Imperial Oil (Esso) developed a creative promotional strategy around its sponsorship of Team Canada, leading up to the 2006 World Junior Championships and the 2006 Olympic Games. While the company did not infringe on any of the Olympic rights, VANOC publicly condemned Esso's promotion through an aggressive public/media relations campaign using a high-profile Olympian as a spokesperson. The company was described as engaging in "unethical" behaviours (e.g., ambush marketing) which were damaging to VANOC's future potential to secure sponsorship agreements. They argued that such

---

[13] Hoek, J. & P. Gendall (2003) Ambush marketing: More than just a commercial irritant? *Entertainment Law*, 1(2): 72–91.

[14] Crow, D. & J. Hoek (2003) Ambush marketing: A critical review and some practical advice. *Marketing Bulletin*, 14(1). Retrieved May 3, 2005 from http://www.marketing-bulletin.massey.ac.nz

[15] Crompton, J.L. (2004) Sponsorship ambushing in sport.

[16] Seguin, B., M. Lyberger, N. O'Reilly, & L. McCarthy (2005) Internationalizing ambush marketing.

[17] ibid.

activities could lead to fewer dollars going to Canadian athletes (stealing from athletes) and jeopardizing VANOC's revenue potential. While Hockey Canada quickly responded in defence of its sponsor, Esso refocused its promotional strategy and terminated its campaign. In turn, this gave VANOC's sponsor, Petro-Canada, a clean marketplace in which to conduct its Olympic promotions.

Techniques of Ambush Marketing

The Olympic Games are arguably the world's most powerful property, generating billions of dollars in sponsorship and broadcast fees. As such, they also have the most to lose if ambush marketing flourishes in coming years. In fact, Payne[18] takes this issue so seriously that he argues that ambushing could destroy Olympic sponsorship all together: "If sport organizations and their corporate sponsors do not learn how to effectively protect the exclusivity of sponsorship, they will lose this source of revenue." Before we contemplate potential solutions to this issue, we first need to understand how ambush marketing works.

Event organizers and sponsors understand that ambush marketing efforts are essentially promotional tactics: the more variety of promotional opportunities tied to a sport event, the more suitable the environment for ambush marketing activities to take place. Meenaghan[19] and Crompton[20] identify a number of potential ambush opportunities. We will focus our attention on:

- sponsoring the media coverage of the event (including broadcast) and/or purchasing advertising in and around event broadcast
- sponsoring subcategories within the event and exploiting this investment aggressively
- engaging advertising space at locations that are close to the event
- thematic advertising and implied association

In the context of an event, it is not uncommon that all of these ambush techniques are used together to maximize the desired effect. And for the most part, the context in which these techniques are used is perfectly legal[21]. However, from an event organizer (e.g., Olympics) point of view, ambush activities may result in complaints from official sponsors suggesting that there is a reduction in the value of their investments. If sponsors truly believe that the value is less, there is the potential risk of event organizers losing revenue and, in the end, of damaging the event's brand.

---

[18] International Olympic Committee (1993) Ambush marketing: A risk to Olympic sponsorship and sports. *Marketing Matters*, 2: 2.

[19] Meenaghan, T. (1998) Current developments and future directions in sponsorship. *International Journal of Advertising*, 17: 3–28.

[20] Crompton, J.L. (2004) Sponsorship ambushing in sport.

[21] Crow, D. & J. Hoek (2003) Ambush marketing.

Sponsoring the Media Coverage of the Event (Including Broadcast)

A number of sport properties include media extensions such as television broadcasts and commercials. At times, a company may have the opportunity to purchase advertising during the broadcast of an event, without being a sponsor of that event, as for the Super Bowl and sometimes the Olympic Games. By purchasing and/or sponsoring the broadcast of such events, an ambusher may not be doing anything illegal but may create the impression that it is a sponsor of that event. For example, at the 1996 Olympic Games, as the official broadcaster for Canada, CBC sold advertising packages to a number of companies that became "sponsors" of the broadcasting and received recognition in the opening segment of the broadcast—"the 1996 Summer Olympics Games broadcast is brought to you by Compaq"—when, in fact, the official worldwide sponsor of the Olympic Games was IBM. While the on-site spectators are unaffected by such advertising, the much larger television audience of the event may be fooled. In this context, it is important that event organizers either control the broadcast tied to the event or develop a **sponsor recognition program** to increase consumer awareness of who the official sponsors are. In fact, there are important differences between the official sponsor of an event and the official sponsor of a broadcast of that same event: The first provides resources directly to the event organizers and, in effect, buys a licence to spend more money to exploit this; the latter buys airtime during the broadcast of the Games and employs the tactic of "ambush marketing."

A similar tactic may be to purchase **advertising inventory** during or around the broadcast of an event. While some properties may have arranged with the broadcasters to offer sponsors first right of refusal to the advertising inventory (e.g., Olympic sponsors and CBC), it remains a popular tactic among competitors, especially if they use sport images in their commercials. Thus, buying of television advertising inventory by a competitor of an official sponsor could be considered ambush marketing as it confuses the consumers about who the real sponsor of the event is. Research in this area suggests that consumers do not differentiate between advertiser and sponsor[22].

Sponsoring Subcategories in the Event and Aggressively Exploiting This Investment

The proliferation of sponsorship categories has resulted in many opportunities for corporations that do not wish to pay the fees of top-category sponsors. With the number of events and the number of teams participating in an event such as the Olympics, the opportunities for exploiting a subcategory sponsorship are substantial. Aggressive campaigns related to subcategory status have the potential for great effectiveness at a significantly lower cost.

Subcategory conflicts present a growing problem for sport properties. By sponsoring individual athletes, teams, and/or national sport federations, corporations can gain the type of associations they seek without paying the

sponsor recognition program: promotional activities developed by sponsees to increase consumer awareness of who the official sponsors are and to help them differentiate between official sponsor and non–official sponsor.

advertising inventory: advertising opportunities available for purchase during or around the broadcast of an event, such as 30-second commercial spots, in-program graphics, opening and closing segments of a broadcast.

---

[22] Seguin, B., M. Lyberger, N. O'Reilly, & L. McCarthy (2005) Internationalizing ambush marketing.

Important Strategic Elements of Sport Marketing in Canada

cost of a full-event sponsorship. Another concern of Olympic organizers is at the lower end of the sponsorship categories, where some companies may be overexploiting their rights and "claiming the space" of major sponsors. For example, when Roots became a supplier for the Canadian Olympic Team competing at the 1998 Winter Olympic Games in Nagano, the brand received unprecedented publicity. Although Roots signed a supplier agreement at a much lower fee than official sponsors of the Canadian Olympic Committee (COC), its innovative clothing design and creative marketing strategies quickly became the talk of the Games. In fact, Roots found a successful way to break through the clutter and received tremendous exposure during key broadcast events, including the opening ceremonies, medal presentations, national and international television interviews, newspaper coverage, and even an appearance of Olympian Ross Rebagliatti, fully dressed in Roots clothing, on *The Tonight Show with Jay Leno*. There is little doubt that Roots was prepared to take full advantage of its deal with the COC, giving the company an international stage at a national price. This kind of marketing program presents some special challenges for the COC and for the IOC as well. The IOC insists on a clean venue policy; yet national suppliers like Roots are able to make their way onto the playing field, where national pride and emotions run at its peak. Meanwhile, a major sponsor, Coca-Cola which paid more than $50 million for worldwide rights, is shut out of the field of play. This raises an interesting question about fair play among the various levels of sponsorship. The Roots Olympic program in Nagano and Sydney was so successful that the United States Olympic Committee (USOC) selected it to be the clothing supplier for the US Olympic Team for Salt Lake 2002. The company's deal with the USOC was an important part of its growth strategy in the US.

Engaging in Advertising That Coincides with the Sponsored Event

Corporations may resort to large-scale promotional campaigns directly at or close to the venue of the event. By such methods as displays, billboards, and banners, companies try to get consumers' attention in the surrounding of the event itself. Nike, for example, displayed significance presence at such major world events as the 1996 Olympic Games and the 1998 World Cup soccer finals. It was not a sponsor of either event, but its presence at the venues, combined with its broadcast presence through the athletes wearing Nike products, effectively deflected attention from official sponsors.

The IOC responded to this kind of ambush marketing by demanding new levels of commitment from cities that wished to host the Olympic Games. Bid committees are now expected to demonstrate that they can deliver a "clean city" during the entire month of the Olympic Games. In other words, organizing committees must find a way to acquire all outdoor advertising space, including billboards, bus advertising, and subway ads, for the duration of the Games. This IOC preemptive strike was considered a breakthrough in the fight against ambush marketing as it provided sponsors with additional value through increased presence in the host city.

Using Thematic Advertising and Implied Association

Some events have developed such well-known brands that association with the event and brand is possible without the use of logos or trademarks. This is accomplished by creating thematic advertising that may imply an association with the sponseee. For example, Hockey Canada has been very successful in building a powerful brand and in making associations between its own brand—Team Canada—and the Canadian Olympic hockey team. In fact, since the onset of the participation of professional hockey players in the Olympic Games in 1998, the jerseys worn by the Canadian Olympic hockey team have been branded with Hockey Canada's logo. Over the years, sales of Hockey Canada merchandise have skyrocketed, especially following the gold medal performances of the men's and women's hockey teams at the 2002 Salt Lake City Olympic Winter Games. A number of Hockey Canada's sponsors have been successful in leveraging its brand by integrating it into their promotional activities. For example, the Hockey Canada 'theme' can be observed at the thousands of Esso gas stations across the country.

In general, when promotional campaigns are activated in the months leading to the Olympic Winter Games, some may question the motives behind such timing. This was the case a few months prior to the 2006 Winter Games, when Esso used a creative and effective thematic promotion titled "Cheers for Canada in Torino, Italy."

This promotion was executed at the pumps of all Esso stations across Canada. While Esso was careful to not use the word Olympics or any Olympic symbols, the fact that Torino was the host city for the Games made the connection to the Winter Olympics. This promotional campaign played on Canadians' passion and strong emotional connection to hockey and indirectly to the Olympic Winter Games. Responsible for protecting the Olympic brand in Canada until 2012, VANOC quickly denounced this promotion and ultimately succeeded in stopping it. This example illustrates the complex situation when numerous promotional opportunities are linked to a specific event. The many levels of official sponsorship available with the Olympic Games adds to this complexity, since a company can be a global sponsor, national Olympic sponsor, sponsor of a national sport federation, sponsor of an athlete, or sponsor of a team.

Other Ambush Marketing Strategies

Many ambushers have created highly creative and inventive strategies to suggest involvement in events: "using photographs of recognizable places or implants, tennis rackets, etc, or staged sequences from the same sport as background in advertising which coincides with the event to suggest sponsorship involvement; or undertaking congratulatory advertising in the ambusher's name for athletes and teams who are officially sponsored by competitors[23]."

Many companies seek to associate themselves with the event by creating sweepstakes, give-away tickets, or special prices. Pepsi successfully created a sweepstakes involving five high-profile athletes during the 2000 Sydney Olympic Games. By entering the contest and correctly guessing the athletes' final standings at the Games, consumers had a chance to win up to 1000 pounds of gold. Pepsi carefully placed a disclaimer at the bottom of the form indicating that the promotion was in no way sanctioned or supported by the Canadian Olympic Committee.

Ethics and Ambush Marketing

Whether ambush marketing is ethical, legal, or simply smart business practice has been the topic of a handful of researchers. All have used the Olympic Games as a point of reference to examine the issue.

Meenaghan[24] examines the strategies employed by ambush marketers and the counter-strategies used by corporate sponsors to protect their investments. He claims that[25]: "because such [ambush marketing] activities reduce the effectiveness of the official sponsors' promotional efforts while simultaneously denying the activity owner potential revenue, there is reason to question the morality of this type of competitive practice." On the other hand, O'Sullivan and Murphy[26] state that one has to be careful when examining ethics and the practice of ambush marketing. They note that annoyed sponsees such as the IOC have developed public relation campaigns that claim ambush marketers are using unethical tactics. But is it really unethical or is it just competitive marketing? When reflecting on ambush marketing, former IOC vice-president Dick Pound[27] explains: "Our attitude is that the practice wasn't wrong just because money wasn't paid to be a sponsor, but because someone has appropriated something that did not belong to them." While this attitude may be shared by other sponsees, it is difficult to validate as it represents the viewpoint of one well-known sponsee. O'Sullivan and Murphy[28] suggest that the very ownership of the rights and the exclusive nature and monopolistic exercise of those rights may deserve scrutiny. They argue that[29]: "property

---

[23] Meenaghan, T. (1998) Ambush marketing: Corporate strategy and consumer reaction. *Psychology and Marketing*, 33(3/4): 312.

[24] Meenaghan, T. (1994) Point of view: Ambush marketing: Immoral or imaginative practice? *Journal of Advertising Research*, Sept: 77–88.

[25] ibid: 77.

[26] O'Sullivan, P. & P. Murphy (1998) Ambush marketing: The ethical issues. *Psychology and Marketing*, 15(4): 349–66.

[27] Ettore, B. (1993) Ambush marketing: Heading them off at the pass. *Management Review*, 82(3): 55.

[28] O'Sullivan, P. & P. Murphy (1998) Ambush marketing.

[29] ibid.

rights that are acquired or contractually leased by corporate sponsor must be exercised with due regard for the rights of others, even those of direct commercial competitors."

The greed of organizers must be recognized as contributing to the growth of ambush marketing. Therefore, it may be necessary to eliminate confusing layers of sponsorship by offering sponsors complete vertical and lateral sponsorship rights[30]. The official sponsor would be so pervasive and visible that ambushing would not make sense. Some believe that the official Olympic sponsor should be given the rights relating to everything from the national team federations to the worldwide sponsorship.

Ambush Marketing and Clutter

As previous chapters discussed, the growth of sponsorship is credited, in part, to the clutter found in traditional media[31]. Sponsorship appeared to be an effective and lower-cost way to break through the clutter and reach specific targets. An inherent problem linked to ambush marketing is its contribution to a cluttered environment. However, other factors contribute to the clutter. For example, new sports and events (X Games) and repacked existing sports (beach volleyball) are offering entertaining products that may be attractive to sponsors looking for access to a specific audience. The Canadian sport industry presented in Figure 2-3 has thousands of sport properties available in its five segments—grassroots sports, sporting events, university and college sports, professional sports, and Olympic sports. These segments can be broken down further. For example, in Olympic sport, sponsorship opportunities exist with: Olympic Games, national sport organizations, national teams, individual athletes, coaching programs, multisport organizations, national training centres, and so on. Each opportunity may attract numerous sponsors and at different levels of contribution. All of this increasingly clutters the environment and, if not controlled, can add to confusion in the marketplace. In fact, consumers may not differentiate an Olympic sponsorship from a national sponsorship of an Olympic sport. Thus, rights holders should be concerned with clutter both on its own and as a result of ambush marketing. On its own, clutter leads to a general fragmentation of the market and difficulty in diffusing messages. Clutter is further increased with each case of ambush marketing. In both cases, clutter can diminish the value of a specific sport property or of sport in general.

Recent research on ambush marketing and clutter may shed some light on these closely linked issues. Of particular note is a model published by the authors of this textbook to manage ambush and clutter in Olympic sport.

---

[30] ibid.

[31] Otker, T. (1988) Exploitation: The key to sponsorship success. *Marketing and Research Today*, 16(2): 77–86.

While it acknowledges that ambush marketing is a legitimate strategy that is most likely to continue, the model (Figure 13-1) summarizes how ambush marketing in a cluttered marketplace is related to key stakeholder groups. It identifies brand management strategies for each partner of the Olympic property—IOC, NOC, OCOG, and sponsors—to protect the brand against potential ambush marketing attacks. This model was the result of extensive consumer research and expert opinions in sport marketing. These are some key elements of a brand management system.

1. Managing and protecting the Olympic brand is vital for the future of Olympic marketing programs.
2. A strategic marketing communications program is necessary to develop brand consistency at all levels.
3. Integrated public relations plans play an important role in the Olympic marketing communications program. A team of "brand masters" made up of representatives of IOC, NOC, OCOG, and sponsors should develop the plan, which would then be integrated within each NOC and OCOG.
4. Activation of rights by sponsors: the Olympic brand should be integrated into sponsors' marketing and communications programs. Sponsors must claim their space within the Olympic landscape.
5. IOC, NOCs, OCOG, and sponsors must work closely with each other. All must truly comprehend the Olympic brand and work towards integrated marketing communications. This approach would contribute to making the brand more coherent, an area identified as weak in this research.
6. NOCs must be educated in brand marketing management. NOCs lack competency and expertise in marketing, which caused a lack of coherence and uniformity of Olympic brand worldwide.

Case: Ambush Marketing and the Olympic Brand

To deal with ambush marketing and protect the investment of its corporate partners, the IOC has decided to approach the Olympics as a "brand." In some ways, the IOC has become a brand manager with the ultimate task of protecting, building, and leveraging the Olympic brand. Ambush marketing has been identified as a threat to the brand and the IOC's strategy has been to limit or control the problem. It believes that the value of the Olympic brand will be greatly diminished if the environment is uncontrolled. Ultimately, this could result in the loss of financial support from the corporate partners. TOP sponsors invest large sums of money to receive exclusive rights of association with the Olympic brand and do not want to share the marketing platform with competitors. In fact, sponsors must justify such spending and so are

FIGURE 13-1

Model to Manage Ambush Marketing

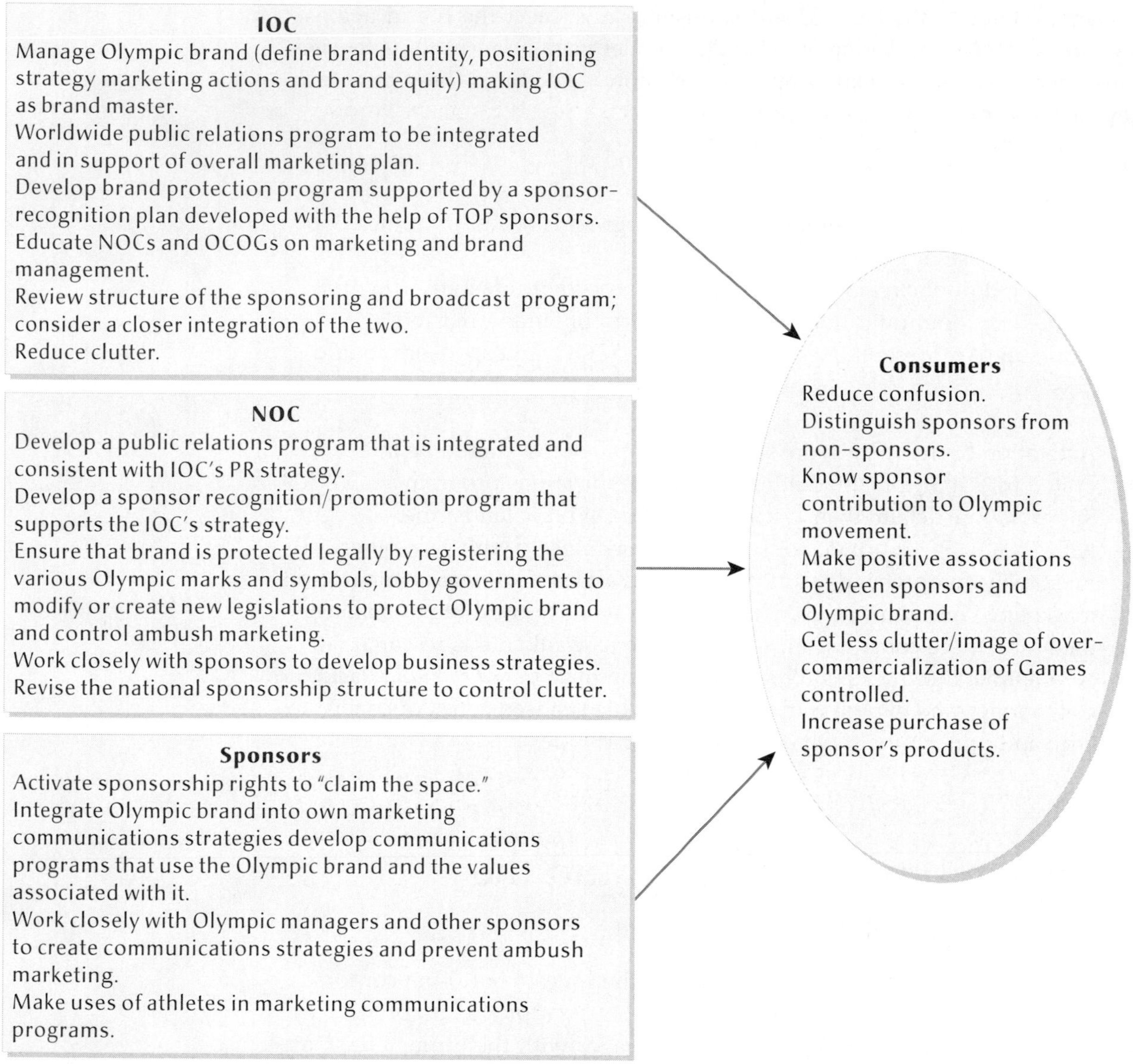

IOC

Manage Olympic brand (define brand identity, positioning strategy marketing actions and brand equity) making IOC as brand master.

Worldwide public relations program to be integrated and in support of overall marketing plan.

Develop brand protection program supported by a sponsor-recognition plan developed with the help of TOP sponsors.

Educate NOCs and OCOGs on marketing and brand management.

Review structure of the sponsoring and broadcast program; consider a closer integration of the two.

Reduce clutter.

NOC

Develop a public relations program that is integrated and consistent with IOC's PR strategy.

Develop a sponsor recognition/promotion program that supports the IOC's strategy.

Ensure that brand is protected legally by registering the various Olympic marks and symbols, lobby governments to modify or create new legislations to protect Olympic brand and control ambush marketing.

Work closely with sponsors to develop business strategies.

Revise the national sponsorship structure to control clutter.

Sponsors

Activate sponsorship rights to "claim the space."

Integrate Olympic brand into own marketing communications strategies develop communications programs that use the Olympic brand and the values associated with it.

Work closely with Olympic managers and other sponsors to create communications strategies and prevent ambush marketing.

Make uses of athletes in marketing communications programs.

Consumers

Reduce confusion.

Distinguish sponsors from non-sponsors.

Know sponsor contribution to Olympic movement.

Make positive associations between sponsors and Olympic brand.

Get less clutter/image of over-commercialization of Games controlled.

Increase purchase of sponsor's products.

Source: Seguin, B. & O'Reilly, N. (Forthcoming) Managing the Olympic Brand in the Era of Ambush Marketing and Clutter. International Journal of Sport Management and Marketing © Inderscience Publishers.

demanding greater returns on their investment. This, in turn, has put tremendous pressure on the IOC to exercise more control over its property. The IOC came under intense criticism following the "flea market" environment of the Atlanta Games in 1996. The "Coca-Cola Games," as many referred to them, were condemned as being over commercialized, or Americanized.

Some perceived the IOC as a money-making machine that sold its soul to the corporate world. In some ways, the Atlanta Games acted as a wake-up call for the Olympic movement. The IOC attempted to regain control on the commercialization of the Games and on the ambush marketing by making major revisions to the contracts with organizing committees and with cities interested in hosting the Games. During the four years that preceded the 2000 Sydney Games, the IOC and the organizing committee undertook a series of precautionary measures to educate various constituents and the public on the negative ramifications of ambush activities.

Case Questions

1. Is the IOC overly concerned about ambush marketing?
2. Are the Olympic Games too commercialized?
3. How can clutter be a problem for the Olympic Games?
4. Develop an ambush marketing plan for the Olympics.

Chapter Summary

Although the prospects for sport properties and sponsorship remain optimistic, the increased cost of sponsorship combined with a highly cluttered sponsorship environment has raised concerns. The emergence of ambush marketing as an alternative to sponsorship is a serious threat to sponsorship. If sport properties do not effectively respond to ambush marketing, the benefits and ultimately the value to sponsors may be diminished. While some have questioned the ethics of ambush marketing, sport organizations should reconsider the way they conduct business and adopt sound marketing strategies that protect exclusivity and combat ambush. The use of a brand management system is a useful tool to manage ambush marketing.

Test Your Knowledge

1. Why is ambush marketing considered a problem by both sponsees and sponsors?
2. What is clutter? Why is clutter an issue in sponsorship?
3. Do you consider ambush marketing an ethical or a business issue? Explain your position.
4. If you were in a position to employ an ambush marketing strategy, would you do it? Why or why not?
5. Have you noticed any ambush marketing activities? If so, what are they? Bring some examples of advertising or promotional materials you consider ambush marketing and present them to your classmates.

For more review questions, go to http://www.sportmarketing.nelson.com.

Key Terms

advertising inventory   exclusivity
ambush marketing   property
brand management   sponsor recognition program
clutter

 A full glossary of key term definitions is located at
http://www.sportmarketing.nelson.com.

Internet Resources

Ambush marketing, http://en.wikipedia.org/wiki/Ambush_marketing

Ambush marketing: The off-field competition at the Olympic Games,
http://www.law.northwestern.edu/journals/njtip/v3/n2/6/

The importance of protecting the Olympic brand, http://www
.vancouver2010.com/en/LookVancouver2010/ProtectingBrand

Université Laval, http://www.ulaval.ca/

True Sport, http://www.truesportpur.ca

SPORTFIVE, http://www.sportfive.com/index.php?id=708&L=0

Ambush marketing: What it is, what it isn't, http://www.poolonline.com/
archive/issue19/iss19fea5.html

CBC Media Report: Some ads violating Olympic copyright, COC says,
http://www.cbcwatch.ca/?q=node/view/423 broken link

Ambush marketing and the Sydney 2000 games, http://www.murdoch.edu
.au/elaw/issues/v8n2/kendall82nf.html

**Canada's new government moves to protect the Vancouver 2010 Olympic
and Paralympic Winter Games brand,** http://www.ic.gc.ca/cmb/welcomeic
.nsf/cdd9dc973c4bf6bc852564ca006418a0/85256a5d006b9720852572920059a745!
OpenDocument

Bill C-47 not in the spirit of Olympics, http://www.thestar.com/
printArticle/193405

Source: Joy Brown / Shutterstock

Chapter 14

Technology in Sport Marketing

Learning Objectives

- To understand the importance of technology in the contemporary sport environment
- To acquire a basic understanding of IT components and the current trends in IT
- To be aware of the types of technologies that can affect steps of the sport marketing cycle
- To understand the business of sport broadcasting

Introduction

Zeros, ones, and everything in between

It may seem that the world of zeros and ones is far from that of sport marketing, but innovations in television broadcasting, large-screen video displays, handheld devices, radio technologies, and the Internet have all altered the ways in which sport is consumed. Today, **information technology** (IT) and **information systems** (IS) now affect each step of the marketing cycle, from market research through to marketing strategy. Sport managers are increasingly emphasizing technology, realizing that to manage technology is to manage the business.

Managing technology is quite different from managing other operations. One must balance the needs of the tangible (computers, printers, network cables), the intangible (software, communication, knowledge), the process,

information technology: the hardware and software that supports communication.

information system: any electronic device or apparatus that manages, stores, and shares data.

and, most important, the person. Sport marketers who are successful in this endeavour ensure that their management decisions and actions are congruent with the environment within which they operate.

EXECUTIVE PERSPECTIVE

Terry Kell, President, Kanatek Technologies Inc.

Over the next few paragraphs, I intend to share with you exciting highlights of how my organization, Kanatek Technologies, leveraged information technology, innovative marketing events, and professional sports to successfully meet its marketing and business objectives.

Company Overview

Incorporated in 1982, Kanatek Technologies is a Canadian-based computer and data storage systems integration company headquartered in Ottawa. When I say a "data storage systems integration company," I mean an organization that keeps track of, backs up, and finds lost data—comparable to insurance for data. In 2007, it employed 75 people and had branch offices in Mississauga and Montreal. Over the years, the company had evolved from being a local supplier of computer and data storage solutions to an international supplier in over 15 countries. For more details on the company, visit the website (http://www.kanatek.com).

Target Market

Kanatek's target market is composed primarily of large Canadian-based organizations with a national or international presence. These organizations, generally with over 1000 employees, are in government, financial, insurance, telecommunications, or manufacturing sectors. A key success factor in Kanatek's market is developing strong relationships with technology partners and clients. The company's competitors are typically international technology and service providers with multimillion dollar marketing budgets and large teams of marketing personnel.

Kanatek's marketing programs focus on raising its profile in the market to appear on the same playing field as its multinational competitors. Its objectives were to achieve this while strengthening the relationships

with its existing customers and developing additional relationships with new customers. Kanatek was able to accomplish its objectives by (i) creating some innovative sports-based marketing events that used the latest in information technology applications and (ii) building marketing promotions around professional sports. These are some examples of marketing programs that were not only highly successful but also exhilarating to be a part of.

Kanatek Silicon Valley Challenges

The Kanatek Silicon Valley Challenges were a series of fantasy hockey events developed in collaboration with the management of the Ottawa Senators NHL hockey team. These were the first events of their kind, where nonprofessional players, Kanatek's customers, would be able to play with NHL alumni at the same venues as the pros. The players would participate in a game with many of the attributes of a regular-season NHL game including equipment. Between periods, interviews were broadcast over the Internet. For Kanatek's clients who did not play hockey but wanted to be a part of the experience, there were also non-hockey-player positions, including president, general manager, head coach, assistant coach, equipment manager, and goal judge.

The Kanatek Silicon Valley Challenge I 1997 (SVCI)

1997 was the 25th anniversary of the 1972 Canada–Russia Summit series. Kanatek's NHL guest player was Paul Henderson, the legendary scorer of the winning goal in the 1972 series. Paul's fame gave the Kanatek event huge television and newspaper coverage leading up to and during the event. The SVCI game, the first live broadcast of a hockey game over the Internet, was viewed by over 1000 people.

Trends in Information Systems

Whether you work with a large sport organization or a grassroots recreation club, you will almost certainly encounter all the basic components of information systems. Specific to business environments, *information systems* comprise five elements: **hardware**, **software**, data, communications, and people. Only two of these elements are inherently technical—hardware and software, or *information technology*. The remaining three can be affected by IT, enabled through IT, or partially consist of IT depending on the specific situation. In the following section, we look at each of these elements.

hardware: technical information technology objects like servers and printers that you can physically touch.

software: programs and applications that run on the hardware.

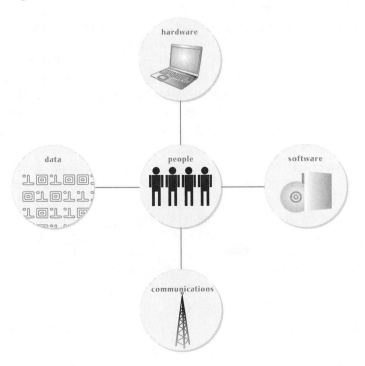

Hardware refers to tangible parts of IT—computers, printers, servers, monitors, keyboards, and mouses. Hardware technology moves significantly faster than software technology. In the past two decades or so, the power of home computers has been increasing exponentially, and software has yet to use or harness this power.

For the IT manager, these circumstances make it difficult to decide how much to spend on hardware. Many firms have taken the approach of purchasing inexpensive, generic hardware rather than expensive, proprietary hardware. However, this practice must be exercised with caution, as insufficient investment in hardware may suboptimize other elements of the information system. Intricate software running on slow computers risks crashing; e-mail capabilities are useless without a capable network and server; and unreliable disk drives can destroy weeks, months, or even years of data collection. The key, therefore, is to balance and make investments in hardware that are in line with the company's resources and organizational strategy.

In addition to inexpensive IT products, we are also seeing a move toward convenience. Handheld and mobile devices enable work on the go, often incorporating cell-phone-type features with wireless connectivity to the Internet and office-style applications. Nowadays, you can check e-mail, write a text document, and update a spreadsheet on your personal digital assistant (PDA). On a much smaller scale (in terms of physical space, but not capacity), organizations are experimenting with radio frequency identification (RFID) whereby computer chips no larger than a grain of sand are placed on products to enable tracking and verification. While this has already helped to reduce costs for organizations, the large social impact will be realized only when consumers themselves can use this technology post-purchase. Consumers will then be able to know how many soft drinks are left in their refrigerator or when they bought their last football jersey.

Software refers to the programs and applications that run on the hardware. Organizations use software to support their processes, enable their employees, and support decision making. Many early business applications were written, modified, and supported almost exclusively by in-house programmers. But as packages made by large specialized software companies became more powerful (e.g., Microsoft Office), the role of programmers quickly shifted from all-in-one software engineers to systems integrators. This new breed of IT employee worked to make new software purchases compatible with other software packages the organization was using. Overlapping this evolution, *web services* began to appear in organizations as a new in-house programming paradigm. This allowed modules of code to be "exposed" and accessed by other developers anywhere in the world through Internet technology. Each module has a *uniform resource locator* (URL) on the Internet and can be called upon to fulfill requests. A module, for example, could perform the risk calculation for automotive insurance firms given specific parameters or calculate the distance between the organization and the customer given the locations of both. This meant that reinventing the programming wheel was no longer necessary since it was possible to use existing codes from other developers. Moving forward, web services are expected to shift ad hoc and simple programming from the systems staff to the user, including the sport marketer.

The **enterprise resource planning (ERP) system**, a common business software package, consists of many linkable application modules purchased from a single vendor and meant to draw from a single repository of data. The goal of ERP systems is to integrate the functions of an organization, from finance to logistics, under one unified systems architecture so that the organization's processes become streamlined and more efficient—a task that is often easier said than done. There are abundant cases of organizations that could not make the cultural and functional integration with these systems, which reflect the difficulties of managing elements of change and uncertainty in the business environment. Thus, both technical *and* change management consultants are typically hired for ERP installation. This, coupled with the price of the software, make the investment in ERP a critical decision. Typically, a detailed cost–benefit analysis of tangibles, intangibles, and risks is recommended before undertaking such an installation.

What does technology help us do? The answer depends on whom you ask, but most organizations agree that it helps them manage data. This is fairly intuitive, as information is really data that have been processed and assigned a meaning. For example, "five hats" means little to any of us, but "Jimmy has five hats" has meaning because the data (number of hats) has been put into context.

Enabling this central function of managing the data is the **database**. The most common form, the **relational database**, stores data about such things as students, employees, and transactions and the relationships that unify them. Each entity is represented by a table with a series of records, stored as rows in each table, which identifies specific instances of that entity. Across each column are the attributes that each entity might hold. For example, we could have an entity named "NHL player," which stores data about all the players in the NHL. Each row would represent a different player, while the columns could include such attributes as "years-in-league," "team," or "position." This database might be used in its raw form for NHL employees to keep track of each player or as a table on the NHL website where customers can look up information about their favourite player.

Now that we can store the data, we have to get it somewhere. Thus, communication plays a large part in the use of an IS. Technologically, we can accomplish this by using a *network* that connects computers and other peripheral hardware through cabling or radio waves. This can occur on many different geographical levels from locally to globally. The global data network that supports intercontinental communication for the Internet relies on *fibre optic cabling* (or simply *fibre*), and uses flashes of light to transmit data from one end to the other. Until recently, only one millionth of the capacity of fibre laid around the world could be used; however, new developments in network technology are predicted to make **bandwidth**, the rate at which information can be passed over a cable, the next technological commodity.

enterprise resource planning system: linkable application modules purchased from a single vendor and meant to draw from a single repository of data.

database: a data management system.

relational database: common database that stores data about entities and the relationships that unify them.

bandwidth: the rate at which information can be passed over a cable.

The projected impact of fibre commoditization—the global use of fibre optic cabling—is tremendous, as there is currently a "bottleneck" in the global network—the last mile to your home. This occurs since it is expensive for telecommunication companies to extend their networks to each residence. To keep costs down, the inputs to your home are likely *twisted-pair wiring* (phone cables) or *coaxial cabling* (TV cables), which are much slower than fibre. As a solution, fibre is beginning to be deployed closer to the end user—to the curb, to the home, and rarely even within the home.

Telecommunication companies are experimenting with wireless technologies to solve this problem. Currently, these technologies are found in local area environments such as within one's house or office. Trends in these technologies are looking inward for future development as the standardization of personal area networks, where high-speed interconnections between one's camera, personal digital assistant, cell phone, and media player can be concurrent and wireless.

Although the idea of object-to-object communication is endearing in IT circles, we often think of technological communication as connecting *people*. People work with software, make decisions based on data, and communicate using the network. People are the component that brings value to the information system in an organizational context and therefore must be managed as its most crucial asset.

Earlier we alluded to the cultural failures of the ERP systems. This holds true for any technological investment. Users must first buy into the idea of using the technology and then be taught how to use it. Without support in both areas, any technology will fail. In this regard, two trends are set to continue in the foreseeable future. First, younger generations are entering the workforce with higher levels of technological knowledge—both a boon and bane for organizations, as the decrease in training costs may be offset by the threats felt by older workers leading to tension, disputes, and change of management issues. Second, and as a partial response to the previous point, lifelong technological learning is becoming more prominent in organizations. Some employees are learning as a way of coping with the increasing demand on users to be more technologically proficient while others see technology as a way to make their jobs easier. In either case, supporting this personal growth with adequate resources is a healthy investment for organizations.

Information Systems in the Marketing Cycle

With our basic understanding of the IS, we can look more closely at how it fits into the specific context of the marketing cycle. Previous chapters covered the three general zones in the marketing cycle—the information mainland (situational analysis), the bridge (STP), and the strategy mainland (4 Ps). Technology enables and supports activities in each zone. This section breaks down technology's role in each and shows how both understanding and managing these technological components are critical in sport marketing. Figure 14-1 describes the process of marketing strategy development from a technology focus.

FIGURE 14-1

Technology-Based Marketing Strategy Development

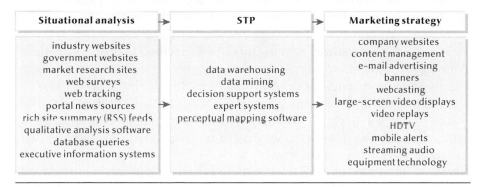

Situational analysis	STP	Marketing strategy
industry websites government websites market research sites web surveys web tracking portal news sources rich site summary (RSS) feeds qualitative analysis software database queries executive information systems	data warehousing data mining decision support systems expert systems perceptual mapping software	company websites content management e-mail advertising banners webcasting large-screen video displays video replays HDTV mobile alerts streaming audio equipment technology

Source: Developed by O'Reilly,N & Rahinel,R. (2006)Forecasting the Importance of Media Technology in Sport. The Case of the Televised Hockey Product in Canada pg. 82-94 International Journal of Sport Marketing & Sponsorship © Inderscience Publishers.

Situational Analysis

Technology performs the role of gatherer and compiler in the situational analysis. Secondary data on anything from NHL playoff television ratings to performance metrics of the Canadian sport fishing industry are available on the Internet. A good and often overlooked source of secondary information is the federal government. For example, on the Industry Canada website for businesses and consumers, Strategis[1], you can find such information on specific industries as total market size, labour characteristics, major organizations, and total output. However, even if the information you need isn't free, paying for it electronically and having it e-mailed to you reduces your time and effort. Websites offering market research services are wide and varied, and prices for reports (both custom and standard) have dropped in the midst of e-competition. Nevertheless, well-established securities and consulting firms are likely the best choices should you choose to take this route.

Some less formal routes for acquiring secondary data are news sites offered by major media or web portals. Google News[2], for example, compiles its news using algorithms to determine what is most prominent and pressing among a large and representative sample of news websites. News is also flexible and can be personalized to your interests and needs. Another way to acquire news updates is to use rich site summary (RSS) feeding. This not only allows you to personalize your news, but also to have it delivered to your desktop, akin to a newspaper delivery. Specially designed aggregator software automatically accesses RSS feeds you have subscribed to and retrieves them. These feeds contain snippets of information and sometimes small

[1] See http://www.strategis.gc.ca/.

[2] See http://www.google.ca.

pictures about new updates. More in-depth information is usually available at the click of your mouse. Overall, RSS feeds are an efficient and personalized way to stay on top of news sites with irregular updating cycles.

Technology also supports gathering primary data. The simplest way to do this is to ask website visitors to complete a short questionnaire. Responses can be collected automatically by a back-end database and downloaded to your local computer for analysis. A more unobtrusive method to obtaining primary data on the Internet is to track customer movement through your website. Webtrends[3] is an example of software that helps you do this. Not only can you track how many hits and visits your site has accumulated, Webtrends also lets you track the path of pages visited by customers, where those customers drop off the site, how well an ad campaign did on an external site, and how long each visitor spent on a page.

What if gathering data in these ways doesn't suit the questions you are trying to answer? Perhaps you are trying to gather qualitative data, for example, and you are planning to do this via in-depth interviews. It's not likely that everybody you'd like to talk to is within physical access or even a regional telephone call away. Skype[4] is a new form of computer telephony that allows users to call each other through the Internet without amassing long-distance charges. Using a sound card with two outputs can let you digitally record the interview with much better quality than a mini-cassette recorder. If many interviews are conducted and a cadre of research assistants is not available, you may want to consider speech recognition software (e.g., Nuance's Dragon Naturally Speaking) that can transcribe your interviews into text by just listening to your voice. Qualitative data can then be processed by qualitative analysis software like QSR's NVivo. If you have a multitude of transcribed interviews, such software can help you group statements into themes or categories. As demonstrated above, technology is available to support your research needs regardless of collection style or methods of analysis.

Aside from Internet-centred solutions, technology can help keep you organized. Many executives are noting the organizational impact of technology and are using *executive information systems*. Often called "dashboards," these bring the summaries of the latest news updates and organizational happenings to the executive's computer upon request.

Segmentation, Targeting, and Positioning (STP)

In the STP process, considerably more focus is placed on technology's ability to analyze data and aid in decision making. Segmentation requires that we establish both mutually exclusive and homogeneous groups of people. This process implies that data about a given population is available to the

---

3 See http://www.webtrends.com.

4 See http://www.skype.com.

marketer and can be analyzed. Two database technologies are especially helpful in the segmentation analysis—data warehousing and data mining. A *data warehouse* is a large repository of historical data that allows an organization to analyze trends in financing, market performance, or consumer taste over a specified time and on a broader scale than a regular medium-format database, that typically used by organizations and individuals, such as an Access database of baseball statistics. Note that real-time decision making is not supported by data warehouses, as they are often updated on a weekly schedule. *Data mining* involves uncovering previously unknown trends in the data warehouse. Often this is fully or semi-automatic and relies on complex algorithms or statistical methods. The role of data mining in segmentation is to uncover relevant bases of segmentation for the sport marketer, as chunks of data about consumers are often lost in the depths of a data warehouse. For example, a data mining project could reveal that fathers with male children under ten years old are more likely to attend Major League Baseball games. MLB can therefore include age of child and gender of child as two relevant bases of segmentation and subsequently choose to target this segment. As a cautionary note, however, data mining comes with a host of ethical issues. Sport marketers should familiarize themselves with regional data mining and customer privacy laws before proceeding with this method of analysis.

Choosing the method of targeting is often complex and cumbersome without adequate support from technology. Technology offers several tools to sport marketers to aid specifically with this decision making. The most common of these is the *decision support system* (DSS), which uses mathematical models to represent complex decisions. The systems often use data warehouses, summary data from transaction databases, and user input as the data component to arrive at decisions. They can help marketers answer questions related to the size, profitability, and measurability of a segment. *Expert systems* (ES) provide yet another supplement to the targeting process. As the name implies, their purpose is to deal with problems the way an expert would. Expertise can be stored in these systems in three ways:

1. *Case-based reasoning:* A repository of past cases is kept on reference for access by the ES engine. This reasoning is particularly useful for complex situations with many variables and nuances.
2. *Neural networks:* The system "learns" as it goes along by noting which factors have determined success and failure in previous situations.
3. *Tree structures:* Decisions are made by running data through a series of simple if–then programming structures formulated collaboratively with experts.

Competitive positioning involves developing perceptual maps to visualize your brand versus other brands in your industry. Many Internet sites offer free software to complete this task, differing only in minor respects. In fact, these applications can often be created by novice programmers. For a first look at positioning software, check out PERMAP, a free perceptual mapping application developed by Professor Ronald Heady at the University of Louisiana at Lafayette[5].

Marketing Strategy

Technology performs the role of distributor and enabler in marketing strategy. While marketers who understand consumers' propensity to use and purchase technology capture only incremental customers today, they almost certainly stand to capture large and fruitful segments of consumers tomorrow. From a consumer perspective, we take advantage of these impacts almost carelessly: We buy online, buy technological products, and tell people about products using technology. This section will cover the ways in which the product, price, place, and promotion have been altered by the technological revolution and its impact on sport from both marketing and consumer perspectives.

The dynamics of promotion and pricing have changed considerably as a result of technological change. Marketers now include Internet advertising in their integrated communications mix. The most common and wide-reaching tool that marketers use in this capacity is the organization website. As evidence of its pervasiveness, the FIFA World Cup 2006 website[6] recorded 5.7 million visitors during April 2006, over a full month before the tournament final was scheduled to begin. Much of this activity can be attributed to a website's ability to transcend time and space.

In response to this, increasing importance has been placed on *content management*, which includes all the activities related to the creation, modification, collection, maintenance, organization, and publication of text and other media for the web. Most organizations with web channels include processes and employees to oversee each content management responsibility. While some have taken the approach of hiring functional experts to create content and publish it to the web, many consider that this endeavour should be a joint responsibility between functional experts and web-writing/editorial specialists.

E-mail advertising is another way marketers are using the web to promote their products. In this approach, e-mail addresses of the target market are gathered and included in a mailing list. The mailing list is sent advertisements—new product updates, special one-time promotions, or notifications of in-store events. This has drawn much controversy from consumers, as some organizations have simply chosen to purchase e-mail addresses from other organizations, resulting in large batches of unwanted junk e-mail, or spam, in consumers' e-mail inboxes. Organizations engaging in these practices run the risk of generating negative consumer perceptions.

---

[5] See http://www.ucs.louisiana.edu/~rbh8900/permap.html.

[6] See http://www.fifa.com.

A less controversial form of technology advertising is the use of banners, "online billboards" often promoting products related to the website. For example, a banner promoting an open university's masters degrees may be found on a popular web portal devoted to collegiate sports. Banner effectiveness can be optimized by making it *dynamic*. For example, the same banner could be displayed only when a user types "masters degree" or "online university" into a search engine, while other, more appropriate banners would be displayed upon the entry of other keywords. Although banners offered innovative potential in the early 1990s because of their relatively low cost, the marketing literature suggests that online consumers now rarely pay attention to them.

In terms of pricing, products are generally less expensive online. The reasons include reduced costs due to no brick-and-mortar presence and heightened competition in the online market. Even prices for privileged content, which provides special value to the reader (e.g., detailed market research data, census information on Statistics Canada website), are relatively lower than in other channels. For example, MLB.tv webcasts cost much less than similar television-based options provided by regional cable companies. The savings of transporting the sport product via the Internet have been passed on to the consumer. However, technology also has the potential to interact with the product itself, leading to several advantages for sport marketers. Consider, for example, the impact that online ticket purchases for sporting events has had on the marketing of those products.

Technology can be directly or indirectly involved with product. With many consumer technologies like DVD players and cell phones, it is the whole product and thus directly involved. In indirect cases, technology enhances or complements a core product, as is the case in live sport. Think of the last time you went to a professional league game. Whether it was hockey, baseball, soccer, basketball, or football, technology enhanced the live experience (product) of attending a game. On one level, equipment technology has made players better. Golfers hit longer than they ever did before, and this is due in part to advances in golf club and golf ball technology. Yet even holding player performance constant, the live experience has been enhanced through the incorporation of media technologies. Large-screen video displays let fans catch important plays no matter where they are sitting in the audience, and video replays ensures both fair play and accurate refereeing. In mediated contexts, televised and radio broadcast sports have been positioned in the sport management literature as products in their own right. As such, technological developments (e.g., HDTV) fundamentally increase the quality of the mediated sport product. We will delve deeper into this merger between the sport product and media technology later in the chapter.

The most wide-reaching impact of technology has been in the distribution of products. With the advent of the Internet, the reach of both small and large organizations is worldwide. Some sport organizations, including

Diving Canada[7] and the International Paralympic Committee[8], have recently used webcasting as an alternative to television broadcasting of their events, including the recent 2006 Paralympic Winter Games from Torino, Italy. Combining this with other aspects of globalization and the relative specialization of nations in their media consumption interests, we are seeing a persisting focus on supply chain management issues related to the sourcing of inputs from foreign nations. Some broad challenges for supply chain managers include products taking longer to arrive, complex power dynamics, and intercultural communications. ERP and other logistical systems are contributing to coordination, but only so much can be done on the technological front. Good supply chain management ultimately requires good technology management as much as good technology. In the mediated sport context, technology is creating new channels altogether. Major League Baseball incorporates traditional television (including extra channels branded MLB Extra Innings for out-of-market games), mobile alerts, streaming audio, and, most notably, streaming video[9] in its distribution strategy. Clearly, we can deduce that MLB wants fans to have access to the baseball product in as many ways as possible. But underpinning this decision is a host of questions that must first be answered:

- Is the product conducive to such a strategy?
- Do different regions require different mixes of distribution channels?
- Does the governance structure permit the league to make such a decision for each of its teams?
- How do we manage investments in each of the distribution channels?

As an example of how one organization addressed some of these questions, the following case describes how an NHL team recently evaluated investments in its media distribution channels.

In the Know

HDTV and Ice Hockey[10]

In sports leagues of media interest, revenue generation for both broadcasters and leagues follow a standard pattern. First, rights to broadcast sporting events are sold to broadcasters, usually through a set contract

---

[7] See http://www.diving.ca.

[8] See http://www.ipc.org.

[9] See http://mlb.mlb.com/mlb/subscriptions/index.jsp?c_id=mlb.

[10] O'Reilly, N. & R. Rahinel (2006) Forecasting the importance of media technology in sport: The case of the televised ice hockey product in Canada. *International Journal of Sport Marketing and Sponsorship*, 8(1): 82–94.

where the broadcaster is granted exclusive or joint rights to broadcast a specified number of games. One league may have concurrent contracts with many broadcasters, and one broadcaster may have concurrent contracts with many leagues and sports. In turn, broadcasters sell advertising to cover the costs of the content rights. The more viewers the event can garner, the more a broadcaster can charge for advertising fees. Thus, the ability to attract sizable audiences is a key component in a league and broadcaster's ability to generate revenue. The size of audience watching an event is calculated by Nielsen Media Research in the form of *ratings*.

In comparing trends in rights fees and television ratings, an interesting result emerges. While rights fees have increased, television ratings for all the major professional sports leagues in North America have declined noticeably over the past decade. None of the leagues have felt this recession as hard as the National Hockey League (NHL). Over the course of the NHL's recent six-year television deal with ABC/ESPN (1999–2004), regular-season cable ratings decreased 31 percent on ESPN and 38 percent on ESPN2, with network broadcast ratings on ABC slipping 21 percent over that period[11]. Further, a league of comparable size and growth patterns, the National Basketball Association (NBA), has been and is clearly continuing to outperform the NHL. In 2002–2003, the NBA had ratings of 1.2 (ESPN regular season), 2.6 (ABC regular season), and 6.5 (NBA finals), compared to the NHL with 0.46 (ESPN regular season), 1.1 (ABC regular season), and 2.9 (NHL finals). In all three cases, the NBA is drawing at least double the viewership of the NHL—a gap that is continuing to widen.

The NHL team, the Toronto Maple Leafs, recognized this gap and sought to reclaim its piece of the ratings pie by looking to new media technologies. Richard Peddie (CEO of Maple Leafs Sport and Entertainment) and Tom Anselmi (COO) identified five major media technologies with the potential to have an impact on the televised ice hockey product:

- *High-definition television (HDTV):* Provides a superior view (wide screen), better sound, and a crisper image of the game
- *Interactive television (iTV):* Allows fans to check pool statistics, league standings, or player biographies on a TV screen while watching the game or ice-hockey-related programming
- *Video on demand (VoD):* Allows viewers to order sporting events using their television and remote

---

[11] The Sports Network (2005) TV Ratings Report. Retrieved March 10, 2006 from http://www.tsn.ca.

- *Personal video recorder (PVR):* Also known as digital video recorders (DVRs), allows fans to record a game and watch/rewatch it on command
- *Mobile multimedia devices (MMDs):* Include personal digital assistants (PDAs) and cellular phones (with storage and/or viewing capacity for audio and video) that enable consumption of ice hockey wherever a fan may be

The Toronto Maple Leafs sponsored a study[12] to answer the questions: "Which of the five technologies will have the most impact on televised hockey?" and "Will this technology affect hockey more than other televised programs (news, sitcoms, etc.)?" Through a series of data collection and analysis efforts, including reviews of secondary materials, expert interviews, content analyses of televised hockey, and diffusion forecasting, researchers arrived at two key findings:

1. *HDTV has the most potential to have an impact on televised hockey:* Surround-sound capabilities, increased picture depth, and smoother motion adapt to televised ice hockey and current ice hockey viewer characteristics.
2. *Canadian HDTV consumer adoption will reach a peak in 2007:* An approximate 2007 peak gives a deadline for broadcasters, leagues, and other stakeholders involved in the broadcasting of ice hockey to align themselves with consumer tastes.

In addition to exploring the central question, the research holds other, more general implications for managers, including the importance of forecasting and understanding technology trends in sport, the capacity of technology as a source of competitive advantage, and the use of a mixed-method approach to investigating complex and multitiered questions.

Case: TELUS Corporation[13] and 2001 World Athletics

Background

TELUS Corporation is both a new company and one with a long history in Alberta and British Columbia. Following the 1999 merger of Alberta-based TELUS Corporation and BC-based BC Telecom, the new corporation became Canada's largest telecommunications company. It provides a full range of

---

[12] O'Reilly, N. & R. Rahinel (2006) Forecasting the importance of media technology in sport.

[13] The authors thank Marlene Malyj, TELUS event marketing manager, and Mike Killick, TELUS enterprise marketing, for their time and contribution to this case.

communications products for Canadians at home and at work, as well as a comprehensive array of mobility provisions through its two arms, TELUS Mobility and TELUS Communications. TELUS Mobility is a national facilities-based wireless provider with 2.6 million subscribers (as of 2001); TELUS Communications provides nationally, comprehensive local and long-distance wireline services, data, Internet protocol, and managed services, as well as telecommunications equipment.

TELUS is well known for its support of charities through large donations and its strong support of sport in Canada. The organization also encourages and assists its employees in their volunteer activities and, though the TELUS volunteer involvement fund, makes a donation of $200 for a minimum of 60 hours of voluntary service. The company leverages its expertise in technology and communications with the TELUS Community Investment Program, which sees it support local communities with donations of expertise in technology and equipment rather than money.

2001 World Athletics Championships

The World Athletics Championships is the third largest sports event in the world: Only the Olympic Games and the World Cup of Football attract more attention. In 2001, Edmonton was the first North American city in host the event.

TELUS, Technology, and the 2001 World's

TELUS became the national partner category sponsor in the telecommunications category as a way to build awareness, gain competitive advantage over Bell, stimulate sales, and, most important, demonstrate its technology as a means of differentiation. It provided a state-of-the-art telecommunications network to the event, incorporating everything from audio and video broadcast circuits to cellular phones and Internet service.

In seeking to leverage its technology advantage message and attain its objectives, TELUS implemented an ambitious program:

- It performed promotional activity pre, during, and post event.
- Advertisements were strategically placed in newspapers, magazines, transit/outdoor advertising, on-site displays/signage, and promotional contests.
- The Invite a Friend Contest encouraged contestants to make a long-distance call to invite a friend or relative to the championships, with the winner awarded an expense-paid trip for two to a site of previous World Championships.
- It sponsored sporting events pre-World's to communicate sponsorship of the 2001 World's.
- Miniature footballs were given away at Edmonton Eskimo games and baseballs at Edmonton Trappers AAA baseball games, all with TELUS and World Championship branding.
- During the event, TELUS had the naming rights to the Stage at Worlds Plaza, the main venue for cultural and entertainment activities during the Championships.

- During the competition, it distributed 50 000 Canadian flags with its brand on them.
- For the opening ceremonies, it recruited 250 volunteers and provided clothing and cost of training.
- TELUS launched the Athlete ambassador program, recruiting athletes to speak to guests in its VIP tent, and the Legends of Gold dinner, at which winners of an associated charity fundraiser sat with a Canadian Gold Medal winner at their table.

Source: Institute for Sport Marketing Case Studies. Laurentian University 2003-2005

Case Questions

1. Why would TELUS sponsor the 2001 World Athletics Championships to demonstrate its capacity and competency in telecommunications?
2. In general, why would technology companies use sport marketing? In addition to this case, refer to the executive perspective at the beginning of the chapter.
3. If TELUS was seeking to demonstrate its technology, why did it spend so much on leveraging activities?
4. Who is TELUS's main competitor, and why could this sponsorship help them achieve a competitive advantage?
5. Visit http://www.telus.ca. What is TELUS doing today to market its technology? Is it involved in sport marketing? Which properties? What does this tell you?
6. Visit http://www.bell.ca and answer the same questions posed in Question 5.

Chapter Summary

This chapter introduces the concept of technology (information technology or IT) to sport marketing. It provides sport marketers with a perspective on technology and knowledge of the tools of IT applied to all business environments. The chapter outlines and describes key IT components, including the leading media technology trends, that have an impact on or have the potential to affect all steps of the sport marketing process. Of particular note is HDTV and its potential role in the future marketing of ice hockey.

Test Your Knowledge

1. Define technology.
2. List and describe at least four current trends in information systems.

3. Define and give examples of hardware and software? Which is more important in sport marketing?
4. What is webcasting? Do you see a future for it in sport marketing?
5. If you were a marketing director for Swim Canada, what technology trends/changes would you watch out for?
6. Define and describe each of these media technologies:

    a. HDTV
    b. iTV
    c. VoD
    d. PVR
    e. DVR
    f. MMD
    g. PDA

7. Select any two of the media technologies listed above and forecast their future impact on a sport of your choice.

For more review questions, go to http://www.sportmarketing.nelson.com.

Key Terms

bandwidth
database
enterprise resource planning system
hardware

information system
information technology
relational database
software

A full glossary of key term definitions is located at http://www.sportmarketing.nelson.com.

Internet Resources

National Hockey League, http://www.nhl.com/

Webcast, http://en.wikipedia.org/wiki/Webcasting

Kanatek: Everest Expedition, http://www.kanatek.com/everest/

Sport and Technology, http://www.sportandtechnology.com/page/0001.html

TSN Report: 2006 CFL season goes live online, http://www.tsn.ca/cfl/news_story/?ID=169448&hubname

Will technology ruin sports?, http://www.csmonitor.com/2004/1216/p13s01-stct.html

New technology in sports information, http://multimedia.olympic.org/pdf/en_report_60.pdf

Chapter 15

Social Marketing in Sport

Learning Objectives

- To understand what social marketing is and its potential in the sport context
- To know when to use social marketing
- To be able to adapt commercial marketing concepts to social marketing
- To be aware of the complications arising from this adaptation

Introduction

Behaviour change in the business of behaviour

Sport's impact on society is tremendous: It contributes to economic vitality; it fosters activity and exercise in the population; and it boosts municipal, regional, and national morale. Just like any other industry, however, sport is not without flaw. Behaviour change, trivial or major, is sometimes necessary of key stakeholders, whether they be athletes, potential athletes, coaches, administrators, media, funding agencies, or regulatory boards. This is where marketing is most useful. Marketing *owns* the business of **behaviour** influence. Thus, in these situations where the "purchase" of new *behaviours* is required, we can use *social marketing*. Examples of behavioural change where social marketing has been used effectively are practising safe sex, avoiding drinking and driving, quitting smoking, and curbing alcoholism.

behaviour: the actions of human beings.

As marketers, we are expert coordinators, strategists, microeconomists, and psychologists, which allows us to approach the field of behaviour management with a holistic and integrated perspective. Finding situations where social marketing can be applied, assessing the context of the "product" and organization, understanding the various segments of "consumers," choosing a target segment, and executing a behaviour-management strategy are all marketing processes. In doing this, we just have to take the relatively small step from one field of exchange to another.

EXECUTIVE PERSPECTIVE

SPORT MATTERS 🍁
Where Canadian sport connects

Ian Bird, CEO, Sport Matters Group

Social Marketing and the Sport Matters Group: Building on Our Success Together

A Platform for Shared Success

"Sport matters" is an expression used to say we care about the future of sport in Canada. In some ways sport matters is a spoken promise to one another, an affirmation of shared values. The Sport Matters Group (SMG) is, not surprisingly, a group of sport and physical activity leaders from across Canada who have come together to think about the future of sport and physical activity in Canada and to collaborate on public affairs and policy matters that affect sport and physical activity.

Over time, it has become evident that people participate in SMG activities for three common reasons.

- To do something good for sport and physical activity
- To exercise some leadership
- To influence public policy

People participate in the SMG because it is a place we have created for ourselves to connect, to park our respective agendas and escape the daily preoccupations for awhile, to talk and learn about the things that can make a difference for the sport sector as a whole. The story of the SMG is the story of the sport sector becoming master of its own destiny. It has produced a new kind of leadership that gets things done collectively and through the individual contributions of those who participate.

Much of the work of the SMG is about sector development, paying attention to how we work together, changing relationships within sport networks, and what is happening in the environment. This identity—a participatory identity grounded in shared values—is what first brought 12 of Canada's sport leaders together six years ago and continues to galvanize hundreds of leaders and citizens today.

Common Ground

Beginning in 2001, the SMG focused on two main objectives: helping ourselves learn more about the public policy process and getting directly involved in that process. But along the way, a third activity took hold: developing our ability to work together—our common ground—on issues of common interest. Our new collective approach, operating under the banner of Sport Matters, has achieved a remarkable number of policy and advocacy objectives for the benefit of the entire sector. In spring 2005, our collective efforts resulted in a doubling of Sport Canada's budget, with an infusion of new money for sport and physical activity equivalent to $350 million over five years.

Our collective work on the 2006 federal election campaign brought forward unprecedented attention to sport and physical activity, driven by a record level of sector engagement in the election process. The new government's platform included the allocation of one percent of federal health funding on physical activity and sport (now indexed at $435 million a year), tax credits for sport registration fees (equivalent to $160 million in foregone revenues), and a $50 million annual fund for youth-at-risk programs, which includes sport. Canada's new government has already implemented the tax credit program, allocated $20 million a year for youth-at-risk programs, and introduced a heritage sport fund valued at $1.5 million.

It is now clear that, along with other efforts, the Sport Matters approach has helped to create the conditions for action and success on sport policy. An online community has also been established to allow us to connect with each other and work together more effectively (http://www.sportmatters.ca). Policy capacity groups, such as the SMG, are another way that leaders from across the sector connect when they have an interest and a willingness to engage around a specific policy issue, to bring or to develop their policy expertise, or to work to advance a policy goal or to help build policy capacity within the sport and physical activity sector. These groups keep on top of a diverse range of sport matters, like charitable tax status and the relationship with CRA (Canadian Revenue Agency), social development and sport, enhancing the role of public broadcasting and amateur sport, and responding to the sport infrastructure crisis.

As a gathering place for sport leaders, SMG also seems to have spawned another group of willing collaborators—the Friends of Canadian Sport. Friends come from Canadian towns and cities and counties, and work together to connect the dots between sport at all levels, especially in their communities. They value sport and physical activity, and many are already actively supporting and promoting a sporting Canada. It may be that Sport Matters is more of a place and method for people and leaders to connect, while Friends is an expression of that connection in our communities. All this has been achieved through pooling contributions, including financial resources, to pursue campaigns, projects, and activities of common interest.

Strategic Opportunities

Compared to five years ago, the sport sector is now much more confident and comfortable with the public policy process. We have developed new abilities and experiences in influencing the environment in which we work. Never before has sport been able to carry out so much collective work with such impressive results. And there's more.

Just over a year ago, a consortium of research partners, including Statistics Canada, revealed that more than 34 000 sport and recreation organizations exist in Canada, thus making sport and recreation the single largest group of voluntary organizations in the country. Not long after, the Conference Board of Canada released *Strengthening Canada*, a study confirming the powerful socioeconomic benefits of sport participation in Canada. Among other things, sport spending by Canadians totals almost $16 billion a year, and sport accounts for about 2 percent of jobs in the country.

In June 2007, the *Canadian Survey on Giving, Volunteering and Participating* was released, highlighting the trend-setting way that Canadians make sport the largest citizen participation endeavour of the nation. We now know that more people—over 3 million Canadians—volunteer in sport than in any other sphere of volunteer life Through Sport Matters, the sport sector now has a comprehensive policy platform entitled Sport and Physical Activity: A New Direction for Canada. This gives us a common set of policy objectives and a frame of reference for collective action.

We also made possible an innovative project that examined citizen participation in communities, with an in-depth look at sport's role in that process. In exploring citizen and community participation, the Investing in Canada project—a plan developed by the SMG to show the importance of investing in sport infrastructure—demonstrates the power of sport to generate human and social capital, the kind we need for strong and healthy communities to flourish. At two consecutive meetings of federal, provincial, and territorial ministers responsible for sport and physical activity, sport and physical activity infrastructure continues to be the top priority. This is in addition to their goal of increasing physical activity by 10 percent in each province by 2010.

The big cities mayors' caucus has followed suit, making sport and physical activity infrastructure part of their $60 billion municipal infrastructure proposal. Adding to this momentum is the Council of the Federation, the place where Canada's 13 premiers meet to advance shared provincial interests. At their August 2006, promoting Canada through sport emerged as one of their 13 key priorities.

Once converted into action, the new federal government's sport plan offers the greatest potential yet, including broader investments, tax measures, and strengthened infrastructure—a kind of comprehensive approach to make sport better and to give Canadians a chance to shape the future of sport in Canada.

And most recently, Sport Matters has connected the dots between a new kind of leadership around sport and social development with the interests and wherewithal of one of Canada's most innovative, engaged, and generous private foundations. New opportunities and resources for sport, active living, and recreation groups which are addressing community concerns and social inclusion are now rolling out.

These achievements and strategic opportunities have come about through contributions made by many organizations and individuals on various policy initiatives and advocacy campaigns. Moreover, in pursuing these achievements, we have learned a lot about how to work together, how to be effective policy players, without creating new structures or organizations that divert resources or get in the way of achieving our common interests.

The Best Contribution Is the One You Want to Make

All participation and contributions have been voluntary and generally based on level of interest, specific issues of common interest, and resources needed to have any impact. Many leaders have offered money, an essential ingredient of success. By pooling financial resources, we have been able to collectively undertake effective campaigns that have paid tremendous dividends for sport and physical activity.

Another contribution has been the involvement of the senior management of sport organizations. Over the past few years, CEOs and key decision makers have invested time to attend SMG meetings and to help shape public policy on sport and physical activity. During the most recent federal election, over 500 Canadians took part in the Sport Matters campaign, covering over 200 ridings and generating over 1300 letters to election candidates. There are always opportunities to contribute expertise and content for policy papers and media releases, to the online community and policy capacity group, and in government relations.

Some have contributed to the costs of office space, travel, printing, data collection, communications, meetings, fiduciary functions, and the operations and administration of the SMG. Organizations and individuals have also lent their names as endorsements for policy positions and campaigns, significantly increasing the power and credibility of activities designed to show the sector's interest in certain positions. Some have reached out to others to expand the network, and community, of those who care about the future of sport and physical activity.

In the end, the best contribution is the one you wish to make.

What's Next?

- We are now in the process of converting Canada's new government policy from commitments into action.
- We continue our work together to implement the Canadian sport policy and to look for new approaches to the governance and leadership of sport.
- We build on our work to connect Canadian sport, using online technologies, policy capacity groups, and services that make it easier for us to work together.
- We begin to make sense of the whole sport and physical activity infrastructure file, which reaches communities across Canada.
- We connect with others to maximize the value and contribution of Canadians who volunteer in sport.
- We vigorously promote some of the important ideas that are emerging from within the network of sport leaders, such as the road to excellence, the sport we want, population sport, youth engagement, social inclusion, and public leadership.
- And perhaps most important, we keep the Sport Matters approach going. It's always been up to us to make these things happen, and we've found a very effective way of doing it. So we build on our success by continuing to combine our efforts.

Ian Bird is the senior leader of the Sport Matters Group, a voluntary group of over 100 national, provincial, and community organizations that have come together to collaborate on issues that affect sport and physical activity in Canada.

What Is Social Marketing?

Social marketing is a relatively new subfield of marketing that was born in 1969[1] as part of a thrust to broaden the field of marketing. Many definitions have been offered since then; however, there is still no consensus on what social marketing is. Some writers have taken a narrow approach, arguing that social marketing is present only where a clear mutual exchange of value has taken place; others have taken a wider approach, arguing that social marketing is any sort of application of commercial marketing principles for behaviour change. In fact, the question of what is social marketing is often the topic of discussion in keynote speeches and panels at social marketing conferences. For the purposes of this chapter, we will adopt a definition from Alan Andreasen[2], a leading scholar in the field who conceptualized social marketing as "the adaptation of commercial marketing technologies to programs designed to influence the voluntary behavior of target audiences to improve their personal welfare and that of the society of which they are a part." Thus, social marketing involves all these pieces, which this chapter will further examine:

1. *an adaptation of commercial marketing technologies:* The 3 Cs (company, competition, and customer), 4 Ps (marketing strategy), and STP (segmenting, targeting, and positioning) as the bridge between the two concept islands are all transferred into the new context of behaviour management. We use this two island and bridge analogy as a guiding schema for this chapter.
2. *influencing voluntary behaviour of target audiences:* The goal is not to coerce or force target audiences to act in a way that is in line with your goals. As you might know from casual experience with your parents or supervisors at work, negative effects often arise when this approach is used.
3. *improving the personal welfare of target audiences and that of the society of which they are a part:* The impetus of a social marketing program is usually to foster behaviours that sustain or improve the social welfare of the target audience or society at large—social marketing is good-spirited.

In adopting this definition, we note that competing definitions of the field are neither right nor wrong, but simply that this definition is better suited to this book. Using this definition, we are able to explore a wide range of situations where social marketing has been or might be used and an array of tools and tactics to go about it. However, before we can embark on the adaptation of commercial marketing principles for social marketing programs, we must first address the issue of when to apply social marketing.

---

[1] Kotler, P. & S. Levy (1969) Broadening the concept of marketing. *Journal of Marketing*, 33(1): 10–15.

[2] Andreasen, A. (2002) Marketing social marketing in the social change marketplace. *Journal of Public Policy and Marketing*, 21(1): 3–13.

When Is Social Marketing Appropriate?

In a landmark social marketing article, Michael Rothschild[3] compares three tools for social change: education, social marketing, and law. Education refers to the change agent's messages that attempt to convince the target audience to change or behave in a specific way but don't offer rewards or punishments in return. Education is the least persuasive of the three tools and will work on its own only when the target audience can perceive that its self-interests will be served. For example, an educational message might read: "Engage in physical activity; it's good for you." According to Rothschild, law is "the use of coercion to achieve behaviour in a non-voluntary manner ... or to threaten with punishment for noncompliance or inappropriate behaviour." Law is the most persuasive tool and will work even when the target audiences does not perceive that its self-interests will be served. For example, a change agent's message might read: "Those who do not exercise regularly will not receive health-care benefits." In the middle ground between these two approaches is social marketing, which was defined earlier. In this context, Rothschild adds that social marketing involves the reinforcement of incentives and consequences to shift the balance of costs and benefits so that voluntary exchange is encouraged. For example, a social marketing message might read: "Tell us your address, and we'll drive you to the gym." Here, the additional costs that one would incur from driving to the gym (cost of gas, physiological effort, and psychological effort) are taken away by the social marketer's offer to take on this responsibility. And so, the question persists: In what situations should one use education, social marketing, or law?

Table 15-1 shows that this largely depends on three characteristics of the target audience: *motivation*, *opportunity*, and *ability* (MOA[4]). Target audiences are *motivated* when they believe their self-interests will be served by engaging in the behaviour. In using our first example, the target audience might see the benefits to increasing their engagement in physical activity—getting healthier, living a better life, reducing stress. These people are motivated. Conversely, someone may be very content just sitting on the couch watching television and playing video games, and might not see the benefits: In other words, this person has no **motivation**. Target audiences have the *opportunity* to behave when a known environmental mechanism is at hand. For example, consider children in underprivileged families. They may not have access to recreational programs and so may be more likely to engage in deviant behaviours (e.g., gangs, drugs). These children are said to have a deficient level of positive opportunity. Finally, *ability* includes the basic skills of the target audience to counter peer pressure, break a habit, and comprehend rational appeals. This also includes the self-confidence of the target audience to make the behavioural change. For example, a coach may be too easy on his players and may not have the "heart" to tell them that they are performing below expectations, even if it is in the team's best interests. This coach lacks the ability (or at least the willpower) to behave in a way to best achieve the team's goals. Depending on the mix of motivation, opportunity, and ability in the target audience,

motivation: the desire to change behaviour after being convinced that the change will lead to self-benefit.

opportunity: known environmental mechanism at hand allowing target audiences to behave.

ability: basic skills of the target audience to counter peer pressure, break a habit, comprehend rational appeals, have the self-confidence to make the behavioural change.

---

[3] Rothschild, M. (1999) Carrots, sticks, and promises: A conceptual framework for the management of public health and social issue behaviors. *Journal of Marketing*, 63(4): 24–37.

[4] ibid.

different combinations of education, marketing, and law are suggested. As shown, social marketing's potential as a tool of social change is vindicated by its recommendation in six of the eight possible situations.

TABLE 15-1

Applications of Education, Marketing, and Law

Motivation	Yes		No	
Opportunity	Yes	No	Yes	No
Ability	#1	#2	#3	#4
Yes	prone to behave education	unable to behave marketing	resistant to behave law	resistant to behave marketing, law
	#5	#6	#7	#8
No	unable to behave education, marketing	unable to behave education, marketing	resistant to behave education, marketing, law	resistant to behave education, marketing, law

Source: Rothschild, M., (1999) Carrots, Sticks and Promises: A Conceptual Framework for the Management of Public Health and Social Issue Behaviours. Journal of Marketing, Vol.63, No.4 (Oct.1999) pp.24-37.

Rothschild MOA Framework Issues

Some social marketing scholars have taken the approach of comparing and contrasting Rothschild's work with other frameworks or approaches to behaviour change. However, we feel that this comparison is somewhat unfair as the aims of such competing frameworks are divergent as they were developed for a variety of purposes. Whereas Rothschild looked at where social marketing is appropriate, many other scholars merely describe the best ways to go about social marketing once it has been chosen as a tool for social change. Thus, many (if not all) of the frameworks make a unique and desirable contribution to the field of social marketing.

Some issues have been raised over the Rothschild MOA framework. One issue is the difficulty in evaluating each of motivation, opportunity, and ability as binary constructs[5,6]. For example, in looking at college athletes who binge drink, one can discern that motivation to change one's behaviour may differ widely among the target audience. Some students may see the health benefits in halting their excessive drinking; while others may not, considering binge drinking a part of the university experience. Even assuming that the other two dimensions—opportunity and ability—are the equal across the target audience,

[5] O'Reilly, N. & J. Madill (2007) The World Anti-Doping Agency: The role of social marketing. *Journal of Nonprofit and Public Sector Marketing*, 17(1/2).

[6] Rahinel, R., N. O'Reilly, & J. Madill (2006) Public urban gun use behaviour and social marketing: Balancing theoretical and practical considerations. Social Marketing Advances in Research and Theory (SMART) Conference, Banff.

what the change agent decides to be the motivation will determine which tools are chosen. This decision is further confounded by the difficulty and expense of research in social marketing. One can take the approach of using more tools than necessary, but this has a tremendous impact on resources—money, time, and people—which are often scanty in social marketing environments. This brings us to our second criticism of the model. Often, deciding on social marketing requires significant coordination and buy-in from several different agencies, from internal administration to the media. This entails the commitment of many resources, some of which the change agent may not have. Thus, although an MOA analysis might confirm that social marketing is appropriate in a situation, careful planning and budgeting is still needed to ensure the resources to execute a social marketing strategy. In other cases, sufficient resources may be available, but the societal costs of the behaviour might not warrant such expenditure. In these situations, change agents must question why they are interested in such behaviour change and the nature, recipient, and volume of benefits accrued. In answering such questions, change agents will be able to move toward developing a behaviour management program they know can work.

Understanding the Company and Customer

Chapters 3 and 4 discussed sport marketing research and the sport consumer. As with any other subset of marketing, social marketing is highly customer focused, and tapping into the needs and wants of each customer is paramount when formulating any marketing strategy. In doing this, the company and its ability to meet those needs and wants must also be assessed.

The Company

Analyzing the company in a social marketing context is similar to that activity in commercial contexts. The main difference is that the findings are often more unpleasant. Organizations engaging in social marketing are often in the non-profit sector and rely largely on volunteer employees. Even those organizations that are in for-profit industries often only have limited and dispersed resources (if any) devoted to behaviour management. For those organizations without dedicated resources, the first step involves moving the problem up the organizational or governmental agenda, so that people start to care about behaviour management in the first place. Thus, if you do not head up your organization or if behaviour management is not a normal activity for your department, someone else—an individual, group, or organization—will have to support your cause with the resources you need. Good candidates for this may include parties whose interest in curbing behaviours are perhaps less altruistic than yours. For example, Queensland Health in Australia funded a project to encourage the residents of the Rockhampton region to increase their number of steps they walk each day to 10 000. In doing this, they partnered with Yamax to manufacture a special 10 000 Steps project pedometer. Locations of retailers and instructions on how to use the pedometers are given on the 10,000 Steps website (http://10000steps.org.au).

Another hurdle that social marketers encounter on this crusade is resistance from individuals from other intellectual disciplines who dislike taking a "business approach" to a good-spirited activity[7]. Overcoming this resistance will not be easy; but arming yourself with data and knowledge is a step in the right direction. How you frame the social problem, your persuasiveness versus that of your opponents, and other miscellaneous company- and political-centred factors will determine how you fare.

The Customer

Regardless of the characteristics of your target audience, every target audience member goes about the process of change in a stepwise fashion. Andreasen[8] calls these four steps the *stages of change*:

1. *Precontemplation:* Target audience members have decided against or are unaware of the social marketer's desired behaviour. In either case, they are not thinking about behaviour change.
2. *Contemplation:* Members of the target audience are weighing the benefits and costs of changing their behaviour. Self-efficacy is an important influencer at this time.
3. *Preparation and action:* Some target audience members are ready to act and do so. Others, however, sit on the edge of change and need the final push. Andreasen suggests that a potential motivator toward action may be offering some sort of trial behaviour.
4. *Maintenance:* Social marketers often seek to encourage repetition of the behaviour, similar to a habit. For example, it is really no good if an athlete changes his unsportsmanlike behaviour or conduct the first time he is reprimanded. This change has to be turned into a long-standing record of emotional control and self-discipline. The difficulty of achieving this goal often depends on the type of behaviour, how behaviour change was accomplished, and how constant the change was.

Andreasen notes that sometimes the goal will be not to move members of the target audience from the precontemplation to the contemplation stage, as some purchases are low involvement, but rather directly to the preparation and action phase. These differences between classes of consumers will be addressed in the "product" section of the chapter.

STP for Social Marketers

STP has implications for resource allocation and competitive strategy, which are important in light of generally low budgets and often intense competition in the market, respectively. Therefore, the ignorance of segmentation in particular could lead to a mass misallocation of resources, which could ultimately go unnoticed in the light of positive (though suboptimal) program results.

---

[7] Andreasen, A. & P. Kotler (2003) *Strategic Marketing for Nonprofit Organizations*, 6th ed. Prentice Hall.

[8] Andreasen, A. (2006) *Social Marketing in the 21st Century*. Sage Publications.

Segmentation and Targeting

Segmentation in social marketing requires thinking outside the box and analysis. Although traditional bases of segmentation might provide information on which segments are larger or growing fast, usually these provide little insight about which segments are most susceptible to social marketing programs or how prevalent the behaviour is in each segment. Lifestyle and psychographic bases are much more likely to provide the necessary insight into these matters.

Social marketing targeting usually involves choosing between two strategies—differentiated targeting and concentrated targeting. As with commercial marketing, undifferentiated targeting is not recommended, especially in light of resource constraints. In differentiated targeting, two scenarios are possible. First, if the target can select from a number of alternative behaviours, you may wish to concentrate on different offerings for different segments. For example, the My Anti-Drug campaign[9] suggests many different behaviours to convince different segments of teenagers to abstain from drugs. These offerings range from ballet to beatboxing and from shopping to surfing. With minor exceptions, the former are framed as offerings for females and the latter for males in the target audience. In the second situation, you may wish to sell the same product to all segments, as when the primary concern is engaging in the social marketeter's behaviour rather than leaving behind the undesirable behaviour. The sport social marketer must consider both behaviour maintenance and behaviour change in any social marketing strategy.

Positioning

Similarly, positioning depends on the social marketer's objective—to entice the target audience to leave behind a behaviour or to engage in a new one. If the former, then positioning is relatively easy. The only rational appeal a social marketer must make is that the costs of the existing behaviour clearly outweigh the benefits and that other alternative behaviours are much better. In commercial marketing, this is referred to as *demarketing*. The quantity and nature of these other behaviours are irrelevant (as with the My Anti-Drug campaign); however, it is important to allow sufficient opportunity for the target audience to try and eventually adopt one (or more) of them. If the objective is for target audience members to engage in a new behaviour (e.g., a league executive would like athletes to be more active in the community), this will have to be positioned in consumers' minds versus alternative behaviours, which presumably do not fit with the social marketer's objectives. A target audience must realize that engaging in the behaviour is congruent with their desired self-image.

---

[9] See http://www.whatsyourantidrug.com.

Social Marketing Strategy

Product

In commercial marketing, products evolve with the ever-changing needs and wants of the market and, thus, many ultimately fail: Sometimes, the market doesn't want what you have to sell. The same is true for social marketing. No matter how many resources are dedicated to convincing a target audience that they should undertake one behaviour or cease another, sometimes people just resist. The difficulty in this situation, however, is that behaviours are behaviours: You can't make a behaviour out of better material or put more gadgets on it. All you can control is how the behaviour is *framed*[10]: Is the behaviour called 'unsportsmanlike conduct' or 'trash talking'? Which of these is more politically correct? Which of these is more likely for people to notice? Which of these is more likely to help you in your social marketing crusade? Recognizing that the way by which you define your social marketing product may be your only leverage point is deceivingly important to your product strategy.

Price

In social marketing, price is a simpler construct than in commercial marketing. Chapter 6 explained that a product can be initially priced in several ways—low to penetrate the market and capture market share, or high to skim the segment of users who are willing to initially pay more for a product. Social marketing *always* takes the former approach. The objective is to frame or design replacement behaviours and products, while keeping target audience costs as low as possible. In fact, this "let's make a deal" mentality is largely at the heart of social marketing. For example, if the government's objective is to encourage youth to engage in sport, then free lessons in hard-to-reach neighbourhoods may be a viable product offering. Because it is free, the target audience will be more motivated to participate: Costs have been more than offset (for most) by the benefits (e.g., having fun, getting outside, spending time with friends, being active), With audiences who are more resistant, this product might be augmented with other cost-reduction strategies, such as providing transportation, equipment, babysitting (if the target audience includes parents), or free league membership.

Promotion

The same promotional tools of commercial marketing are available to social marketing. You can choose from advertising, public relations, sales promotions, and personal selling, although some contextual differences do exist. Table 15-2 summarizes the potential advantages and disadvantages of each tool.

---

[10] Andreasen, A. (2006) *Social Marketing in the 21st Century.*

TABLE 15-2

Promotional Mix Assessment

PROMOTIONAL TOOL	ADVANTAGES	DISADVANTAGES
Advertising	Wide reach Control the message	Costly Longer development process May not be as credible
Public relations	Not as costly Unbiased third party may signal credibility Ability to leverage brand equity of third party Wide reach	No control on message Must have human resources resources with contacts Long-term process
Sales promotions	Immediate effects Target gets to try desired behaviour Engage third party (corporate) into promotion	Incur extra costs of communicating sales promotion
Personal selling	Can reach socially "detached" audience members Message can be tailored for specific member Ideal for high-involvement decisions Power of speech	Very expensive Limited reach Variance of sales agent skills Time consuming

Depending on the target audience, a social marketer also has to choose the kind of appeal to make—rational or emotional. In rational appeals, the social marketer lays out objective costs and benefits for the audience to show that leaving behind old ways for new behaviours is a logical decision: Everybody wants to believe they act rationally. In an emotional appeal, the social marketer appeals to the emotions of the targets, whose behaviour they are seeking to maintain and/or change.

Place

Place is a relatively minor strategic element in social marketing, although it still requires attention. In seeking behaviour change in sport environments, the distribution of "change" may work through other individuals such as coaches, referees, technical experts, parents, and teammates. In these cases, each member of the chain must also be convinced of the value of the behaviour.

Case: World Anti-Doping Agency

Hurdling Barriers to the Adoption of Social Marketing: What Are Your Options?

Background

Sport faces an enormous threat from doping. In recognition of this threat, the International Olympic Committee (IOC), in collaboration with numerous sport organizations and governments worldwide, founded (in 1999) and continues to support the World Anti-Doping Agency (WADA) and its mission to eradicate doping from sport. WADA was formed with a structure based on equal representation of the Olympic Movement and public authorities, with a funding model of 50 percent provided by the Olympic Movement and 50 percent by various governments around the world[11]. WADA[12] defines doping as "the occurrence of one or more of the anti-doping rule violations" outlined in eight articles of its World Anti-Doping Code. These broad rules include: "the presence of a prohibited substance or its metabolites or markers in an athlete's bodily specimen," "tampering, or attempting to tamper, with any part of doping control," and "administration or attempted administration of a prohibited substance or prohibited method to any athlete, or assisting, encouraging, aiding, abetting, covering up or any other type of complicity involving an anti-doping rule violation or attempted violation."

Target Market: High-Performance Sport

Sport, as an industry, is not homogeneous, and this is particularly important from an **anti-doping** perspective. The segment of sport that is most likely to be affected by doping is the high-performance stream of sport. High-performance sports are those in which performance is the principal goal (Olympic Games, professional sport) rather than development or participation. This stream is not limited to elite international athletes: It includes any athlete who is on the 'track' to high performance, beginning at quite young ages depending on the sport. In practical terms, the stream includes varsity athletes, national-level athletes, development-level athletes, and participation-level athletes in high-performance training environments with the objective of achieving performance success (junior national athletes). WADA's programs must target not only the athlete but also their entourage—coach, trainer, family, doctor, masseuse, and so on.

anti-doping: the movement, led by the World Anti-Doping Agency in partnership with governments and sport organizations worldwide, to eradicate doping (or cheating through the use of banned substances) from sport.

WADA's Current Strategy and Approaches to Behaviour Change

WADA's business activities include conducting unannounced out-of-competition doping control among elite athletes, funding scientific research to develop new detection methods, observing the doping control and results management programs of major events, and providing anti-doping education to

---

[11] Pound, R. (2004) Personal communication.

[12] WADA (2006) *WADA 2006 Annual Report*. Retrieved from http://www.wada-ama.org/rtecontent/document/2006_Annual_Report_En.pdf.

athletes, coaches, and administrators. WADA has a physical presence in four cities—headquarters in Montreal, Canada, and regional offices in Lausanne, Switzerland, Tokyo, Japan, and Cape Town, South Africa.

WADA works through national Olympic committees, government authorities, and national anti-doping organizations (NADOs) to administer its programs. Its 2006 budget was US$22 356 150, of which 46.87 percent (about $11.1 million) came from the Olympic movement, 46.87 percent (about $11.1) from public sector contributions, and 6.26 percent (about $1.5 million) from other sources[13].

WADA's raison d'être is to eradicate doping from sport, which involves changing behaviours at many levels in over 200 countries and dozens of sports. Its 2006 budget reveals that sanctions (law) and education are its priority. Of the 2006 expenditure budget (about 92% of budgeted income), 60 percent was slotted for research, 15 percent for out-of-competition testing, 15 percent for education, and 10 percent for contingency fund. WADA's 2004–2009 strategic plan further demonstrates its focus on the legal and education approaches to social change. As well, the tenets of the World Anti-Doping Code are strongly rooted in the law and education as ways to effect behaviour change.

Social Marketing: Barriers to Use at WADA

barriers: structural or political elements that limit the influence and adoption of social marketing.

The social marketing literature suggests eight **barriers** to the adoption of social marketing (Table 15-3), of which seven have limited its consideration as part of WADA's strategy to social change:

TABLE 15-3

Barriers to the Adoption of Social Marketing

#	BARRIER	DESCRIPTION	WADA SITUATION
1	Reliance on education and the law as approaches to social change	Marketer needs to show relevance of social marketing as a complement to education and the law.	Analysis of WADA documents described previously support this barrier.
2	Difficulty in distinguishing social marketing from education	Education can suggest an exchange but cannot deliver the benefit of the exchange explicitly. Targets must figure out how to meet their own needs.	"Yes [we consider our education programs to be a form of social marketing], because they are designed to alter behaviour and bring about certain outcomes." (Comment by WADA CEO).

[13] ibid.

3	Managers lacking formal marketing training	Managers lack an appreciation for the self-interest of the client, the benefits of an exchange, and an understanding of power and competition.	"Less than 10 percent [of WADA's directors and managers have formal marketing training]." (Comment by WADA CEO).
4	Ethics of social marketing	It requires a tradeoff between the rights and responsibilities of the individual and society.	No related comment.
5	Lack of appreciation of social marketing by top management	Research has shown acceptance of social marketing primarily at the practitioner level.	"I haven't the faintest idea [what social marketing is]." (Comment by WADA CEO).
6	Poor "brand positioning" of field, which some perceive as manipulative and not community based	It has a fuzzy image, no clear definition, and no differentiation from other approaches to change.	No related comment.
7	Lack of formally documented and publicized successes	There is a need to demonstrate the effectiveness of social marketing and its superiority to alternatives.	No evaluation or evidence available at WADA.
8	Lacks of academic structure in social marketing	There is a lack of courses, programs, faculties, and journals.	"Not as such, but I don't often get into that level of curriculum." (Comment by WADA CEO when asked: "Are you aware of any universities that offer courses in social marketing?"

Source: adapted from: Rothschild, M., (1999) Carrots, Sticks and Promises: A Conceptual Framework for the Management of Public Health and Social Issue Behaviours. Journal of Marketing, Vol.63, No.4 (Oct.1999) pp.24-37 : and Andreasen,A. (2002) "Marketing Social Marketing in the Social Change Marketplace", Journal of Public Policy and Marketing, 21 (1), 3-13.

Case Questions

Take the position of the executive director of WADA. You and your education committee (there is no formal social marketing structure) are discussing how to improve your strategies and tactics, given the continued growth in funding and support from governments and the sporting community. The topic of social marketing comes up as a potential strategy to employ. Many are interested, many don't understand what it is, and many are hesitant as they express concerns over its effectiveness and, more important, the time frame to effectiveness. Many questions emerge:

1. What do you do?
2. Can social marketing work here?
3. How diverse are your targets? Can they all be reached?
4. If you were to include a social marketing effort, what would you do? Where do you start?

Chapter Summary

Social marketing is a field of study in marketing that has received sporadic attention over the years. However, its effectiveness in encouraging behaviour change in health-related issues (e.g., safe sex, drinking and driving, smoking, alcoholism) is widely accepted and supported empirically. Some marketing theorists and practitioners believe strongly that, as a product form, a behaviour should receive as much attention as a tangible good, service, or idea. This chapter applies the situational analysis, sport marketing mix, and STP concepts to social marketing and uses Rothschild's MOA (motivation, opportunity, ability) framework to describe behaviour change. The chapter closes with the case of WADA and its work in anti-doping behaviour in sport, where social marketing strategies and tactics could be applied to support its overall mission.

Test Your Knowledge

1. Define social marketing.
2. Provide at least three examples of a social marketing product in sport.
3. Distinguish between social marketing and education.
4. If you were the CEO of the World Anti-Doping Agency, would you invest in social marketing expertise? Support your decision.
5. Provide an example for each of the eight boxes in Rothschild's MOA framework.
6. Explain why the law and legal sanctions are often ineffective in achieving these social change objectives:

    a. anti-doping
    b. drinking and driving
    c. safe sex

 For more review questions, go to http://www.sportmarketing.nelson.com.

Key Terms

ability

anti-doping

barriers

behaviour

motivation

opportunity

social marketing

A full glossary of key term definitions is located at
http://www.sportmarketing.nelson.com.

Internet Resources

Social marketing, Health Canada,
http://www.hc-sc.gc.ca/ahc-asc/activit/marketsoc/index_e.html

Social Marketing Institute, http://www.social-marketing.org/

Sport Matters Group, http://sportmatters.ca/Content/home.asp

Social marketing, http://en.wikipedia.org/wiki/Social_marketing

World Anti-Doping Agency, http://www.wada-ama.org/en/

Sport Canada, Investing in sport participation 2004–2008,
http://dsp-psd.pwgsc.gc.ca/Collection/CH24-16-2004E.pdf

Sport Canada, Implications for future action,
http://www.pch.gc.ca/progs/sc/pubs/socio-eco/10_e.cfm

Social marketing in health promotion...The Canadian experience,
http://www.hc-sc.gc.ca/ahc-asc/alt_formats/cmcd-dcmc/pdf/marketsoc/
experience_e.pdf

The Sport We Want Symposium,
http://www.cces.ca/pdfs/CCES-REPORT-TSWWRegCon-E.pdf

VERB—A social marketing campaign to increase physical activity among
youth, http://www.cdc.gov/PCD/issues/2004/jul/04_0043.htm

Right to Play, http://www.righttoplay.com

Calgary civic sport policy strategic plan,
http://www.calgarysportcouncil.com/pdf%20folder/
CSPStrategicPlan16082006.pdf

Chapter 16

Sport Marketing Strategy Implementation and Evaluation

Source: supplied by the author, Norm O'Reilly

Learning Objectives

- To know the key steps in turning the marketing mix into marketing action
- To articulate how managers and marketers in sport organizations allocate their resources
- To understand that strategy needs a plan to implement it
- To explain how a marketing program is evaluated by using such metrics as sales date, profitability analyses, return on investment, and return on objectives
- To adapt the example of scouting as the product to other sport products

Introduction

There is no room on the shelf for another strategy!

This chapter represents the final, and most important, step in the strategic marketing process—putting your research, creativity, and strategy into action. Initially, this sounds like an exciting step and one that most sport organizations would be willing to embark on immediately. However, this is often not the case: Many strategies, white papers, and planning documents collect dust on the shelves with no money or work allocated to make them reality.

Taking strategy to action involves three general steps, the three key components of this chapter: developing the strategy into resourced action (allocating resources to the proposed strategy), implementing the strategy (e.g., who, when, how, resources), and evaluating the effectiveness of that strategy to determine future action. This chapter reviews each step and presents possible tactics.

Marketing Strategy Implementation in Sport

An Introduction to Implementation

implementation: operational excellence, activation, or marketing action, the act of putting a developed strategy in place.

Whether termed **implementation**, operational excellence, activation, or marketing action, the act of putting a developed strategy in place is important to any business including sport. At its roots, implementation involves the allocation of resources, both human and financial, to a developed strategy.

Stotlar[1] points out that the effort of all human resources assigned to the effort—the team—is vital to the successful implementation of any marketing strategy. Quite simply, coordinated action across the entire organization is necessary for implementing both efficiently and effectively. Certain skills are required within the team, so recruiting and involving particular individuals are crucial. For example, if television is an element of the marketing plan for the Canadian Diving Championships finals of the women's three-metre springboard competition, expertise in television production is required. Similarly, the activation of an in-stadium T-shirt giveaway at a Toronto Blue Jays home game requires a large number of trained, part-time staff who are energetic, safe, and engaging with children.

Budget realities are equally important to implementation and affect the human resources involved as a function of salary, incentives, or bonuses. Sport organizations struggle to allocate resources to implementation, a difficult process: A poor forecast of resources required during the development stage of a strategy will often lead to a failed implementation. In an attempt to overcome this challenge, sport marketers use several budget techniques[2], including maximum allocation (aggressively supporting the implementation with as many financial resources as possible), percentage of revenue allocation (forecasting potential sales, then using actual sales, to determine budget based on a preset number, say 10%), objective based (allocating budget to each objective of the sponsorship based on its importance and priority), and fixed budget (using an amount based on past budgeting in similar activities). No one tactic is preferable over the others: The budget for implementation should ideally be based on an assessment of the amount required to achieve the objectives of the marketing activity.

---

[1] Stotlar, D. (2001) *Developing Successful Sport Marketing Plans.* Fitness Information Technology.

[2] Stevens, R.E., D.L. Loudan, W.E. Warren, & B. Wrenn (1997) *Market Planning Guide.* Haworth Press.

Marketing Strategy Implementation Defined

Marketing strategy implementation is the process that turns marketing plans into actions and ensures that such actions are executed in a manner that accomplishes the plan's stated objectives[3]. Since an excellent and well-planned marketing strategy is worthless if not implemented properly, marketing scholars[4] have suggested guidelines for successful marketing strategy implementation:

- Ensure that marketing objectives and schedules are clearly understood, accepted across the organization, fair and attainable, and measurable.
- Develop a reward system that recognizes those who successfully perform their implementation duties.
- Develop a project calendar that outlines clearly these three items for each specific action:

  > task to be accomplished;
  > name of the person(s) responsible for completing the task;
  > date(s) by which by the task must be completed.

- Develop systems to avoid "paralysis by analysis"[5] so that analysis is sufficient but not excessive. This will ensure that resources are balanced between strategy development and strategy implementation, and that decisions are made promptly.
- Include a communications plan to encourage open dialogue around issues or problems that may arise in implementation. A suggested course of action to marketers includes these actions:

  > Develop an open system of problem identification, where:
  >
  > - problems are identified and communicated quickly;
  > - individuals feel comfortable and safe in bringing forth such issues;
  > - anonymity is offered;
  > - solutions are developed efficiently and ethically.

  > Provide and communicate resources available to help with problems or issues including mentors, coaches, and resource people.

  > Foster the development of an environment of problem solving, rather than one that seeks to attribute blame.

Activities of Marketing Strategy Implementation

According to Sommers[6], marketing strategy implementation typically includes three activity areas. First, the organization must be staffed with people with the needed skills, competencies, dedication, work ethic, motivation, and

---

[3] Goetsch, H.W. (1993) *Developing, Implementing and Managing and Effective Marketing Plan.* American Marketing Association NTC Business Books.

[4] Crane, F.G. (2006) *Marketing,* 6th Cdn ed. McGraw-Hill Ryerson.

[5] Crane, F.G. (2006) *Marketing.*

[6] Sommers, M.S. (1998) *Fundamentals of Marketing,* 8th Cdn ed. McGraw-Hill Ryerson.

knowledge. They will form the team or group that will be the 'implementers' of the given marketing strategy. If the team lacks any of the required skills or abilities, the likelihood of successful implementation decreases significantly. Second, management will determine who from the team compiled in the first step will be allocated to which roles in implementing the marketing effort. Here, the relationship between the organization's functional divisions (e.g., marketing, accounting, human resources) and any cross-functional teams will be defined. Third, management will direct the execution of the implementation by communicating, delegating, and motivating the implementers by defining and allocating tasks, setting deadlines, and allocating the necessary resources.

Tools for Activity Scheduling

Activity scheduling is a method most organizations use to effectively organize tasks, set time lines, and allocate resources. The wide array of tools available in the marketing literature include Gantt charts, project calendars, operational plans, the program evaluation review technique (PERT), and the critical path method (CPM). The last two methods use critical path analysis to define the order of tasks in the most efficient way to support implementation.

Although we present only two methods here, we encourage you to learn more about the others. The project calendar tool is easy to use and adaptable for many implementation situations. The PERT is an example of a critical path method that is more sophisticated and therefore suitable for larger and more complex marketing situations.

A project calendar can be created with any calendar software on a desktop computer, laptop, or a PDA. It can also be developed with a hard-copy calendar or spreadsheet. Whatever the recording mechanism, the content of the calendar involves four things: identification of all tasks required to implement the marketing strategy, timing and order of these tasks, estimation of the time required to complete each task, and recognition of tasks that can be performed simultaneously and those that cannot. The PERT involves multiple stages. Anderson and colleagues outline a nine-step approach:

1. Develop a list of activities that make up the project.
2. Determine the immediate predecessor(s) for each activity in the project.
3. Estimate the completion time for each activity.
4. Draw a project network depicting the activities and immediate predecessors listed in steps 1 and 2.
5. Use the project network and the activity time estimates to determine the earliest start and earliest finish time for each activity by making a forward pass through the network. The earliest finish time for the last activity in the project identifies the total time required to finish the project.
6. Use the project completion time identified in step 5 as the latest finish time for the last activity and make a backward pass through the network to identify the latest start and latest finish for each activity.

7. Use the difference between the latest start time and the earliest start time for each activity and determine the slack for each activity.
8. Find the activities with zero slack; these are critical activities.
9. Use the information from steps 5 and 6 to develop the activity schedule for the project[7].

EXECUTIVE PERSPECTIVE

Gavin Roth, Senior Director, Partnerships

Marketing through Partnerships

Take a moment to flash back to December 2005. Imagine an awards banquet in downtown Toronto where the Canadian Football League (CFL) is being recognized as one of the marketers that matter by *Marketing Magazine*. It was an honour for the CFL to be nominated alongside Coca-Cola, WestJet, Procter & Gamble, and Cold-fX. We joked at our table that those brands spent more in a week on external brand marketing than we do in a year.

So, why were we receiving this honour? Was it our record ratings and attendance? Sure. Our own promotional TV spots on TSN and CBC and in CanWest newspapers across the country played a role too. But much more than that, it was our surging profile in the media and our feature position in promotional campaigns and various retail environments across Canada—the support and activation programs of our corporate partners.

Let me give you a few examples from that time:

• Purolator was garnering national broadcast and print press for its Tackle Hunger program, whereby every time a CFL quarterback was sacked, his weight in food was donated to local food banks.

• Frito-Lay was running the Fritos Fandemonium promotion, a program that used national TV spots and millions of bags of chips in retail channels to search for the number 1 fan in each CFL market and reward them with a VIP experience at Grey Cup.

• Scotiabank had created four commercials, one of which was an award-winning spot, and aired them on CBC. The spots creatively demonstrated how

Scotiabank employees were fans of the CFL.

• Crown Royal ran a national key account program in support of its web-based fan poll to vote for the greatest play in Grey Cup history.

Fantastic support and enhanced marketing muscle, to be sure. But this also presented a challenge that's not uncommon for sports properties: When you rely on others to market your brand, you don't fully control the message. With scarce internal marketing funds, we needed to refine our approach to partnership marketing to ensure our brand message was being carried forward. Looking back, here are the steps we took:

• To begin, we targeted partners who aligned with our values, goals, and brand image. Here, you need to balance the essence of your property's brand with the acquired brand equity of your partners, sort of like the old saying: "If you're not happy with yourself, you're probably not ready for a relationship."

• We targeted partners who were not only interested in investing in rights fees, but who also wanted to activate our brand. Why buy a beautiful new car only to keep it in the garage under a tarp? Take it out for a spin. Show it off. Get some enjoyment out of it.

• We established goals for the partnership up front, well before committing to the partnership. Very importantly, we worked with our partners to develop goals for both sides. This process included identifying common and distinct objectives at all

---

[7] Anderson, D.R., D.J. Sweeney, & T.A. Williams (2005) *An Introduction to Management Science: Quantitative Approaches to Decision Making*, 11th ed. Thomson South-Western: 466–7.

levels (e.g., human resources, sales, B2B, trade partners) since it is not uncommon for the property to just accept the sponsor's goals without sharing their own. Note that sponsors generally want to help the property achieve its goals as well.

- We insisted on being a part of the activation planning process—the brainstorm sessions and the plan development. Properties often hand over the rights to a partner and let them develop their own game plan in isolation, which is not ideal. Better plans materialize from a collaborative approach to the process.
- Finally, we reviewed all creative before it went to production. This ensured our marks were being used properly and that our brand was reflected in a positive manner.

In early 2007, our commissioner, Mark Cohon, led us through an exercise to define who we want to be—what our brand stands for and should embody. From that foundation, core initiatives emerged that projected those values (e.g., development of a central league 'cause' built around improving the health and wellness of Canadian families and kids). These types of meaningful initiatives made like-minded marketers stand up and say: "Hey, I want to be a part of that." And this led to brand and revenue growth.

Back to that event in December of 2005.... Did we win the marketer of the year award? Regrettably, no. That honour went to a very deserving Cold-fX. However, this was truly one of those cases where being nominated was more than sufficient.

About the Canadian Football League

Building on a strong past toward a stronger future, the CFL celebrates the best of Canada's game with fans across the nation. The 96th Grey Cup will be played in Montreal on November 23, 2008. For additional information, visit http://www.cfl.ca.

Gavin joined the CFL in 2004 and soon assumed leadership of the partnership team, helping to grow the business to record levels via new innovative partnerships. Before joining the CFL, Gavin spent five years with World Wrestling Entertainment in a variety of senior marketing and sales positions.

Marketing Strategy Evaluation

An Introduction to Evaluation

Once the implementation of a marketing strategy has begun, the evaluation of that implementation should already be well under way[8]. Although the importance of evaluation is well known to researchers and practitioners in marketing, it is also considered one of the most difficult tasks to accomplish[9]. McDaniel and Kinney[10] strongly critiqued marketers for not tracking their promotions, while Berrett and Slack[11] found that most Canadian companies in their study had no clear idea of the benefits they received from sponsorship and that most evaluations were relatively informal and fairly infrequent.

[8] Sommers, M.S. (1998) *Fundamentals of Marketing: 570–2.*

[9] Harvey, B. (2001) Measuring the effects of sponsorships. *Journal of Advertising Research,* 41(Jan–Feb): 59–65.

[10] McDaniel, S.R. & L. Kinney (1998) The implications of recency and gender effects on consumer response to ambush marketing. *Psychology & Marketing, 15(4): 385–403.*

[11] Berrett, T. & T. Slack (1995) *Approaches to Corporate Sponsorship in Canada's National Sport Organizations.* A report submitted to Sport Canada. Faculty of Physical Education and Recreation, University of Alberta.

Others[12] have pointed out that those who do evaluate often use only such ad hoc procedures as media impressions, television ratings, and print coverage, which do not necessarily capture the true objectives (e.g., sales, intent to purchase, brand repositioning). In turn, the calls from organizations for viable tools for measuring marketing effectiveness have increased[13].

Evaluation, sometimes referred to as **control**, involves examining feedback from target market reactions to the marketing mix and then fine-tuning the mix based on the feedback. The benefits of a properly planned and implemented evaluation are clear. The results will show what factors are contributing to the success or failure of the overall marketing strategy and provide direction for future marketing activities. To successfully evaluate a marketing strategy, the marketer must assess all factors that influence the reaction of targets (e.g., customers, employees, potential customers, partners): Did sales or intent to purchase increase? How did employees respond to an internal marketing program? Did the organization meet customer expectations? How did it respond to customer complaints? How did it analyze customer feedback? How did it manage relationships with its customers.

control: feedback loop to test the effectiveness of marketing programs.

Measures of Evaluation

Several studies have identified different methods for evaluating marketing activity. From surveys of customer or employee satisfaction to analysis of sales figures and the opinion of experts, these are applicable to a broad range of marketing objectives which might need to be evaluated. Canadian researchers Thwaites and colleagues[14] studied objectives in sport marketing and assessed the extent to which selected Canadian organizations adopted the prescriptions for effective sport marketing identified in the literature. They found that 82 percent of companies set specific objectives; however, only 69 percent sought to formulate objectives in a quantifiable manner.

Methods of evaluating marketing activity include brand recall levels, image transfer, image enhancement, relationship building through hospitality, awareness improvement, media equivalency, sales, purchase intention, location dependency[15] (or the geographical location of the venue or facility where the sponsored property is held), consumer loyalty, employee satisfaction, media exposure, prompting product trials, repeat purchase, donations encouraged, inquiries generated, ability to reach specific target market(s), altering public perception, blocking competition, and increasing general public awareness of the sponsor. Sometimes, developing a measurement metric is difficult. For example, the link between sponsorship and long-term sales is difficult to measure; however, consumer attitudes can be gauged more easily[16].

---

[12] Marshall, D. & G. Cook (1992) The corporate sports sponsor. *International Journal of Advertising*, 11: 307–24.

[13] Milne, G.R. & M.A. McDonald (1999) *Sport Marketing: Managing the Exchange Process.* Jones and Bartlett.

[14] Thwaites, D., R. Aguilar-Manjarrez, & C. Kidd (1998) Sports sponsorship development in Canadian companies: Issues and trends. *International Journal of Advertising*, 17: 29–49.

[15] Westerbeek, H.M. & A. Smith (2002) Location dependency and sport sponsors: A factor analytic study. *Sport Marketing Quarterly*, 11(3): 140–50.

[16] Nicholls, J.A.F., S. Roslow & S. Dublish (1999) Brand recall and brand preference at sponsored golf and tennis tournaments. *European Journal of Marketing*, 33(3/4): 365–86.

Case: Marketing Strategy Implementation and the Toronto Blue Jays Scouting Department

Introduction

Major League Baseball (MLB) is one of the most established and followed professional sport leagues in the world. *Forbes* currently values its top franchise, the New York Yankees, at well over US$1 billion, and its annual TV contracts bring billions to the league. Founded in 1977, the Toronto Blue Jays became the only Canadian franchise in MLB following the relocation of the Montreal Expos to Washington in 2004. *Forbes* values the Toronto franchise at US$344 million.

Of all the professional sport leagues in North America, MLB takes the most 'open-market' approach to its business. Thus, the amount of money available to spend on players is an important driver to team personnel. The Blue Jays opening-day team payroll increased from $46 million in 2005 to $72 million in 2006, which moved them from twenty-fifth place in team payroll to sixteenth. A further increase to $90 million was implemented for the 2007 season. These payroll increases allow the Blue Jays to pursue star free agents and high-profile prospects in the amateur draft. However, as the Blue Jays director of scouting, Jon Lalonde, points out, salary is not the only driver attracting players to the team. Players consider a variety of other factors when deciding where to play and what type of contract (e.g., length, trade clauses, salary) to sign. In this regard, Lalonde points out that the Blue Jays understands that it has three target markets of potential players to market itself to: draft picks, free agents, and current players. With respect to its current players, the Blue Jays seek to keep them satisfied and happy to increase the chances that they will re-sign with the team in the future, while strategies around draft picks and free agents are more about attracting players to the team and are the focus of this case. It is here where the Blue Jays scouting department takes on a major role.

Scouting in Major League Baseball Is a $45 million Industry

Scouting can be defined as the identification and acquisition of talent. When deciding which players to select to become part of their team, professional sports teams use scouting as a form of talent identification. The scouting process involves observing players during games and then filing scouting reports on each player's strengths and weaknesses. These reports are sent to team management, which then uses them for player evaluation.

Each MLB team employs about 27 full-time and 8 part-time baseball scouts. The full-time scouts work as area scouts, cross checkers, or pro scouts. Area scouts, assigned to a specific geographic area, are responsible for scouting all of the draft-eligible high-school, junior college, and college players in their region. The average number of area scouts for each MLB team is 15. Cross checkers are scouts who are not assigned to a geographic area but who view certain players that the team has targeted. Each team employs an average of four cross checkers. Professional scouts evaluate major and minor league baseball players so that management of the team has information on players who are offered in trades or are available via free agency. The average number of professional scouts for each MLB team is eight. Both area scouts and cross checkers receive an average annual salary of US$44 275; the average annual salary for a pro scout is US$83 630.

The Toronto Blue Jays amateur scouts file reports on about 600 prospects a year; the professional scouts report on the vast majority (about 98%) of the nearly 8000 minor league players and the 1200 major league players. These reports are continually updated to give the team the most recent information possible to support player personnel decisions. After an area scout has completed a scouting report, the information from that report is entered into the team's database on all players. A cross checker then reviews the player to provide the scouting department with a "second set of eyes" to reduce error.

Marketing the Toronto Blue Jays to Draft Picks

MLB consists of 30 teams in major metropolitan areas throughout North America. Since 1965, the first-year player draft has been held annually in June. During the draft, teams take turns selecting amateur players from the US, Canada, and Puerto Rico. Under the current format, the draft consists of 50 rounds. The order for the draft selections is based on the team's win–loss record from the previous season, with the team with the fewest number of wins having the first selection. Before each draft, all of the amateur scouts get together with team management and rank all the players for the upcoming draft. The list is then used as a guideline when deciding which players to select (and at what time) during the draft.

If the Blue Jays are interested in drafting a player, an area scout will meet with that player and his family before the draft since many families have a major influence on where their son will play professional baseball and the route they will take. Families want reassurance from the team that it will look after the player, providing a safe place to live, an environment with positive surrounding influences, supportive coaching, and sometimes a mentorship program. The size of a player's signing bonus and the availability of the MLB scholarship program are also key considerations. The scout is looking at the player's personality, his compatibility with the team, his likely attitude in the clubhouse, and his salary demands.

Deciding which players to draft is a very important decision for the Blue Jays, with expensive and long-term financial consequences. Luke Hochevar, the top pick in the 2006 amateur draft, received a four-year contract worth a guaranteed $5.25 million, before even playing one inning in the major leagues. Note that only 8 percent of all players drafted in the first 10 rounds of the draft go on to play in the MLB.

Just because the team has drafted a player, this does not mean that he will necessarily begin his career with the Blue Jays. After a player is selected, the team has 15 days to offer a minor league contract, or else the player can become a free agent. In 1996, four first-round picks became free agents after the teams that drafted them missed the 15-day deadline. All four players received substantial contracts on the open market. The largest of these contracts went to pitcher Matt White who received a $10.2 million contract from the Tampa Bay Devil Rays after being selected seventh overall by the San Francisco Giants. If a minor league contract is offered, the team holds exclusive negotiation rights for that player up until a week before next year's draft. A player who is drafted and does not sign with the club that selected him is open for selection by any franchise at a future year's draft, as long as he is eligible for that year's draft. A club may not select a player again in a subsequent year unless he has consented to the reselection.

After signing their first professional contract, first-year players are given an information booklet by the Blue Jays. This booklet contains information on the team's minor league affiliates and on other minor league personnel, as well as the guidelines and procedures for minicamp.

Marketing the Toronto Blue Jays to Free Agents

The second group of players that the Blue Jays market themselves toward are free agents. Pro scouts spend significant time and energy scouting players on other MLB teams who are in the final years of their contracts. They report to management so they can consider action about the future free agents.

Any player with six or more years in the major leagues is eligible to become a free agent at the conclusion of the final year of his contract. Free agents can then sign with any MLB team that offers him a contract. The criteria a player uses when deciding which team to sign with may include financial compensation, contract length, proximity of the city to his family, recent team success, likability of the coaching staff, and opportunity for increased playing time.

In the off-season, if the Blue Jays wants to sign a particular free agent, the general manager contacts the representative or agent for the player and lets the agent know that the team is interested in gaining the player's services. In some cases, the player visits Toronto and receives an information package about Toronto and the Blue Jays organization—information the player and his family may not have known but which may help persuade him to sign a contract with the team.

Being the only MLB team outside of the US, the Blue Jays are in a unique situation. Many American-born players do not want to live in Canada for such reasons as patriotism, income taxes, and climate. To combat this, the Blue Jays strive to treat its players well and to employ knowledgeable, talented, and hardworking baseball people. The Blue Jays believe that this will attract players to come play on the team because it is a well run and successful organization.

Marketing Strategy Implementation and Scouting

MLB players come from a variety of social, economic, and geographic backgrounds. The one trait they all possess is the talent to play baseball at a high level. The Blue Jays marketing plan must meet the needs of this diverse group to have all major league players want to play in Toronto and view the Blue Jays as a successful organization with a strong chance of winning the World Series. Further, with $45 million invested in scouting salaries and the average annual MLB player salary nearing $2.5 million[17], teams must make sure that their marketing strategy is implemented in a way to mitigate financial risk.

Target markets: The Toronto Blue Jays scouting department is attempting to reach two target markets in player personnel: prospects who will develop into talented major league players and talented MLB-calibre free agents. In both cases, MLB teams all have different lists of players they are seeking. Lalonde identifies four main factors why a MLB team would exclude a player from its choice set: talent, mental makeup, signability, and position.

Talent: One of the key success factors of MLB teams is having a roster full of highly skilled players—the more talent a team has, the more likely it is to win. Therefore, one could assume that all MLB managers desire to have talented players on their roster to be successful on the field. Similarly, general managers are expected to work toward continuously acquiring players they deem to be highly talented, while disposing of players they believe are less talented, either through trade, waivers, or the outright release of the player.

Mental makeup: Teams often remove a player from their target market if the player is deemed to have "bad makeup." Bad makeup typically includes mental disorders, social problems, personality disorders, or a criminal record. Teams will avoid players with bad makeup due to the distractions and negative publicity associated with having those types of players on the team[18].

Signability: A player's signability refers to his financial expectations in negotiating a contract. Some teams will refuse to draft a player they deem to be unsignable, even if they believe him to be the best available prospect when it is their turn to pick[19]. Teams will not contact the representatives for a free agent whose contract demands do not fit within their payroll budget. Teams will also attempt to trade away their own players whose contracts expire at the end of the season, so they can receive players back in exchange for them rather than compensatory draft picks for losing the players to free agency.

Position: A certain player may be excluded from a team's target market due to a lack of need for a player at that position. For instance, a team with a star second baseman will not pursue a free agent second baseman who becomes available. In a case like this, the team's resources (payroll budget) may be better used in acquiring a player at a different position to fill a current weakness on the team.

---

[17] mlbplayers.com (2005) MBLPA Info. Retrieved December 5, 2006 from http://mlbplayers.mlb.com/NASApp/mlb/pa/info/faq.jsp

[18] Lewis, M. (2003) *Moneyball.* W.W. Norton.

[19] ibid.

Draft Strategy of MLB Teams

Typically, MLB teams have adopted the strategy of drafting the best available amateur player regardless of position. The reasoning for this is that newly drafted amateur players must develop their skills in the minor leagues before they are ready to be an everyday player in the major leagues. For first-round draft picks, the average number of years spent in the minor leagues are[20]:

- Regular player: 3.13 years
- Good player: 2.88 years
- Star player: 2.22 years

Since 1965, only 20 players have advanced directly to the major leagues without playing in the minors[21]. Due to the continuous change among major league rosters from year to year, MLB teams do not draft by positional need since their needs may be much different by the time the player drafted reaches the major leagues.

Case Questions

1. Apply the 4 Ps to how the Blue Jays markets itself to players.
2. What kind of (a) activity schedule and (b) evaluation plan would you recommend to Jon Lalonde?
3. How would using a PERT or CPM model have helped the San Francisco Giants following 1996 draft?
4. What group of major league players does the Blue Jays have a competitive advantage in attracting?
5. How should a MLB team position itself in the minds of the target market (prospect or free agent)?
6. Using the marketing strategy implementation guidelines in the chapter, outline how the Blue Jays should implement its marketing strategy for scouting.
7. In considering its marketing implementation activities, what must Lalonde do to:

   a. ensure the necessary skill-sets are available at his department?
   b. organize his implementers in the marketing efforts?
   c. direct the execution of the marketing strategy?

---

[20] Burge, J.D., R.D. Grayson, & S.J.K. Walters (2006) *Initial Public Offerings of Ballplayers. International Association of Sports Economists. Working paper series, paper no. 06-24: 31.*

[21] mlb.com (2006) Straight to the majors. Retrieved December 6, 2006 from http://mlb.mlb.com/NASApp/ mlb/mlb/history/draft/index.jsp?feature=straight.

Chapter Summary

The process of implementing and evaluating the implementation of a marketing strategy is vital to a sport organization. Based on the principles of performance and feedback, these processes are actions that must not be neglected by marketers; however, they often are. This chapter provided content, direction, and tools for implementing and evaluating marketing action. It should be clear that no marketing action is implemented without a detailed plan, which includes tasks, human resources, financial recourse, time, and evaluation, the last occurring at all stages.

Test Your Knowledge

1. Define scouting.
2. Describe the marketing implementation strategic process.
3. Name the three types of full-time baseball scouts.
4. How big (in terms of dollars) is the scouting industry in Major League Baseball?
5. Define marketing strategy implementation.
6. What three elements should specific implementation actions include?
7. What three guidelines does marketing strategy implementation encompass?
8. What two critical path analysis methods are used for activity scheduling?
9. When should evaluation of the marketing strategy start?

For more review questions, go to http://www.sportmarketing.nelson.com.

Key Terms

control   implementation

A full glossary of key term definitions is located at
http://www.sportmarketing.nelson.com.

Internet Resources

Toronto Blue Jays,
http://toronto.bluejays.mlb.com/NASApp/mlb/index.jsp?c_id=tor

CFL, http://www.cfl.ca/

MLB Scouting Bureau,
http://mlb.mlb.com/NASApp/mlb/mlb/official_info/about_mlb/scouting_
overview.jsp

Nation branding and place marketing,
http://samvak.tripod.com/nationbranding7.html

The Economist, http://www.economist.com/index.html

Evaluation of the school sport sponsorship programme,
http://www.lboro.ac.uk/departments/sses/institutes/iys/pages/School%20
Sport%20Part%20pdfs/SchSportPartReport2005pdf/
Partnership%20D05.pdf

Canadian strategy for ethical conduct in sport: Action plan,
http://www.truesportpur.ca/files/Secretariat/Documents/GOC-Policy-
EthicsStrategyActionPlan-E.pdf

The Canadian sport policy,
http://www.pch.gc.ca/progs/sc/pol/pcs-csp/action/action_e.pdf

Vancouver city council: Implementation plan for Olympic legacy,
http://vancouver.ca/ctyclerk/cclerk/20031021/a5.htm

Development of PEI sports strategy,
http://www.gov.pe.ca/photos/original/cca_sportstrate.pdf

Pan Territorial sports strategy, http://www.maca.gov.nt.ca/sport/sport_
and_rec/PanTerritorialStatusReportJune2005.pdfbroken link

Chapter 17

Olympic Marketing

Source: CP Photo / Chuck Stoody

Learning Objectives

- To appreciate the history of Olympic marketing
- To understand the place of television in the Olympic Movement
- To understand the sponsorship (TOP) program and its significance for the Olympic Movement
- To understand the role of branding in the Olympic Movement
- To learn the structure of the Olympic Movement in Canada
- To appreciate the gigantism of hosting the Olympic Games and its impact on Canadian sport—VANOC 2010

Introduction

Olympics are big business

The Olympic Games have become a global icon of sport. Held every two years—alternating the Olympic Games and the Olympic Winter Games—this multisport spectacle draws thousands of the world's best athletes, millions of attending fans and tourists, and billions of television viewers worldwide. It has evolved into a big business. This chapter provides a historical perspective of the development of the Olympics including the role of marketing (television and sponsorship), key events that have had an impact on the **Olympic Movement**, and its state going into the 2010 Olympic Winter Games in Vancouver.

Olympic Movement:
an umbrella term that includes all entities who are involved with the Movement (e.g., athletes, coaches, administrators, fans, owners).

David Bedford, Canadian Olympic Committee

Canada has provided the Olympic Movement with many rich, tumultuous moments since the modern Olympic Games were started in 1894 by Baron Pierre de Coubertin. In fact, it is safe to say that, based on its small size among the world's countries (number 36 in population), Canada has had a disproportionate impact on the Olympic Movement. Some of these moments have been triumphant; some are iconic images of sport gone awry. One thing is sure, however, and that is the Olympic Games would never have been the same without Canada, and Canada would not be the same country without the Games.

When the 2010 Vancouver Olympic Winter Games are completed, Canada will have been host to three Olympic Games: The 1976 Montreal Games and the 1988 Calgary Winter Games round out the triumvirate. Only two countries have had more Olympic Games on their soil, the United States with six and France with five (Germany, Italy, and Japan have each had three).

When Montreal hosted the 1976 Olympic Games, the Movement was desperately short on cash and exceptionally long on excesses. The Montreal Games suffered many of the afflictions that were common to the Olympic Movement during that era, including building of extravagant facilities meant to eclipse those of any preceding Games. Political intrigue reared its head as well, as Montreal 1976 was the first Games to suffer a boycott (many African nations boycotted in protest over apartheid in South Africa). And yet, when the Montreal Olympic Games were all over, they not only proved to be a shining success on the field of play, but also provided a legacy for Olympic sport in Canada that survives to this day. Many of the venues built for the Montreal Games are still in use (e.g., Olympic Pool, Claude Robillard Centre) as high-performance training grounds for today's generation of Olympic hopefuls.

After the boycott of the 1980 Moscow Games (many nations, including Canada and US, boycotted in protest of the Soviet Union's occupation of Afghanistan) and the rampant commercial success of the 1984 Los Angeles Games, the International Olympic Committee (IOC) realized that they had to put the Olympic Movement on much more sound financial footings. President Juan Antonio Samaranch listened closely to the commercial partners of the Olympic Movement. Knowing that the future of the Olympic Games rested on financial stability, he created the New Sources of Finance Commission. Samaranch asked Canadian IOC member Richard Pound to lead the charge to find new sources of financing for the Olympic Movement. Pound helped create, and launch, the TOP sponsorship program, which is still the cornerstone of IOC revenue.

The year 1988 illustrated the best, and worst, of Olympism to Canadians. In February 1988, the Olympic torch was lit in McMahon Stadium, signifying the start of the magical Calgary Olympic Winter Games. The Calgary Games were the first to reap the benefits of the TOP sponsorship program, and what a benefit it was to Canadian sport. Its share of profits from the Calgary Games is still fuelling the Canadian Olympic Committee (COC). Just as important, a share of those same profits has been keeping Canada Olympic Park and many of the 1988 Olympic venues producing Olympic champions ever since. Unfortunately, 1988 also saw Ben Johnson stripped of his 100-metre gold medal for doping (Seoul, Korea). The national embarrassment Canada felt has also led to good, however, as the world sat up and took heed of the call to fight doping in sport, with Canada at the forefront of that movement. The IOC created the World Anti-Doping Association (WADA), installed Dick Pound as the leader of this important fight, and named Montreal as its headquarters.

Controversy was never far from the Canadians after Ben Johnson's downfall in Seoul. In 1992, Sylvie Frechette was denied a 1992 Barcelona Games gold medal in synchronized swimming by a judging mistake, only to be awarded her gold medal a number of years later. In 1998, Ross Rebagliati won the gold medal in snowboard but, testing positive for marijuana, had his medal removed. Upon appeal, Rebagliati's medal was reinstated as marijuana was not on the IOC list of performance-enhancing substances. In 2002, figure skaters Jamie Sale and David Pelletier were victims of a judging scandal that saw them placed second in the pairs competition. Fortunately, the scandal was uncovered, and Sale and Pelletier were rightfully awarded the gold medal they had earned. Also at the 2002 Salt Lake City Games, Beckie Scott became the first Canadian cross-country skier to win a medal, a bronze. After the gold and silver medal competitors tested positive for doping infractions and a long fight by Beckie and the COC, the IOC awarded Beckie with the gold medal she had rightfully won.

Triumphs for the ages, however, have far outstripped the controversies: Barbara Ann Scott's figure skating gold in 1948 (St. Moritz); Nancy Greene winning gold and silver in skiing in 1968 (Grenoble); Gaetan Boucher's four Olympic medals (a silver in 1980 at Lake Placid and two gold and a bronze in 1984 in Sarajevo); Mark Tewksbury's race of a lifetime to swimming gold in 1992 (Barcelona); Marnie McBean and Kathleen Heddle taking gold in rowing pairs in 1992 and 1996 (Atlanta); Donovan Bailey becoming the world's fastest man in the 100 metre in 1996 (Atlanta); Marc Gagnon winning five Olympic medals in short track speed skating over three Winter Games in 1994 (Lillehammer), 1998 (Nagano), and 2002 (Salt Lake City); and most recently, Cindy Klassen being named the "Queen of the 2006 Torino Games" by IOC President Jacques Rogge for her five medals.

As you can see, Canada's history in the Olympic Movement is chock full of suspense and political intrigue, disappointment and excitement. Canada has contributed to the greatest show on earth as a wonderful host, as an exciting competitor, and even as a tremendous builder of the Olympic Movement. Vancouver 2010 will undoubtedly add another stirring chapter to the story that unfolds of Canada and the Olympic Movement.

David Bedford brings over 25 years of sports and entertainment sponsorship and promotional marketing expertise to his role as executive director, marketing and communications for the Canadian Olympic Committee.

History of Olympic Marketing

The Early Years—1896–1932

Baron Pierre de Coubertin's dream of reviving the Olympic Games was to establish a broadly based social movement which, through the medium of sport, would celebrate physical culture and art, promote international understanding, and inspire people to reach higher and farther while growing stronger in mind and body[1]. He was convinced that the Olympic ideal would help promote universal values such as mutual understanding, friendship, and tolerance that, in turn, would contribute to build a better and more peaceful world[2].

Since the revival of the Olympic Games in 1896, the commercialization of the Olympic Movement has led to many strong and heated debates. Yet, this was not a new phenomenon. The ancient Olympic Games, held in the honour of the god Zeus, could not have been celebrated without the financial support from various Greek states and from wealthy Greek men. As far back as

---

[1] Muller, N. (1986) (dir) *Pierre de Coubertin. Textes choisis.* Tome II: *Olympisme.* Weidmann.

[2] ibid.

525 BCE, commemorative medals were sold to finance the Games[3]. This suggests that even in those days, the organizers of the Games were concerned about how they could stage the event.

Like the Greeks of ancient times, de Coubertin was concerned about the cost of hosting the Olympic Games and the source of financing. It should be no surprise to you that marketing would play a vital financial and supporting role in the Olympic Movement from the beginning. The 1896 Athens Games were funded by stamps, ticket sales, commemorative medals, program advertisements, and private donations[4]. The donation by Greek philanthropist George Averoff of $390 000 combined with the issuance by the Greek government of the first series of commemorative stamps of the Olympic Games to provide the funds necessary for the success of the Games[5]. The American firm Kodak, one of the current worldwide partners of the Olympic Movement, was already among the advertisers in the official Olympic program of the 1896 Games. The Games of 1900, 1904, and 1908 were closely connected with international trade. The 1900 Olympic Games in Paris were conducted within the program of the International Universal Exposition in Paris, whose central objective was the promotion of industry and trade. Its financing was assured mainly by the French state through global subsidies granted by the Ministry of Commerce and Industry[6]. The 1904 Olympic Games in St. Louis were held adjacent to the St. Louis World's Fair. The 1908 London Olympic Games were linked with the Anglo-French exhibition, which covered all capital costs of the Games—£60 000, or 75 percent of their total costs[7].

Financing the Olympic Games continued to be a challenge through the years. Since no standard provision was made in the development of the Olympic charter for raising these funds[8], the responsibility was left up to each organizing committee. The 1912 Stockholm Games were a milestone as they marked the beginning of true marketing in the Olympic Movement. The Games were a financial success[9]. It was reported that the direct contributions from the states and the city of Stockholm accounted for only 2.5 percent of the total revenues, while sponsorship contributed twice as much to the revenues of the Organizing Committee for the Olympic Games (OCOG). However, the major part of the revenues (51%) came from the establishment of a lottery

---

3   McMahon, E.A. (1996) The evolution of Olympic commercial partnerships. Olympic Message—Sources of financing sports, 3: 14–18.

4   ibid.

5   Landry, F. & M. Yerlès (1996) *The International Olympic Committee. One Hundred Years. The Idea—The Presidents—The Achievements*. Vol. 3. IOC.

6   ibid.

7   ibid.

8   McMahon, E.A. (1996) The evolution of Olympic commercial partnerships.

9   Landry, F. & M. Yerlès (1996) *The International Olympic Committee*.

managed by the Swedish Central Association for the Promotion of Athletics[10]. De Coubertin was pleased with the Stockholm Games but the financial costs of hosting them continued to concern him[11]:

> Around the Games began a veritable dance of the millions: Imaginary millions and real millions because although the papers sometimes exaggerated or imprecisely quoted the figures that were being handed out, these figures were nevertheless based on one exact datum, i.e. the enormous efforts that governments, municipalities, and sport groups were willing to make to ensure the celebration of the Olympiads.... The question that arises is not whether they will be celebrated, but how and at what cost?

De Coubertin was troubled with the escalating financial consideration of hosting the Games and the potential cost that commercialization could have on the Olympic ideals. He was also concerned about the excessive usage of the title "Olympic Games" in many countries. This led the IOC to protect the title and establish these guidelines in 1913[12]: "the title 'Olympic Games' could only be used in connection with the IOC's Olympic Games and the intermediate Athens Games taking place between the Games of the third and fourth Olympiad."

Inevitably, **commercialism** grew over the years, uncontrollably at times. It was reported that the official program for the 1920 Antwerp Olympic Games was "so cluttered with advertising that the reader had to examine the book very carefully to find information about the Games[13]." Four years later, commercialism hit a milestone at the 1924 Paris Olympics with venue advertising permitted for the first and only time.

commercialism: corporate interests that penetrate the Olympics (e.g., sponsorship, broadcasting, licensing) for commercial purposes.

In the 1928 Amsterdam Games, revenues from ticket sales, rights fees, and various contracts were able to cover over 60 percent of the total costs of the Games[14]. Based on the insight that businesses could use the Olympic rings to increase sales, the first forms of merchandising took place[15]. The many requests received from businesses wishing to associate their products with the Amsterdam Games prompted the organizing committee to have certain names (Olympic Games, 1928 Olympiade) and items (a design of the five intertwined rings) registered and copyrighted by the government authorities to protect and commercially exploit those marks[16].

---

[10] ibid.

[11] ibid.

[12] Martyn, S. (1996) Toward an impasse: An examination of the negotiations behind the inclusion of the United States Olympic Committee in the Olympic Programme. International Centre for Olympic Studies: Third International Symposium for Olympic Research: 107–20. Page 108.

[13] McMahon, E.A. (1996) The evolution of Olympic commercial partnerships.

[14] Landry, F. & M. Yerlès (1996) *The International Olympic Committee.*

[15] Preuss, H. (2000) *Economics of the Olympic Games.* Walla Walla Press.

[16] Landry, F. & M. Yerlès (1996) *The International Olympic Committee.*

During the 1932 Los Angeles Games, the relationship between businesses and the Olympics continued and was largely responsible for the success of the Games[17]. The Olympics became a platform for businessmen, hotels, and travel agencies to boost tourism in the area. Several advertising agencies were contracted by the organizing committee for the right to use Olympic symbols and emblems for a variety of advertising campaigns. However, the word "Olympics" and "Olympiad" continued to be abused by various entities.

Television and Its Impact on Commercialization (1936–1972)

The first live coverage of an Olympic Games for people watching at home was provided by the British broadcaster BBC at the London Games in 1948. Only 80 000 homes in Britain could receive the signal, and the BBC paid about $4000 for the television rights. Although the organizers never cashed the cheque, the concept of television rights was born[18].

In 1956, television executives refused to pay for the rights to telecast what they perceived as news footage on a tape-delayed basis. This resulted in a virtual **blackout**[19]. After Melbourne, the IOC added to its charter a new rule governing publicity. Rule 49 provided strict controls on bona fide news coverage, reading, in part[20]: "The direct, or what is commonly called Live Television Rights, to report the Games, shall be sold by the OCOG, subject to the approval of the IOC, and the proceeds shall be distributed according to its instructions."

This probably paved the way, almost accidentally, for high future payments for the "exclusivity" of rights. When network executives realized that the Olympics attracted great numbers of viewers, they became open to the concept of paying right fees[21]. Television networks were able to charge ever-increasing advertising fees to companies eager to reach a large audience, thus justifying the payment of a **rights fee**. This proved to represent a key turning point as television shifted its coverage of the Olympics from news to entertainment. By the 1960 Squaw Valley Olympic Winter Games and Rome Olympic Games, the principle was established that the Games were entertainment and therefore could be sold.

The emergence of communication satellites is perhaps the most important recent step in the relationship between television and the Olympics. The growth of the television industry internationally had strengthened its ability to act as a global outlet of the Olympic ideal. IOC president Avery Brundage recognized the value of television in promoting and expanding the Olympic Movement worldwide. Prior to the sale of the 1960 Rome television rights, he

blackout: broadcasting restriction imposed by broadcasters, professional sports teams, their leagues, and/or other sport federations (e.g., IOC).

rights fee: amount charged for the rights to exclusively broadcast a given sport property/sponsee.

---

[17] Trumpp, E., 1998. Les enjeux des Jeux: L'impact des Jeux Olympiques de 1932 sur la ville de Los Angeles. In Loudcher, J.-F. & C. Vivier (eds) *Le sport dans la ville*. L'Harmatta: 29–38.

[18] Landry, F. & M. Yerlès (1996) *The International Olympic Committee*.

[19] Wenn, S. (1994) An Olympic squabble: The distribution of Olympic television revenue, 1960–1966. *Olympika*, 3: 27–47.

[20] Schantz, O. (1995) La présidence d'Avery Brundage (1952–1972). In Gafner, R. & N. Muller (eds.) *Un siècle du Comité International Olympique* , Vol. 2. IOC: 72–200.

[21] Slater, J. (1998) Changing partners: The relationship between the mass media and the Olympic Games. International Centre for Olympic Studies: Fourth International Symposium for Olympic Research: 49–68.

said[22]: "Much more is involved than just financial returns. Through television there is a wonderful opportunity to develop public interest in the Olympic Movement along the rights line. We are just as interested in this as we are in the price sale."

However, the IOC did instruct the Squaw Valley and Rome OCOGs to sell the television rights to the Games for the "highest tariff[23]." The revenues from television rights sold by the Rome organizers totaled a record $2 880 000[24]. The Games were shown live in 18 countries throughout Europe. Before satellite communications, which provided live coverage, the drama of events in the Olympic arena could only be shared by those lucky enough to be seated in the Olympic stadium[25]. Others had to wait for the films of the Games shipped by plane. Once available in cinemas, people already knew the results, and the drama were lost[26]. The 1964 Tokyo Games were truly memorable as, for the first time, the Games were transmitted across the world "live." Live transmission created new dynamics, and entertainment became an integral part of the Olympics. Millions of people worldwide could experience the Games and consume the drama as it unfolded from the comfort of their homes. This truly gave the Olympics the status of a "global event."

The rapid evolution of technology helped improve the production and transmission of the Olympics. In the US, the 1960s also brought a fundamental shift in television network policies, when ABC decided to make sports a centrepiece of its programming[27]. This resulted in high-quality sport programming, which in turn offered improved entertainment value to the audience. With fast-growing audiences, television responded by doing the only thing that made sense—televising more.

In fact, the number of countries and the number of hours devoted to Olympic coverage increased with each Olympics. The popularity of the Olympic Games made for strong ratings, which made for top-dollar advertising rates, which in turn made for healthy profits for the networks. The value of acquiring the television rights for ABC was demonstrated in 1968, when it secured $20 million in advertising revenue from corporations such as Coca-Cola, Ford, Texaco, Pan American Airlines, and Goodyear. ABC's acquisition of the US television rights for only $4.5 million was a worthwhile investment[28]. The increased accessibility to real-time sports programming spurred the growing demand for sport, including Olympic sport, on television, and the cost of television rights skyrocketed. In 1972, television rights replaced ticket sales as a principal source of income[29].

---

[22] Wenn, S. (1994) An Olympic squabble.

[23] ibid.

[24] Slater, J. (1998) Changing partners.

[25] Downing, T. (1996) A historical perspective. Olympic Message—The Olympic Movement and the mass media, 1: 26–30.

[26] ibid.

[27] ibid.

[28] Wenn, S. (1995) Growing pains: The Olympic Movement and television, 1966–1972. *Olympika*, 4: 1–22.

[29] ibid.

Since little was known outside the trade about the true value of TV rights, the IOC created the finance commission in 1967. This became closely involved in negotiations for the sales of television rights, consulting with numerous executives from media and entertainment sectors to increase the IOC's knowledge of the value of television rights and the negotiation process[30]. The finance commission pursued a policy of "maximum profit" in negotiating with the television networks.

This enabled the IOC to drive up the prices for the rights to televise the Olympic Games. However, Brundage was concerned about the loss of autonomy due to the increased influence exerted by economic (e.g., television, advertisers) and political interests. His strong opposition to the commercialization and the professionalization of the Olympic Games led to a struggle between those defending the traditional Olympic ideology and those adapting to the reality of marketing and sponsorship in the Olympic world itself. Brundage's efforts to achieve two divergent aims—the pursuit of commercial television revenue for the IOC and its affiliated organizations and the preservation of the IOC's image—made for some interesting debates during the 1960s. Money was a dominant topic of discussion in the Olympic Movement. The troubled Brundage questioned the commitment of the international federations (IF) and National Olympic Committee (NOC) to amateur sport and to the Olympic ideals. To him, they seemed more interested in pursuing a sizable share of Olympic television money. The IFs, in Brundage's mind, had adopted a disgraceful profit-making stance with respect to television revenue generated at both the Olympic Games and the World Championship[31]. Brundage was also displeased with the lax enforcement of the rules of amateurism by a number of IFs in such sports as football (soccer), figure skating, skiing, and basketball. Television contributed to making athletes in those sports huge celebrities. It became very difficult for athletes and for some sports to resist to the temptation of cashing in on their successes and popularity.

With the Munich Games in 1972, the Olympics became the target of many difficult situations, including political interference, threat of terrorists, and the escalating cost of hosting the Games. Preuss[32] noted that Munich reported a deficit of $667 million, while Montreal's was $1.2 billion. These figures were not encouraging for the IOC and cities interested in bidding for the Games.

Financial Stakes of Hosting Olympic Games—1976 Montreal Olympic Games

Montreal won the rights to host the 1976 Olympic Games over Los Angeles and Moscow by promising very modest Games with a price tag of $125 million. In 1973, Mayor Jean Drapeau stated: "The Games could no more have a deficit than a man could have a baby[33]."

---

[30] ibid.

[31] Wenn, S. (1994) An Olympic squabble.

[32] Preuss, H. (2000) *Economics of the Olympic Games.*

[33] Ludwig, J.B. (1976) Five ring circus. In Senn, A.E. *Power, Politics, and the Olympic Games.* Human Kinetics: 164.

This proved to be an ironic statement. The expenditure directly related to hosting the organization of the Olympic Games amounted to about US$1.581 billion—$1.2 billion for the Olympic Park and Olympic Village and $380 million for the OCOG operating costs and related expenses[34]. The official report of the Montreal Games established the overall deficit of the OCOG at US$981 million as of April 1977. The fact that the cost of the Olympic facilities increased more than ten-fold between the forecast in 1969 and the reality in August 1976, with a gap equivalent to US$1.2 billion, received much press coverage and did little to enhance the Olympic Movement[35]. When including the interest paid on the debt over the years and the additional $537 million required to complete the facilities after the Games, the Olympic debt totalled $2.729 billion[36]. The debt was finally paid off by municipal and provincial tax dollars in 2006.

The financial situation tarnished the otherwise well-organized and successful 1976 Olympics. The Montreal Games were also an impetus for developing amateur sport in Canada through government funding. It brought tremendous publicity for sports, and the television coverage of amateur sport greatly increased after the Games. Despite the many positive outcomes of the Games, the Olympic Movement was hurt by the notorious financial fiasco. For years, public opinion seemed to be consistent worldwide: Hosting the Olympics was not worth the financial risk. This was clearly demonstrated when only Los Angeles bid for the rights to host the 1984 Olympic Games, the organizers promising that they would be financed by the private sector and that no subsidies or loans would be obtained from the local, state, or federal public administrations.

IOC's Opening to Marketing

Under Lord Killanin's presidency, the IOC gradually embraced the influence of marketing on the Olympic Movement. Some of the changes made by the IOC in the mid-1970s paved the way to the commercialization of the Olympic Games. In 1973, the IOC decided to grant permission to the Montreal Organizing Committee (COJO) to use the Olympic emblems for publicity or commercial purposes[37]. This was followed by a marketing program with the goal of helping achieve "the self-financing of the Games." In Montreal, COJO created an innovative three-tier sponsorship program:

- Official Sponsor: $150 000 or more
- Official Supporter: $51 000–149 000
- Official Promoter: up to $50 000

---

[34] Landry, F. & M. Yerlès (1996) *The International Olympic Committee.*

[35] ibid.

[36] Levesques, K. (2001) Il y a 25 ans les Jeux: une monstrueuse aventure financière. *Le Devoir*, 7 juillet; http://www.ledevoir.com/public/client-css/news-webview.jsp?newsid=2792;

[37] Landry, F. & M. Yerlès (1996) *The International Olympic Committee*

A total of 628 companies with branches in 47 countries signed sponsorship agreements with the OCOG: Forty-two companies were recognized as "official sponsors[38]." About $20 million ($7 million in cash and $13 million in-kind) was raised through the sponsorship program. Had the organizers recognized the potential of marketing sooner than one and a half years prior to the Games, this figure could have been much higher[39].

In 1974, the IOC introduced the new eligibility Rule 26, which made each IF responsible for determining who would be eligible to participate in the Olympic Games. This decision opened the door to the true professionalization of the Olympic Games. With increased financial incentives from television networks and sponsors to stage the Games that included "the best athletes in the world," the IFs structured eligibility requirements that gradually allowed athletes to compete while receiving money from sponsors, governments, and universities. It was no surprise, therefore, when the IOC decided in 1987 that professional tennis players would be eligible to compete in the 1988 Olympic Games. This was followed by the 1992 "dream team," made up of professional basketball players including Michael Jordan. The Olympic Games entered into a new era of sporting "spectacle," where practicality and monetary consideration clearly dominated.

Beginning of a New Era—Los Angeles Olympic Games

Olympic marketing:
revenue generating programs including sponsorship, broadcasting, ticket sales, and licensing.

Olympic marketing has been part of the modern Games since their beginning in 1896. However, "the new era of Olympic Marketing" coincided with the 1984 Olympics in Los Angeles. After Montreal, Los Angeles was the only city making a formal bid to host the Games, promising that their Games would be financed totally by the private sector. Under the guidance of Peter Ueberroth, sound business principles were applied to the organization of the Games, which marked a "turning point for the Olympic Movement representing the development of a structured partnership between commerce and sport[40]." For the first time in their history, the Olympic Games were totally organized, administered, and financed by private enterprise.

Television and corporate sponsors became the two pillars on which the Olympic Games were organized. The potential value of the Olympic Games as a vehicle for commercial sponsorship became clear. The Los Angeles Olympic Organizing Committee (LAOOC) sold the Games on the premise that companies were willing to pay to be involved with the Olympic Games for such benefits as: "an improved public image, increased product name recognition, improved employee morale, and the exclusion of competitors from similarly associating themselves with the Games[41]." The LAOOC developed a three-tier program for corporations to become sponsors, suppliers, or licensees. In

---

[38] ibid.

[39] Stauble, V.B. (1994) The significance of sports marketing and the case of the Olympic Games. In P.J. Graham (ed.) *Sport Business—Operational and Theoretical Aspects.* WCM Brown & Benchmark: 14–21

[40] McMahon, E.A. (1996) The evolution of Olympic commercial partnerships: 15.

[41] Los Angeles (1985) *Official Report of the Games of the XXIIIrd Olympiad Los Angeles, 1984*: 233

most cases, the sponsors were large multinational firms, which paid at least $4 million to the LAOOC in cash, goods, and services[42]. The suppliers were companies that provided a combination of products, services, and cash needed by the LAOOC in staging the Games. Finally, the licensees were companies authorized by the LAOOC to manufacture and sell souvenir products featuring all LAOOC symbols: On average, the licensees paid 10 percent royalty fees to the LAOOC[43].

The sponsorship program was based on a new concept of offering corporations exclusivity within a limited number of product categories. In return, corporations were given certain rights to use Games symbols in their advertising and marketing. As early as 1979, the LAOOC signed sponsorship agreements with Coca-Cola and Anheuser-Busch worth more than $20 million[44]. These early signings served as a benchmark for other negotiations and indicated that privately financed Olympic Games were possible. This resulted in fewer sponsors paying more money to be associated with the Games. The organizers signed 35 companies as sponsors, 64 as suppliers, and 65 as licensees—164 companies in all. The marketing program of the LAOOC took in $157 million, almost 10 times that generated by Montreal in 1976. Television revenue also reached new heights with revenue of $236 million compared to $35 million in Montreal. The final result was an unprecedented $222.7 million in profit[45]. Los Angeles clearly demonstrated that, with sound business practices, the Olympic Games could make a profit.

Olympic Marketing

Shortly after becoming president, Juan Antonio Samaranch expressed serious concerns about 95 percent of the IOC revenues coming from selling television rights for the Olympic Games, with 83 percent of this deriving from American networks. As a result, the IOC established the New Sources of Finance Commission in 1982 to identify potential areas of opportunity for the generation of revenues for the Olympic Movement[46]. In 1985, the IOC, with the help of International Sports, Culture and Leisure (ISL) created its first worldwide sponsorship program, TOP (The Olympic Programme), to establish a more diversified revenue base for the Olympic Movement and Games. The first TOP sponsor was Visa, a TOP sponsor to this day. In 1989, the commission led by Canadian Richard Pound reported that TOP had achieved its objective of diversifying the IOC's revenues and reducing dependence on television. Following the resounding success of TOP I, the percentage of television revenues had gone down to slightly to about 50 percent of total revenue[47].

---

[42] ibid.

[43] ibid.

[44] ibid.

[45] Landry, F. & M. Yerlès (1996) *The International Olympic Committee.*.

[46] Martyn, S. (1996) Toward an impasse.

[47] IOC Commission Report (1989) *Olympic Review*, 263: 441–6.

Olympic marketing quickly evolved into one of the world's most sophisticated and successful sport marketing programs. Recognizing the increased importance of marketing, the IOC gradually played a significantly greater role in coordinating all aspects of marketing the Olympic Games and the financial health of the Olympic Movement. In 1989, the IOC executive board decided to create its own marketing department, primarily to generate income for the Olympic Movement on a stable, long-term basis in accordance with the general policy of the IOC[48].

Olympic marketing generates revenue from a variety of programs. The Olympic Movement generates most of its revenue from Games broadcasting and sponsorship. The IOC has been exploring a new international licensing program, which may become a third base of funding for the Olympic Movement[49]. However, the IOC believes that the promotional and educational benefits of using licensing to communicate the ideals of the Movement are more significant than the potential revenue (http://www.olympic.org). Ticket sales have also become an important source of revenue for OCOGs. For example, Vancouver 2010 expects to sell nearly $200 million in tickets. Since 1980, Olympic Marketing has generated revenue of over US$10 billion[50]. Figure 17-1 shows the rise in Olympic marketing revenue since 1980.

FIGURE 17-1

Olympic Marketing Revenue by Quadrennium, 1980–2004

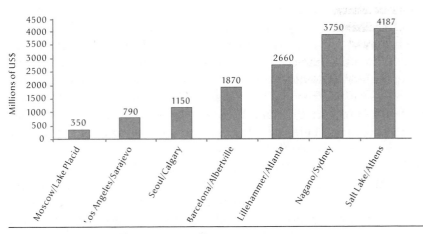

Source: International Olympic Committee 2006 Marketing Fact File (www.olympic.org)

[48] ibid.

[49] Preuss, H. (2000) *Economics of the Olympic Games.*

[50] Rozin, S. (2000) Olympic marketing: Striking balance between business and sport. *Fortune*, July 24: S2–S10.

The IOC distributes 93 percent of Olympic marketing revenues to the OCOGs, IFs, NOCs, and such other sport organizations as the International Paralympic Committee and the World Anti-Doping Agency.

In addition to programs for generating revenue, the IOC is developing new ones to broaden the promotional efforts of the Olympic Movement—an extensive Internet site, worldwide Olympic exhibitions, and special Olympic films and television programs. The IOC has also introduced a series of promotional public service announcements (PSA) to increase awareness and understanding of the principles of the Olympic Movement—excellence, fair play, friendship, unity, hope, and peace. Supported by Olympic broadcasters, these PSAs have been televised worldwide since 1996[51].

Olympic Broadcasting (1984–2008)

"Dear Friends, we in the IOC have done well without TV for 60 years and we will do so certainly for the next 60 years, too"—Avery Brundage, IOC President, 1956 Cortina Winter Olympic Games[52].

Despite Brundage's tireless efforts to keep commercialism out of the Olympic Games, the marriage between television and commercial interests and the Olympic Movement was inevitable. During the 1950s, sport became a significant advertising vehicle for television. With more sporting events on television, new fans were created, while the interest among existing fans increased. Hence, television served as powerful promotional and marketing tools[53]. Sport and television relied on one another and enjoyed a symbiotic relationship which benefited both sides. Schantz[54] noted that "the spiraling effect of media exposure, popularization and commercialization had been set in motion: the popularity of sport increased, and, with it, financial interest in sport as a commodity; this in turn intensified its media exposure which ultimately helped to promote sport itself." This resulted in the acceleration of the commercialization of sport. Despite strong resistance from some of its members, the IOC finally embraced commercialism and went from a practically bankrupt organization to a multibillion dollar business.

The first significant revenue from broadcasting rights was obtained in 1960, when American broadcaster CBS paid US$660 000 to broadcast the Rome Olympics in the US. Broadcast rights revenue continued to increase with each Olympics; however, beginning in 1984, it started increasing dramatically. Under IOC president Samaranch, cumulative broadcast revenue

---

[51] http://www.olympic.org

[52] International Olympic Committee (1999) *Olympic Marketing 1999 Fact File*. IOC.

[53] Mullin, B., S. Hardy, & W. Sutton (2000) *Sport Marketing*, 2nd ed. Human Kinetics.

[54] Schantz, O. (1995) La présidence d'Avery Brundage: 51.

from 1984 to 2008 has been reported to be about US$10 billion[55]. The broadcast revenue for the Olympic Games has grown more than 15-fold from US$101 million for Moscow 1980 to over US$1.7 billion for the 2008 Olympics to be held in Beijing. The growth of Olympic Winter Games broadcast revenue has been even more impressive, increasing more than 40-fold from US$21 million for the 1980 Lake Placid Games to $832 million for the 2006 Torino Games[56].

While Brundage mentioned that the Olympic Movement could do without television, he was well aware of television's potential in developing public interest in the Olympic Movement. In fact, television has been recognized as the medium that has globalized the Olympic Games. The IOC's policy on television coverage has aimed to maximize the global coverage of the Games, both in number of countries and overall global reach: "The world experiences the Olympics through television and the IOC wants to guarantee that if there is a television available, every family, every child can watch—*not* that he/she has to pay. It should be everyone's right to watch the Olympic Games free of charge[57]."

This strategy has been very successful for the Olympic Movement. The number of countries broadcasting the Olympics nearly doubled from 111 during the 1980 Moscow Games to 220 during the 2000 Sydney Games[58], the most watched sport event ever with over 3.7 billion viewers tuning in. This represented a 20 percent increase over the Atlanta Olympic Games in 1996[59]. By maximizing the television audience, the IOC has provided sponsors and advertisers with a unique platform that reaches huge audiences. In turn, sponsors and advertisers have been willing to pay a premium to acquire exclusive advertising inventory during Olympic Broadcast. Ultimately, this has ensured that the IOC has maximized revenues from its number 1 source of revenue—the broadcasters.

As the broadcasting rights revenue rose rapidly in the 1980s, the role of the IOC in negotiating those rights changed from one of partnership with the OCOGs to one of sole negotiator. Since the 1992 Barcelona Games, the IOC has assumed full control on the negotiation of television rights. As indicated in Olympic Charter, Rule 11[60]:

> The Olympic Games are the exclusive property of the IOC which owns all rights relating hereto, in particular, and without limitation, the rights related to their organization, exploitation, broadcasting and reproduction by any means whatsoever.

As the owner of all broadcasting rights to the Games, the IOC has been negotiating the broadcast agreements directly with each broadcaster. It negotiates the rights on a territorial basis, selecting broadcasters that provide the

---

[55] International Olympic Committee (2001) *Marketing Matters.* 18: 1–12. IOC.

[56] ibid.

[57] Payne, M. (1998) IOC marketing policy: Marketing programmes and the broadcaster. In *Television and the Olympic Games: The New Era.* IOC: 107–12.

[58] International Olympic Committee (2001) *Marketing Matters.*

[59] International Olympic Committee (2001) *Sydney 2000 Marketing Report.* IOC.

[60] International Olympic Committee (1999) *Olympic Charter.* IOC.

widest and best possible coverage. With total control over the negotiation, the IOC embarked on a new long-term broadcast strategy. As a result, broadcasters in all major television markets signed contracts to air the Olympic Games in their countries/territories through 2008, including the broadcast rights to five Olympic Games—2000 (Sydney), 2002 (Salt Lake City), 2004, 2006, and 2008. (The agreement was signed before locations had been selected for the last three.) The long-term broadcast strategy has guaranteed the IOC over US$6 billion in revenue.

There appears to be no limit to the sums broadcasters have been willing to pay to secure the rights to the Olympic Games. Following the long-term agreements, many observers questioned the value of such a strategy, especially for broadcasters. It is interesting to note that this was also the case 20 years ago when the cost of broadcasting rights for the Olympic Games jumped by nearly 400 percent in two quadrennials (1984, 1988). Slater[61] found that observers in the mid-1980s suggested that broadcasting rights for the Olympic Games became[62] a:

> virtual test of manhood, rather than a carefully designed element in the overall business plan.... The networks have allowed the Olympics to become so emotional an issue, so much a matter of pride and self-importance, that they no longer measure it by any reasonable business standard that are normally applied to programming decisions ... many observers predicted that the prices simply couldn't go any higher ... the selling price of broadcasting rights to the Games in the United States has no doubt reached its peak.

Similar sentiments were expressed by many following the signing of long-term broadcast agreements for over US$5.5 billion in 1997. Although right fees may appear excessive, investing billions of dollars in broadcasting rights is a business decision based on economic projections. The Olympic Games remains one of the few properties where advertisers can reach large audiences. The impressive increase in audience watching the Games has placed a premium price on advertising during them. Broadcasters are in business to make profits, and it appears that the Olympics contribute to reaching that objective in many ways. For the 2000 Sydney Games, NBC paid the IOC US$705 million for the broadcasting rights, and it cost the network an additional $125 million in production costs. However, NBC reported record sales of more than $900 million in advertising and expected a profit in the tens of millions of dollars from the Games[63].

The IOC's marketing strategy of increasing the number of countries broadcasting the Olympic Games and the number of hours each network devotes to Olympic programming has paid dividends for the Olympic Movement

---

[61] Slater, J. (1998) Changing partners.

[62] ibid: 57.

[63] Fendrich, H. (2000) NBC's coverage turned back the clock; network says future rosy. *American Press*, Retrieved October 2, 2000 from http://www.wire.ap.org.

(Figure 17-2). It resulted in higher audience ratings, which in turn increased revenues from corporations eager to reach this growing audience. The result has been an increase in broadcast rights revenue, which permitted the IOC to maximize its marketing revenue (Table 17-1).

Traditionally, broadcasters and sponsors have enjoyed two separate programs. But, they have been supporting each other in many ways. For example, Olympic broadcasters offer Olympic sponsors preferential advertising opportunities. As a result of these marketing advantages, advertising airtime bought by Olympic sponsors accounted for a substantial percentage of a broadcaster's total advertising inventory. This has helped broadcasters recoup a large part of their broadcasting rights fees. It is reasonable to assume that broadcasters were prepared to pay the IOC higher broadcast rights fees because they knew that Olympic sponsors were going to support their coverage and purchase considerable advertising airtime. This strategy may have helped the IOC maximize its revenue from both the broadcasters and sponsors. However, more studies are needed to determine the impact of such a strategy on Olympic sponsors.

FIGURE 17-2

IOC Formula to Maximize Revenue

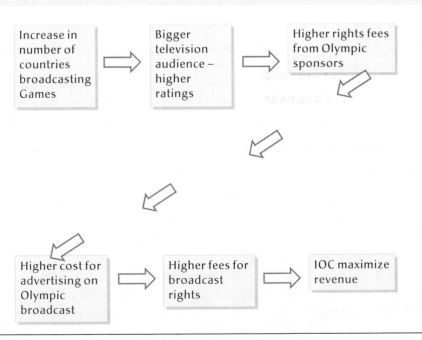

Source: Séguin, B. (2003) *Représentations d'acteurs sociaux sur les relations entre le marketing et les Jeux olympiques.* Unpublished doctoral dissertation, Université Marc Bloch (Strasbourg II).

TABLE 17-1

Evolution of the Olympic Marketing at Games at a Glance

	1980	2004
Number of countries broadcasting	111	220
Host broadcaster hours (summer)	500	35 000
Global broadcaster revenue (quad, winter/summer)	$122 million	$2230 million Salt Lake City/Athens
Percentage of total broadcast revenue (summer) from US network	84%	54%
Total international sponsorship revenue (quad, winter/summer)	$0	$663 million Salt Lake City/Athens
Total ticketing revenue (summer)	$13 million	$228 million
IOC summer Games support (TV and marketing revenue) to OCOG	$60 million	$1000 million
Olympic solidarity (quad)	$8 million	$210 million (2001–2004)

Note: All figures in US dollars
Sources: International Olympic Committee (2001) Olympic Marketing 1980–2001, Marketing Matters, Issue 19 (July): International Olympic Committee. International Olympic Committee (2006), 2006 Marketing Fact File: International Olympic Committee.

The TOP Sponsorship Program

"The media and commentators of the late 1970s were writing the Olympic Movement's obituary, as bankruptcy, disunity and political challenges threatened the future of the Games."—Michael Payne[64]

"Take away sponsorship and commercialism from sport today and what is left? A large, sophisticated finely-tuned engine developed over the period of 100 years—with no fuel."—Richard Pound[65]

These two quotes reflect the phenomenal financial turnaround of the Olympic Movement in fewer than 20 years. The 1980 Moscow Olympic Games had 381 sponsors who paid an average of $10 000[66]. Too many companies were involved in sponsoring those Olympic Games, and too few benefits were realized.

[64] Payne, M. (1996) Olympic marketing in the next millennium. *Olympic Message: Sources of Financing Sports*, 3: 19–24.

[65] Pound, R.W. (1996) The importance of commercialism for the Olympic Movement. *Olympic Message Sources of Financing Sports*, 3: 10–3.

[66] Stotlar, D.K. (1993) Sponsorship and the Olympic Winter Games. *Sport Marketing Quarterly*, 2(1): 35–43.

TOP (The Olympic Program) was the IOC's response to the difficulties experienced by OCOGs and sponsors with their international marketing activities in connection with the Olympic Games. At that time, Canadian IOC member Richard Pound, who was also the chair of the New Sources of Finance Commission, argued that it was virtually impossible for OCOGs and sponsors to engage in efficient marketing activities[67]. The Olympic charter stipulated that no sponsor could use the OCOG marks without permission of the local NOC. Sponsors were forced to negotiate with the NOC of each country to use the emblems of the OCOG, making the sponsorship much less attractive as a marketing proposition.

Changes in politics, economies, technologies, and communications caused major companies to seek platforms for marketing their products and services on a global basis[68]. Major international sponsors involved with the Olympic Movement indicated that they would be willing to contribute "much more" to the Movement if the IOC could make the process of international sponsorship much simpler and deliver exclusivity on a worldwide basis[69]. The IOC responded to the needs of the sponsors by creating TOP and allowing multinational corporations to promote their associations with the Olympics on an exclusive basis worldwide. Exclusivity was going to be the rule that future sports marketing programs would have to respect to be successful.

The creation of TOP was a challenge for the IOC, which had to convince 167 NOCs to give up certain marketing rights to launch the worldwide program. This proved to be particularly difficult with the USOC and a few other NOCs that had developed successful marketing programs. Following long and complex negotiations, especially with the USOC, 159 NOCs (92%) agreed to participate in the program[70]. As part of the agreement with NOCs, the IOC reserved 44 product categories for TOP sponsors, many of which remain today. The program was launched in 1985 as TOP I. In total, nine multinational companies became worldwide sponsors and provided the Olympic Movement with US$96 million. The **TOP program** was a great success and rapidly evolved as one of the largest revenue sources of the modern Olympic Games. In 1996, sponsorship provided 32 percent of the revenue of the Atlanta Games, while 34 percent came from the television rights. The TOP VI program, which covers the 2005–2008 quadrennium (Torino and Bejing), is expected to bring in US $866 million in revenue to the Olympic Movement (Table 17-2)[71].

TOP Program: The Olympic Partner Program consists of agreements with companies that are based on a quadrennium structure and therefore require at least four years' commitment; TOP partner companies are multinational organizations that provide direct support, sponsor services, or expertise for staging the Games.

[67] Pound, R.W. (1986) The international Olympic marketing program. *Olympic Review*, 220: 84–6.

[68] International Olympic Committee (1998) *NOC Olympic Marketing Guide*. IOC.

[69] Pound, R.W. (1986) The international Olympic marketing program.

[70] Landry, F. & M. Yerlès (1996) The International Olympic Committee.

[71] International Olympic Committee (2006) 2006 Marketing Fact File: IOC.

TABLE 17-2

Evolution of the TOP Program

	TOP I 1985–1988	TOP II 1989–1992	TOP III 1993–1996	TOP IV 1997–2000	TOP V 2001–2004	TOP VI 2005–2008
Number of companies	9	12	10	11	10	12
Number of NOCs	159	169	197	199	202	202
Revenue generated in US $million	96	172	279	579	663	866

Source: International Olympic Committee (2006), Marketing Fact File: International Olympic Committee

The TOP program brings together in a single package the marketing rights and the benefits of the IOC, NOCs, and OCOGs. In exchange for exclusive worldwide marketing rights, the sponsors provide state-of-the-art technology and services to Olympic organizers, athletes, and spectators[72]. The IOC's primary objective for sponsorship is to ensure the enhancement of the Games, allowing for efficient running of the Games, increased attendance by athletes, and increased viewership both at the venue and around the world.

In 1997, TOP became "The Olympic Partners" program. This indicated the evolution in the relationship (partnership) between the Olympic family and the companies involved in Olympic sponsorship. Specifically, the sponsorship program of the IOC was designed to meet these objectives[73]:

- Ensure the independent financial stability of the Games and the Olympic Movement
- Create a long-term structure that ensures continuing and substantial support
- Guarantee equitable revenue distribution throughout the Olympic Movement
- Prohibit uncontrolled commercialism of the Games.

As official partners, TOP sponsors were to receive these benefits[74]:

- Exclusive rights and opportunities within their designated product category;
- Worldwide rights to develop marketing programs with members of the Olympic family;
- Rights to use Olympic imagery, designation of products, hospitality opportunities at Olympic Games, direct advertising and promotional opportunities, including first right to Olympics broadcast advertising;

[72] International Olympic Committee (1995) *Marketing Matters*, 6.

[73] International Olympic Committee (1993) *Marketing Matters*. Summer: 1.

[74] International Olympic Committee (1998) *Facts File*. International Olympic Committee: 49–50.

- On-site concessions/franchises, product sale/showcase opportunities, ambush marketing protection, and broad Olympic sponsor recognition program.

By diversifying the revenue base of the IOC, TOP has helped bring financial stability to the Olympic Movement. TOP is also considered to[75]:

- Generate long-term, independent sources of revenue for the OCOGs, NOCs, and the IOC.
- Offer TOP partners a simple and unique solution for acquiring the Olympic marketing rights and the execution of a global Olympic marketing strategy.
- Provide TOP partners with a broad marketing platform from which to communicate worldwide the powerful messages about their support of the Olympic Movement.
- Harness the marketing power of the partners to communicate Olympic ideals to people worldwide.
- Provide integrity to Olympic marketing and the Olympic brand through a greater authority over the use of Olympic marks and imagery.

The rights fee for sponsors of TOP V (2001–2004) averages about $75 million in cash, equipment, and/or services. The sponsors' cost associated with leveraging this investment creates a much higher total cost of Olympic sponsorship. Leveraging activities may include Olympic-related advertising (Olympic broadcast and others), promotional programs, athletes' appearances, sponsorship of international and national sport federations and national teams, Olympic day runs, and other cultural/educational programs. It is estimated that TOP V will bring in more than $650 million[76]; it is reasonable to assume that more than US$1.5 billion will be spent in Olympic-related marketing/promotion programs.

In return for their financial commitment to the Olympic Games, sponsors seek to achieve a multitude of objectives including audience awareness and image enhancement. The sponsorship role permits marketing communicators to talk more directly to particular market segments in a manner that may be more efficient and less costly than traditional media advertising. The return on investment may take the form of improved profit figures, elevated employee morale, perceived status elevation in the public perception, and more. These benefits come from an association with the imagery of the Games as the most important event in the world, from the recognition of the Olympic symbol as the best known "symbol" in the world, and from the qualities of Olympism[77]. A special article in *Fortune*[78] mentioned that whatever gain companies might realize is contingent upon the universally held view that the Olympics are good, and the ability of each company to tie itself to that position image. The

[75] International Olympic Committee (1998) *NOC Olympic Marketing Guide.*

[76] International Olympic Committee (2001). *Marketing Matters* July.

[77] Pound, R.W. (1996) The importance of commercialism for the Olympic Movement.

[78] Rozin, S. (1998) Sponsorship—Good for business and good for the Olympics. *Fortune*: S2–S14.

Olympic Movement has established an enduring and valuable image. The Olympic rings and other symbols are essential to the long-term viability of the Olympic Movement. According to the IOC[79]: "these symbols and ideals that they embody are the cornerstones of all Olympic marketing programme." Thus, protecting these symbols and ideals has become a critical element in the IOC marketing management.

Olympic Brand

The foundation of the Olympic system has been established on a set of Olympic ideals promoted as its core values. Over the years, these ideals have been "packaged" and "communicated" to a mass audience via extensive worldwide television coverage. The Olympic symbols (e.g., rings, torch relay, lighting of the flame, athletes' oath, Olympic truce) seem to be well recognized and accepted by people of diverse cultural backgrounds. In fact, these symbols have contributed to making the Games a celebration of values and aspirations that have resulted in universal appeal and power. This has made the Olympic brand an attractive proposition for a multitude of corporations (broadcasters, firms from various industries) hoping that such Olympic brand values transfer to their own brands.

Since the concept of positioning is closely related to association and image concepts, these ideals and values have differentiated the Olympic system from other professional sport systems. As a result, a well-positioned Olympic brand can have a competitively attractive position supported by strong associations. Ultimately, these associations will create value for the firm and its customers by helping to process/retrieve information, differentiating the brand, generating a reason to buy, creating positive attitudes/feelings, and providing a basis for extensions.

Branding a product that has the potential to be a dominant global player requires strategic management in addition to superior marketing skills. The consistent reinforcement of market positioning and brand identity requires an extremely high level of management integration and discipline. In defining and communicating the essence of the Olympic brand (e.g., ideals), management consciously or unconsciously makes a commitment to certain values. Thus, any action perceived to dilute, confuse, or betray the ideals will inevitably undermine and damage the Olympic brand and, by extension, the sponsor's own brand(s). Thus, scandals such as doping, corruption, and fixing of events all have damaging effects on the Olympic brand.

While a number of brand studies have been conducted in traditional industries such as packaged goods and services over the years, the concept of "brand" in the Olympics context is fairly new. The IOC's decision to embrace commercialization and create an innovative marketing program has, in some ways, changed the essence of the organization. On the verge of bankruptcy in the 1970s, the IOC went from an amateur-run sport organization to a

---

[79] International Olympic Committee (1998) *Olympic Marks and Imagery Usage Handbook.* IOC: 16.

multibillion dollar international corporation. The building of a close relationship with industry—in 1985 when TOP started and in 1988 when the television rights deal obtained for the Calgary Olympic Winter Games—eventually led the IOC to rethink its operating structure and adopt sound business/brand management principles. To protect and maximize the return on investment for its partners, the IOC decided in 1998 to adopt an innovative marketing approach for a sport organization—strategic brand management[80]. Hence, the IOC initiated intensive and extensive brand studies in 1998 and after every Olympic Games since. These studies are conducted in more than ten countries each time. In addition, the number of academics paying attention to Olympic marketing has increased worldwide. All of these studies have helped the IOC to:

- understand how people feel about the Olympic image today and confirm that the original words of the Olympic Charter (1896) are being upheld;
- put practices in place to protect the image, enhance it and to ensure that the Olympic image is marketed consistently worldwide;
- leverage the power of the brand for long-term financial stability by making it a valuable property for its partners (sponsors, broadcasters, others) to invest in.

With the amount invested by partners in the Olympic brand (counted in billions of dollars since 1984), it is no surprise that they want and need a strong Olympic brand. It is the IOC's responsibility to keep the Games a viable and strong investment choice. The brand research infuses sponsors with much-needed brand information and provides NOCs and OCOGs with supportive evidence to use in selling to national sponsors. Broadcasters also get information on the appeal and power of the Olympic image, which is critical to their programming and to their goal of maximizing television ratings. This in turn maximizes revenue from advertisers. Thus, a well-defined brand provides partners, broadcasters, and OCOGs with the foundation for building their Games-time image and Olympic-associated activities.

What Is the Olympic Brand?

The five interlocking rings is the symbol representing the Olympic brand; the five rings also represent the five continents. The Olympic brand enjoys incredible awareness worldwide. Results from the various studies conducted since 1998 are fairly consistent, suggesting that the Olympic rings symbol is the most recognized symbol in a group of both commercial and non-commercial logos as well as other sporting international symbols tested[81]. The research also found that the respondents associated the Olympic rings with success, high standards, international cooperation, a continuous tradition of excellence, a force for world peace, and a source of national pride. Besides the rings, the Olympic oath and Olympic flame are powerful symbols closely linked to the brand, representing a combination of sport and community attributes. According to previous

---

[80] International Olympic Committee (1998) *The Olympic Marketing Guide for NOCs.* IOC.

[81] International Olympic Committee (1997) *Olympic Marketing Research Analysis Report.* IOC.

research[82] the torch and flame represent peace, unity, and hope. The results of brand studies conducted by IOC since 1998 suggest that the strongest attributes of the Olympic brand go beyond sport to feature the Olympic values.

The consumer-defined attributes from the IOC internal brand study are summarized as: "A peaceful and festive forum for cultural exchange and fair play" and "Ideals of equality, tradition, honor, and excellence[83]." These brand equities possess multiple dimensions, increasing the breadth and the depth of their value. For example, friendship's dimension includes friendship between athletes, between cultures, and between nations. Similarly the peaceful dimension includes peaceful events, peaceful spectators, peaceful hosts. The study concludes that the Olympic brand derives power from its ability to combine the ideals of the Olympic Movement with the intensity of its sport values[84]. In fact, values like peaceful, fair, friendly, and honourable convey the ethical and social values lacking in commercial brands (e.g., Disney, Nike). Others such as competitive, striving, dynamic, and inspirational deliver the excitement and dynamism lacking in cause-related brands (e.g., Red Cross, UNICEF). These equities were found to closely match the basic principles of the Olympic charter created in 1894.

This combination of uniform and universal appeal may provide Olympic partners with a powerful marketing advantage. In fact, the alignment with the Olympic values allows for a single message to appeal across multiple markets worldwide and broad simultaneous appeal across diverse demographic segments[85]. Recent brand strategy by the IOC suggests that the essence of the Olympic brand consists of three pillars[86]: "The first of these is *Striving for Success*, which is founded upon the ideals inherent in sport—such as striving, excellence, determination, being the best. Attributes that define the Olympic Games as a global festival, such as global, participation, celebration, unity, festive, constitute the second pillar, *Celebration of Community*. The third pillar, *Positive Human Values*, is composed of the attributes that fulfill our understanding of, and aspiration to, universal ideals—optimism, respectful, inspirational. These three pillars support a powerful, emotive brand that transcends sport and resonates strongly with the people of the world[87]."

In an effort to support the brand essence, the IOC has developed three communication platforms[88]:

- *Excellence*: The Olympic Games offer examples of the pinnacle of sporting achievement, inspiring us to strive to do, and be, our best in our daily lives.
- *Friendship*: The Olympic Games provide examples of how humanity can overcome political, economic, religious, and racial prejudices and forge friendships in spite of these differences.

---

[82] International Olympic Committee (2006) *2006 Marketing Fact File*.

[83] International Olympic Committee (2001) *The Olympic Marketing Guide for NOCs*. IOC.

[84] ibid

[85] ibid

[86] International Olympic Committee (2006) *Marketing Report: Torino 2006*. IOC.

[87] ibid: 24.

[88] ibid.

- *Respect*: The Olympic Games present examples of the profound meaning of "respect," as a life lesson for humanity—respect for yourself, respect for others, and respect for the rules

These communication platforms helps differentiate the Olympic brand from competitive brands such as FIFA World Cup, Super Bowl, and any other major international events—amateur or professional. Note that the Olympics is not positioning itself only as a sporting event but also as a cultural event: This may help to differentiate the brand and for the Olympic Games to remain true to its origins. The Games have strong heritage, having survived the ancient times, which in fact makes them unique. But what makes them different from other properties? What is the true point of differentiation in branding terms? First, it is a truly global event that unites people from around the world. With over 200 NOCs, thousands of athletes taking part in the Games, and billions watching on television, the Olympics are truly a global event uniting the entire world. The Games are the pinnacle of sporting achievement—a celebration of sports, cultures, and humanity. The values and ideals associated with the Olympic brand also make it unique.

Threats to the Olympic Brand

While it is clear that the Olympic brand has created incredible brand equity, the recent crises that have plagued the Olympic Movement have led to growing concerns on the part of commercial partners and the public. Séguin and colleagues[89] suggest that failure to live up to the brand promise could lead to serious problems for the Olympic brand. For example, the doping concerns are significant threats as they relate directly to the competition and to the athletes whom sponsors often use as a communication medium in their market strategy. In fact, doping may be the biggest threat to the brand. The increased role and importance of the World Anti-Doping Agency (WADA), created by the IOC, may have been a response to this threat. WADA is engaged in a legitimate effort in the fight against doping with the support of a number of professional sport leagues and governments worldwide. Since the Olympic brand is closely linked to values, any kind of crisis—doping (Ben Johnson, 1988 Seoul Games), corruption (IOC members), or event fixing (figure skating, 2002 Salt Lake City Winter Games)—is a potential liability.

Given the global nature of the brand, controlling it is important to the IOC and all involved in the Olympic Movement. One inherent problem is the Olympic system's inability to protect the exclusive rights of sponsors. Legislations protecting symbols, marks, and image association differ from one country to the next, making it nearly impossible to protect the brand worldwide. This is a serious concern when examining the brand as a legal instrument[90]. Over the years, the IOC and TOP sponsors have invested large

---

[89] Séguin, B., A. Richelieu, & N. O'Reilly (2007) Leveraging the Olympic brand through the reconciliation of corporate consumers brand perceptions. *International Journal of Sport Management and Marketing*

[90] de Chernatony, L. & F. Dall'Olmo Riley (1998) Modelling the components of a brand. *European Journal of Marketing*, 32(11/12): 1074–90.

sums of money in the brand, and therefore the IOC, OCOGs, and NOCs must seek legal ownership of the title as protection against imitators[91]. Given the ambush marketing activities taking place, the IOC must continue to work closely with its partners to influence governments worldwide to pass legislation to protect the Olympic brand.

The Olympic landscape has become cluttered with multiple tiers of official affiliations—sponsors, suppliers, licensees—at all levels of the Olympic Movement (IOC, NOC, OCOG). Adding to the clutter (while not directly under the control of NOCs) are international sport federations, world championships, national sport federations, and athletes. As a result, sponsors face a challenge making their messages understood by consumers. In addition, unofficial affiliations (ambush marketing) are gaining in popularity, making overcommercialization a serious concern. In this cluttered environment, previous studies on the Olympics have found high levels of confusion among consumers[92]. However, even the large number of official associations with the Olympic brand worldwide (IOC, NOCs, OCOGs) is a major concern: An increasing number of "hands" touch the Olympic brand with different professional levels and capability, leading to a lack of brand consistency and weakening the brand. In fact, the power of strong brands is in the continuity and uniformity of approach. Consistency makes the brand grow. Keller[93] suggests that "consistency involves ensuring that diverse brand and marketing mix elements share a common core meaning, perhaps in some cases literally containing or conveying the same information." For example, brand elements may be designed to convey a certain benefit association that is further reinforced by a highly integrated, well-branded marketing communications program. However, there are many "part timers" involved in the brand management process of the Olympics, which poses a great risk to the brand. This leads to another issue—the lack of understanding in the meaning and managing of the brand.

Previous studies (Séguin, et al.[94]) suggest that a large number of NOCs may lack the core skills needed to bring the brand to life. The failure to fully understand the brand and its management at all levels of the Olympic hierarchy is a growing concern for the future. Given Keller's[95] premise that consumers "own" the brand, it is essential to have an understanding of "what they think and feel" about the brand and plan and implement marketing programs accordingly. While some NOCs such as the Canadian Olympic Committee have a thorough understanding of brand management, a large number lack this expertise. As a result, they may make decisions based on mistaken beliefs about what consumers really think. They may neglect the full range of tangible and intangible associations that characterize the brand.

---

[91] ibid.

[92] Séguin, B., M. Lyberger, N. O'Reilly, & L. McCarthy (2005) Internationalizing ambush marketing: The Olympic brand and country of origin. *International Journal of Sport Marketing and Sponsorship*, 7(3): 216–29.

[93] Keller, K. (2003) *Strategic Brand Management: Building, Measuring, and Managing Brand Equity*, 2nd ed. Prentice Hall: 733.

[94] Séguin, B., M. Lyberger, N. O'Reilly, & L. McCarthy (2005) Internationalizing ambush marketing

[95] Keller, K. (2003) *Strategic Brand Management*.

However, as presented above, the IOC has committed to implementing an ongoing research program which benefits the brand. However, there are challenges in communicating and educating stakeholders on brand management. The IOC, NOCs, and OCOGs must spend the money, time, and energy necessary to develop and grow the Olympic brand. A greater use of public relations could help to identify, anticipate, and prepare strategies to offset threats to the brand.

Managing the Olympic Brand

Developing a brand management program is crucial to the growth and leveraging opportunities of the Olympic brand. As the owner, the IOC has the responsibility for educating the Olympic family on the meaning and importance of brand management. The "power" of the brand provides partners with benefits that are not available in other sport properties. Furthermore, interest from consumers, corporations, broadcasters, governments, and bidding cities are at an all-time high. As a result, the financial stability of the Olympic movement is quite secure for years to come. Despite the great successes of the Olympic brand, it can be threatened by clutter, lack of public relations, ambush marketing, lack of sponsor protection/recognition, increasing rights fees, doping, and lack of added-value initiatives[96].

Brand values like harmony, global peace, excellence, and friendship are frequently mentioned as a point of differentiation for Olympic brand. The Olympic ideals have well-defined meanings and values that consumers can relate to, thus providing a platform unavailable in other properties. The protection, enhancement, and communication of the Olympic brand were all identified as key factors to the continued success of the Olympic marketing program. However, as discussed earlier, the Olympic movement is made up of over 200 Olympic committees and three OCOGs, and the emphasis on marketing and brand management is still at an early stage. A true understanding of brand management is necessary if the decision makers are to allocate the investment on the brand (money, time, and energy). While the IOC, and some NOCs and OCOGs have strong marketing programs, a large number of NOCs do not recognize the value of marketing and the importance of brand management to the future of the Olympic Movement.

The threat posed by clutter must be dealt with by a brand management program. When hundreds of companies have official associations with a brand like the Olympics, some variance will be found in the levels of professionalism of those entities associating themselves with the brand. In addition, a large number of NOCs with little marketing expertise may lack the core skills needed to bring that brand alive. In many ways, such lack of knowledge and expertise could do more damage to the brand than good. The advantage

---

[96] Séguin, B., A. Richelieu, & N. O'Reilly (2007) Leveraging the Olympic brand through the reconciliation of corporate consumers brand perceptions.

of a strong brand like Coca-Cola is in the continuity and uniformity of the organization's approach to brand management. Consistency is the essence of a great brand. Making sure that the image, message, look, and feel are true to the brand essence are key elements of a successful campaign.

An integrated public relations program is an important aspect of brand management. A good PR program anticipates, prepares for, and manages problems in a positive manner. In the case of the Olympics, past practices have been more reactive (damage control) than proactive in enhancing the brand[97]. The Salt Lake City scandal in 1999 acted as a wake-up call for the IOC and the entire Olympic family. At the time, the IOC did very little PR: Much of the communications efforts were in the form of media relations. In Canada, the emphasis on PR (community affairs) by the COC is quite recent. A proactive PR program should diminish the impact of such threats as doping, bidding scandals, overcommercialization, and ambush marketing.

A key benefit of the Olympic marketing program for TOP sponsors is their ability to associate with each NOC worldwide. This provides opportunities to develop targeted programs using multitudinous associations. However, these benefits are possible only if the exclusive rights of sponsors are protected. Ambush marketing and clutter remove the ability of sponsors to differentiate themselves from others, which diminishes the value of their sponsorship investment. Since revenue generation and brand association are key benefits of association with the Olympic property, a lack of sponsor protection could compromise future revenue growth (and sponsorship renewals).

The relevance of the Olympic brand to the youth of the world is an important consideration for the Olympic family. Corporations are facing fragmented television audiences and other market factors that may make the Olympics less relevant. With the fragmentation of entertainment options, it would be more difficult for properties such as the Olympics to attract young consumers. The failure to position the brand to the youth segments could have consequences for generations of consumers. Thus research on the youth segment is paramount.

Olympic Marketing in Canada

Canada's contribution to the Olympic movement is significant. Despite the financial difficulties of the 1976 Montreal Games, Canada's reputation in hosting capabilities is well-recognized internationally. Since Montreal, Canada has hosted numerous multisport events—Olympic Winter Games, Commonwealth Games, Pan American Games, FISU (world student) Games, FINA World Aquatics Championships, as well as world championships in gymnastics, athletics, figure skating, hockey, speed skating, alpine skiing, and FIFA U-20, and World Cup events of various sports. With the hosting of the 2010 Vancouver Olympic and Paralympic Winter Games, Canada will have organized three Olympic Games: Olympics in 1976 (Montreal) and Olympic

---

[97] ibid.

Winter Games in 1988 (Calgary) and 2010 (Vancouver). Of all NOCs, the COC has one of the most sophisticated marketing programs, consisting of sponsorship, licensing, fundraising events, communications, and public relations. Revenue generated from these programs account for over half of total revenue. The COC agreed to transfer all commercial sponsorship and licensing rights to its marks from 2004 through 2012 to the Vancouver Organizing Committee for the Olympic and Paralympic Winter Games (VANOC). This joint marketing program is mandated by the IOC to control the Olympic brand to ensure that the NOC does not sell rights to companies competing with OCOG sponsors. Meanwhile, the COC may not sell its brand in the marketplace for sponsorship or licensing. As a result, it has refocused its marketing strategies to fundraising through special events, community programs, and PR initiatives. In return for assigning its commercial marketing rights to VANOC, the COC receives a payment of $73.5 to $110 million, the final value based on the marketing revenue VANOC generates from sponsorship and licensing (excluding broadcast revenue).

Brand management is a key component of COC's operations. Since 1998, the COC has conducted consumer research on a variety of topics including sponsor recognition, attitudes toward sponsors, interest of consumers in the Olympic Games and various sports, television consumption patterns, and consumer attitudes toward the Olympic brand. Since the selection of Vancouver as host of the 2010 Olympic Winter Games, the IOC has also implemented a research program in Canada.

Olympic Broadcasting in Canada

Since the IOC negotiates broadcasting rights, the COC has little control over the choice of broadcaster. The CBC has been the longest-standing Olympic broadcaster, having televised the Games since 1956. CTV held the broadcast rights for the 1988 and 1994 Olympic Winter Games and the 1992 Olympics. In 2000, CBC agreed to a five-Games package by securing the rights from 2000 to 2008. In 2005, the IOC awarded the broadcasting rights to the 2010 and 2012 Olympic Games to an alliance of CTV and Rogers Communications, which bid US$153 million, an increase of 110 percent over the $73 million the CBC paid for the Canadian broadcasting rights for the 2006 and 2008 Games[98]. Led by Bell Globemedia, the CTV-Rogers consortium offered $90 million for the rights to the 2010 Games alone and $63 million for the 2012 London Games, a considerable increase over the $28 million spent for 2006 Torino Games. Note that this is the first time that payment for the Olympic Winter Games has exceeded that for the Olympics. CTV's subsidiaries include TSN, the French-language RDS, and the Outdoor Life Network. Rogers's holdings include Sportsnet and the Omni and 43 radio stations. In Quebec, TQS will be the main carrier, with RDS helping out in coverage. The IOC's strategy went from having one broadcast partner per country to a diversification of partners, or multiple broadcasters (e.g., CBC, TSN, RDS), thus maximizing the

[98] CBC Sports (2005) TV wins 2010 and 2012 Olympic broadcast rights. Retrieved January 15, 2007 from http://www.cbc.ca/sports/story/2005/02/07/ctv050207.html..

hours broadcast on television. By having a national carrier like CTV, it also accomplishes its policy of ensuring that the Olympic Games are available free of charge to the largest audience possible. If consumers want more, they can turn the specialty channels.

The total hours devoted by the broadcaster to Olympic coverage depends on a number of factors, the most important being the location of the Games. Hours and ratings are affected by the time zone (e.g., North America versus Asia) in which the Games take place. For example, the 1998 Olympic Winter Games in Nagano seriously challenged the CBC. The 10- to 12-hour difference meant that none of the finals took place in television prime time. Despite the time zone differences (middle of the night in Canada), CBC decided to carry a number of events (e.g., ice hockey) live. Of note, an agreement between the NHL and the IOC gave the opportunity for professional hockey players like Wayne Gretzky to make their Olympic debut. With Team Canada's version of the dream team, CBC was able to generate a large audience especially for the time of the coverage. At the Salt Lake City Olympic Winter Games, the Canadian men's gold medal hockey game against the US drew over 9 million viewers, an all-time record for a television program in Canada. Similarly, the women's gold medal hockey game—Canada versus the US—also had a huge audience of more than 6 million viewers in Canada, a breakthrough for women's sports.

On average, Canadians are big consumers of the Olympic Games: Their appetite is reflected in the number of hours devoted by CBC and TSN to Olympic coverage. During the Olympic Games in Torino, the CBC provided 313 hours of Olympic coverage, an increase of 18 percent over Salt Lake City in 2002[99]. Of this coverage, 58 percent was live. In addition, 100 hours of coverage was shown on sport channel TSN. Canadian viewers over the age of four consumed an average of over 10 hours of Olympic Winter coverage throughout the Games period. Canadians are huge followers of hockey; and despite the men's hockey team's loss in Torino, ice hockey maintained its status as the most popular winter sport in Canada, providing all of the top five audiences on Canadian television (over 3 million viewers per game despite non-prime-time coverage)[100]. More than 3 million Canadians watched the gold medal performance of the women's hockey team in Torino; more than 2 million watched the opening and closing ceremonies.

VANOC Marketing

In July 2003, IOC president Jacques Rogge announced that Vancouver was the city chosen to host the 2010 Olympic Winter Games. Led by John Furlong, Vancouver edged out bids from Pyeongchang, Korea and Salzburg, Austria. These games will be the second Olympic Winter Games organized by Canada in 22 years, the previous one being Calgary in 1988. Canada also hosted the 1976 Olympic Games in Montreal.

---

[99] International Olympic Committee (2006) *2006 Marketing Fact File.*
[100] International Olympic Committee (2006) *2006 November: Sponsor Workshop. IOC.*

There are a few significant differences this time around. Unlike the 1976 Olympic Games and the 1988 Olympic Winter Games, where Olympic marketing was in its infancy, the IOC now generates nearly $5 billion in marketing revenue. Since the IOC provides nearly 50 percent of revenues to OCOGs, VANOC can budget about $1 billion in revenue from the IOC. VANOC works closely with the IOC in planning the Games and in managing the Olympic brand. In a few years, VANOC has developed the most sophisticated and successful sport marketing program in Canada, including sponsorship, licensing and merchandising, and ticketing.

Sponsorship

VANOC's sponsorship sales and marketing strategy is to build mutually beneficial relationships, to offer a superior client services program by being proactive, dedicated, and professional, and to have an extensive sponsor protection program[101]. In terms of sales, VANOC has decided to go for quality over quantity. Given that TOP sponsors have identified clutter as one of the greatest threats to the Olympic brand[102], this is a strategy welcomed by TOP and national partners alike. VANOC plans to limit the number of domestic sponsorship to 50 partners by implementing a three-tier system. Tier I consists of national partners, six companies that have committed about $600 million for the rights to be associated with the 2010 Olympic and Paralympic Winter Games, as well as the Canadian Olympic Team (2006, 2008, 2010, and 2012). All national partners have also made a financial commitment to the "Own the Podium" initiative. The six partners have been very dynamic in activating their associations with the Olympic brand through various marketing communication programs. It appears that most partners are building marketing communication strategies around athletes. Since athletes are at the heart of the Olympic brand and Canadian consumers are much more receptive to support companies that clearly demonstrate financial support for athletes[103], sponsors are pursuing a number of new initiatives, including:

- Bell Real Champions Program, Bell Athletes Connect Program
- Run for Canada (Husdon Bay Company)
- Growing with Our Athletes (RONA)
- FACE—Fueling Athlete and Coaching Excellence (Petro-Canada)
- Making Dreams Possible (General Motors)
- Olympians Program (RBC)

The sponsorship goals for Tiers II and III are to assemble a valued group of companies to provide products and services that will help VANOC stage the Games. Tier II will consist of about 15 supporters, while Tier III will con-

---

[101] International Olympic Committee (2006) *November: Sponsor Workshop. IOC.*

[102] International Olympic Committee (1997) *Olympic Marketing Research Analysis Report.*

[103] Séguin, B. & N. O'Reilly (forthcoming). Managing the Olympic brand in the era of ambush marketing and clutter. *International Journal of Sport Management and Marketing.*

sist of about 30. Given the investment provided by TOP and national sponsors, Tiers II and III will have more limited access to the marks. The same will apply for access to tickets, transportation, accommodations, and other benefits. Finally advertising and promotion using Vancouver 2010 marks will also be restricted to prevent Tier III companies from accessing the marks at a lower cost than Tier I sponsors but then aggressively leveraging their rights to gain the same benefits.

An account management team is administering sponsor relationships, providing such services and support as regular communication and update to partners; marketing activations; marketing approvals and brand protection; workshops and meetings; hospitality, operations, accommodations, and showcasing; and facilitates partnerships with the Olympic family.

Licensing

VANOC is also in the business of managing a comprehensive licensing and merchandising program. By granting companies the right to use VANOC and the COC marks on goods for retail sale, a licensing program enables VANOC to maximize revenue and consumers to connect with the Olympic brand. With all the attention on brands in recent years, licensing programs have emerged as a major source of revenue for organizing committees. The success of licensing and merchandising lies in the ability of OCOG to control the brand and create product authenticity. Thus, much effort goes into protecting the brand against counterfeit merchandise.

Ticketing

After sponsorship and broadcasting, ticketing programs are the third base of revenue for OCOGs[104]. VANOC has an ambitious goal to sell out every single Olympic and Paralympic event in 2010. To reach this goal, it has to sell a total of 1.8 million tickets—for about $220 million in revenue.

Brand Protection

The power of the brand is directly linked to the ability of the IOC and VANOC to protect it. This is a difficult task, given the numerous organizations with access to the brand (IOC, OCOGs, NOCs, sponsors). Forty percent of VANOC's operating budget will come from sponsorship agreements. Thus preventing unauthorized companies and individuals from creating an association with the Olympic Movement in Canada and the 2010 Winter Games is directly linked to the success of the brand protection program.

Almost four years before the Games, VANOC hired a number of individuals dedicated to brand protection. Such commitment is a first for Olympic Games marketing. In addition, VANOC has created a comprehensive education program to provide its stakeholders information about the meaning and importance of protecting the brand. VANOC executives present at conferences

---

[104] Séguin, B., M. Lyberger, N. O'Reilly, & L. McCarthy (2005) Internationalizing ambush marketing.

in sponsorship/marketing, advertising, and media (e.g., Sponsorship Forum, Canadian Promotional Marketing Conference, *Strategy Magazine* conference, and CAN/CCMA Conference) and in specific industries (e.g., Automotive Dealer Association, CTIA—Canadian Telecommunications Industry Association)[105]. In addition, VANOC is working on a proposed anti-ambush legislation aimed at increasing its effectiveness in protecting the Olympic brand from grey ambush. Bill C-47, the *Olympic and Paralympic Marks Act*, protects marks related to the Olympic and Paralympic Games and protects against certain misleading business associations, and makes a related amendment to the *Trade-marks Act*. The VANOC website (http://www.olympic2010.com) has extensive information on brand protection, including a section on this topic—Respect the rings and support the Games. VANOC must work proactively with the winter and summer NSOs and the media to ensure the brand protection message is delivered to prevent ambush, rather than police it reactively after the ambush has taken place.

Own the Podium

Since companies are looking for ways to leverage their rights, a number of programs to provide high-performance athletes with additional funding have been created. These programs provide sponsors with the opportunity to connect with the athletes and activate their sponsorship in a way that Canadians can appreciate and support. Research has shown that Canadians are more supportive of Olympic sponsors if they can clearly demonstrate that their financial support of the Olympics helps athletes in a tangible way (money directly to the athletes)[106].

The Own the Podium (OTP) high-performance technical program aims to make Canada the number 1 nation in total medals won at the 2010 Olympic Winter Games. A total of $110 million is committed to OTP, $50 million coming from sponsorship and fundraising, with $55 million coming from the federal government and $5 million coming from the government of British Columbia. OTP, supported by all 13 of Canada's winter NSOs, is a partnership between the COC, the Canadian Paralympic Committee (CPC), Sport Canada, and VANOC. An extensive public relations campaign has been launched around this program. Sponsors are already integrating messages of Own the Podium into their own communication programs.

Beyond VANOC

Moving forward, the challenge for the COC will be to create meaningful programs that will connect with sponsors, their employees and consumers, and the general public in its fundraising efforts. Equally as important to the COC

---

[105] Preuss, H. (2000) *Economics of the Olympic Games*.

[106] Seguin, B., Lyberger, M., O'Reilly, N., and McCarthy, L. (2005) "Internationalizing Ambush Marketing: The Olympic Brand and Country of Origin," International Journal of Sport Sponsorship and Marketing, 6(4), 216–230.

will be to nurture enduring relationships with its corporate partners, because once the 2010 Vancouver Winter Games are over, all of the sponsor relationships revert back to the COC. The COC will need to develop strategies to help sponsors activate their investment through 2012 and to keep sponsor interest after the 2010 Games are over. Although this is the most exciting time in the history of the Olympic Games for Canadians, maintaining the level of enthusiasm about the Olympics and sports in general will be difficult. Sponsors became very active in the marketplace almost four years before Vancouver, and sponsor fatigue could set in. The risk is not so much of losing interest after the 2010 Vancouver Games, but more that some sponsors may feel they have tried every idea, developed every promotion, and created every advertisement they possibly can. In short, what would they do for an encore?

Case: Mélanie Turgeon and RONA

RONA is the largest Canadian distributor and retailer of hardware and home renovation and gardening products. It operates a network of about 530 franchised, affiliated, and corporate stores of various sizes and formats. RONA has over 20 000 employees working under its family of banners across Canada and 12 million square feet of retail space. With close to $4 billion in annual sales, RONA offers Canadian consumers a national network of stores of all formats.

RONA bases its strategy on the conviction that consumers have varied needs and that no retail sales format can satisfy them all. RONA's ambition is to offer consumers the best of both worlds: personalized service as found in small stores and the efficiency of a large national network. The organization has grown through a number of acquisitions in eastern Canada (Cashway Building Centre in Ontario) and in western Canada (Revy, Revelstoke, and Lansing). Each store shares a common objective—to be the category leader in its market.

An important part of RONA's strategy is its association with the Olympic Movement, the COC, various sports federations, sporting events, and athletes. RONA's interest in sports is demonstrated by a number of key sponsorships and partnerships. For example, the organization has contributed to developing amateur sport; to professional sports, athletes, and teams; and to promoting cycling as a participation sport. RONA sponsors: the professional cycling team Team RONA; national team cyclist Geneviève Jeanson, the Hamilton 2003 Road Cycling World Championships and the Montreal Cycling World Cup Challenge; the Quebec Federation of Cycling Sports, a number of biking events in Quebec (e.g., Montreal Bike Fest, Quebec Games); professional sport teams (e.g., Montreal Alouettes, Ottawa Renegades); and specific athletes such as Mélanie Turgeon.

Mélanie is a national team member in the sport of alpine skiing. Her talent is unquestionable. She first made the national team in 1992 at age 16. She won five medals at the World Junior Championships in 1994, won medals at numerous world cup events in downhill and giant slalom events, and was world downhill champion in 2003, which greatly increased her value to sponsors. Mélanie's sponsors included such organizations as Home Depot, Salomon, and Quebec's Parks and Recreation. In return for their supporting her training and competing, Mélanie provided these sponsors with promotional space on her headgear, clothing, or equipment.

RONA's relationship with Mélanie began in 2000 when Renot-Depot (acquired by RONA in 2003) signed a deal. RONA extended the sponsorship in 2004, signing a six-figure, three-year contract. RONA spends considerable resources leveraging this sponsorship to build its brand and drive its sales. It spends three times as much on leveraging the sponsorship than on the sponsorship fee they pay here. Leveraging activities include such promotional tactics as a comprehensive in-store program with visits, meetings with employees, and displays; newspaper advertising; sponsorship of team Québec; and sposorship of a number of national and provincial events. The sponsorship requires that Mélanie be involved in many aspects of the company: She visits RONA dealers and recently spent an entire week with executives to better understand the company. Banners with Mélanie's picture are placed in all RONA stores.

Source: Institute for Sport Marketing Case Studies. Laurentian University 2003–2005

Case Questions

1. Why is RONA so interested in Mélanie?
2. Why does RONA invest so much energy in Mélanie rather than the Canadian alpine ski championships, national team, Canadian Olympic Committee, or Vancouver 2010 Winter Olympic Games?
3. What makes this sponsorship an example of Olympic marketing?
4. In your opinion, is RONA a good sponsor for Mélanie?

Chapter Summary

From modest beginnings in 1896, the Olympic Games have grown to be the biggest and most important sporting gathering in the world. Given the billions that are generated in Olympic marketing revenue today, it is hard to imagine that less than 30 years ago, the Olympic Movement was on the verge of bankruptcy. While the commercialization of the Olympics is the result of a long and often painful process, the emergence of television in the 1950s played a significant role in making the Olympics the global icon it is today. Television provides the Olympic Games with a global platform that attracts billions of viewers worldwide. With the help of a Canadian lawyer Richard Pound, the IOC was able to develop an exclusive sponsorship program (TOP) that interested multinational corporations in investing hundred of millions of dollars in the Olympics. These corporations have been instrumental in developing and communicating the Olympic brand. Canada has played a significant role in developing the Olympic Movement by hosting the 1976 Montreal Olympic Games and the 1988 Calgary Olympic Winter Games. In addition, the 2010 Olympic Winter Games will be hosted by Vancouver. VANOC has developed the most sophisticated marketing program in the history of Canadian sport.

Test Your Knowledge

1. Why is Olympic marketing important?
2. Why are Canadian corporations willing to invest hundreds of millions of dollars in VANOC rather than other promotional activities?
3. Are the Olympics worth what sponsors pay for them?
4. If you were a marketing manager of an Olympic sponsor, how would you maximize the benefits of the sponsorship?
5. Do you agree with the commercialization of the Olympics? Why or why not?
6. Test the Olympic brand by asking five people to name three things they associate with the Olympic Games. Record and bring back to class for discussion.

For more review questions, go to http://www.sportmarketing.nelson.com.

Key Terms

commercialism   TOP program
Olympic marketing   virtual blackout
Olympic Movement
rights fees

A full glossary of key term definitions is located at http://www.sportmarketing.nelson.com.

Internet Resources

IOC, www.olympic.org

COC, www.olympic.ca

IOC marketing support information,
http://www.olympic.org/uk/utilities/reports/level2_uk.asp?HEAD2=
21&HEAD1=8

Objectives of Olympic marketing,
http://www.olympic.org/uk/organisation/facts/introduction/
objectives_uk.asp

100 Years of Olympic Marketing,
http://www.olympic.org/uk/organisation/facts/introduction/
100years_uk.asp

IOC 2006 marketing fact file,
http://multimedia.olympic.org/pdf/en_report_344.pdf

IOC Marketing Commission,
http://www.olympic.org/uk/organisation/commissions/marketing/
index_uk.asp

Beijing 2008 Olympic marketing plan overview,
http://en.beijing2008.com/46/72/column211717246.shtml

Marketing and promotion of the Olympic Games,
http://www.thesportjournal.org/2005Journal/Vol8-No3/lee-aug1.asp

Olympic marketing,
http://www.chinadaily.com.cn/2008/2006-08/27/content_675174.htm

Are the Olympics really worth it?,
http://www.copernicusmarketing.com/about/docs/sponsorship_roi.htm

BBC Sport—2012 Olympics,
http://news.bbc.co.uk/sport1/hi/other_sports/olympics_2012/default.stm

Chapter 18

Marketing Plan Example

Source: compiled by Jeff Barsevich, Alex Campbell, Tim Horton, Allison King and Brandon Mazerall. Students of Laurentian University Sports Administration (April 2007).

The Desert Dry Rack
A Product by Desert Sports Limited

Introduction and Acknowledgment

This chapter gives an example of a marketing plan developed from the teachings in this book. The plan, including product concept and supporting research, was created, developed, and articulated by Laurentian University sports administration students Jeff Barsevich, Alex Campbell, Tim Horton, Allison King, and Brandon Mazerall between September 2006 and April 2007. The full marketing plan of over 200 pages was updated and shortened by Dr. Ann Pegoraro, Laurentian University marketing professor with the ISM summer research assistants.

Executive Summary

Desert Sports Limited has developed a product that will help hockey players dry and deodorize their equipment. This product addresses the lack of quality and durability offered by current products in the industry in an attempt to fill consumer wants and needs. The Desert Dry Rack will be successful because we ensure consumer satisfaction on every product that we build. Through market research, we have uncovered a market niche that we feel we will be able to capture. We have chosen as our target market male hockey parents aged 26 to 40. We feel this market will purchase our product because not only do parents in this segment still play hockey themselves, their children play in some of the age groups with the highest registration numbers. Purchasing our product will allow them to preserve their child's equipment for a longer period of time.

We are entering this industry at a time where there is no firm standing out as an industry leader. By creating a quality product and brand name, we hope to develop customers who are loyal to our brand, which will eliminate competitors and substitutes from our consumers' choice set. With the help of personal financial investments in the business and an initial bank loan, we will be able to supply over 110 retailers nationwide with about 60 units per year at a selling price of $75 per unit to our distribution centre. In our projections, we estimate a net income level of $27 631 after our first year of operations.

Market Research

The first step in developing our marketing plan was collecting primary and secondary data. This information was to form the basis from which we would make our marketing plan decisions. The first type of information collected were data from secondary sources such as Statistics Canada. Primary data were then collected through the use of questionnaires. The two types of data, method of collection, and results are discussed in the following section.

Secondary Data Acquisition

Objectives

The main objective of our secondary data acquisition was determining where we would market our product. The province with the highest number in such categories as population, income levels, and hockey registration numbers would be the province to target. Our second objective was to find the best city in the province to introduce the product.

Sources

Our sources of information were the 2001 Census from Statistics Canada, CBC Sports data, Hockey Canada statistics, retailer locations, and principal city populations. Statistics Canada provided us with population per province, urban and rural populations, median income levels, age, and sex per province. CBC Sports provided a 2007 minor hockey player breakdown per province, as well as a 2003 article on trends in hockey registration in selected provinces. Hockey Canada held key information on all registered hockey players per province in 2006. Last, a principal city population breakdown was used to find Ontario's largest cities.

Discussion of the Data

The first piece of data we looked at was from the 2001 Canadian Census. From this, we learned that Ontario has about 33 percent of the Canadian population. We then looked at age and sex data for Canada and its provinces. We assume that there are more children playing hockey than adults in Canada; however, the consumer groups targeted will be parents and young adults. Therefore, the potential market is any parent aged 33 to 46 or any individual aged 19 to 33 because they are likely to buy their own equipment. Finally, we looked at census information on median family incomes per province in Canada. When analyzing the data of families with two earners, we can see that the Northwest Territories has the highest median family income. The next highest median family income in the country is for Ontario.

Next we looked at the number of hockey players per province. Of the 551 655 hockey players registered with Hockey Canada, almost half of them play in Ontario. Data were then pulled from two CBC articles about Hockey Day in Canada from 2003 and 2007. One article noted that at least 85 percent of hockey players in selected provinces are children. Therefore, we decided to direct marketing activities toward the parents of child hockey players, who represent a majority. We estimated that there are potentially 6500 new customers (increase in hockey registration, from 532 435 participants in 2003 to 551 656 in 2006) every year.

We looked at sports store locations in Canada and determined that the best opportunity for the launch of the product is SportChek, which has the second greatest number of locations in Ontario.

In conclusion, it appears Ontario is the best province to begin to market our product. It has the highest population of the provinces, higher median family income, more hockey players, and more store locations of the major Canadian sports retailers.

We are considering three cities in Ontario as potential areas to begin to market our product: Toronto, Ottawa, and Sudbury.

The final piece of data we collected is on expenditures in Sudbury. Sports and athletic equipment generally accounted for 0.3 percent of total expenditures during the year 2002 for an individual living in Sudbury.

Limitations

The many limitations we encountered were due to lack of information on the number who play hockey in certain cities in Canada, the number of minor hockey players for every province, store locations of some major sporting good retailers, and expenditures for residents of Toronto and Ottawa. Another limitation we encountered, which unfortunately applies to most of our data, is that the newest Canadian Census has not been released so most of our data is outdated by at least five years.

Primary Data Acquisition

Background

We used two methods of gathering primary research. First, we administered two different surveys to gather primary research for Desert Sports Limited—one directed at current hockey players and the other at parents of current hockey players regardless of whether they themselves played. The objectives of our survey were to give us a better understanding of consumer buying behaviours and favoured and disliked product features and to identify our target market.

Objectives

The objectives of the consumer survey were to determine our potential target market, usefulness of the product, and popular retailers. We will look for trends in different target markets and will determine the most important purchasing factors. Objectives for our retail research included determining industry markup standards, identifying competition and success of competition, and determining the methods of distribution to retailers.

Methodology

Hockey Player and Parent of Hockey Player Questionnaire

The hockey player questionnaire was distributed based on a simple random sampling technique. Participants included spectators of hockey games, hockey players, and parents. Surveys were handed out at hockey arenas in Sudbury and at Laurentian University's residence league practices. We had predetermined that a sample size of 40 would be suitable to gain sufficient knowledge of our consumers.

In the Greater Sudbury region, we targeted three stores to gain information for market research: SportChek, Skater's Edge, and Play It Again Sports. We asked all of the interviewees (experienced sales associates) the same general questions, with follow-up questions to certain answers and individual questions specific to each store. Topics included who generally buys equipment, whether they carried a product similar to ours, whether they felt people would buy our product, and what kind of markups they charged on hockey equipment.

Conclusions of Hockey Player Questionnaire

We can conclude that older players' equipment lasts longer since they are no longer growing and generally use their equipment less frequently. The reasons older players buy new equipment are mainly mould, wear, and tear. Unlike younger players, many older players do not own an equipment rack, which has lead to quicker equipment decay.

Adults were found to be less price sensitive about equipment racks as long as quality matched their dollar spent. Younger players are more sensitive to price and space for the actual product.

Based on the surveys, quality and efficiency were the most important aspects of the rack for all age groups, while price and portability were less important. This will support the effort in ensuring good quality and efficiency while we develop and market our product.

Conclusions of Parent of Hockey Player Questionnaire

Conclusions from the parent survey were similar to those from the player survey. Older parents have children who play more frequently, which increases the need for equipment care. As well as frequency of use, children tend to outgrow their equipment within one to three years, while parents were able to keep their equipment for five or more.

When ranking the attributes of the equipment rack, in all different segments, quality was ranked first and portability was ranked last. This will once again support developing a good-quality product, with a higher pricing ceiling.

The most visited hockey equipment retailer based on our primary data is Skater's Edge.

Conclusions of Retail Store Interviews

All interviewed retailers believed that this product has the possibility of selling on the market. The only difficulty they mentioned is creating a demand for the product. Currently, only casual sales are made; and there is no noticeable high demand for this type of product.

Markups on this type of item tend to vary from store to store: Larger franchise stores have a much higher markup compares to the smaller individualized stores.

Situation Analysis

Consumer Analysis

Through experience, local retailers have noticed the main sports and athletic equipment buyers are older men, mainly fathers purchasing for their children and themselves. However, middle-aged men, younger males, and females are also avid equipment buyers.

Our data revealed that some consumers claimed to already own an equipment rack because they built their own. Most individuals are motivated to purchase an equipment rack to help dry their equipment efficiently. However, our data show people were skeptical about purchasing their equipment racks from retailers due to the lack of quality of store-bought equipment trees. Customers perceive existing equipment racks to be of poor quality and value.

Consumer Market Analysis

Based on the Sudbury summary statistics from the regional business centre, 0.3 percent of the expenditure per year for people living in the city goes to sports and athletic equipment. Through experience, local retailers have noticed the main sports and athletic equipment buyers are middle-aged men, mainly fathers purchasing for their children and themselves. As well as middle-aged men, younger males and females with their own source of income, mainly from part-time jobs, are also avid equipment buyers.

However, to build a solid marketing plan, we must also look at the larger cities and regions of Ontario. Toronto's population has increased during 1996 to 2001, and this trend can only continue with the expansion of cities within the Greater Toronto Area such as Mississauga and Brampton. Generally, citizens of this area earn more per year, which could provide them with more disposable income to spend on our product than someone in a smaller city like Sudbury. Citizens of Ottawa actually earn more per year than citizens of Toronto, but the population of Ottawa is smaller than Toronto. However, the growing trend is for people to live in urban areas, so we can assume that all three populations will be increasing over time.

For young hockey players under 18 years of age, we found most hockey equipment lasts an average of one to three years, mainly due to players growing out of their equipment or wear and tear because of constant use. Older individuals and parents tend to have their equipment last longer since they do not play as often and will not grow out of their equipment. The only thing that spoils equipment is wear and tear, mould or rust.

According to our primary data, Skater's Edge seems to be the most popular Sudbury-based retailer in our survey questionnaire. The second most popular retailer for hockey equipment and accessories was SportChek. Though people may visit these retailers, our data also revealed that some consumers who claimed to already own an equipment rack do so because they built their own. Most individuals are motivated to purchase an equipment rack to help dry their hockey equipment efficiently. However, our data show people were skeptical about purchasing their equipment racks from retailers due to their poorly perceived quality and value. We view this as an opportunity: If we are able to market a quality product, it may entice individuals to purchase our product from retailers rather than making one at home.

Another interesting point about the consumer is the recent introduction of a tax break for parents of Ontario children involved in minor sports. This tax break would entice more parents to register their kids in sports, mainly hockey because the cost of involvement in hockey is so high. This would also entice parents to spend money on our product because it would preserve their children's equipment longer. Because of growing registration of hockey players, on average about 6500 per year, a larger market year after year could increase sales of our product over the same time period.

One final note about our potential consumer, the hockey player: Hockey players generally like to play with dry equipment. Our product will not only help hockey players get dry equipment but it will also allow them to have equipment that does not smell of sweat. Since our product offers a deodorizer, hockey players will have dry, nice-smelling equipment, which will allow them to preserve it for a long period of time.

Situation Analysis

SWOT Analysis / Key Success Factors

The following provides our analysis of strengths and weaknesses of the Desert Dry Rack as well as the opportunities and threats that exist in the market we will operate in.

Strengths: There are many unique aspects to our product. There is nothing similar to our product on the hockey accessories market. Our product is an easy-to-assemble, efficient, and durable rack with an Arm & Hammer deodorizer included for customer ease—a major selling point. This product has proven to be better quality than competing racks. The Desert Dry Rack is an efficient solution for drying and deodorizing hockey equipment.

Weaknesses: Our product requires the purchase and use of very durable and quality materials, which makes our costs higher than our competitors'. Another potential weakness for this product is that it will have high advertising costs to create awareness.

Opportunities: Some opportunities for our product include the rapidly growing sports market, especially now that the Ontario government has begun to grant $500 tax breaks for families with younger children participating in minor sports. The female hockey player market is also growing rapidly, which increases the total number of potential users of our product.

Threats: A major threat is that a competitor will enter the market and find much lower material costs and begin to charge less for a similar product. This will force us to lower our price and have virtually no margin left, eventually driving us out business.

Competition Analysis

Direct Competition

Our findings from our primary market research show that fewer than half of the individuals surveyed do not own an equipment rack. This is partially due to the lack of effective market penetration and inferior quality of existing products. The market for hockey equipment accessories in the sporting goods industry does not have a dominant player, leading to a wide-open market potential.

With respect to our direct competition, these product offerings do not show a distinct competitive advantage. Most equipment trees are similar, without any qualities that would separate an industry leader from the rest of the pack. From the retailers we visited, we only encountered two different models of hockey equipment racks, with prices ranging from $35 to $45. The first of these models was constructed out of wood and the second of metal, the more expensive of the two. We were unable to identify the producer of the racks because there was no brand name on the packaging. This lead to the assumption that the retailers produce and sell their own customized equipment racks. For example, the Forzani Group sells its equipment rack under its own name; Sport Mart equipment rack. The representative from SportChek, however, had equipment racks in stock but not on display. This would result in the customer having to make a special request to see the product, and the company would not gain any visual advertising. The sales representative did not know the name of the manufacturer of the equipment rack. Based on our market research, those consumers who do currently own an equipment rack are unhappy with the overall design of it, commenting on a lack of stability and durability. Figure 18-1 shows a general design of the metal equipment rack; the wood design is very similar.

FIGURE 18-1

Patented Hockey Rack

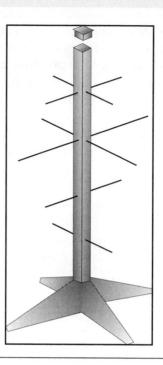

An online US competitor—Sticklocker—has been on the market since 2002. This very small and lightweight product uses a player's hockey stick as its main mast and attachable aluminum brackets which clamp to the players stick as equipment holders. However, the product does not have a spot for skates, pants, or shoulder pads; therefore, these pieces of equipment would still need to be laid out to dry. The stability of the product is also in question since the base is very narrow and flimsy. Since 2002, Sticklocker has received only 15 000 hits on their website, and we can assume only a fraction of these hits lead to purchases because they have not developed a proper brand image. If we developed a brand image, we should be able to surpass a 15 000-unit sales level very quickly in our company's life.

Substitutes

There are numerous substitutes for equipment racks. Equipment owners have been known to simply spread their equipment out on the floor, which eliminates any need for our product. Home-made equipment racks are also frequently used; however, like some manufactured racks, they lack stability and durability. The most extreme substitute for equipment owners is frequently replacing equipment before it begins to deteriorate. An innovative hockey bag recently appeared on the market: The Shock Doctor is a heavy-duty hockey bag which can accommodate a fan to air dry the equipment in the bag. It includes a filtration system to get rid of smells in the bag. The fan is sold separately from the bag, which itself sells for US$129.95. There is no information on the price of the power-dry blower. The cost of the bag is well above the industry average, as most quality hockey bags sell for less than half its price.

Future Competition

In the future, we predict the entry of a lot of similar products with slight variations. Due to the innovativeness of our product, there are bound to be some copycats. To keep up with the market's more innovative products, our product will remain adaptable to the market, and continuous research will be performed to further enhance it.

We are primarily concerned with competitors who will create products similar to ours but will find improvements in fan power and potentially lower costing materials. Our material costs are nearly 70 percent of our proposed price. If a competitor is able to decrease this margin to 50 percent, they will either make a higher profit or will lower their prices and steal a large market share. Competitors may also add new features such as portability and lightweight materials, all of which would lead to higher quality products than ours. There may also be a market expansion in children's and goalie racks, or even market development into different sports such as football or lacrosse.

Product Offering

The design of the Desert Dry rack is unique. Both the operation and structure set it apart from any competitive product. The core structure is a dome-shaped plastic base and central pole of ABS tubing which extends upward from the base to about 5.5 feet tall. Extending off the central pole are limbs made of ABS tubing, each designed for a separate piece of hockey equipment to hang on. These limbs have tiny holes to allow air to escape from the inside of the tubing to the equipment. In the base is a fan, eight inches in diameter, mounted inside to blow air into the central pole for distribution to each of the limbs. The size of the fan allows the air to funnel into the central pole and create enough pressure to successfully flow to each part of the equipment. Also mounted near the base of the central pole will be a deodorizer that will be distributed through the rack to the equipment as part of the air flow. A diagram of the product can be seen in Figure 18-2.

Chapter 18: Marketing Plan Example

FIGURE 18-2

Product Concept Diagram

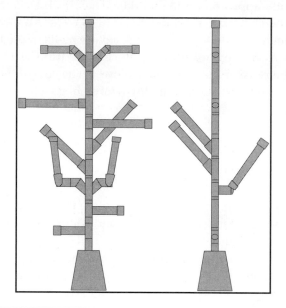

Innovation

We feel that our product is innovative in the equipment rack industry. One, it is constructed of different materials. The current products on the market have a wood base and wood branches. However, customers have been complaining of the quality and stability of these wood products, and some have even decided to make their own equipment racks. With our innovativeness in the tubing, the fan, and the fact our product eliminates hockey equipment odours, customers should be happy a quality product is on the market and begin to purchase it. No other product on the market is built with ABS tubing, which allows airflow to each piece of equipment and can take the weight of hockey equipment, use after use. Two, customers will be impressed with the fan that will allow their equipment to dry faster in between uses. Three, our product is the first of its kind to include an item that will help remove the sweat smell in hockey equipment. Our strategic alliance with Arm & Hammer will help both companies: our company because of brand association and Arm & Hammer because consumers will have to go purchase another Arm & Hammer product once the initial product runs out.

Marketing Strategy

Mission

Our company name is Desert Sports Limited (DSL). We believe our company name will help the customer associate our product with the dryness of the desert. The DSL mission is to produce high-quality sporting goods for the sporting-good consumer. By producing a high-quality product, our company aims to sell our product to the consumers complaining about the quality of other products on the market. Using our competitive advantage, our company looks to gain large market share quickly in these markets.

Segmentation, Targeting, Positioning

Segmentation

Our segmentation begins by dividing consumers into two categories: hockey players and non-hockey players. Our mass market is generally targeting hockey affiliates. By segmenting hockey players from non–hockey players, we are able to separate possible consumers from those who would have no interest or need for our product. Next we segment hockey parents from non–hockey parents. Parents can be both hockey players and have children who play hockey. Non-parents are primarily singles or couples who play hockey but do not have children who play hockey. From this we separate into males and females, which will coincide for both mothers and fathers of children, as well as male and female hockey players. Last, we segment into our five identified age groups: 0–18 years old, 19–25, 26–40, 41–60, and 61+.

The 0–18 age group represents children who would be unable to purchase their own hockey equipment. Also, people in this age group generally do not have children, but in the rare chance that they do, the child will be of proper age to play hockey once the person is outside of this segment. The 19–25 age group represents people in university and not married or in a common-law relationship. This group is young and has not started to work full time so they do not have much of an income. The 26–40 age group includes people starting to settle down by getting married and having children as well as people who have been married for some time and have preteen children. This age group is also generally involved in playing hockey if they participate in adult hockey leagues after work. Part of the segment—those 35–39—is the highest population segment in Ontario. The 41–60 age group represents parents of older children who are getting ready to start high school or move on to university. These children are generally participating in hockey more often due to representative leagues within their community. Also, the parents are generally the older players of adult hockey leagues. The 61 and over age group represents grandparents or parents of adults who are just starting to get married and have children. People in this age group generally do not play adult hockey any more. Our complete segmentation charts can be seen in Tables 18-1a, 18-1b, and 18-1c.

TABLE 18-1A

Segmentation Chart: Males and Females Who Play Hockey but Do Not Have Children Playing Hockey

AGE GROUP	0–18	19–25	26–40	41–60
Who	Youth, children, teenagers	young adults	middle-aged adults	older adults
What	something to refresh & dry equipment	something to refresh & dry equipment	something to refresh & dry equipment	something to refresh & dry equipment
When	seasonal: late summer to early fall	seasonal: late summer to early fall	seasonal: late summer to early fall	seasonal: late summer to early fall
Where	department stores	department stores & specialty sporting goods stores	department stores & specialty sporting goods stores	department stores & specialty sporting goods stores
Why	dry & preserve equipment/ remove odour	dry & preserve equipment/ remove odour	dry & preserve equipment/remove odour	dry & preserve equipment/remove odour
How	parents/guardians supply equipment	purchase at department/ sporting goods stores	purchase at department/sporting goods stores	purchase at department/ sporting goods stores

TABLE 18-1B

Segmentation Chart: Males and Females Who Play Hockey and Have Children Playing Hockey

AGE GROUP	19–25	26–40	41–60
Who	mothers & fathers who play & have very young children just starting to play	mothers & fathers who play & have young children/teenagers who play	mothers & fathers who play & have teenagers/ young adults who play
What	something to refresh and dry equipment	something to refresh and dry equipment	something to refresh and dry equipment
When	seasonal: late summer to early fall	seasonal: late summer to early fall	seasonal: late summer to early fall

Where	department stores & specialty sporting goods stores	department stores & specialty sporting goods stores	department stores & specialty sporting goods stores
Why	dry & preserve equipment/remove odour	dry & preserve equipment/remove odour	dry & preserve equipment/remove odour
How	purchase at department/sporting goods stores	purchase at department/sporting goods stores	purchase at department/sporting goods stores

TABLE 18-1C

Segmentation Chart: Males Who Play Hockey but Are Not Parents of Children Who Play Hockey

AGE GROUP	0–18	19–25	26–40	41–60
Who	n/a	mothers & fathers with very young children who are just starting to play	mothers & fathers with young children/teenagers who play	mothers & fathers that have teenagers/young adults who play
What	n/a	something to refresh & dry equipment	something to refresh & dry equipment	something to refresh & dry equipment
When	n/a	seasonal: late summer to early fall	seasonal: late summer to early fall	seasonal: late summer to early fall
Where	n/a	department stores & specialty sporting goods stores	department stores & specialty sporting goods stores	department stores & specialty sporting goods stores
Why	n/a	dry & preserve equipment/remove odour	dry & preserve equipment/remove odour	dry & preserve equipment/remove odour
How	n/a	purchase at department/sporting goods stores	purchase at department/sporting goods stores	purchase at department/sporting goods stores

Targeting

The target market we decided to pursue was the segment of male and female parents aged 26–40. We had to examine the criteria for selecting a target market in depth to fully justify our choosing this segment as our target market.

Ensuring that our target market has compatible goals with the organization was the first criterion we looked at. The male and female segment of parents aged 26–40 responded to our survey by saying they wanted a quality product, stating the main reason they are not currently in the market for equipment racks was due to their poor quality. This clearly aligns with the organizational goal of producing a quality product, therefore creating compatible goals with our chosen target market.

The second criterion states the market opportunity must match company resources. Our company is currently very confident that we will be able to supply our target market with all the product and resources needed to be successful.

The third criterion is the target market must have an opportunity to generate enough sales to earn a profit. We strongly believe that selecting the male and female segment of parents aged 26–40 gives our organization potential to earn a profit. One of the reasons is because the majority of the males and females surveyed in this specific segment stated they are actively playing hockey, meaning they are potential consumers for an equipment rack. As well, the children's age group involved in this segment has some of the highest registration numbers in the country. For instance, the tyke age groups have the most hockey players in Canada, accounting for 20 percent of the total registration numbers for the country. As tykes are five to six years of age, they would fit perfectly into our chosen target market providing that the parents have their first child near the age of 26 or older, placing them at 31 years of age or older when registering their children. Also, the number of hockey players registering in Canada is increasing year after year. Combined with this fact, a recent tax break offered to the parents of children in minor sports in Ontario further attracts parents to register their children in hockey. As hockey is considered to be the most expensive sport to get a child involved in, a product such as ours that can help preserve equipment as long as possible would be a very persuasive offer.

The final criterion states that the target market we select must allow us to have a competitive advantage. Our organization believes we will be able to establish a competitive advantage by targeting the male and female segment of parents aged 26–40 because this specific segment is frustrated with the quality of current equipment racks on the market. Since quality is an important component of our product, this gives us a competitive advantage over our competition. We believe consumers will purchase our product because it is superior to our competitors' products and longer lasting, saving consumers money in the future. Another competitive advantage we possess is that we are targeting the parents of children as soon as they begin to play hockey. If we can successfully gain consumer loyalty early on in their children's hockey career, the potential benefits in the future could be enormous.

Positioning

With the many types of competition in the market, both direct and indirect, positioning the product in the minds of our target market correctly will be key to the success of our company. Our primary data acquisition helped us decide how to position ourselves. Our questionnaires showed that our target market was primarily concerned with the quality of the product. They also believed that some of the direct competitors' products were very unstable and poorly constructed. This information led us to take two positioning strategies and combine parts of both of them. We will use the "set apart" strategy to focus on the innovation and differences of our product from the market's current products (specifically the fan and ABS piping) but also incorporate the "against competition." These two strategies combined will show that our product is superior to the competition based on quality because of the difference from the competition. We would like to stress how the differences of our product create a higher quality and innovative product.

We used this information to create a product position map to illustrate how our product would compare to the competition. The results of how this process are presented in Figure 18-4, which illustrates how the consumer will perceive our product in terms of price and quality compared to the competitors in the industry. Our placement on the perceptual map will be high in both price and quality. There is not much competition in this market of high-quality products with the exception of one substitute, the Shock Doctor hockey bag, which is much more expensive. This bag tries to incorporate a fan like our product does; however, is not sold with a fan and has a combined cost of about double our proposed retail price. The other competitors have all adopted low-cost strategies that have resulted in low-quality products.

FIGURE 18-3

Positioning Chart

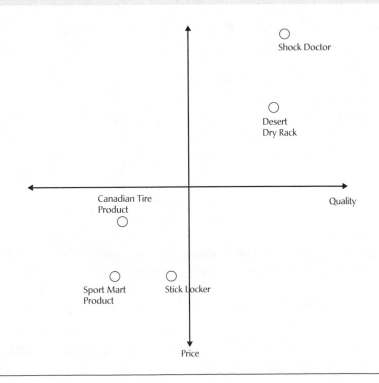

Marketing Strategy and 4 Ps

Product Strategy

The Desert Dry Rack will be a new tangible shopping good on the market. While there are similar products already on the market, the Desert Dry Rack has obvious differences in terms of quality and efficiency. Because there are similar products, this product will be entering this market segment in the market growth stage. This will help early sales as customers will gain awareness of our product while investigating more established yet less effective products that are used to dry hockey equipment and prevent odour. Customers have adopted the idea of the rack but have been displeased with the quality, which has led to a deterioration of the potential market size. With an emphasis on quality and efficiency, we will still be able to capitalize on part of the early adopters as well as the early majority consumers.

We are essentially a B2C company; however, we are using an intermediary retailer to sell the product to the consumers. Therefore, a large part of our integrated marketing plan is devoted to B2B selling.

TABLE 18–2

Key Elements of Marketing Plan

PRICE	PLACE	PROMOTIONAL EMPHASIS	PURCHASE BEHAVIOUR
Premium pricing to offset the costs of technology development	More selective outlets (e.g., SportChek)	Differentiation from competitors based on quality and enhanced features	Infrequently purchased product; comparison shopping used; consumers spend time making the decision

Since our market is already established and aware of similar products, we will attempt a product modification strategy by altering a current product to meet the needs of customers, as well as adding new features and packaging. Through this strategy, we hope to entice new customers to try the product as well as grab part of the existing market share.

Price Strategy

Our market is based primarily on monopolistic competition, in which there is strong competition over price and product differentiation. From our primary data, however, we have concluded that our potential target market is not very price sensitive and is willing to spend extra dollars to ensure high quality and a product that will last.

Our pricing window has a very high floor price due mainly to the high material costs of nearly $55 per unit. After fixed costs and advertising are added on, our floor price nears $63 per unit. The ceiling price per unit was projected to be near $100 per unit sold; however, this will severely reduce the number of units sold. Therefore, our target selling price to retailers is about $75 per unit. Considering a significant margin and their costs, a manufacturer's suggested list price (MSLP) of $99 is recommended to retailers. This will provide sufficient contribution per unit but still have a low enough price to appeal to consumers.

The value of our product relies heavily on the perception of quality by the consumer. We will emphasize the improved quality of our product in comparison to competition, which will substantiate our chosen price. However, there are constraints on our pricing because we are in monopolistic competition.

In the early years of production, our cost and volume analysis will not be based entirely on margins. We will be mostly focusing on break-even volume and secondly on cost reduction. Unfortunately, our company has very little automation, leading to high production costs due to the labour to produce the product.

Our pricing strategy is premium pricing. Competitive pricing is not justifiable since we have an innovative product with additional features competitors. Moreover, since our return per unit is low, we need to recuperate our costs based on the initial investment. We are charging a reservation price on market entry meaning the highest price a consumer is willing to pay based on perceived quality. We are aiming to associate higher price with higher quality.

In the short-term plan, our higher price is helpful in testing the market for price sensitivity as well as developing customer's perception of high quality and efficiency. In the long run, as economies of scale grow, the production prices will drop, leading us to consider a more competition-oriented pricing strategy.

Promotion Strategy

Print material: To create awareness of our new product, we plan weekly print material to create a demand for it. Developing standard templates for advertisement style, logo, and slogans will make it easier for product recognition. Our main print material focus will be on weekly Ontario Minor Hockey Association (OMHA) magazine advertisements, which reach nearly 105 000 hockey player households across Ontario. They are available for purchase by subscription or individual sales at hockey arenas. Quarter-page ads will be placed in these magazines to advertise our product to Ontario residents. These ads will also notify the customer they can purchase the product at their nearest SportChek. The budget and timing for these materials is found in Table 18-3.

TABLE 18-3

Advertising Cost Breakdown

	DURATION IN MONTHS	COST PER MONTH	TOTAL EXPENSE	TYPE OF ADVERTISEMENT
Magazine ads*	5	$1 467	$7 335	Total cost for 8 ads and an article in 2 different magazines
Hockey tournament	1		$5 000	January
One-time cost	1		$16 500	Promo displays
Strictly Visual	1		$3 000	Design of all promotional materials, logo, etc
Website	12	$20	$240	Basic website design for an information page
Total			$32 075	

*because of confidentiality agreement, no more information can be disclosed

Publicity: Newspaper articles and possible news coverage will provide DSL with further awareness to the public. To facilitate news coverage, various press releases will be sent to relevant media. As well, in any way possible, networking will be done with journalists, especially through existing connections in sports, to convince them to publish articles on the product.

Sponsorship in-kind: A strategic alliance will be formed with Arm & Hammer to create a sponsorship in-kind. We will be supplied with Arm & Hammer's new Fridge Fresh product that will be part of our product bundle. The Fridge Fresh will be suctioned cup to our rack as a deodorizer for the hockey equipment. Arm & Hammer is in nearly 60 percent of households across the US and will help DSL expand our reach to more potential consumers. The only criterion that Arm & Hammer considers when looking to create a business relationship is that the product must be ranked either number 1 or 2 in its market. By establishing a relationship between Desert Sports and Arm & Hammer, not only will our firm profit from having a strong product supporter, but Arm & Hammer will also be getting more frequent reach into the sports market. Also, once the initial Arm & Hammer product has been used by the consumer, the consumer will need to go to the store to buy a new Arm & Hammer product if they want the smell to continue to be removed from their equipment. This benefits Arm & Hammer by driving their sales up if the product is effective.

Promotional material: Each sales location will have a sample display of the product, which consumers can examine and test to see how our product works. Hopefully with a visual sample of the product, consumers will realize the quality the product offers and will help raise their perceived value of the product.

Personal selling: Since our success relies heavily on the compliance of SportChek, Arm & Hammer, and our suppliers, the majority of the personal selling will be devoted to keeping strong and healthy distribution channels. We will need to use push strategies to sell our products to retailers, since we do not yet have enough financial or market pull in our industry.

Our goal is to have about 20 percent of the market share after the first two years of operation. This would equate to about 100 000 consumers across Canada, with the majority of our sales in Ontario. Since our product is very seasonal with peak sales occurring during August through December, the majority of our advertisements will be posted during near the beginning of the season.

Place Strategy

Our main retailer will be SportChek, which gives us nationwide reach of about 110 stores. In the early stages of our development, however, we will focus our marketing efforts on Ontario, which gives us 57 store locations to sell our product. The majority of these are located in densely populated areas such as the GTA and Ottawa.

Our two intermediaries are the SportChek distribution centre and SportChek retail stores themselves. However, we have will establish a strategic channel alliance, where our product ships through the SportChek distribution centre to the retailers themselves.

Each part of our product has a separate supply channel, ranging from the ABS tubing, all-purpose glue, rack base, fan, and box. These suppliers are relatively close to our production warehouse, the majority being based in GTA. This will reduce the stress of maintaining long-term business relations, where we can frequently communicate with our supplier to ensure quality parts are shipped.

Financials

Break-even Analysis

The material costs are about $55 per unit. After fixed costs and advertising are added, our floor price nears $63 per unit. The ceiling price per unit was projected to be near $100 per unit sold; however, this would severely reduce the number of units sold. Therefore, our target selling price to retailers is about $75 per unit. This will provide sufficient contribution per unit, but still have a low enough price to appeal to consumers. Using these figures, our break-even sales point at the most likely sales estimate of 4638 units (Figure 18-4).

Chapter 18: Marketing Plan Example

FIGURE 18-4

Break-Even Analysis

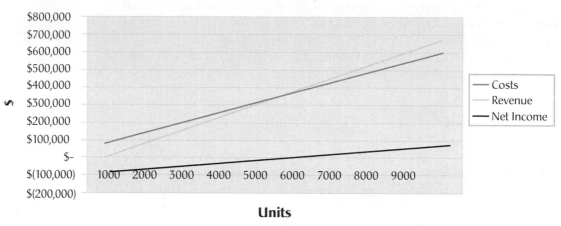

Breakeven Analysis

Sales Forecasts

To fully analyze sales potential for our product, we developed the three sales estimates detailed below.

Pessimistic sales estimate: This estimate included each of the 110 stores selling 30 units, for a total of 3300 units. This would produce sales of $242 550, with cost of goods sold totalling $175 347 for a gross margin of $67 203. The result would be a negative net income of $3654. This amount decreases in the second year showing a promising net income for the third year.

Most likely sales estimate: This estimate included each of the 110 stores selling 60 units, for a total of 6600 units. This would produce sales of $485 100, with cost of goods sold totalling $350 695 for a gross margin of $134 405. The result would be a net income of about $27 000. In the second year, there would be a net income of about $34 000.

Optimistic sales estimate: This estimate included each of the 110 stores selling 90 units, for a total of 9900 units. This would produce sales of $727 650, with cost of goods sold totalling $526 042 for a gross margin of $201 608. The result would be a net income of about $58 000. In the second year, there would be a net income of about $68 000.

Expenses

A warehouse lease cost was found through an online broker for a warehouse in Mississauga. Our insurance costs were estimated by reviewing similar costs of local retailers; however, we took into consideration that retailers carry more inventory than manufacturing businesses. Utility costs were estimated in the same way. Because of our central location to all of our suppliers and our distributor, we have estimated freight costs to be three percent of the merchandise cost. Office supplies have been estimated at $125 due to our small office space and reduced distributor paperwork. Selling expenses would include all travel and meeting costs. We have estimated an accounting cost of $5000 for the year: We got an estimate from a retailer at $3500, and we are going to have our accountant do more than what this retailer currently does. We have estimated legal fees of $10 000 for the first year on the basis of all start-up fees. With further discussions with our legal advisors a more exact figure will be acquired. We have also estimated miscellaneous costs as a percentage of sales. This allows for unforeseen costs related to increases in sales. A break down of our expenses can be seen in our projected income statement in Table 18-4.

TABLE 18-4

Projected Income Statement 2008

BUDGETED INCOME STATEMENT
YEAR ENDING APRIL 30, 2008

Sales	$242 550.00	
Cost of goods sold	$175 347.48	
Gross margin		$67 202.52
Operating Expenses		
Rent	$13 800.00	
Insurance	$3 600.00	
Utilities	$6 000.00	
Freight	$5 395.43	
Office supplies	$1 500.00	
Selling expenses	$1 680.00	
Accounting expenses	$5 004.00	
Legal fees	$9 996.00	
Miscellaneous	$7 276.50	
Advertising	$15 575.00	
Total Expenses		$69 826.93
Income from operations	($2 624.41)	
Interest	$3 465.00	
Income before taxes	($6 089.41)	
Taxes (40%)	($2 435.76)	
Net Income	$3 653.65	

Chapter 18: Marketing Plan Example

Implementation and Control

Following the product development stage (Figure 18-9), we will be shipping our product to be sold through SportChek stores. To facilitate this, we will advertise in the Ontario Minor Hockey Association Magazine to generate interest. But to ensure the success of this plan, we must do considerable work to ensure that the advertising dollars are well spent. Among the necessary steps are interviewing salespeople at SportChek stores in the GTA once the product is in store to obtain customer feedback and to develop techniques for best selling the product. Additionally, depending on the information these salespeople provide and the levels of sales of the product, modifications and/ or increases to the level of advertising may be required.

Contingency Plan

If our outlined strategy has not succeeded and our efforts at control and revision of marketing is insufficient to propel the company to success, some changes in the marketing plan may be required. If in-store sales are low, one alternative is altering the target market. Currently, the plan is to target the male hockey parent aged 26–40, but the higher-income 41–60-year-old male hockey parent could provide a viable substitute target market. Like the 26–40 year olds, this market would primarily be purchasing for their children; however, there are several critical differences in the demographics of the children that could contribute to success. For instance, these children tend to be older and have been playing longer, and accordingly parents may be more likely to invest larger

FIGURE 18-5

Implementation and Control

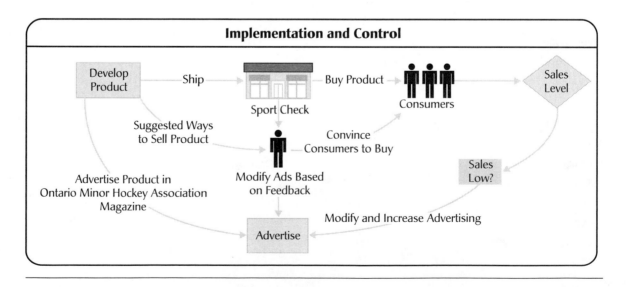

amounts in preserving their sporting equipment. Additionally, since these children are reaching maturity, they will no longer replace equipment as regularly, increasing the necessity and desirability of taking better care of it. In our interviews with local retailers, many noted that it is generally older males who come in to buy equipment for their children.

A second strategy would be to switch to a different distributor. Many large department stores, such as Wal-Mart and Canadian Tire, have sporting goods sections. There are also sports specialty stores that may be a worthwhile choice. Based on a preliminary analysis, the best option for our company would be Canadian Tire. As this is a nationwide retailer with considerable hockey sales, it could provide a prime alternative location should SportChek sales not be as high as anticipated.

Index

company, 6, 322–323
company image, 232, 233–235
competition, 6
    analysis, 389–392
    global, 181
    professional sport, 19
competitive positioning, 305–306
complementary product price setting, 177
concentrated targeting, 110, 324
consumer analysis, 387
consumer brand partnerships, 98–99
consumer demand, 178–179
consumer goods, 133
consumer market, 105–106
consumer market analysis, 387–388
consumers, 6
    See also sport consumers
    decision-making process for, 79–81
    gateways to sport, 76–79
    influencers on, 79
    needs and wants of, 5
    perceptions of, 97–98, 233–235
    psychological relationship between sport
        and, 76
    target, 101
consumption decisions, 81–87
content management, 306
contests, 197
contingency plan, 404–405
contingency tables, 62
contribution margin, 180–181, 182
control, 339, 404
CORFing, 39–40
corporate objectives, sponsorship and, 232–242
corporations, leveraging by, 261–262
co-sponsor, 258
cost-oriented price setting, 175
costs
    controlling, 181–182
    estimating, 179–180
    vs. price, 184–186
cost-volume-profit (CVP) analysis, 180
Coubertin, Baron Pierre, 349–351
crisis management, 210, 215–216
Crosby, Sidney, 135
crowded markets, 114
CTV, 375–376
Cuban, Mark, 75
cultural entrée, 67–68
culture
    concept of, 83
    importance of, 66
cultured individualists, 92
curling, sponsorship of, 47–49
customers
    See also consumers
    loyalty of, 158–159
    in social marketing context, 323
customized marketing messages, 100–101
Cuthbert, Linda, 42–43

dashboards, 304
data
    analysis, 62–63, 68
    display, 62
    gathering, 303–304
    qualitative, 304
databases, 301

data collection, 62, 68
data mining, 305
data warehouses, 305
decision makers, 87
decision-making process, 79–87
decision support systems (DSS), 305
decline stage, of product life cycle, 129, 130
demand
    elasticity of, 179
    estimating, 178–179
demand-backward price setting, 176
demarketing, 324
Department of Canadian Heritage, 27
descriptive research, 58, 61
Desert Dry Rack, 383–405
differentiated targeting, 110, 324
direct competitors, 6, 389–390
Direct Energy, 275–277
discounts, 183–184
disinterested consumers, 75
distribution
    concept of, 209
    key influences in, 218
    in sport, 216–218
    technology and, 307–308
distribution channels, 217–218
Diving Canada, 308
doping, 371
doping scandals, 30
draft strategy, for MLB teams, 340–344
Dupré, Jean R., 224–225, 248–251
DVD players, 307
dynamic ads, 307

Edmonton Sport Council, 40
education, 320, 321–322
Egan, Sean, 144–147
elasticity of demand, 179
electronic media, 211–212
e-mail advertising, 306
emotional attachment, 132–133, 140, 151–152
enterprise resource planning (ERP) system, 301
environment, external, 6
ethics
    ambush marketing and, 291–292
    pricing and, 178
    research, 68
evaluation
    of marketing strategy, 338–339
    measures, 339
evaluation framework, for sponsorship, 264
evaluators, 87
events. See sport events
exchange, 1, 4
exclusivity, 232, 239–240, 273
executive information systems, 304
executive summary, 383–384
expenses, 402–403
experience curve price setting, 175–176
experiments, 61, 65
expert interviews, 61, 64–65
expert systems (ES), 305
exploratory research, 58
external environment, 6
external influences, on decision making, 83–84
extreme sports, 91
EZ chair quarterbacks, 92

facilities, 137
family, 84
FANatics, 75
fan cost index (FCI), 185–186
fan identity, 39–40
fans, 91–92, 132–133, 140, 151–152
Federal Policy for Hosting International Sports
    Events (2000), 32
fibre optic cabling, 301–302
figure skating scandal, 216
Firestone, Bruce, 21
fit, of sponsorship, 260, 273
Fitness and Amateur Sport Act (1961), 29
fitness services, 137–138
fixed costs, 180
focus groups, 61, 65
follow-up, after promotion, 202–203
football
    CFL, 17–18
    Montreal Alouettes, 165–170
    R&O, 242–245
form, 4
Formula One, 19
Fuji, 284
full-line price setting, 177
functional discounts, 183
funding
    of hosted sport events, 32
    of national sports, 28–30, 32–33
future competitors, 6, 391

Game Plan 1976, 30
Games Program, 120
gatekeepers, 87
gateways to sport, 76–79
Gatorade, 99
General Mills, 201, 268–269
Gladden, Jay, 155
global competition, 181
golf, 19
goods, 128, 133
government policies, 29–31
graphs, 63
grassroots organizations, 40–43
grassroots sport, 14, 36–41
    participation in, 37–38
    spectatorship, 38–40
    sponsorship of, 47–49
Greenlaw, Andrew, 119, 121–122
Gretsky, Wayne, 133, 135
Grey Cup, 39
group dynamics, 132
group memberships, 84
group sales, 193
growth stage, of product life cycle, 128–130

handheld devices, 300
hardware, 299–300
Harrison, Mark, 2–3
health-related services, 137–138
Hellstrom, Peter, 24–25
high-definition television (HDTV), 308–310
histograms, 62
hockey
    AHL, 18
    Canadian culture and, 66
    HDTV and, 308–309